THE
LIFE OF MOSES

the Smart Guide to the Bible™ series

BE SMART · BE INSPIRED ·

Larry Richards

THOMAS NELSON
Since 1798

NASHVILLE DALLAS MEXICO CITY RIO DE JANEIRO BEIJING

The Life of Moses
The Smart Guide to the Bible™ Series
Copyright © 2008 by GRQ, Inc.

Published in Nashville, Tennessee, by Thomas Nelson. Thomas Nelson is a trademark of Thomas Nelson, Inc.

Thomas Nelson, Inc. titles may be purchased in bulk for educational, business, fundraising, or sales promotional use. For information, please e-mail SpecialMarkets@ThomasNelson.com.

General Editor: Larry Richards
Managing Editor: Michael Christopher
Associate Editor: Karen Artl Moore
Scripture Editor: Deborah Wiseman
Assistant Editor: Amy Clark
Design: Diane Whisner

ISBN 10: 1-4185-1009-2
ISBN 13: 978-1-4185-1009-1

Printed in the United States of America
10 11   9 8 7 6 5 4 3

Introduction

Meet Moses

Picture an old man striding into Egypt some fourteen hundred years before Christ. His beard and hair are white, his face weathered by the hot desert sun. Bright eyes peer out from under bushy white eyebrows, and as he walks he leans now and then on a long, hooked shepherd's staff. You might see old men who look much as he did in the Middle East today. But this old man carries his eighty years of life well, and his pace suggests he's a man on a mission.

Moses has had a checkered past. He was born a slave but grew up as a prince of Egypt, one of the ancient world's Great Powers. Later he defected from his adopted race and identified with his slave heritage. At forty, he murdered an Egyptian and fled into the desert. Moses spent the next forty years of his life as a shepherd, passing lonely days and nights caring for his father-in-law's flocks. At eighty he had an encounter with God, and was commissioned to return to Egypt. Now he's about to confront Pharaoh, the ruler of Egypt, arguably the most powerful individual in the world. Moses will demand that Egypt free its slaves—and when Pharaoh refuses, this old man will call on God to perform a series of miracles that will ruin prosperous Egypt and bring grief to every Egyptian household.

It's an unlikely story. Yet it's a true story, and this solitary old man has had a greater impact on our lives—and on our concept of God—than any individual other than Jesus Christ himself.

Moses is honored as the man who . . .

1. delivered Israel from bondage in Egypt.

2. wrote the first five books of the Old Testament.

3. revealed the personal name of God.

4. was Israel's first and greatest prophet.

5. transformed a slave people into a disciplined, united people.

6. gave Israel the law by which many Jews still live.

7. gave humankind the Ten Commandments.

And the Winner Is . . .

If we were to name one man, other than Jesus, whose influence has had the greatest continuing impact on Western civilization, we'd have to pick Moses. No one else has helped shape the conscience of the human family as much as Moses did. No one else has helped establish the Western world's concept of who God is and what He is like to a comparable extent. And no one else—via both his own character and the *messages he delivered directly from God*—has so clearly defined a people that they've maintained their distinctive identity over the course of nearly four millennia.

The Hebrews, the children of Israel, the Jews—all common names for the people Moses led—still remain, separate and distinct. Practically all the other distinct "people groups" that interacted through the centuries with the people Moses represented before God have long since been absorbed into the surrounding world.

As we study Moses, the man and his mission, we'll explore his impact on sacred history and on our own personal histories. And we'll discover something else as we follow his journey through the pages of the five Bible books tradition tells us Moses wrote. We'll find that Moses, far more than any other Old Testament figure, had an intimate relationship with God—literally, a "working" relationship that is unparalleled in the Bible. And as we look at encounter after encounter between Moses and the Lord, in effect we'll be "mentored" by Moses in our *own* relationship with God.

Through Moses we'll come to know God better and better.

> ## what others say
>
> ### Gene Getz
> Moses was a man who literally walked and talked with God. In turn, God spoke to him face-to-face, as man speaks with his friend (Exodus 33:11). No leader in Israel ever experienced God's presence like Moses.[1]

Benefits Galore

What are the benefits of studying Moses the man, and learning about his mission? Here are just a few:

- *You'll be mentored in your relationship with God by Moses*, who knew God intimately. This study of Moses will enrich and deepen your personal relationship with the Lord.

- *You'll discover the significance of Moses's contributions to our faith*, most notably:
  - *in the revelation of the name Yahweh.* God told Moses, "This is My name forever" (Exodus 3:15 NKJV). Understanding this name can give you comfort and confidence in your daily life.
  - *in the performing of the Exodus miracles.* Miracles help us define who God is and how we can expect Him to work in our lives today.
  - *in the making of the Law Covenant given at Sinai.* We need to know what the law is and what it isn't if we're to live godly, guilt-free lives.
  - i*n the presentation of Moses as the Bible's prototype prophet.* Prophets play a significant role throughout the Old Testament. You'll come to understand the role of prophets, and what takes their place in your life today.
  - *in the establishment of the Old Testament worship system.* No Old Testament institution better foreshadows and helps to explain the significance of Christ's death on the cross.
- *You'll develop a better understanding of the first five books of the Old Testament.* These five books lay the foundation of Judeo-Christian faith, a foundation every Christian needs to understand.
- *You'll grow in your appreciation for the Lord.* The clearer our understanding of God's revelation of Himself in Scripture, the less confused we are about who He is—and the better we love Him.

Hard, or Easy?

If this sounds like a lot of work, take heart. Each book in The Smart Guide to the Bible™ series is designed to help you master the Bible—and make the process as easy as possible! Each author is an expert in his or her own field; each has carefully researched his or her subject matter. You get the benefit of years of research without having to do that research yourself. And, as each author highlights the most important elements in the Bible, he or she will also help you see the relevance of these elements to your own life.

Many tools built into this book also provide significant help. These are designed to further clarify what the author is saying. No other commentary or study material available provides as many aids to understanding God's Word.

I (Pre) Suppose

Actually, everyone who writes about the Bible begins with presuppositions. Indeed, we *all* start off with assumptions or beliefs about the nature of Scripture and the historical reliability of its accounts. All too often these presuppositions aren't stated, even though they shape everything that is said about Bible text itself. I believe that it's important to make such presuppositions clear, so let me explain mine.

Is Scripture "God's Word"?

My answer to that one is a resounding "Yes." More than twenty-six hundred times, Old Testament writers make assertions such as "God said" and "the Word of the LORD came to so-and-so." The writers of the Old Testament, and the community of faith that grew up around the Old Testament, were convinced that the biblical text was indeed revealed by God Himself.

This doesn't mean that the men who wrote the Bible books recorded word for word what God dictated. The human authors of the Old Testament books were active participants in the process, and their writings reflect their different styles and their personalities. But somehow the finished product remained "God's Word."

The technical name for what most Jews and Christians believe happened is "inspiration." Inspiration affirms that God was also actively involved in the writing of the Bible. In fact, He was so involved that the finished product, the words actually put on paper, convey exactly what God intended. The apostle Peter in his second New Testament letter simply says that "holy men of God spoke as they were moved by the Holy Spirit" (2 Peter 1:21 NKJV). God was moving, and the result was that what these men recorded was a reliable and relevant word from God Himself.

That Was a Long, Long Time Ago!

Yes, it was. In fact, the first five books of the Old Testament, the books we'll be looking at in our study of Moses, were probably written down nearly fourteen hundred years before the birth of Christ. How do we know that the Scriptures we have today are accurate copies of words first recorded nearly three and a half millennia ago?

Part of the answer lies in the deep reverence that the Jewish people have historically held for what we call the Old Testament. Making copies of these Scriptures called for the greatest possible care. Each time a copyist wrote down a line of Scripture, he went back and counted each letter to make sure that the middle letter in that line was the same in his copy and in the text he was duplicating. When he finished a page, he went through the same process of counting every letter and verifying that the middle letter of the copy and the original text were the same. When he finished copying an Old Testament book, he again went back and counted to verify the middle letters were the same. Finally, several experts examined every single copied page upon completion; if they found even one mistake, they buried the page and the scribe started over.

For centuries, the earliest Old Testament text in existence dated from about AD 1100. Then a cache of Bible scrolls was found in a cave near Israel's Dead Sea. Among them was a scroll of the Old Testament book of Isaiah that dated from two hundred years before Christ. When that scroll of Isaiah was compared with the text of Isaiah recorded thirteen hundred years later, they were essentially the same!

It's true that we don't have the original writings themselves. But we can be completely confident that what we do have are extremely accurate copies of the original.

But I Don't Read Ancient Hebrew

What we have are English translations of copies of the original Hebrew text. So it's fair to ask, "How good are our English translations?" The answer to that is, "Very good."

It's true that there are words and expressions in the Hebrew that no one today really understands. But there are very few of these. Thousands of both Jewish and Christian scholars have dedicated their lives to studying ancient Hebrew, to comparing words and expressions to those found in similar ancient languages, and to clarifying difficult passages.

Similarly we have a number of English translations of the Bible that are dedicated to expressing in our language what the original texts expressed in Hebrew. We can be very confident that such English versions as the Revised Standard Version (RSV), New International Version (NIV), the New American Standard Bible (NASB), and The New King James Version (NKJV) reliably reflect what was in the original Hebrew manuscripts. For this series of books we've chosen to use the NKJV as our basic version, although at times other versions may also be quoted.

To sum it up, the first presupposition I make in writing this book is that the text we'll rely on in studying the life and mission of Moses really is God's reliable and relevant word, and that the English versions we read accurately convey what was in the original manuscripts.

One More Biggie: When?

There's another presupposition that has to be stated. That's a presupposition concerning when Moses lived. The "when" question isn't an easy one to answer, and believing scholars disagree.

In part the debate results from the fact that the first date in Hebrew history that can be fixed with certainty is the year that Solomon became king, 971 BC. In part the debate also reflects uncertainty about the exact dates of the reigns of the pharaohs of Egypt.

Another aspect of the debate rests on disagreements concerning the dating of pieces of pottery found in a burned-out level at ancient Jericho, which the Bible tells us the Israelites took and burned when they invaded Canaan.

The traditional view, based in large part on Scripture's testimony to the number of years between certain events, is that Moses led the Israelite slaves out of Egypt approximately 1,447 years before Christ. This would put Moses's birth around 1527 BC.

More recently, a date for the Israelites leaving Egypt of approximately 1275 BC was proposed, based primarily on archaeological evidence. This would place Moses's birth around 1305 BC.

The proponents of both dates cite archaeological evidence, and support their views with arguments based on what was happening in Egypt at the time. Unfortunately, the evidence on either side is far from conclusive. For this reason I've chosen to stick with the traditional biblical dating, and references to rulers and events taking place in Egypt reflect conditions in the 1500s–1400s BC.

In one sense, dating the Exodus has little relevance to the story of Moses's life and mission. While the precise "when" might be in doubt, the "what" is spelled out clearly in the pages of Scripture. And it is the "what" that concerns us most in this book.

Getting the Most Out of Moses

Moses is the most prominent individual in no less than four Old Testament books: Exodus, Leviticus, Numbers, and Deuteronomy. In the NKJV Bible I'm using as I write, those four books take up just a little less than one-sixth of the entire Old Testament (233 of 1,371 pages)! That's a lot of Bible, and I won't ask you to read everything on those pages. Here's what I will do:

1. I'll often sketch the "big picture" with overviews of many of the events and teachings recorded in these four books. If you find any of this information fascinating, feel free to go to the Bible and read any "Big Picture" section(s) that interests you.

2. I'll identify shorter core Bible passages that describe events or teachings that you really should look at for yourself. I'll summarize what's in them, but I encourage you to read these core passages thoughtfully.

3. I'll quote some Bible passages in this book, and we'll examine them closely together. Frequently these quoted passages will involve dialogue between Moses and God that enables Moses to mentor you in developing a closer personal relationship with the Lord. At other times these quoted passages will contain pivotal information that you need in order to understand foundational biblical truths. These are passages that you'll want to read again and again until you feel you understand their significance.

Of course, nothing I've just written should keep you from simply reading through the entire four books. But if your time is limited, the approach outlined above will help you learn what's in each Bible book, and you'll understand what's most significant in each one.

One other thing. Please don't hurry to get through this book. It will be most helpful to you if you work through one chapter at a time, and then take a day off to think about what you've learned. To help you really understand what you've read, I've included questions at the end of each chapter. These aren't really test questions—you can't "fail" them. They're simply intended to help you recall what's most significant. And you can check your answers against mine by flipping to the back of this book, where an answer key is provided.

So blessings, then, as we start off together on our study of Moses the man, and of his mission: a man and a mission that have shaped not only our society, but also you and me far more than we probably realize.

About the Author and the General Editor

Dr. Larry Richards is both the author of this book and the general editor of the series of which it is a part. Larry is a native of Michigan who now lives in Raleigh, North Carolina. He was converted to Christianity while in the Navy in the 1950s. Larry has taught and written Sunday school curriculum for every age group, from nursery through adult. He has published more than two hundred books that have been translated into twenty-six languages. His wife, Sue, is also an author. They both enjoy teaching Bible studies as well as fishing and playing golf.

Understanding the Bible Is Easy with These Tools

To understand God's Word you need easy-to-use study tools right where you need them—at your fingertips. The Smart Guide to the Bible™ series puts valuable resources adjacent to the text to save you both time and effort.

Every page features handy sidebars filled with icons and helpful information: cross references for additional insights, definitions of key words and concepts, brief commentaries from experts on the topic, points to ponder, evidence of God at work, the big picture of how passages fit into the context of the entire Bible, practical tips for applying biblical truths to every area of your life, and plenty of maps, charts, and illustrations. A wrap-up of each passage, combined with study questions, concludes each chapter.

These helpful tools show you what to watch for. Look them over to become familiar with them, and then turn to chapter 1 with complete confidence: You are about to increase your knowledge of God's Word!

Study Helps

The thought-bubble icon alerts you to commentary you might find particularly thought-provoking, challenging, or encouraging. You'll want to take a moment to reflect on it and consider the implications for your life.

Don't miss this point! The exclamation-point icon draws your attention to a key point in the text and emphasizes important biblical truths and facts.

death on the cross
Colossians 1:21–22

Many see Boaz as a type of Jesus Christ. To win back what we human beings lost through sin and spiritual death, Jesus had to become human (i.e., he had to become a true kinsman), and he had to be willing to pay the penalty for our sins. With his <u>death on the cross</u>, Jesus paid the penalty and won freedom and eternal life for us.

The additional Bible verses add scriptural support for the passage you just read and help you better understand the <u>underlined text</u>. (Think of it as an instant reference resource!)

How does what you just read apply to your life? The heart icon indicates that you're about to find out! These practical tips speak to your mind, heart, body, and soul, and offer clear guidelines for living a righteous and joy-filled life, establishing priorities, maintaining healthy relationships, persevering through challenges, and more.

This icon reveals how God is truly all-knowing and all-powerful. The hourglass icon points to a specific example of the prediction of an event or the fulfillment of a prediction. See how some of what God has said would come to pass already has!

What are some of the great things God has done? The traffic-sign icon shows you how God has used miracles, special acts, promises, and covenants throughout history to draw people to him.

Does the story or event you just read about appear elsewhere in the Gospels? The cross icon points you to those instances where the same story appears in other Gospel locations—further proof of the accuracy and truth of Jesus's life, death, and resurrection.

Since God created marriage, there's no better person to turn to for advice. The double-ring icon points out biblical insights and tips for strengthening your marriage.

The Bible is filled with wisdom about raising a godly family and enjoying your spiritual family in Christ. The family icon gives you ideas for building up your home and helping your family grow close and strong.

Isle of Patmos
a small island in the
Mediterranean Sea

something significant had occurred, he wrote down the substance of what he saw. This is the practice John followed when he recorded Revelation on the **Isle of Patmos.**

What does that word really mean, especially as it relates to this passage? Important, misunderstood, or infrequently used words are set in **bold type** in your text so you can immediately glance at the margin for definitions. This valuable feature lets you better understand the meaning of the entire passage without having to stop to check other references.

the big picture

Joshua
Led by Joshua, the Israelites crossed the Jordan River and invaded Canaan (see Illustration #8). In a series of military campaigns the Israelites defeated several coalition armies raised by the inhabitants of Canaan. With organized resistance put down, Joshua divided the land among the twelve Israelite

How does what you read fit in with the greater biblical story? The highlighted big picture summarizes the passage under discussion.

what others say

David Breese
Nothing is clearer in the Word of God than the fact that God wants us to understand himself and his working in the lives of men.[5]

It can be helpful to know what others say on the topic, and the highlighted quotation introduces another voice in the discussion. This resource enables you to read other opinions and perspectives.

Maps, charts, and illustrations pictorially represent ancient artifacts and show where and how stories and events took place. They enable you to better understand important empires, learn your way around villages and temples, see where major battles occurred, and follow the journeys of God's people. You'll find these graphics let you do more than study God's Word—they let you *experience* it.

Chapters at a Glance

Chapter 1
The First Eighty Years

Chapter Highlights:
- Along the Nile
- Getting Here from There
- In Egypt's Royal Court
- Pick a People
- Off to the Sinai

Let's Get Started

The three-year-olds I taught when I was editor of nursery curriculum at Scripture Press loved the story of <u>baby Moses</u>. They'd place Moses's chubby figure in the basket-boat we fashioned, and wait eagerly for a princess to appear to rescue him from the river. They didn't understand why Moses had been hidden in his floating cradle fashioned of reeds. And they didn't realize that this babe would grow up to become one of history's most famous individuals. But they loved the story. And they loved baby Moses.

Later, most Sunday schoolers went beyond the stories of Moses's infancy and learned something of the man and something of his mission. But despite his fame, few have a sense of Moses as a human being. I can't recall ever hearing a sermon preached on Moses. Even commentaries on the biblical book of Exodus, where Moses is a central character, tend to ignore Moses the man and focus on his mission.

Yet it's fascinating to look at Scripture and consider the impact of the events related there on the development of this man, whom so many honor as one of Scripture's greats. But before we can understand Moses as a person, we have to know something of his times.

baby Moses
Exodus 2:1–10

Hebrews
Jews, Israelites, descendants of Abraham, Isaac, and Jacob

Semitic
eastern Mediterranean people living north of Egypt, Asiatics

Toughing It Out Along the Nile

Moses was born a slave in Egypt. His parents were slaves. His brother Aaron and sister Miriam were slaves. They were **Hebrews**, members of a slave race—**Semitic** peoples who had been in Egypt for centuries but who were distinctively different from the native Egyptians. As is often the case with slavery, Moses's people were persecuted, worked to exhaustion—and feared.

Chapter 1 of the book of Exodus provides a vivid picture of the relationship between the Egyptians and their slaves.

Pharaoh
the title of Egypt's
rulers

supply cities
treasure cities

rigor
severity, harshness

paranoia
unreasonable fear

Pure Paranoia?

EXODUS 1:9–14 *And he [the king] said to his people, "Look, the people of the children of Israel are more and mightier than we; come, let us deal shrewdly with them, lest they multiply, and it happen, in the event of war, that they also join our enemies and fight against us, and so go up out of the land." Therefore they set taskmasters over them to afflict them with their burdens. And they built for **Pharaoh supply cities**, Pithom and Raamses. But the more they afflicted them, the more they multiplied and grew. And they were in dread of the children of Israel. So the Egyptians made the children of Israel serve with **rigor**. And they made their lives bitter with hard bondage—in mortar, in brick, and in all manner of service in the field. All their service in which they made them serve was with rigor. (NKJV)*

On first reading it looks as though, when Moses was born, Pharaoh and the Egyptians were in the grip of pure **paranoia**. But in fact Pharaoh's speculation that the Israelites might join a potential enemy had a solid historical basis. During what's called the "second intermediate period" of Egypt's history (1759–1539 BC), an Asiatic peoples we call the Hyksos had ruled the delta region of Egypt. The Egyptians called these rulers *hegakhases*, "rulers of foreign lands." They had been finally driven out by Ahmose I, who founded the first of the New Kingdom dynasties in 1567 BC.

Josephus, the first-century Jewish general-turned-historian, claims to quote from Manetho, an Egyptian whose writings have been lost, in describing the Hyksos invasion.

key point

what others say

Josephus

There came, after a surprising manner, men of obscure birth from the east, and had the temerity to invade our country, and easily conquered it by force, as we did not do battle against them. After they had subdued our rulers, they burnt down our cities, and destroyed the temples of the gods, and treated the inhabitants most cruelly, killing some and enslaving their wives and children. . . . They all along waged war against the Egyptians, and wanted to destroy them to the very root.[1]

While archaeology suggests this picture of Hyksos rule is over-drawn, we can understand why, after the Hyksos were expelled, the Egyptians were suspicious of the large Hebrew population in their land. After all, the Hebrews came from the same part of the world as the Hyksos.

What is harder to understand is Pharaoh's concern that the Israelites might join their enemies and "so go up out of the land" (Exodus 1:10 NKJV). If the Egyptians were uneasy about the Hebrews, why not just expel them? The most logical explanation is that the Hebrews were already being used as slave labor. Even though the Egyptians were frightened by the Hebrews' numbers, they were addicted to the free labor the Israelites provided.

ratcheting up
marked increase

The Tough Get Tougher

The Egyptians were already tough on the Hebrews. But they were about to get tougher. They had put the Israelites to work on the massive building projects that were so dear to all the Egyptian pharaohs. Now they "set taskmasters over them to afflict them with their burdens" (Exodus 1:11 NKJV). This phrase marks a **ratcheting up** of the pressure on the Hebrew slaves, and the phrase "lest they multiply" (1:10 NKJV) suggests that Pharaoh intended to work these slaves to death. While it's probable that thousands died working on such projects as the building of Pithom and Raamses, the strategy didn't succeed. "The more they afflicted them, the more they multiplied and grew" (1:12 NKJV).

Pharaoh's Oppression of the Israelites

	Pharaoh's Effort	Biblical Reference
Step 1	Enslave the Israelites	Exodus 1:10b (implied)
Step 2	Afflict them with their burdens	Exodus 1:11
Step 3	Make their lives bitter with hard bondage	Exodus 1:13–14
Step 4	Order midwives to kill male infants	Exodus 1:15–16
Step 5	Command the whole Hebrew population to throw their newborn sons into the Nile	Exodus 1:22

go to

brutal Babylonians
Ezekiel 7:24–25;
Habakkuk 1:5–11

**principles of
judgment**
natural conse-
quences of evil
behavior

pledges
The poor would
often leave their
cloak as a guarantee
they would repay a
loan. OT law
required that this
pledge be returned
at night, as it was
used as a blanket
(Exodus 22:26;
Deuteronomy
24:10–12).

Brutality Brings Dread

There's no doubt that the increasing brutality of the Egyptians
had an impact on the Israelites. But that brutality had an impact on
the Egyptians as well. While the Israelites must have felt both hatred
and resentment, the excesses of the Egyptians filled the Egyptians
themselves with . . . fear!

Centuries later the prophet Habakkuk would question God when
he learned the Lord intended to permit a <u>brutal Babylonian</u> army to
conquer Judah. Habakkuk realized that the behavior of God's people deserved punishment. But, he asked, how could the Lord let a
people like the pagan Babylonians, who were certainly worse than
the people of Judah, get away with crushing God's own people?

In chapter 2 of the biblical book of Habakkuk the prophet records
God's surprising answer. No wicked ever "get away with" doing evil.
It may look as though they're on top of the world. Their successes
and their riches may provoke others to envy. But we live in a moral
universe. God has built into it **principles of judgment** that are constantly at work. One of those principles is that the successes of the
wicked, however great, can never bring them satisfaction (Habakkuk
2). Another principle is that when we oppress others we create a hostility which not only will destroy us in the future, but which creates
a present fear of those we harm.

> HABAKKUK 2:6–7
> *Will not all these take up a proverb against him,*
> *And a taunting riddle against him, and say,*
> *"Woe to him who increases*
> *What is not his—how long?*
> *And to him who loads himself with many **pledges**"?*
> *Will not your creditors rise up suddenly? (NKJV)*

This is what happened to the Egyptians. Their oppression of the
Israelites made the Egyptians afraid of their slaves. The fear made
them treat their slaves even more brutally. And, as the cycle of fear
leading to increased brutality leading to even greater fear spiraled
out of control, the Egyptians found themselves "in dread of the children of Israel" (Exodus 1:12 NKJV).

Good, but Not Good Enough

It's good for each of us to realize that those who do evil to others aren't really getting away with it, however well-off they may seem. It's also important for us to realize that any inner, psychological impact on those who do evil isn't punishment enough. This is a moral universe, and God is committed to "'render to each one according to his deeds' . . . to those who are self-seeking and do not obey the truth, but obey unrighteousness—indignation and wrath" (Romans 2:6, 8 NKJV).

Remember this as we move deeper into the book of Exodus and see the destructive plagues God brings on Egypt and its people. The once-fruitful land will be devastated and lie in ruin, and anguished wails will rise from those who have lost their firstborn. All these will be consequences of the systematic oppression of the Israelites by the Egyptians and their rulers. The fear with which God punished the oppressors was good—but not good enough.

Beyond Oppression

> EXODUS 1:15–16 *Then the king of Egypt spoke to the Hebrew midwives, of whom the name of one was Shiphrah and the name of the other Puah; and he said, "When you do the duties of a midwife for the Hebrew women, and see them on the birth-stools, if it is a son, then you shall kill him; but if it is a daughter, then she shall live." (NKJV)*

Dread of the slave race drove Pharaoh beyond oppression to attempt the extermination of the Hebrew people. Without the technology available to the Nazis in Germany, Pharaoh took a simpler but potentially more effective approach. He ordered that every boy born to Hebrew parents be killed at birth. If the Egyptian solution had worked, within a generation there would have been no Hebrew people.

Like every other attempt to exterminate the Jews, from <u>Haman's</u> in the time of the Persian Empire to Hitler's in the past century, Pharaoh's attempt failed. God used two unlikely people to thwart the powerful ruler's plan.

Haman's
Esther 3:8–13

Semitic
the racial group of
which the Hebrews
were a part

feared
respected, honored

Are Two Plenty?

Archaeologists frequently develop lists of common names given to people in different eras. The lists are aids in dating monuments or documents where the names appear. And the names Shiphrah and Puah were in fact common **Semitic** names in the second millennium BC. Still, critics have challenged the reliability of the biblical text, arguing that if there really were multitudes of Israelites in Egypt, they could hardly have been served by just two midwives. In posing this argument the critics overlook the Egyptian love of bureaucracy. It seems far more likely that Shiphrah and Puah headed a guild of midwives who served both Hebrew and Egyptian mothers-to-be.

When the two were given orders by Pharaoh they determined not to follow them. As Egyptian women would hardly stoop to do a task assigned the slave race, it must have been easy for Shiphrah and Puah to enlist the many Hebrew midwives of Egypt in their plot of passive resistance. They did not defy Pharaoh. They simply didn't carry out his orders.

It Was Right, but Did They Do Wrong?

EXODUS 1:17–21 *But the midwives* **feared** *God, and did not do as the king of Egypt commanded them, but saved the male children alive. So the king of Egypt called for the midwives and said to them, "Why have you done this thing, and saved the male children alive?" And the midwives said to Pharaoh, "Because the Hebrew women are not like the Egyptian women; for they are lively and give birth before the midwives come to them." Therefore God dealt well with the midwives, and the people multiplied and grew very mighty. And so it was, because the midwives feared God, that He provided households for them.* (NKJV)

Some people seem to take great delight in finding supposed factual contradictions in God's Word. Typically their arguments are flawed. Like those who assumed that because only two midwives were named there were only two midwives in all of Egypt, critics leap too quickly to their conclusion and shout, "See! Here's a mistake!" Usually, as in the case of Shiphrah and Puah, the two midwives, there's a logical explanation for the supposed contradiction.

key point

Others look for supposed moral contradictions, either to discredit Scripture or to whittle away at its **moral imperatives**. So it's not surprising to find Exodus 1 charged with moral inconsistency for the report that "God dealt well with the midwives" for what they did. "How," the critics say, "can the Bible say that <u>lying is wrong</u>, when God obviously rewarded those two for lying to Pharaoh?"

But did the midwives lie? What they told Pharaoh was, "The Hebrew women are not like the Egyptian women; for they are lively and give birth before the midwives come to them" (Exodus 1:19 NKJV). In all likelihood this was the exact truth! What better way to thwart the king's orders and protect themselves at the same time than to delay when called to assist at a Hebrew birth? Shiphrah and Puah found a way to honor God and at the same time to protect Egypt's midwives . . . without having to lie.

This isn't the place to go into a detailed discussion of **ethics**. But the story does remind us that most ethical **dilemmas** can be resolved without violating revealed standards of right and wrong. And where it is impossible to avoid painful consequences for doing the right thing, we need to be willing to follow Scripture's <u>exhortation to do good</u>. As 1 Peter 2:19 reminds us, "This is commendable, if because of conscience toward God one endures grief, suffering wrongfully" (NKJV).

lying is wrong
Proverbs 19:5;
Ephesians 4:25

exhortation to do good
Romans 13:1–5;
1 Peter 2:12

moral imperatives
biblical teachings on what is right and wrong

ethics
principles guiding moral behavior

dilemmas
difficult situations

Back to the Main Point

For all the possible distractions in the biblical text, we need to keep the main point in view. When Moses was born, probably around 1527 BC, his people were slaves whose numbers terrified their Egyptian masters. That fear had driven Pharaoh and his people to treat the Israelites more and more brutally. Pharaoh's command that the midwives kill all male infants had been thwarted, leading the ruler to issue a final, ultimate decree. Pharaoh "commanded all his people," literally the "whole population," saying, "Every son who is born you [the Israelite] shall cast into the river" (Exodus 1:22 NKJV).

Now the whole community was responsible. As infants developed in their mothers' wombs, the parents must have looked at each other and wondered: Would it be a girl, and live? Or would it be a son, condemning them to murder their own child or face possible punishment?

Abraham
the founder and
father of the
Israelites, the Jewish
people

Canaan
modern Israel and
Palestine, the Jewish
homeland

This was the pressure under which the Hebrew people lived when Moses entered the world. They were brutalized, afflicted, their lives bitter—and they had been ordered to exterminate every hope of a future for their race.

Getting Here from There

the big picture

Genesis 12–50

The descendants of **Abraham**, who came to the land of **Canaan** some two thousand years before Christ, have lived there for three generations. Abraham's grandson Jacob, also known as Israel, fathered a dozen sons. Eleven live with him now, and Jacob mistakenly believes that his youngest, Joseph, has been killed by wild animals.

What actually happened, however, is that his jealous brothers have sold Joseph into slavery. Joseph has then been resold to a high Egyptian official, and after a series of disasters has come to the attention of Pharaoh as a reliable interpreter of dreams. When Joseph explains that two dreams of Pharaoh foretell a terrible famine in the Egypt and the whole Middle East, Pharaoh appoints Joseph to supervise Egypt and store up food supplies. When the predicted famine strikes, only Egypt is prepared. Back in Canaan, Jacob and the brothers of Joseph are starving.

When Jacob reluctantly sends his sons to buy food in Egypt, Joseph recognizes them. After his brothers make a third trip to Egypt, Joseph finally tells them who he is. He invites the whole family to move to Egypt, both to be near him and to survive the drought, and they are welcomed by Pharaoh himself. The family settles down on choice land, and prospers. But their numbers grow and grow, and after the Hyksos are driven out of Egypt the suspicious and fearful Egyptians make the descendants of Jacob/Israel slaves. This history lies behind the opening words of the book of Exodus.

How did the Israelites come to Egypt in the first place? We're told the story in the book of Genesis, chapters 37–40.

The Trip to Egypt

EXODUS 1:1–8 *Now these are the names of the children of Israel who came to Egypt; each man and his household came with Jacob: Reuben, Simeon, Levi, and Judah; Issachar, Zebulun, and Benjamin; Dan, Naphtali, Gad, and Asher. All those who were descendants of Jacob were seventy persons (for Joseph was in Egypt already). And Joseph died, all his brothers, and all that generation. But the children of Israel were fruitful and increased abundantly, multiplied and grew exceedingly mighty; and the land was filled with them.*

Now there arose a new king over Egypt, who did not know Joseph. (NKJV)

And with this last sentence reporting "a new king over Egypt," we are launched into the situation that existed when Moses was born.

Moses Is Born, and Adopted

EXODUS 2:1–10 *And a man of the house of Levi went and took as wife a daughter of Levi. So the woman conceived and bore a son. And when she saw that he was a beautiful child, she hid him three months. But when she could no longer hide him, she took an ark of bulrushes for him, daubed it with asphalt and pitch, put the child in it, and laid it in the reeds by the river's bank. And his sister stood afar off, to know what would be done to him.*

Then the daughter of Pharaoh came down to bathe at the river. And her maidens walked along the riverside; and when she saw the ark among the reeds, she sent her maid to get it. And when she opened it, she saw the child, and behold, the baby wept. So she had compassion on him, and said, "This is one of the Hebrews' children." Then his sister said to Pharaoh's daughter, "Shall I go and call a nurse for you from the Hebrew women, that she may nurse the child for you?" And Pharaoh's daughter said to her, "Go." So the maiden went and called the child's mother. Then Pharaoh's daughter said to her, "Take this child away and nurse him for me, and I will give you your wages." So the woman took the child and nursed him. And the child grew, and she brought him to Pharaoh's daughter, and he became her son. So she called his name Moses, saying, "Because I drew him out of the water." (NKJV)

sages
highly respected
scholars

Both the "bulrushes" and the "reeds" mentioned in this verse are papyrus plants, which grew along the Nile and whose pulp was used to make paper. Reeds woven together were also used to fashion baskets, and bundles of buoyant papyrus reeds were bound together to fashion boats.

The phrase "when she could no longer hide him" is significant. Apparently there was no organized attempt to hide infants in the Israelite community. There may even have been informants eager to curry favor with the oppressors. At any rate, the danger seemed significant enough that Moses's mother felt she had to act.

There's an irony in what she chose to do. Pharaoh had commanded the Israelites, "Every son who is born you shall cast into the river" (Exodus 1:22 NKJV). Now Moses's mother obeyed the letter of that command—but made sure that his life would be preserved by placing him in a watertight basket first! It's also possible to see in the text a likelihood that Moses was purposely placed in an area where Pharaoh's daughter was known to bathe. Thus the princess did appear, "saw the ark among the reeds" (2:5 NKJV), and discovered the child.

key point

The next event suggests that Moses's mother really had foreseen what might happen. Moses's older sister, Miriam, had been posted to watch the baby. When the princess saw the child, Miriam immediately spoke up. "Shall I go and call a nurse for you from the Hebrew women, that she may nurse the child for you?" (2:7 NKJV). If the princess had not thought of adopting the baby, Miriam's words planted the idea in her mind. And she quickly agreed.

Four Formative Years

EXODUS 2:9b–10 *So the woman took the child and nursed him. And the child grew, and she brought him to Pharaoh's daughter . . . (NKJV)*

Everyone agrees that the brief time Moses stayed with his mother strongly influenced his life. Church fathers—early and influential writers and theologians in the Christian church—echo Jewish sages in emphasizing the importance of the first years of life. One church father in particular, Chrysostom, a fourth-century Christian bishop and the patriarch of Constantinople, stressed the importance of telling stories from the Bible: Surely Moses's mother must have related many of the stories found in early Genesis to her child! The stories of a God who spoke to Abraham and Isaac and to Jacob, and who used Joseph to save the family from starvation, shaped Moses's sense of identity. As an adult he would take a stand with the slave population and reject his privileged position as a prince of Egypt.

Moses's mother made the most of his early years, after he was brought back to her for nursing. The stories she told took such deep root that they shaped the man.

something to ponder

Insight from the New Testament

EXODUS 2:10 . . . *she brought him to Pharaoh's daughter, and he became her [the princess's] son.* (NKJV)

The New Testament book of Acts picks up the story and adds to the Exodus record. In a speech given before the Jewish ruling court, an early Christian leader named Stephen says, "Pharaoh's daughter took him away and brought him up as her own son. And Moses was learned in all the wisdom of the Egyptians, and was mighty in words and deeds" (Acts 7:21–22 NKJV). And the writer of the book of Hebrews indicates that Moses carried the title of "son of Pharaoh's daughter" (Hebrews 11:24 NKJV). We'll return to these passages later. But already they provide important clues to Moses's life in the court of Egypt, and to the possible future that Moses abandoned when he took sides with the enslaved Israelites.

Amun
an Egyptian deity

Meet Hatshepsut

Many scholars believe that the princess who discovered baby Moses was Hatshepsut, who became the first female pharaoh of Egypt. If so, the day she came down to the river to bathe and found Moses she would only have been seven or eight years old.[4]

We can imagine the little girl's excitement, and her impetuous decision to keep the doll-like child. We also know something of her father, Thutmose, and his affection for his daughter, his only surviving child by his principal wife. Women played a significant role in the Egyptian court, and marriage to a king's daughter solidified a pharaoh's claim to Egypt's throne. This was especially the case with Thutmose, who designed his daughter as heiress to the throne. In Egypt it was the heiress who actually conveyed the throne to her husband when they married.[5]

Hatshepsut was fifteen, and her son and friend Moses eight or nine, when she married Thutmose II and became the queen of Egypt. The two had no children, although Thutmose II had a son by a secondary wife. When Thutmose II died, Hatshepsut married her underage nephew, Thutmose III, and she ruled the country. Egyptian Internet services provide this summary of her career:

> Hatshepsut, the fifth ruler of the 18th Dynasty, was the daughter of Thutmose I and Queen Ahmose. As was common in the royal family, she married her half-brother, Thutmose II, who had a son, Thusmose III, by a minor wife. When Thutmose II died in 1479 B.C. his son Thutmose III was appointed heir. However, Hatshepsut was appointed regent due to the boy's young age. They ruled jointly until 1473, when she declared herself pharaoh. Dressed in men's attire, Hatshepsut administered affairs of the nation with the full support of the high priest, Hapuseneb and other officials. When she built her magnificent temple at Deir el Bahan in Thebes she made reliefs of her divine birth as the daughter of **Amun**. Hatshepsut disappeared in 1458 B.C. when Thutmose III, wishing to reclaim the throne, led a revolt. Thutmose had her shrines, statues and reliefs mutilated.[6]

Despite Thutmose III's attempts to wipe out all references to Hatshepsut, records do remain, such as this inscription cut in the stone of a government official named Ineni. Having ascended into heaven, he [Thuthmose II] became united with the gods, and his son, being arisen in his place as king of the Two Lands, ruled upon the throne of his begetter, while his sister, the god's wife Hashepsowe governed the land and the Two Lands were under her control; people worked for her, and Egypt bowed the head.[7]

As the "son of Pharaoh's daughter" and of Egypt's first female pharaoh, Moses would have been a significant member of the royal family. Should anything have happened to Thutmose III, there's a possibility that Moses might have married his "mother" and become pharaoh himself! Certainly Moses had every educational and other advantage available to a member of the royal family, and the later contention that "Moses was learned in all the wisdom of the Egyptians" (Acts 7:22 NKJV) is no overstatement.

key point

Egypt and the Bible

Dates (BC)	Egypt	The Bible
2040–1759	Middle Kingdom Strong, prosperous Influence in Canaan	Abraham enters Canaan The Hebrews move to Egypt
1759–1539	Second Intermediate Period Hyksos control Egypt's delta	
1539–1070	New Kingdom Hyksos expelled Hebrews enslaved Emenhotep II Pharaoh Egypt's power limited, 150 years	Moses born, 1527 Exodus takes place, 1447

The Wisdom of the Egyptians

The Egyptians valued learning, and the educated man was thought to have a great advantage over the uneducated. Adolph Erman, in *Life in Ancient Egypt*, asserts that "learning . . . divided the ruling class from those who were ruled."[8]

Indications are that "all the royal sons received the education of a potential pharaoh since no one could know whom fate had in store for the succession."[9] In the palace school, Moses would have studied not only the literature of Egypt, but would have learned to read and write other languages as well. His curriculum would have included stories of the gods of Egypt and all the myths of that ancient land. Moses would also have learned basic mathematics. And, as the practice was in the New Kingdom, Moses would have been given military training and, quite likely, a military command.

As the "son of Pharaoh's daughter"—especially such a daughter as Hatshepsut—Moses would have received the best possible education and would have been given truly significant posts in the administration of Egypt. He certainly would have had an education that equipped him to write down the bulk of the first five books of the Old Testament, as long-established tradition insists that he did. But, surprisingly, as we'll discover as we continue our study, his Egyptian education did little else to equip him for his mission. Nor did the theology of Egypt provide any ideas for the radically different revelation he was to receive from the God of the Hebrews.

Pick a People

> EXODUS 2:11–12 *Now it came to pass in those days, when Moses was grown, that he went out to his brethren and looked at their burdens. And he saw an Egyptian beating a Hebrew, one of his brethren. So he looked this way and that way, and when he saw no one, he killed the Egyptian and hid him in the sand.* (NKJV)

When Moses was forty years old, an event occurred that shaped his future and still shapes our lives today. Prince Moses committed a crime that led him to abandon Egypt, and perhaps to abandon a long-held secret dream.

Despite all his privileges as a prince of Egypt, Moses continued to **identify with** the Hebrew slaves. These people, not the Egyptians, were his true "brethren." The stories his mother had told him had gripped his heart, and witnessing their suffering was too much for him. When he observed a fellow Hebrew being beaten by an Egyptian he felt driven to act. He was cautious—he didn't want anyone to know where his sympathies lay just yet—but still he acted.

Moses had made his choice. He had picked the Hebrew slaves over Egypt.

The murder of the Egyptian reveals traits that most of us tend to admire. Moses was a man of action, not talk. Perhaps he acted impetuously, but he did act decisively. He was resolute in holding his convictions, clear-thinking in the heat of the moment. One would imagine that these would be the very traits God would value in a man He might choose to deliver His people.

In fact, these are the very traits that kept the forty-year-old Moses from being usable by God! It's a very different Moses we meet at age eighty; and it's that different Moses whom God found usable, and whom God did in fact use.

I Have a Dream

ACTS 7:23–25 *Now when he was forty years old, it came into his heart to visit his brethren, the children of Israel. And seeing one of them suffer wrong, he defended and avenged him who was oppressed, and struck down the Egyptian. For he supposed that his brethren would have understood that God would deliver them by his hand, but they did not understand. (NKJV)*

The book of Acts adds an insight. Stephen's words help us understand that Moses had dreamed of delivering his people from slavery! In his dream Moses saw himself as the instrument God would use to free Israel. And Moses embraced the dream. Moses became convinced that he truly was God's man for the job.

We don't know whether God had revealed this to Moses, or whether the dream bubbled up through his consciousness, stimulated by the stories told by his mother when he was a child. It seems likely that Moses viewed the murder of the Egyptian as the first blow to be struck in his battle to free the Israelites. If so, the events that followed on the next day certainly shattered Moses's dream.

They Know What I Did!

EXODUS 2:13–15a *And when he went out the second day, behold, two Hebrew men were fighting, and he said to the one who did the wrong, "Why are you striking your companion?" Then he said, "Who made you a prince and a judge over us? Do you intend to kill me as you killed the Egyptian?" So Moses feared and said, "Surely this thing is known!" When Pharaoh heard of the matter, he sought to kill Moses. But Moses fled from the face of Pharaoh . . . (NKJV)*

From a historical point of view, Moses had good reason to run. When Moses was forty, the pharaoh was none other than Thutmose III, whose hatred for Hatshepsut surely extended to her adopted son, Moses. Although Hatshepsut controlled the nation, Thutmose had his own competing court and adherents. The murder Moses committed provided all the grounds that Thutmose needed to act against him, and through Moses to strike at his hated wife.

But there's more to the story of Moses's flight than we can deduce from the Exodus text. Once again the New Testament provides insight, first into Moses's "by faith" choice of a people, and second into Moses's surprising "by faith" flight.

Not Afraid of Whom?

HEBREWS 11:24–27 *By faith Moses, when he became of age, refused to be called the son of Pharaoh's daughter, choosing rather to suffer affliction with the people of God than to enjoy the passing pleasures of sin, esteeming the* **reproach of Christ** *greater riches than the treasures in Egypt; for he looked to the reward. By faith he forsook Egypt, not fearing the wrath of the king; for he endured as seeing Him who is invisible.* (NKJV)

That phrase "not fearing the wrath of the king" truly is surprising. If Moses wasn't afraid of the king, why did he rush out of Egypt?

This is a question we can't answer with certainty. But we can suggest possibilities. For one, the reaction of the Hebrews may have led Moses to question his dream. Was he really intended to deliver the Israelites? Or was it all his imagination? The sudden loss of our dreams often leads to a time of despair and depression. It's possible that Moses was so shaken by the experience that he felt he simply had to get away for a time, and reevaluate.

A more likely possibility seems to be that in murdering the Egyptian, Moses confronted something in himself that shook him. Moses undoubtedly was an idealist. He saw himself as a deliverer, not a killer. But then he had felt nearly uncontrollable anger and hatred surge when he saw the Egyptian beating one of his own people. Controlled by powerful emotions, he murdered another human being. It was an act that we might try to justify. But it's likely that Moses refused to make excuses; he saw in himself something that he did not like, and he feared it.

If this is what happened, Moses's flight from Egypt makes perfect sense. Moses simply had to leave—to get away and search his own soul in a painful effort to **reconcile** his image of himself as a deliverer with the fact that he was now a murderer.

There's no way for us to know for sure why Moses fled. But flee he did. And he hid himself away in one of the most desolate places on earth for the next forty years!

Off to the Sinai

go to

the Sinai
Exodus 16:1; 19:1–2

Gershom
stranger

EXODUS 2:15b–17, 21–22 *Moses fled from the face of Pharaoh and dwelt in the land of Midian; and he sat down by a well.*

Now the priest of Midian had seven daughters. And they came and drew water, and they filled the troughs to water their father's flock. Then the shepherds came and drove them away; but Moses stood up and helped them, and watered their flock . . . Then Moses was content to live with the man, and he gave Zipporah his daughter to Moses. And she bore him a son. He called his name **Gershom**, *for he said, "I have been a stranger in a foreign land." (NKJV)*

In the time of Moses, nomadic groups of Midianite peoples wandered northwestern Arabia and parts of the Sinai peninsula. Some of them, like the family that Moses fell in with, followed herds of sheep from place to place. Others were traders, while some were miners. We know that the group Moses joined wandered <u>the Sinai</u>. We also know that although the twenty-four-thousand-square-mile Sinai was hot and dry, wandering herdsmen had lived there for thousands of years, and that as early as the 2600s BC the Egyptians had mined turquoise there.[10]

key point

For forty long years Moses would wander that desert, caring for his father-in-law's flocks and pondering his circumstances. The chances are that during those forty years Moses's dream died. Certainly, as we'll see in the next chapter, Moses himself was deeply affected, for the Moses who came out of the Sinai wilderness was a very different person from the Moses who entered it.

Now, for Some Real Help

EXODUS 2:23–25 *Now it happened in the process of time that the king of Egypt died. Then the children of Israel groaned because of the bondage, and they cried out; and their cry came up to God because of the bondage. So God heard their groaning, and God remembered His covenant with Abraham, with Isaac, and with Jacob. And God looked upon the children of Israel, and God acknowledged them. (NKJV)*

Moses may have misplaced his dream of delivering Egypt's slave population. But back in Egypt the continual persecution of the Israelites drove them to turn to the Lord.

covenant
commitment,
promise

Three things in these verses are particularly significant: (1) the cry of the Israelites, (2) the **covenant** God had made with Abraham, and (3) God's "remembering."

1. *The Cry of the Israelites*

We can't tell how greatly the Israelites' time in Egypt had corrupted their knowledge of God. It's likely that a great many looked to Egypt's gods. Ancient peoples evaluated the power of deities by the prosperity of the nation that worshipped them. Certainly on this basis the gods of mighty Egypt appeared more powerful than a god of slaves! And yet, appeals to Egypt's gods brought the Israelites no relief. Finally, unable to bear their bondage any longer, the Israelites looked to the true God. And God "heard their groaning."

2. *The Covenant with Abraham*

The text tells us that God "remembered His covenant with Abraham" (Exodus 2:24 NKJV). In biblical times, "covenants" served as legally binding instruments. A covenant made between two nations was a "treaty." A covenant made between two businessmen was a "contract." A covenant made between a ruler and his people was a "constitution." The concept of covenant, then, was very broad and applied to many different situations. So, what is the "covenant" that God made with Abraham?

---

the big picture

Genesis 12–20

It's about 2100 BC. Abraham, known as Abram, is a wealthy businessman in Ur, a major Mesopotamian city. Without warning, God speaks to Abram. God tells him to leave his homeland and go to a place that God will show him. At the same time God makes a number of promises to Abram, each time pledging himself by stating "I will . . ." The promises, later recorded in Genesis 12 and before that engraved on the minds of Abram's descendants, are:

I will make you a great nation;
I will bless you
And make your name great;
And you shall be a blessing.
I will bless those who bless you,
And I will curse him who curses you;
And in you all the families of the earth shall be blessed.
(Genesis 12:2–3 NKJV)

---

go to

covenant ceremony
Genesis 15:4–21

remembered
Deuteronomy 7:18;
Psalm 78:35;
Jonah 2:7

forgot
Judges 3:7;
Jeremiah 23:27

Abram leaves Ur and finally comes to the land of Canaan. There God confirms His promises in a special <u>covenant ceremony</u>. After Abraham dies the covenant promises are passed on to his son Isaac and his grandson Jacob, also known as Israel. Israel's twelve sons then inherit the covenant promises, and they are passed on through these sons to the whole Hebrew people.

The desperate Israelites are then driven by suffering to turn to the God of their fathers, to the God of the covenant.

God Remembers

The word *remember* is special in Scripture. Its emphasis isn't on recall, but rather on action. Remembering is no mere mental activity. Remembering is *acting on what is recalled.*

As you read the Bible you may come across phrases like "And Israel <u>remembered</u>" God and His law. In such cases, the writer is telling you that God's people worshipped Him and kept the laws and precepts He taught them. If the text says "And Israel <u>forgot</u>" God or the law, the writer is telling you the Israelites were worshipping pagan deities and were violating God's laws.

key point

Here, where the text says, "and God remembered His covenant with Abraham" (Exodus 2:24 NKJV), the meaning is that God is about to do what He has promised! The Israelite slaves are about to discover what it means to have a God who commits Himself. And Moses, now an aged man of eighty living in one of the true backwaters of the ancient world, is about to fulfill his destiny.

Chapter Wrap-Up

- When Exodus opens, the Israelites are slaves in Egypt.
- Moses, a son born to a slave couple, is adopted by an Egyptian princess.
- After spending four years with his mother, Moses enters the Egyptian court.
- Moses is educated and trained as a prince of Egypt.
- As an adult, Moses takes sides with *his own people*, the Hebrew slaves, and dreams of freeing them.
- After Moses murders an Egyptian who was beating an Israelite, he flees to the Sinai desert, where he lives for forty years.
- When the Israelites appeal to God, He determines to act on the promises made earlier to Abraham—what is called the "Abrahamic Covenant."

Study Questions

1. How did the Israelites happen to be in Egypt?

2. What events led up to their enslavement?

3. How drastic was the situation for the Israelite slaves when Moses was born?

4. What were two primary influences on Moses's development?

5. What event caused Moses to flee Egypt?

6. Where did he go, and how long was Moses there?

7. What are several promises in the covenant God gave Abraham?

8. What was happening in Egypt that caused God to "remember" His covenant with Abraham, Isaac, and Jacob?

Chapter Highlights:
• Holy Ground
• I Know Their Pain
• What's in THE NAME?
• Moses Gets a Look
• Take Off Your Sandals

Chapter 2
The God Who Is with Us

Let's Get Started

Forty years have passed since Moses fled Egypt. He's now eighty years old, still sturdy but weathered from years spent beneath the desert sun. Moses is no longer a prince of Egypt. He's simply a shepherd, caring for flocks of sheep owned by his father-in-law. But Moses's life is about to take another radical turn. Before you go on in this chapter, take a few minutes and read Exodus 3 and 4.

go to

many angels
Psalm 148:2;
Matthew 26:53

named
Daniel 8:16;
Jude 9

holy
set apart, sacred, not common or ordinary

Holy Ground

EXODUS 3:2–5 *And the Angel of the LORD appeared to him in a flame of fire from the midst of a bush. So he looked, and behold, the bush was burning with fire, but the bush was not consumed. Then Moses said, "I will now turn aside and see this great sight, why the bush does not burn." So when the LORD saw that he turned aside to look, God called to him from the midst of the bush and said, "Moses, Moses!" And he said, "Here I am." Then He said, "Do not draw near this place. Take your sandals off your feet, for the place where you stand is **holy** ground." (NKJV)*

Meet the Mystery Angel

GOD AT WORK

The "Angel of the LORD" shows up frequently in the Old Testament. He spoke to Abraham and Isaac (Genesis 22:15–18) and also to Jacob (Genesis 31:11–13). Here He appears to Moses. Scholars have debated the identity of the "Angel of the LORD." We know that the Hebrew word translated "angel" means "messenger" or "representative," and that there are <u>many angels</u>, some of whom are <u>named</u>. But what distinguishes being identified as the Angel of the Lord from other divine messengers?

First we need to note that at times a similar phrase, "an angel of the LORD," also shows up in Scripture. This second phrase is simply descriptive, and means "an angel who came from the LORD," or "an

go to

essential glory
Exodus 33:18–23

angel the LORD sent." But "the Angel of the LORD" is a name or title rather than a description. So the question of who this particular "Angel of the LORD" is becomes important.

The best answer seems to be that "the Angel of the LORD" is God Himself, appearing to human beings in cloaked form rather than in His <u>essential glory</u>. The evidence for this identification is found here and in parallel passages:

> EXODUS 3:2
> *"The Angel of the LORD appeared . . ."*
>
> JUDGES 2:1
> *"Then the Angel of the LORD came . . ."*
>
> EXODUS 3:4
> *"God called to him from the midst of the bush . . ."*
>
> JUDGES 2:1
> *"I led you up from Egypt and brought you to the land of which I swore to your fathers . . ."*
>
> EXODUS 3:6
> *"I am the God of your father—the God of Abraham . . ."*

In the Exodus passage, the text identifies the Angel of the Lord as "God." In the second, the Angel of the Lord claims that "I" led you up from Egypt, and that "I" swore the covenant promises given to Abraham. This kind of evidence strongly indicates that "the" Angel of the Lord is a cloaked appearance of God Himself, in contrast to "an" angel of the Lord.

what others say

J. Vernon McGee

The angel of the Lord who appeared to Moses is none other than the preincarnate Christ.[1]

Appearances of the Angel of the Lord

Reference	Appearance	Purpose of the Appearance
Judges 2	the Israelites	To announce judgment for disobedience
Judges 6	Gideon	To commission him to deliver Israel
Judges 13	Samson's mother	To announce Samson's birth
Judges 13	Samson	To empower
1 Kings 19	Elijah	To strengthen
1 Chronicles 21	Gad	To give him a message for King David
Zechariah 1	Zechariah	To reveal the future of Israel

Take Off Your Sandals

miracles
Exodus 7–10

sorrows
pain, suffering

Before Moses can approach the bush he's told to take off his sandals, "for the place where you stand is holy ground" (Exodus 3:5 NKJV). In the Old Testament, "holy" is a technical religious term that identifies places, persons, things, and even times that are set apart as sacred.

The "holy" is distinguished from the common and ordinary, and is considered sacred because of its association with God.

In the Old Testament, the seventh day, the Sabbath (Saturday) is holy because it is set aside for worship and rest. No ordinary tasks are to be undertaken on the Sabbath day. Here we're told that the very ground around the burning bush from which God spoke is holy; it is associated with God's presence and is not to be walked on as though it were ordinary ground. Moses must remove his sandals and walk on it barefoot.

key point

Tremendous stress is placed throughout the Old Testament on the holy, and as we'll see, the Law Moses later gave Israel insists that God's people scrupulously guard the difference between the sacred and the secular; the holy and the ordinary. The association with God of anything or anyone designated holy made that thing or the person special—forever.

Later, after the Lord works <u>miracles</u> to free the Hebrew slaves, Moses will lead the Israelites back to this sacred site where he now stands barefoot (Exodus 3:12). On the mountain towering above it, God will give Moses the Law, which for all time will set the Israelites apart as His own people.

I Know Their Pain

EXODUS 3:7–10 *And the LORD said: "I have surely seen the oppression of My people who are in Egypt, and have heard their cry because of their taskmasters, for I know their **sorrows**. So I have come down to deliver them out of the hand of the Egyptians, and to bring them up from that land to a good and large land, to a land flowing with milk and honey . . . I have also seen the oppression with which the Egyptians oppress them. Come now, therefore, and I will send you to Pharaoh that you may bring My people, the children of Israel, out of Egypt." (NKJV)*

defining act
an act that reveals
something basic or
essential about God

saving act
an action by which
God delivers his
people

**godly men and
women**
persons who trust in
and seek to please
God

chastening
difficult, painful
experience

It's difficult for us to remember that God not only knows but also feels our pain. When our circumstances resemble those of the Israelites in Egypt, we're likely to feel abandoned and alone—particularly when our suffering seems without end. So it's helpful to note several things about the Israelites in Egypt.

- *First, their suffering led them to cry out to the Lord* (Exodus 3:7). When everything seems to be going well, it's all too easy to ignore God and drift. Later, Moses will warn the Israelites against this very thing, saying, "When you have eaten and are full, then you shall bless the LORD your God for the good land which He has given you. Beware that you do not forget the LORD your God by not keeping His commandments" (Deuteronomy 8:10–11 NKJV).

- *Second, the suffering prepared them to appreciate their blessings.* From the beginning God intended to "bring them up from that land to a good . . . land flowing with milk and honey" (Exodus 3:8 NKJV). Blessing lies ahead, no matter how difficult this is to realize during the darkest of our times.

- *Third, God controlled the timing of the deliverance. He prepared Moses.* And the ready response of the Israelites to Moses's announcement of deliverance indicates He had prepared the hearts of the Israelites as well.

- *Fourth, the intensity of the Israelites' suffering made their rescue all the more special.* For all time this people would look back at what God did for them in Egypt as a **defining act**. For all time God would be known through this **saving act**, and **godly men and women** would have a basis for their confidence in His ability to save them in their time of need.

As the writer of Hebrews reminds us, "No **chastening** seems to be joyful for the present, but painful; nevertheless, afterward it yields the peaceable fruit of righteousness to those who have been trained by it" (Hebrews 12:11 NKJV). Like the Israelites in Egypt, our most painful times can bring us closer to the Lord. Suffering can prepare us to appreciate the blessings that God will bring in His own time. And our experiences can encourage others as well.

apply it

D. A. Carson

All the correct theology in the world will not make a spanking sting less, or make a brutal round of toughening-up exercises fun. Ye it does help to know that there is light at the end of the tunnel, even if you cannot yet see it; to know that God is in control and is committed to His people's good, even though it still does not look like that to you. The suffering is no less real, but perhaps it is less debilitating when the larger perspective is kept in mind.[2]

Ready. Set. Don't Go!

EXODUS 3:10–11 *"Come now, therefore, and I will send you to Pharaoh that you may bring My people, the children of Israel, out of Egypt." But Moses said to God, "Who am I that I should go to Pharaoh, and that I should bring the children of Israel out of Egypt?"* (NKJV)

God was at last ready to act. But Moses, who forty years earlier had viewed himself as Israel's savior, definitely was not ready! "Who am I?" Moses asked the Lord. And that's a question we should ask as well. Remember the brash, impetuous prince of Egypt whose intense passion for his people led to the murder of an Egyptian overseer? Can we imagine that Moses rejecting the offered commission and muttering, "Who am I that I should . . . bring the children of Israel out of Egypt?"

As we read on in these two chapters of Exodus, we see a Moses who is almost the opposite of the man he once was. The confident prince of Egypt who naively expected the Israelites to hail him as their leader is now uncertain, hesitant, and humbled.

The New Moses

Moses's Words of Humility	Passage
"Who am I that I should . . . bring the children of Israel out of Egypt?"	Exodus 3:11 NKJV
"But suppose they will not believe me or listen to my voice . . . ?"	Exodus 4:1 NKJV
"O my Lord, I am not eloquent . . . I am slow of speech and slow of tongue."	Exodus 4:10 NKJV
"O my Lord, please send by the hand of whomever else You may send."	Exodus 4:13 NKJV

made perfect
fully and completely
expressed

It's important for us to remember that the "natural leaders" we tend to admire aren't necessarily people God can use. The old Moses, for all his native strengths, wasn't ready to be Israel's deliverer. Before God could use Moses it was necessary that Moses abandon all reliance on his own strengths. Moses had to become aware of his weakness so that he would rely totally on God.

what others say

Robert L. Cole

"Who am I?" was a pretty good question, but God had a good answer. He did not tell Moses how many talents he had or how great he was. Instead he gave Moses the assurance of the Divine presence.[3]

The apostle Paul expresses this principle in the New Testament. He tells of a time when he was in the grip of a disfiguring illness. He begged God for healing, but God told him, "My strength is **made perfect** in weakness" (2 Corinthians 12:9 NKJV). God still needs people who are so aware of their own weaknesses that they will rely completely on Him.

The strengths of the old Moses were inadequate for the task of delivering the Israelites. That's why God told Moses, "I have come down to deliver them" (Exodus 3:8 NKJV). It would require an act of God to rescue Israel, and it had taken forty years in the Sinai desert to purge Moses of reliance on the "strengths" that would have gotten in God's way.

The new Moses, humbled and deeply aware of his own inadequacies, had become someone that God could and would use as He, the Lord, did the delivering.

We'll see much more of this new, humbled Moses as we trace his story through the pages of Scripture. But already we've discovered the first of many guidelines for a healthy relationship with God.

A healthy relationship with God is marked by a humble reliance on Him rather than on our natural strengths, gifts, or abilities.

Just One Side of the Coin

Moses was now a humble and usable individual. But awareness of weakness is only one aspect of usability. There must also be awareness of who God is and confidence in His great power. So God initiated the first of several revelations that would give the hesitant Moses confidence to rely on the Lord completely.

The revelations that we'll see as we continue on in Exodus 3 and 4 are:

- The revelation of God's name: Exodus 3:13–18
- The revelation of what will happen: Exodus 3:18–22
- The initial revelation of God's power to act: Exodus 4:1–9

What's in THE NAME?

Names have great significance in the Old Testament. They do more than point to a person or thing. Names are intended to bring out something special about the thing named; to give insight into its unique qualities or nature.

Names Do Describe

Many of the Old Testament's names for God are clearly descriptive. They express something special about His identity. For instance, the **generic name** that is translated "God" in our Old Testament is *Elohim*. That name differs from the generic name *El*, which was used by other **Semitic peoples**. And it differs in a peculiar way, for the Israelites adopted *El* and added the plural . . . *him*.

Some scholars have called this addition the "plural of majesty," suggesting it is intended simply to exalt Israel's God above competing Middle Eastern deities. But when we go to early Genesis, far greater significance is suggested. There, in the very first chapter of the Bible, the God *Elohim* speaks to Himself and says, "Let Us make man in Our image" (Genesis 1:26 NKJV). Yet when God speaks to Adam in the same chapter He says, "I have given you . . ." (Genesis 1:29 NKJV).

What we see here is Scripture's first hint that the One God who says "I" to Adam is in fact the Trinity, who when speaking to Himself must say "Us" and "Our." The so-called "plural of majesty" is more than that. It's a name that provides insight into the nature of our God, a <u>Trinitarian nature</u> that is gradually revealed more and more clearly.

Trinitarian nature
John 14:26;
Ephesians 1;
1 Thessalonians 4:8

generic name
common, ordinary name

Semitic peoples
several distinct groups of people who spoke similar Western Semitic languages

R. Laird Harris

A better reason [for the plural ending] can be seen in Scripture itself where, in the very first chapter of Gen., the necessity of a term conveying both the unity of the one God and yet allowing for a plurality of persons is found . . . This is further borne out by the fact that the form *'elohim* occurs only in Hebrew and no other Semitic language, not even in biblical Aramaic.[4]

Many names or titles of God are purely descriptive, where adjectives are added to the basic name *Elohim* or the name we're about to study, Yahweh. You can see these descriptive names, and consider what they tell us about our God, in the chart below. But the most significant Old Testament name of God is the one that's about to be revealed, now, to Moses.

Some Descriptive Names and Titles of God[5]

The Name	Its Emphasis
LORD God	Emphasizes God's Sovereignty
God Almighty	Emphasizes His power, ability
God of Hosts (armies)	Emphasizes His rule over every earthly power
God Most High	Distinguishes Him from competing pagan deities
The Great God	Establishes His superiority to competing deities
God of (places, persons)	Emphasizes His relationship with places, persons
The Eternal God Everlasting God	Emphasizes His consistency, presence
The God of Glory	Emphasizes His uniqueness, our awe, wonder
God in Heaven	Emphasizes His universal rule
The Living God	Emphasizes His ability to exercise all His powers
The LORD, the King	Emphasizes His right to rule
Ancient of Days	Emphasizes His ultimate triumph over enemies
Creator	Describes Him as the source of all that exists
Holy One of Israel	Presents Him as the focus of all that is sacred
God of Justice	Presents Him as the moral ruler of the universe
God of Knowledge	Presents Him as all-knowing
God of My Salvation	Exalts God as able to deliver from every danger
God Our Healer	Describes God as the source of health, peace
God Who Sees	Describes God as aware of every event, thought
Hope of Israel	Describes God as the One who controls the future

Some Descriptive Names and Titles of God (cont'd)

The Name	Its Emphasis
Jealous God	Describes God as passionately concerned for us
Judge of All the Earth	Describes God as One who metes out punishment
Lawgiver	Describes God as the source of morality
Merciful God	Describes God as compassionate, caring
Redeemer	Describes God as One who acts to deliver the helpless
The LORD Our Peace	Presents God as the source of wholeness, harmony
The LORD Who Provides	Presents God as the One who supplies every need

memorial to all generations
literally, how I am to be remembered by all (future) generations

Introduce Me, Moses

EXODUS 3:13–15 *Then Moses said to God, "Indeed, when I come to the children of Israel and say to them, 'The God of your fathers has sent me to you,' and they say to me, 'What is His name?' what shall I say to them?" And God said to Moses, "I AM WHO I AM." And He said, "Thus you shall say to the children of Israel, 'I AM has sent me to you.'" Moreover God said to Moses, "Thus you shall say to the children of Israel: 'The LORD God of your fathers, the God of Abraham, the God of Isaac, and the God of Jacob, has sent me to you. This is My name forever, and this is My* **memorial to all generations***.'" (NKJV)*

The name rendered here as "I AM" and as "I AM WHO I AM" is composed of four Hebrew consonants whose English equivalents are YHWH. All scholars agree that the name is built on the Hebrew verb "to be," although there's little agreement as to its exact significance. The translators of most English versions settle for "I AM" in the Exodus text, and elsewhere represent YHWH by the word "LORD," written with a capital L followed by small capital letters. "LORD" occurs in our English Old Testament some twenty-six hundred times.

The Jewish people view this as the ultimate name of God, and the most holy. Each time Jewish scribes copying an Old Testament text came to YHWH, they took a ceremonial bath to cleanse themselves before daring to write it down.

key point

The name is so holy that it was never spoken aloud. When vowels were finally added to the Hebrew text around AD 1100, no guide to pronouncing this most holy name was provided. Instead the vowels for another word translated "lord," *adonai*, were added. The name was written YHWH, but was pronounced "adonai." The early

conjugate a verb
go through how it is
expressed in past,
present, future, and
other tenses

key point

translators of the English Bible didn't understand this practice, and so they transcribed YHWH into English using the vowels from *adonai*, leading to what most certainly is a mispronunciation of YHWH as "Jehovah." While no one today knows the exact pronunciation, scholars tend to agree that "Yahweh" is close to the way it was originally spoken.

The fact that the name Yahweh truly is special is emphasized in the text itself, for "this is My name forever, and this is My memorial to all generations" (Exodus 3:15 NKJV).

From the time of Moses onward forever, God is defined for His people by the name Yahweh.

The Defining Name of God

Other names of God found in the Old Testament give us insight into characteristics or qualities of God. But the name Yahweh, revealed to Moses, opens our eyes to an essential aspect of who God is that truly does define Him. No ancient peoples conceived of a God like the One who revealed Himself to Moses.

While translating Yahweh as I AM was something of a compromise, it was a brilliant one. YHWH truly is a construction built on the Hebrew verb "to be." Typically when we **conjugate such a verb** we say, "I was, I am, I will be." But the point of God's revelation of this name is that it cannot be conjugated. It is never true to say of God "He was" or "He will be." We must always say of God, "He IS!"

> **what others say**
>
> **Broadman Bible Commentary**
>
> The name Yahweh, and the use of the phrase "I am who I am" when God speaks of Himself, is a declaration of the presence of God. In this regard verse 12 is instructive: "I will be with you. . . ." YHWH is pregnant with meaning and its significance could hardly be overstated.[6]

For centuries the Hebrew people had thought of their God as a God of the past, who had once spoken to their forefathers Abraham, Isaac, and Jacob. Or they thought of Him as a God of the future, who would one day keep His covenant promises and bring Israel back to Canaan. But Moses is told to tell God's people that He is I AM, a God of their present! And the Israelites were about to experience Him in their present in a way that would forever transform their view of who God is.

We see this in our text. God tells Moses to tell the Israelites in Egypt His name, and then to further identify Him as "the God of Abraham, the God of Isaac, and the God of Jacob" (Exodus 3:15 NKJV). Scripture never presents the Lord as the One who *was* the God of the forefathers. God is always viewed as the One who *is* the God of the forefathers. God was present when the forefathers lived. God is present in Moses's time. And God will always be present to and for future generations!

To say that God is the I AM is to define Him as The One Who Is *Always Present*! It's no wonder God comforts us as He comforted His <u>Old Testament</u> people with the promise "I will never leave you nor forsake you" (Hebrews 13:5 NKJV). Of course He will never leave us. God is The One Who Is *Always* Present.

Old Testament
Deuteronomy 31:6, 8;
Joshua 1:5

what others say

John I. Durham

It is inappropriate to refer to God as "was" or as "will be," for the reality of His existence can be suggested only by the present: "Is" or "Ising," "Always Is" or "Am."[7]

John L. Mackay

The most appropriate explanation seems to be that what is said here builds on the earlier assertion, "I will be with you." The verb form "I am" is the same as "I will be" in verse 12 . . . It is not merely the existence of God that is to encourage Moses, but the fact of His active and committed presence to help His people. That is His character, and it is on that basis that they may have confidence for the present and the future . . . Malachi brought out the constancy of the divine commitment to the covenant relationship when he wrote, "I the Lord do not change. So you, O descendants of Jacob, are not destroyed" (Mal. 3:6).[8]

To Moses and to the Israelites, God's presentation of Himself as Yahweh was both new and exciting.

redactors
people who go back
and change ancient
documents to match
their own theories

literary criticism
the analysis of liter-
ary works based on
the choice of words,
themes, and gram-
matical construc-
tions

What Do You Mean, New?

Critics have jumped on the view that the name Yahweh is a new revelation, and have completely discounted God's statement in Exodus 6:3: "I appeared to Abraham, to Isaac, and to Jacob, as God Almighty, but by My name LORD [Yahweh] I was not known to them" (NKJV). In rebuttal the critics point out that *Yahweh Elohim*, "LORD God," appears several times in Genesis 2 through 11, and over three dozen times in the story of Abraham. Abraham even addresses God as Yahweh (Genesis 15:8).

The appearance of the name Yahweh in early Genesis has even been taken as evidence that the first book of the Bible is a patchwork, put together by Yahwist and Elohist **redactors** long after the traditional date these books were written. Applying the tools of **literary criticism**, critics have chopped up Old Testament passages and even verses, and grandly announced that the early books of the Bible were con-structed much later than Moses's time by competing schools of thought. The notion that Jewish scholars who studied the Scriptures intensely in the pre-Christian and Christian eras were too blind to see the supposed contradictions and were blind to the "literary evidence" on which their theories were based never seemed to bother the critics.

However, Exodus 6:3 doesn't say that the forefathers were *unaware* of the name Yahweh. What it says is, "But by My name LORD I was not known to them" (NKJV).

The Difference Between "Know" and "Know"

Every student of Hebrew understands that there's a difference between "know" and "know." Every English speaker understands the same thing. We might say, "Yes, I know Caesar," and everyone would understand that we're simply saying that we recognize the name, have some information about Caesar, or perhaps have read some of his writings. If we'd lived in Rome some forty years before Christ and said, "Yes, I know Caesar," we could have been making a very different claim. We might be claiming to know about Caesar, or we might be claiming to have a relationship with Caesar—to know him as a friend. In the former example, "know" means to possess information; in the latter, "know" means we have personally experi-enced Caesar.

Hebrew tends to emphasize this distinction to an even greater extent. The Hebrew word *yada'*, "know," is used in the sense of possessing <u>information or facts</u>. It's used in the sense of a <u>mastery of skills</u>. But underlying all these uses is the notion that true knowledge is something that is gained by experience. Thus to <u>"know" God</u>, even when it's merely knowing something about God, conveys the notion that we've had some sort of experience through which that knowledge was acquired.

Now, let's go back to the essential meaning of Yahweh as The One Who Is Always Present. When God tells Moses that "by My name LORD I was not known to them," He is not saying that the name Yahweh had never been heard or uttered. What He is saying is that Abraham, Isaac, and Jacob *had never experienced the full implications of the name.* They had never known what it means to have a God Who Is Always with Them.

What the name does mean is about to be experienced by the Israelites in Egypt. What Yahweh does mean will be displayed in the awesome miracles and wonders that force a hostile and hateful oppressor to release his slaves. What it does mean to have a God Who Is Always Present is that this God *is acting* on behalf of His people!

Not only will this generation of Israelites be the first to experience God's exercise of His power on their behalf, but their experiences will forever <u>define who God is</u> for His people. For us, as for Israel, we are to see God as both present with us and acting in our lives.

go to

information or facts
Genesis 19:33;
Exodus 4:14;
2 Samuel 3:26

mastery of skills
Isaiah 7:16

know God
Exodus 4:14;
Psalm 20:6;
Ezekiel 24:24, 27

define who God is
Deuteronomy 7:19;
Psalms 77:14; 135:9

Flash Forward

JOHN 8:52–58 *"Now we know that You have a **demon**! Abraham is dead, and the prophets; and You say, 'If anyone keeps My word he shall never taste death.' Are You greater than our father Abraham, who is dead? And the prophets are dead. Who do You make Yourself out to be?" . . . [Jesus answered,] "Your father Abraham rejoiced to see My day, and he saw it and was glad." Then the **Jews** said to Him, "You are not yet fifty years old, and have You seen Abraham?" Jesus said to them, "Most assuredly, I say to you, before Abraham was, I AM."* (NKJV)

demon
an angel who rebelled against God and now follows Satan

Jews
In John's Gospel "Jews" nearly always refers to the religious leaders, not to the people as a whole.

It's nearly a millennium and a half after I AM spoke to Moses. A group of religious leaders are debating with Jesus of Nazareth, who insists that He speaks and acts for God, and that God is His Father. The hostile leaders charge Jesus with being a **demon-possessed Samaritan**. The debate continues as the religious leaders scoff:

The leaders understood Jesus's claim perfectly . . . that the Man who stood before them was in fact Yahweh, the I AM of the Old Testament, whom they claimed to worship as God. Furious at what they considered **blasphemy**, "they took up **stones** to throw at Him" (John 8:59 NKJV).

In Jesus the great I AM, The One Who Is Always Present, came to be present with us in a new and unique way. And just as I AM acted to deliver Israel from slavery in Egypt, Jesus acted to deliver you and me from our bondage to sin's power and penalty.

Moses Gets a Quick Look Ahead

> EXODUS 3:17–22 *I have said I will bring you up out of the affliction of Egypt to the land of the Canaanites . . . You shall come, you and the elders of Israel, to the king of Egypt; and you shall say to him, "The LORD God of the Hebrews has met with us; and now, please, let us go three days' journey into the wilderness, that we may sacrifice to the LORD our God." But I am sure that the king of Egypt will not let you go, no, not even by a **mighty hand**. So I will stretch out My hand and strike Egypt with all My wonders which I will do in its midst; and after that he will let you go. And I will give this people favor in the sight of the Egyptians; and it shall be, when you go, that you shall not go empty-handed. But every woman shall ask of her neighbor, namely, of her who dwells near her house, articles of silver, articles of gold, and clothing; and you shall put them on your sons and on your daughters. So you shall plunder the Egyptians. (NKJV)*

Earlier I noted that God would provide three sources of encouragement to Moses to enable His reluctant messenger to trust:

- A revelation of His name: Exodus 3:13–18

- A revelation of what will happen: Exodus 3:18–22

- An initial revelation of God's power to act: Exodus 4:1–9

God has revealed the name Yahweh to Moses; it is a name that will soon be filled to overflowing with meaning as Moses and the Israelites experience God's acts on their behalf. In the verses quoted above, God reveals what will happen. Now . . .

pagan
a term referring to all other religions revealed in Scripture

idols
gods of wood or stone

predicted
foretold, described before it happens

God Predicts the Future

God's ability to tell ahead of time what will happen is celebrated in the Old Testament as one of the things that set Him apart from competing **pagan** deities. Isaiah ridicules those who worship **idols**, and holds up Israel's God, who says, "Besides Me there is no God. And who can proclaim as I do? . . . Since I appointed the ancient people. And the things that are coming and shall come" (Isaiah 44:6–7 NKJV). Later the Lord adds,

ISAIAH 46:9–11
Remember the former things of old,
For I am God, and there is no other;
I am God, and there is none like Me,
Declaring the end from the beginning,
And from ancient times things that are not yet done,
Saying, "My counsel shall stand,
And I will do all my pleasure." . . .
Indeed I have spoken it;
I will also bring it to pass.
I have purposed it;
I will also do it. (NKJV)

How can God be so sure of the future? In part, because The One Who Is Always Present is present in our future as well as in our today. In fact, past, present, and future are all "present" to God! Like a person standing on the top of a mountain who sees a river flowing far below, God stands above His universe and views all of human history, from creation to history's end. To a person on the river in a canoe, what lies beyond the next bend is future to him. But to the Person on the mountaintop who sees the whole river, what's beyond that "next bend" is perfectly visible. God speaks with confidence of the future, for our tomorrow is as visible to Him as our today.

So here God speaks to Moses of what lies ahead for him. And, as **predicted** event follows predicted event, Moses will develop greater

rod
a long wooden staff
used by shepherds,
possibly with a
crook, or hook,
at its end

and greater confidence in the Lord. We can look through the predictive verses in these two chapters, and as we do we too will have a preview of what is about to take place in Moses's life.

- God will deliver His people from bondage in Egypt (3:8).
- God will bring them to Canaan, "a good and large land" (3:8 NKJV).
- The elders of Israel will listen to Moses (3:18).
- But Pharaoh will refuse to release his slaves (3:19).
- Yahweh will perform devastating miracles that ruin Egypt (3:20).
- When the Israelites leave, they will carry Egypt's riches with them (3:22).

In these predictions there's encouragement for us as well as Moses. What Yahweh says to Moses reminds us that God knows our future too, and that no matter what happens tomorrow, He will be with us.

apply it

Mini-Miracles

EXODUS 4:1–4 *Then Moses answered and said, "But suppose they will not believe me or listen to my voice; suppose they say, 'The LORD has not appeared to you.'" So the LORD said to him, "What is that in your hand?" He said, "A **rod**." And He said, "Cast it on the ground." So he cast it on the ground, and it became a serpent; and Moses fled from it. Then the LORD said to Moses, "Reach out your hand and take it by the tail" (and he reached out his hand and caught it, and it became a rod in his hand). (NKJV)*

This and two other mini-miracles that God enabled Moses to perform are called "signs." The second was the transformation of Moses's arm from healthy to diseased with advanced leprosy, and back to healthy again (4:6–7). The third "sign" was turning water to blood (4:9). As "signs," these mini-miracles were intended as evidence that Moses was speaking the truth when he presented God's message. In the case of Moses, not even these authenticating signs kindled immediate enthusiasm. He remained reluctant to undertake God's mission.

I Object!

accommodate
to take into account, to adjust demands in view of

God's reluctant servant still raised objections. God intended to send him to Pharaoh, but Moses still didn't want to go. The dialogue between the two provides fascinating insights into relationship with God. Moses is stubborn. But God remains patient. First the Lord reasons with Moses. Then, despite being provoked, God goes a second mile.

God Talks to Moses

Moses	God
"I am not eloquent, neither before nor since You have spoken to Your servant; but I am slow of speech and slow of tongue" (Exodus 4:10 NKJV).	[God, angrily.] "Who has made man's mouth? Or who makes the mute, the deaf, the seeing, or the blind? Have not I, the LORD? Now therefore, go, and I will be with your mouth and teach you what you shall say" (4:11–12 NKJV).
"O my Lord, please send by the hand of whomever else You may send" (4:13 NKJV).	"Is not Aaron the Levite your brother? I know that he can speak well . . . He himself shall be as a mouth for you, and you shall be to him as God" (4:14, 16 NKJV).

God is patient with us. But there are limits to His patience. Yet even when angry, God was willing to **accommodate** Moses's fears.

There's no need for us to hesitate when God calls us to any service for Him, whether that service is speaking or simply coming alongside others to provide emotional support. The God who made our mouths is perfectly capable of filling them with His words.

something to ponder

A Second Guideline

In all this, God is beginning to teach Moses the second of our guidelines for a healthy relationship with God. Remember the first? The second is like it.

A healthy relationship with God is rooted in complete confidence in God's presence, grace, and power.

key point

the ultimate miracle
Exodus 11

Levite
a descendant of
Levi, one of the
twelve sons of
Jacob (Israel)

O Brother

EXODUS 4:14–16 *He [God] said: "Is not Aaron the **Levite** your brother? I know that he can speak well. And look, he is also coming out to meet you. When he sees you, he will be glad in his heart. Now you shall speak to him and put the words in his mouth. And I will be with your mouth and with his mouth, and I will teach you what you shall do. So he shall be your spokesman to the people. And he himself shall be as a mouth for you, and you shall be to him as God." (NKJV)*

Before meeting Aaron, Moses goes back to tell his father-in-law he intends to return to Egypt. Further encouraged by God's revelation that "all the men who sought your life are dead" (Exodus 4:19 NKJV), Moses sets out with his wife and sons. Again God gives Moses a glimpse of what lies ahead. Moses will confront Pharaoh and insist he let God's people go. But Pharaoh's heart will be hardened, and it will take the ultimate miracle to force the stubborn ruler to release God's people.

Meanwhile, Back in Egypt

Back in Egypt, God has already spoken to Aaron, and Aaron is well on the way before Moses sets out. The two meet at the foot of the mountain where God first appeared to Moses. Moses tells his brother all that has happened and shows him the signs God has provided.

Aaron

All we know at this point in the story is that Aaron is Moses's brother. Later we'll learn much more about him. In Exodus 6, the fascinating story of the aftermath of Moses's first confrontation with Pharaoh is interrupted with a detailed genealogy tracing Aaron's ancestry and identifying one of Aaron's sons and one of his grandsons. This genealogy is significant, for Aaron will be appointed Israel's high priest, and every man qualified to serve as a priest must demonstrate his descent from Aaron. Thus Aaron is significant in his role as high priest as well as in his role as Moses's spokesman before Pharaoh.

Aaron is also interesting as a person. If we view Moses as Israel's great leader, we must view Aaron as Moses's great follower. For most of their time together, Aaron faithfully supported his <u>younger brother</u> and stood beside him in the most difficult of times. Only once did Aaron take sides against Moses, and even then he was a follower, <u>influenced</u> by his and Moses's older sister, Miriam. In this case, and one other, Aaron's strength, his readiness to follow a strong leader, was also his weakness.

go to

younger brother
Exodus 7:7

influenced
Numbers 12

greatest of that people's sin
Exodus 32

Aaron lacked the backbone to stand up to pressure without a strong leader's support. The event that reveals this weakness will take place on the plains below Mount Sinai. While Moses is at the top of the mountain meeting with the Lord, Aaron crumbles under pressure from the people and participates as they commit one of the <u>greatest of that people's sins</u>.

It's important to remember that not every believer is called to be a leader. Followers are important people too. It's also important not to expect a person who is a good follower to be a strong leader, or to give those called to be followers leadership roles without providing plenty of support. We should appreciate people like Aaron. But we shouldn't expect more from them than they are capable of delivering.

apply it

<u>On to Egypt!</u>

When the two brothers arrive in Egypt they gather the elders of Israel together. Aaron speaks and Moses performs the signs God had given him. The Bible tells us that "the people believed; and when they heard that the LORD had visited the children of Israel and that He had looked on their affliction, then they bowed their heads and worshiped" (Exodus 4:31 NKJV).

The euphoria of that moment was not destined to last. As God had told Moses, Pharaoh wasn't ready to let Israel go. Before the slaves were free, Moses would have to face not only a hostile Egyptian ruler but also the anger of his own people.

Chapter Wrap-Up

- After Moses has been in the Sinai for forty years, God appears to him in a burning bush.
- God tells Moses he has been chosen to deliver Israel, and tells him to return to Egypt.
- Moses is fearful and reluctant, deeply aware of his own weakness.
- God encourages Moses in a variety of ways: giving him a glimpse of the future, providing him with mini-miracle signs, and finally giving Moses his brother Aaron to serve as spokesman.
- When Moses and Aaron reach Egypt, the Israelites believe Moses's promise of deliverance and worship the Lord.

Study Questions

1. Who is "the Angel of the LORD," and how does he differ from "an angel of the LORD"?

2. What is the meaning of "holy" in the Old Testament?

3. What is the significance of the name Yahweh? Why wasn't God "known by" that name in earlier times?

4. How do we know this name is different from the many other descriptive names of God?

5. Contrast the "new Moses" with the "old Moses." What reveals the change?

6. What did God do to encourage the reluctant "new Moses" to accept His commission?

7. What two principles for a healthy relationship with God were identified in this chapter?

Let's Get Started

Moses and his brother Aaron have arrived in Egypt. They've told the Israelites that God is going to free them and take them home to Canaan. The Israelites are ready to pack up and move out.

The trouble is, Pharaoh, Egypt's ruler, hasn't agreed. And Pharaoh has an army or two to back him up. What's worse, this pharaoh is a stubborn sort, who isn't ready to recognize any God of slaves. It will take more than one exercise of God's miracle-working power to crack Pharaoh's hard heart. Until then, the Israelites are in for unexpected troubles.

The stories of Moses's confrontations with Pharaoh and the miracles that finally won Israel's release are told in Exodus 5–11, stories you will want to read before going on with this chapter.

The Unexpected Happens

EXODUS 5:1–2 *Afterward Moses and Aaron went in and told Pharaoh, "Thus says the LORD God of Israel: 'Let My people go, that they may hold a feast to Me in the wilderness.'" And Pharaoh said, "Who is the LORD, that I should obey His voice to let Israel go? I do not know the LORD, nor will I let Israel go."* (NKJV)

If the Israelites expected Pharaoh to quickly give in and release them, they were disappointed. Pharaoh wouldn't even let them off work for a few days to "hold a feast" honoring God in a nearby wilderness!

Some have thought Moses's demand for a few days off was deceptive. After all, what God really intended was that the slaves leave Egypt for good. Yet the request was evidence of God's grace. The Lord didn't ask for more than Pharaoh should have been willing to give. Pharaoh's response was a revelation of his heart. The Egyptian ruler was unwilling to consider even this reasonable request. Pharaoh's reaction shocked the Israelites, and Moses as well.

Nasty, Nasty

EXODUS 5:6–8 *So the same day Pharaoh commanded the taskmasters of the people and their officers, saying, "You shall no longer give the people straw to make brick as before. Let them go and gather straw for themselves. And you shall lay on them the quota of bricks which they made before . . . They are idle; therefore they cry out, saying, 'Let us go and sacrifice to our God.'"* (NKJV)

Most of us would feel that Pharaoh overreacted. Certainly the Israelites thought so. In Egypt crumbled straw was added to mud to make building bricks. The chemicals in chopped straw made the sun-dried bricks harden more quickly and strengthened them.[1] Before Moses spoke to Pharaoh, the Egyptians had provided the straw. Now the already overworked Israelites were told to go out and find straw themselves—and to make as many bricks as they'd produced before!

key point

The Israelites tried, but there was no way they could gather enough stubble to replace the straw. Desperate because they were being beaten for their failure, the Israelites appealed to Pharaoh. The ruler's answer was to shout them down. They were idle, Pharaoh insisted, and they had to meet their quotas.

His reaction to the slaves reveals an arrogant pharaoh, a ruler filled with pride and void of compassion. He was a man of already hardened heart, and before the Israelites were freed his heart would become even harder.

A Word About This Pharaoh

Those who believe that the Hebrew slaves were finally released about 1447 BC tend to identify Amenhotep II as the pharaoh Moses confronted. The Egyptian propaganda machine, as reflected in stories archaeologists have recovered, pictured Amenhotep II as a sportsman and athlete, who in his youth could drive arrows through copper shields three inches thick. He was supposedly unrivaled as a military leader. The surviving report of one incident states,

His majesty crossed the Orontes on dangerous waters . . .
Then he . . . saw a few [of the enemy] coming furtively,
adorned with weapons of warfare, to attack the king's army.
His majesty burst after them like the flight of a divine falcon.

The confidence of their hearts was slacked, and one after another fell upon his fellow, up to their commander. Not a single one was with his majesty, except for himself with valiant arm. His majesty killed them by shooting (ANET 245).[2]

Whether or not he actually performed such feats, Amenhotep certainly had a reputation to uphold. He could hardly pretend to be strong and powerful if he gave in to the demands of the God of his slaves.

Great Versus Good Gods

There is another reason Pharaoh would have resisted the Lord's demands. In Egypt, Pharaoh himself was regarded as a god. Egypt was a land of many deities. The chief gods, such as Amon, Re, and Horus, were called "the great gods." Pharaohs were considered to be descendants of Re, and while they reigned were typically identified as "the good god." Thus, the Egyptians might have spoken of Amenhotep as "Horus the lord of the palace, the good god, his Majesty, thy Lord" or simply as "One," signifying his sacred power.[3]

In addition, it was Pharaoh's responsibility, as a familiar of the other deities, to maintain harmony between the gods and Egypt itself. The prosperity of Egypt was thought to depend on good relations between Pharaoh and Egypt's gods.

Perhaps it's not surprising, then, that an arrogant pharaoh who thought of himself as one with Egypt's deities should react so strongly to Moses's message.

What About Pharaoh's Hard Heart?

When the Lord first spoke to Moses He told His reluctant messenger, "I will harden his heart" (Exodus 4:21 NKJV). The recurring theme of Pharaoh's hard heart, found in Exodus 4 through 14, has

go to

miracle chapters
Exodus 7–11

troubled many. Check out the chart below, and you can easily see why.

What Exodus (NKJV) Says About Pharaoh's Heart

Verse in Exodus	What It Says
4:21	But I [God] will harden his heart . . .
7:3	And I [God] will harden Pharaoh's heart . . .
7:13	And Pharaoh's heart grew hard . . .
7:14	Pharaoh's heart is hard; he refuses . . .
7:22	And Pharaoh's heart grew hard, and . . .
8:15	He [Pharaoh] hardened his heart and did not . . .
8:19	But Pharaoh's heart grew hard . . .
8:32	But Pharaoh hardened his heart . . .
9:7	But the heart of Pharaoh became hard . . .
9:12	But the LORD hardened the heart of Pharaoh . . .
9:34	And he [Pharaoh] hardened his heart . . .
9:35	So the heart of Pharaoh was hard . . .
10:1	For I [God] have hardened his heart and . . .
10:20	The LORD hardened Pharaoh's heart . . .
10:27	The LORD hardened Pharaoh's heart . . .
11:10	The LORD hardened Pharaoh's heart . . .
14:4	I [God] will harden Pharaoh's heart . . .
14:8	And the LORD hardened the heart of Pharaoh . . .

A quick glance at the chart reveals several interesting facts:

- The text does say that the Lord hardened Pharaoh's heart.
- The text also says that Pharaoh hardened his own heart.
- At times the text simply describes Pharaoh's heart as hard.

As the number of references to Pharaoh's hardness indicates, this is an important theme in the <u>miracle chapters</u>. But what do they really tell us?

Some have taken these references to mean that God forced Pharaoh not to release the Israelites when normally he'd have let them go immediately. Such people charge that God wasn't playing fair. How could God punish Pharaoh and Egypt when Pharaoh had no choice but to do what God made him do?

At least two faulty assumptions underlie this line of thinking: First, that Pharaoh would have released Israel on his own; second, that God somehow coerced Pharaoh into acting against his will.

The First Faulty Assumption

interesting statement
Romans 1:18–23

The more we know about the reputation of Amenhotep II, and the more we know about the Egyptian pharaohs' role as Egypt's "good god," the less likely it seems Amenhotep would have been inclined to give in to God's demand. His reaction to Moses is perfectly in keeping with both his nature and his position. There's really no basis at all to think Pharaoh would have freed Israel immediately if the Lord hadn't made his heart hard.

> **what others say**
>
> **John D. Currid**
>
> It is clear that God does not make Pharaoh evil. Pharaoh is evil in and of himself. What God simply does is harden Pharaoh in his nature by giving him completely over to his sin. Is that unfair of God? Absolutely not . . . Pharaoh is responsible for his condition. It is not as if God is hardening a good person.[5]

The Second Faulty Assumption

The second assumption, that God coerced or forced Pharaoh to act against his will, can be dismissed on the same grounds. There is no basis for assuming that God *forces* anyone to act contrary to his or her own free will. So, if God didn't force Pharaoh, *how* did the Lord harden Pharaoh's heart?

The apostle Paul makes an <u>interesting statement</u> in the New Testament book of Romans. Paul tells us that God has revealed Himself to everyone through what He has created. Through the witness of the creation everyone is touched by God, so that everyone has a basic knowledge of God's existence and His power. But then Paul says that people "suppress the truth." Instead of being thankful and praising God, they become "futile in their thoughts, and their foolish hearts [are] darkened" (Romans 1:18, 21 NKJV).

What Paul is saying is that even the little touch of God humans can sense through the created universe causes a strong reaction. If we viewed God as a lover, when our hands brushed we'd quickly put our hand in His. But sinful human beings don't react this way to God's touch. Instead, we react as if our hand brushed against a hot iron, and we jerk it away.

apply it

evil
in the sense of
harm, bad things

All the Lord had to do to harden Pharaoh's heart was to reveal more of Himself to that ruler. And that is exactly what happened. The very first mention of Yahweh elicited a furious reaction from Pharaoh. As miracle followed miracle, Pharaoh's naturally hard heart was hardened more and more. Just as the sun melts wax and hardens clay, so God's revelation of Himself melts the hearts of believers and hardens the hearts of those—like Pharaoh—who simply will not believe.

> what others say
>
> **James M. Stifler**
>
> It was not from lack of knowledge that men sinned, but in spite of it.[6]

Don't Discount God

EXODUS 5:21 *And they said to them, "Let the LORD look on you and judge, because you have made us abhorrent in the sight of Pharaoh and in the sight of his servants, to put a sword in their hand to kill us."* (NKJV)

When the Israelites realized how furious Pharaoh was about their request, they blamed Moses and Aaron.

Today they might say, "You're killing us, Moses! You've given Pharaoh all the excuse he needs to wipe us out!"

Moses didn't have an answer. In fact, he was just as shaken as the rest of the Israelites. Moses really had made the situation worse. And all Moses had done was follow God's orders.

Unlike the leaders of the Israelites who quickly turned against Moses, Moses had a better idea: He immediately turned *to* God.

What's Going on Here?

EXODUS 5:22–23 *So Moses returned to the LORD and said, "Lord, why have You brought trouble on this people? Why is it You have sent me? For since I came to Pharaoh to speak in Your name, he has done **evil** to this people; neither have You delivered Your people at all."* (NKJV)

It's clear that Moses felt terribly let down. He'd done what God told him to do. But it hadn't worked out the way Moses expected.

The Israelites' first reaction had been to accuse Moses of putting a sword in the Egyptians' hands with the intent of killing them. Yet Moses, as troubled as his fellow Hebrews, turned to God and asked, "Why?"

There's a world of difference between the two responses to the unexpected setback. The Israelites assumed the worst and immediately looked around for someone to blame. In stark contrast, Moses assumed that God had a reason for what happened, and he asked, "Why?" The Israelites reacted in **unbelief**; Moses responded with faith.

Sometimes it's hard for us to deal with life's disappointments. We try to do the right thing. Sometimes we're even sure that God has led us to a particular decision. When things go wrong, we need to follow Moses's example and believe that God has a purpose in what has happened.

go to

Old Testament quote
Psalms 34:12–16;
37:27

unbelief
lacking in trust

apply it

> **what others say**
>
> **Norman Hillyer**
>
> While Christians are not exempt from troubles, neither are they the only ones who face them. But there is a great difference; believers are aware that there are divine resources available to faith. So, unlike nonbelievers, they have no need to be afraid.[7]

This brings us to a third guideline for a healthy relationship with God: When things go wrong in our lives, we need to trust God to have a reason.

A healthy relationship with God is displayed when things go wrong by the assurance that God has a purpose, and that He intends to do us good.

key point

Peter Gets a Word In

The apostle Peter, writing after the resurrection of Jesus, deals with this issue. He begins by quoting the Old Testament:

1 PETER 3:10–11
He who would love life
And see good days, . . .
Let him turn away from evil and do good. (NKJV)

blessed
benefited, treated
well

bondage
slavery

That is, always do the right thing, and you'll enjoy your life and see good days. And Peter gives a reason:

1 PETER 3:12
For the eyes of the LORD are on the righteous,
And His ears are open to their prayers;
But the face of the LORD is against those who do evil. (NKJV)

The reason good results from doing the right thing is that God watches over His people and superintends the outcome of our actions. God is aware of everything in His people's lives. He hears our prayers, and He makes sure that when we do good, good results.

But then Peter introduces an exception: "But even if you should suffer for righteousness' sake, you are blessed" (1 Peter 3:14 NKJV). That "even if" indicates that while doing the right thing *usually* works out to our benefit, there are times when we do what's right and end up suffering. As believers, we have no guarantee that we won't experience pain, even when we do nothing to deserve it.

Now, Moses had done nothing wrong. All he'd done was go to Pharaoh with the message God told him to deliver. He'd done what was right, and everything had gone wrong! Yet Peter says that when such things happen, we're **blessed**! How can that be?

Peter tells us to look at Jesus for the answer. Jesus surely did the right thing, always. Yet He suffered because of sins—not His own sins, but the sins of those who killed Him. But God had a purpose in Jesus's suffering. Jesus suffered "that He might bring us to God" (1 Peter 3:18 NKJV). *Through history's greatest injustice, God worked history's greatest good.*

And this is exactly the point. Normally, doing the right thing produces a good and pleasant life for you and me. But when we do right and it leads to pain and suffering, we can be sure that the God who brought good out of Christ's death intends to bring something good out of our suffering too.

Moses Gets the "Good" News

EXODUS 6:6–8 *Therefore say to the children of Israel: "I am the LORD; I will bring you out from under the burdens of the Egyptians, I will rescue you from their **bondage**, and I will redeem you with an outstretched arm and with great judgments. I will take you as My people, and I will be your God.*

Then you shall know that I am the LORD your God who brings you out from under the burdens of the Egyptians. And I will bring you into the land which I <u>swore to give</u> to Abraham, Isaac, and Jacob; and I will give it to you as a heritage: I am the LORD." (NKJV)

swore to give
Genesis 12:7;
15:7–8

already revealed
Exodus 3:7–8,
20–22; 6:2–5

Usually when things go wrong, and we cry out "Why?" God remains terribly silent. He doesn't explain; He expects us to simply trust Him. In this case, when Moses asked why, God did explain. He patiently went back over things He had <u>already revealed</u> to Moses, and went on to state exactly what He intended to do.

Pharaoh's harshness made it perfectly clear that the Israelites' release from bondage required an act of God. Through the forthcoming miracles of judgment, God would forever fix in His people's consciousness His identity as The One Who Is Always Present. The promises God stated to Moses, and which Moses in turn related to the Israelites, would also identify the God of the Exodus with the God who gave covenant promises to Abraham centuries before.

God's Great "I Will" Promises

Genesis 12 to Abraham	Exodus 6 to the Israelites
I will make you a great nation	I will bring you out
I will bless you	I will rescue you from bondage
I will make your name great You shall be a blessing	I will redeem you with outstretched arm and with great judgments
I will bless those who bless you	I will take you as My people
I will curse him who curses you	I will be your God
In you all the families of the earth shall be blessed	I will bring you into the land which I swore to give to Abraham
To your descendants I will give this land	I will give it to you as a heritage

The Israelites' Response

EXODUS 6:9 *So Moses spoke thus to the children of Israel; but they did not heed Moses, because of anguish of spirit and cruel bondage.* (NKJV)

The Israelites paid no attention to God's promise of a better future; the present simply hurt too much.

In this reaction, we see one of the reasons why the upcoming spate of miracles was necessary. Only through the visible exercise of God's power would His people realize just who He is, and learn to trust Him.

In fact, Exodus gives us three reasons for the "great judgments" God was about to bring on Egypt:

- Exodus 6:7: "Then you [the Israelites] shall know that I am the LORD your God who brings you out from under the burdens of the Egyptians" (NKJV).

- Exodus 7:5: "And the Egyptians shall know that I am the LORD, when I stretch out My hand on Egypt and bring out the children of Israel from among them" (NKJV).

- Exodus 12:12: "Against all the gods of Egypt I will **execute judgment**." (NKJV)

key point

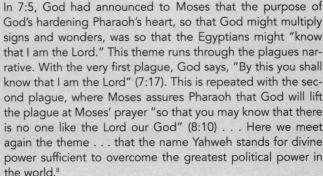

what others say

J. Gerald Janzen

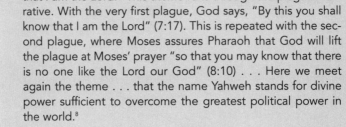

In 7:5, God had announced to Moses that the purpose of God's hardening Pharaoh's heart, so that God might multiply signs and wonders, was so that the Egyptians might "know that I am the Lord." This theme runs through the plagues narrative. With the very first plague, God says, "By this you shall know that I am the Lord" (7:17). This is repeated with the second plague, where Moses assures Pharaoh that God will lift the plague at Moses' prayer "so that you may know that there is no one like the Lord our God" (8:10) . . . Here we meet again the theme . . . that the name Yahweh stands for divine power sufficient to overcome the greatest political power in the world.[8]

The power of the God of the Hebrew slaves would forever demonstrate the powerlessness of Egypt's deities, and Hebrew and Egyptian alike would be forced to confess that the Lord, the Lord is God.

On Bible Miracles

Exodus 7–11 reports a number of events that we call "miracles." Not counting the mini-miracles we looked at in the last chapter, some ten major miracles are reported:

1. The Nile turns to blood.

2. Frogs infest the land.

3. There's an infestation of gnats.

4. There's an infestation of "swarming insects."

5. A deadly disease strikes Egypt's livestock.

6. Everyone breaks out in painful boils.

7. A hailstorm destroys the early crops.

8. A cloud of locusts strips the land of growing things.

9. For three days there's absolute darkness.

10. Every firstborn Egyptian dies.

natural law
descriptions of the way things normally occur

natural events
things that frequently occur again and again

Some people get quite upset at the mention of miracles. A number insist that God doesn't exist, so He could hardly perform miracles. Others are convinced that even if God does exist, He either wouldn't or couldn't violate **natural law** and perform miracles. Both schools of thought tend to look for natural causes to explain away the Bible's stories of miracles. After all, most of the miracles reported in Exodus do involve **natural events**. The fact that history records many swarms of locusts in the Middle East is cited as just one "proof" that the events of Exodus needn't be considered miracles at all. And certainly frogs have always existed along Egypt's Nile River. Just because an unusually large crop of frogs appeared, that needn't be called a miracle. Even the days of darkness are explained away as a darkness caused by dust thrust into the air by the eruption of a volcano somewhere out in the Mediterranean Sea.

There is difficulty with these "natural phenomenon" theories, however. "Natural" events don't generally occur when a Moses calls for them. And they don't just as suddenly disappear when a messenger of God calls them off.

The sequence—one miraculous judgment following another; the intensity of each judgment; the correlation of their appearance and disappearance with Moses's command—marks the Exodus events as miracles indeed.

philosophical
theoretical

Certainly the people who lived through these events viewed them as acts of God. I suspect if the critics had lived through them as well, rather than commenting from the safe distances of a few thousand years, they'd call them miracles as well.

Miracles and "Natural Law"

One of the **philosophical** arguments posed against miracles is that they violate natural law. That is, they go against everything we know about how nature works.

For instance, we all know what the law of gravity is. It's the principle that things that go up will come down. Drop a rock out of a window, and it will always fall. It will never fly upward. All natural laws are alike in that they describe something that invariably happens in nature. There are no exceptions.

Miracles, the skeptic argues, are exceptions that violate natural law. So they just can't happen.

One evening I performed a miracle for a church youth group. We talked about how objects always fall toward the earth until they land on something that stops them. Then I pointed to a screen, and told the group to watch. Immediately a rock flew over the screen and landed on the floor. A miracle! The rock flew!

key point

The young people weren't fooled. They insisted there must be someone behind the screen who threw the rock, and that this wasn't a miracle at all. They were right. Natural law assumes that a rock can't fly *by itself*. But everyone knows that a person can throw a rock, and then it *will* fly.

what others say

C. S. Lewis

In Christianity, the more we understand what God it is who is said to be present and the purpose for which He is said to have appeared, the more credible the miracles become. This is why we seldom find the Christian miracles denied except by those who have abandoned some part of Christian doctrine. The mind which asks for a non-miraculous Christianity is a mind in process of relapsing from Christianity into mere "religion."[9]

Those who accept the possibility of miracles believe that there is a God behind the screen who can act on things in the material world. Miracles don't violate natural law; they testify to a Person who is as free to act on nature as the teen behind the screen was free to throw the rock.

acts in Egypt
Exodus 4:21; 7:3, 9

Bible Words for "Miracle"

Both the Old and New Testaments contain words that describe miracles. Three different Hebrew words and a number of Greek words are associated with these visible acts of God.

- *Pala'*, used seventy-seven times in the Old Testament, means "to be marvelous, or wonderful." In most usages, it describes the awed reaction of people when they witness a miracle and recognize God's hand.

- *Mopet* is used thirty-six times, and means a "wonder" or "sign." It's closely associated with God's <u>acts in Egypt</u>.

- *'ot* is used some eight times, and means "signs." Every one of the plagues that struck Egypt is described as a "sign," evidence that God is acting on behalf of His people.

- *Dynamis*, a Greek word usually translated "miracle," is derived from the Greek word for power. It presents the act it describes as an expression of God's irresistible power.

- *Semeion*, found seventy-seven times, is translated "sign" and views the miracle it describes as evidence that God stands behind the words and actions of the miracle worker.

- *Teras*, used only sixteen times, is rendered "wonder."

- *Ergon*, "work," infrequently has the meaning of miracle, indicating a work of God.

Certainly, then, the Bible does describe events which could only be caused by God, acting in the universe He created. Our God is a miracle-working God, whose freedom to act in this world truly is unlimited.

Modern-Day Miracles?

One thing is certain about Bible miracles: Those who witnessed them had no doubt that God was at work. In the end, not

go to

even the Egyptians
Exodus 8:18–19;
9:20–21; 10:7

Jesus's birth
Isaiah 7:14;
Micah 5:2

Jesus's life
Isaiah 35:5–6a

Jesus's death
Psalm 22:16;
Isaiah 53:6–9;
Zechariah 11:12

Jesus's resurrection
Psalm 16:10;
Isaiah 53:10–12;
Matthew 27:62–63

Jesus's apostles
the men Jesus
appointed to lead
His followers

abnormalities
unusual, uncommon,
seldom repeated

even the Egyptians who refused to acknowledge the Lord had any doubt that He was behind the plagues that struck their land.

There's another thing that's very interesting about Bible miracles. They didn't happen every day. That is, Old Testament believers didn't expect God to perform a miracle every time they or their nation faced a crisis. In fact, there are only three periods of sacred history in which visible miracles were common:

1. The Exodus period (1447–1390 BC). God performs miracles to free the Israelites from bondage in Egypt. He performs miracles during their journey to their homeland. He performs a few miracles during the conquest of that land. These miracles establish His identity as Yahweh, and they usher in the era of Law, which Moses introduced.

2. The time of Elijah and Elisha (875–825 BC). Wicked kings of Israel import pagan priests and prophets in an attempt to wipe out the worship of Yahweh. As the people hesitate, Elijah's miracles turn them back to the Lord. The later miracles of Elisha demonstrate God's power to protect and provide for His people.

3. The time of Jesus and the early church (AD 30–45). Jesus's miracles authenticate Him as God's spokesman as He ushers in a new era for Israel and all humankind. Miracles are performed by **Jesus's apostles** after His resurrection, authenticating their message of salvation through Jesus.

What's fascinating is that these three ages of miracles are *abnormalities*. That is, for most of sacred history God didn't work miracles. Only in the two situations where new revelations were introduced, and in the one situation where worship of God was in danger of being extinguished, were miracles common.

Hidden Miracles

While Scripture concentrates visible miracles into three periods of sacred history, the Bible makes clear that God is always at work in our world through what we might call *hidden miracles*. For instance, the Old Testament is full of specific prophecies concerning Jesus's birth, life, and the events surrounding His death; and His resurrection. All these prophecies were fulfilled, just as foretold. While we believe that God had a hand in guiding events that led to the prophecies' fulfillment, there is usually no hint of a visible miracle.

God worked behind the scenes. Cause and effect followed in natural sequence; the persons involved acted freely, moved by their own passions. No one looking had reason to say, "Look! There's evidence of God's intervention!"

We see the same thing in Old Testament disasters and deliverances. God announces that He will punish His people for their sins. Foreign nations <u>invade and oppress</u> Israel until God's people repent. Or a cloud of <u>locusts come</u> and strip the land. As we look at these events, we can trace the chain of cause and effect that led up to them. There is nothing obviously supernatural about them, and only the eye of faith sees God's hidden hand in the events.

Miracles Today?

"And then," the TV talk show guest says breathlessly, "when the doctor took X-rays again, my cancer was *gone*!" "It's a miracle," the host declares in awed tones. "Yes," the guest agrees. "A miracle."

Those of us who believe in The God Who Is Always with Us have no doubt that God was involved in the guest's healing. God not only is free to act on our behalf; He frequently *does* act.

But we want to be clear that such healings, while **gracious acts**, fall into the category of *hidden miracles* rather than the category of *visible miracles*. The difference is a simple one. Those who do not believe in Scripture's God will view the healing as unusual, but not as a miracle. They will probably dismiss it as a "spontaneous remission," and with that label dismiss any notion that God might have been at work.

There was, however, no way for the Israelites or the Egyptians of Moses's day to label the Exodus events as merely "unusual." They were visible, unmistakably supernatural acts caused by God. And those visible miracles won freedom for the Israelites, forever shaping our understanding of who God is.

invade and oppress
Judges 6:1–6;
Habakkuk 1:5–11

locusts come
Joel 1;
Amos 4:7–10

gracious acts
kindnesses, gifts of God

You're Going Down, Pharaoh!

EXODUS 7:3–4 *I will . . . multiply My signs and My wonders in the land of Egypt. But Pharaoh will not heed you, so that I may lay My hand on Egypt and bring My armies and My people, the children of Israel, out of the land of Egypt by great **judgments**. (NKJV)*

God's Judgments Against Egypt

Judgment	Passage	Pharaoh's Response	Distinctive Elements	Consequence
Nile to Blood	Exodus 7:14–25	Unmoved	Magicians duplicate	Fish die; lack of drinking water
Frogs	Exodus 8:1–15	Asks to remove frogs; promises to let slaves go worship; breaks promise	Magicians duplicate; Pharaoh sets time for frogs to go	Frogs die, rot; the land stinks
Lice	Exodus 8:16–19	Refuses to respond	Magicians can't duplicate; credit "finger of God"	All infested with lice
Swarms	Exodus 8:20–32	Tells Moses to go sacrifice; again breaks promise	Israelite's area has no swarms	Egypt corrupted by the swarms
Disease	Exodus 9:1–7	Refuses to respond	No Israelite livestock die	Egypt's livestock all die
Boils and Sores	Exodus 9:8–12	Refuses to respond		Magicians and "all the Egyptians" suffer
Hail	Exodus 9:13–35	Admits sin; promises to let Israel go; breaks promise	Egyptians who respect God given time to shelter workers and beasts; no hail in Israelite area	Egypt devastated; animals, people killed; crops ruined
Locusts	Exodus 10:1–20	Threatens, then admits sin; promises to release Israel, then refuses	Advisers urge Pharaoh to give in; "Egypt is destroyed"	All vegetation in Egypt is eaten by locusts
Dark	Exodus 10:21–29	Calls for Moses; breaks promise to release Israel; threatens Moses's life		

Pharaoh was **adamant**. He would not consider releasing his slaves for even a few days. In the end Pharaoh's stubbornness would devastate all of Egypt. The "great judgments" by which God brought the children of Israel out of Egypt are summarized in the preceding chart.

As we examine the first nine miraculous judgments Yahweh brought on Egypt, we note a number of interesting things.

Enchanting, Magician

> EXODUS 7:11 *But Pharaoh also called the wise men and the sorcerers; so the magicians of Egypt, they also did in like manner with their enchantments.* (NKJV)

The Egyptians were big on magic and on spells. Spells involved speaking an **incantation** that recalled the story of a god or goddess performing an act that produced a result similar to the result the magician wanted to achieve.[10] Exodus suggests that at least some of Egyptian magic was successful in producing supernatural results. The Bible indicates there are supernatural beings behind pagan deities: <u>demons</u>. So the fact that Egypt's magicians should be able to counterfeit a miracle should not amaze us.

What is amusing, however, is that Egypt's magicians didn't *reverse* the curse on the Nile; they *duplicated* it with fresh water. All the demons could do was make things worse, not better!

Those Nasty Italics

> EXODUS 8:21 *The houses of the Egyptians shall be full of swarms of flies, and also the ground on which they stand.* (NKJV)

In this book I sometimes use italics for emphasis, to make something in sentence stand out and grab your attention. But when the NKJV uses italics, it's for another reason entirely. In the biblical text italics indicate that the word isn't found in the Hebrew text. The italicized word has been supplied by the translators.

The miraculous judgment that Exodus 8:20–32 describes almost certainly isn't millions of buzzing houseflies, as irritating as they can be. The Hebrew indicates the plague was one of "swarming creatures," creatures that not only filled the houses of the Egyptians but also swarmed on the ground and "corrupted" the land (8:24 NKJV). No one can say for sure just what these swarming creatures were. But they were bad enough for a temporary <u>crack to appear in Pharaoh's resolve</u>.

demons
Deuteronomy 32:17;
Leviticus 17:7

crack in Pharaoh's resolve
Exodus 8:25, 28

incantation
a chant, summons, a spell

demons
agents of Satan, the devil

Vive la Différence

Exodus 8:22–23 *I will set apart the land of Goshen, in which My people dwell, that no swarms of flies shall be there, in order that you may know that I am the LORD in the midst of the land. I will make a difference between My people and your people. (NKJV)*

From this fourth judgment miracle on, God differentiates between the Egyptians and His people. When the Israelites entered Egypt some hundreds of years before, they were settled on choice land in a district called Goshen. Much of the Israelite population apparently still lived there, although others had quarters in Egyptian areas (Exodus 3:22).

Given the preceding decades of Egyptian hostility, it may not be too much to say that Goshen was now a ghetto. Yet this Jewish ghetto was now the only safe place in Egypt!

There were no swarms infesting Goshen. When disease decimated the Egyptians' cattle, the cattle of the slaves remained healthy. When boils and sores broke out, it was only "all the Egyptians" who suffered. When hailstones crushed the life from field worker and livestock alike, none died in Goshen. And while the text makes no specific statement about the damage done by the locusts or the three-day dark, it seems that again the Israelites were spared.

More Contradictions?

If we read the miracle accounts carefully, we come across some puzzling things. For instance, Exodus 9:6 tells us that "all the livestock of Egypt died" (NKJV). Yet just two plagues later, the Egyptians who are with livestock out in the field find themselves in danger of being crushed by hailstones (Exodus 9:19). Those Egyptians who'd learned to respect the Lord immediately brought their cattle in from the fields (9:20–21). Where did those livestock come from? The critics scoff and point to the two accounts as more evidence that the Scripture is unreliable, riddled with mistakes. But there's a much better answer.

Exodus tells us that the hailstorm crushed vegetation as well as killed men and animals. In fact, Exodus is very specific: "Now the flax and the barley were struck, for the barley was in the head and the flax was in bud. But the wheat and the spelt were not struck, for they are late crops" (Exodus 9:31–32 NKJV). The very next miracle judgment comes in the form of locusts, which "eat every herb of the land—all that the hail has left" (10:12 NKJV). The result is that there "remained nothing green on the trees or on the plants of the field throughout all the land of Egypt" (10:15 NKJV).

The implication is that while the early crops were destroyed by the hail, enough time passed between the hailstorm and the locust plague for the "late crops" to grow and be destroyed by the locusts!

If we assume an unspecified time period between at least some of the judgment miracles, critics' charge of error in the text is hardly compelling. When the Egyptians' livestock was killed, they got more! They may have purchased livestock from other lands, but it's far more likely that they simply bought or took livestock from the Israelites, whose cattle had been untouched.

Actually such attacks on Scripture's reliability simply display **hubris**. Those who rush so quickly to judgment suppose that they've discovered an "error" that the original writer and hundreds of scholars through the ages have been too ignorant to note. All that has really happened is that the critic has revealed how superficial his reading of the text is. He jumps to the conclusion that what he's observed is an error in Scripture, without seriously considering alternative explanations that treat the Bible with greater respect.

Yet whether a critic challenges the possibility of miracles, or nitpicks in search of supposed errors in detail, an honest examination of the issue ultimately leads to confidence in God's Word.

key point

God's for Real

The miracles recorded in Egypt are real, visible, unmistakable miracles. As we see in them Yahweh, The One Who Is Always Present, we say with the psalmist . . .

PSALM 77:11–15
I will remember the works of the LORD;
Surely I will remember Your wonders of old.
I will also meditate on all Your work,
And talk of Your deeds . . .
Who is so great a God as our God?
You are the God who does wonders;
You have declared Your strength among the peoples.
You have with Your arm redeemed Your people,
The sons of Jacob and Joseph.
Selah (NKJV)

Chapter Wrap-Up

- Moses's first effort to free the slaves led to even heavier oppression for the Israelites.

- Pharaoh's naturally hard heart toward his slaves becomes harder as miracle judgment follows miracle judgment.

- Moses announces nine miracle judgments, each of which comes to pass.

- The miracles devastate the land of Egypt. Pharaoh still refuses to let Israel go.

Study Questions

1. What characteristics of Egypt's pharaoh suggest he would resist releasing his slaves?

2. How did the reactions of the Israelites and Moses differ when Pharaoh insisted they gather their own straw?

3. How did God harden Pharaoh's heart? Why is this method significant?

4. Why aren't miracles really violations of "natural law"?

5. What were the purposes of the miracles God performed in Egypt?

6. List five of the ten miracles described in Exodus 7–11.

7. In what way did several of the miracles demonstrate that the Israelites were God's people?

Chapter 4
Exiting Egypt

Chapter Highlights:
• Death Along the Nile
• Did God Overreact?
• Pass the Passover
• Open Water
• The Blame Game

Let's Get Started

Once green and prosperous, Egypt is now a desolate ruin. No plants grow in the fields along the Nile. Brick buildings seem dilapidated, pitted by the great hailstones. Even the magnificent stone temples erected by previous pharaohs appear shoddy; the bright colors in which the figures of the gods were painted are chipped with the bare stone showing through. Ordinary people wear a stunned look. They move slowly, as though in a daze. The nine devastating miracle judgments God has hurled upon the Egyptians and their gods have taken a terrible toll.

All but Pharaoh. Still defiant, he has quaked and quivered but he hasn't broken. His infamous last words to Moses are, "Take heed to yourself and see my face no more! For in the day you see my face you shall die!" (Exodus 10:28 NKJV).

Pharaoh is right on the money. He will never see Moses's face again. And very soon there will be death aplenty in Egypt. But Moses won't be the one to die.

Death Along the Nile

EXODUS 11:4–6 *Then Moses said, "Thus says the LORD: 'About midnight I will go out into the midst of Egypt; and all the firstborn in the land of Egypt shall die, from the firstborn of Pharaoh who sits on his throne, even to the firstborn of the female servant who is behind the handmill, and all the firstborn of the animals. Then there shall be a great cry throughout all the land of Egypt, such as was not like it before, nor shall be like it again.'" (NKJV)*

what others say

John D. Currid

Although many translations say this will take place at midnight, the Hebrew simply signifies "in the middle of the night." Nighttime was an especially fearful time for the

---

The earlier judgments against Egypt had caused the <u>deaths of animals</u> and <u>men</u>. But now not a single household in Egypt would escape the loss of a loved one. And the one who would die in every family was the firstborn.

In ancient cultures, the word *firstborn* was more than a description. It was also a legal term. The firstborn was the primary heir to a family's fortune. He was the son who was expected to carry on the family's legacy and to guard the family's fortune during his lifetime. Pharaoh's firstborn was the son who was expected to take the throne when his father died. Even in the most humble home—that of the female servant who grinds grain on a handmill—the firstborn was the one on whom the future of that family depended. No wonder the blow God now planned against the Egyptians would cause a "great cry throughout all the land" (Exodus 11:6 NKJV).

Did God Overreact?

When we imagine ourselves in the Egypt of Moses's time, it's fairly easy to **empathize** with the Egyptians. After all, wasn't Pharaoh the one who refused to bow before the Lord? Why should all Egyptians suffer for what Pharaoh did? Wouldn't it be enough to take only Pharaoh's firstborn and let the rest of the firstborn of Egypt live?

Our first response to such questions should be, "Who are we to question God's **justice**?" This is a good question to ask ourselves whenever we find our moral sensibilities offended by any act of God. It's not the place of mere creatures to question the Creator. As someone once said, one of the first things to get straight in our minds is, "He's God." And the second thing is, "We're not."

But in this case, there's another answer to the question "Why should everyone suffer?" To understand that answer, we need to empathize not with the Egyptians but with the Israelites. For possi-

deaths of animals
Exodus 9:6, 25

deaths of men
Exodus 9:25

empathize
feel for, even take
sides with

justice
moral correctness or
righteous actions

bly two centuries, the Israelites had been slaves in Egypt. Remember Exodus 1:13–14? At the beginning of our study of Moses we were told that "the Egyptians made the children of Israel serve with rigor. And they made their lives bitter with hard bondage" (NKJV).

When Pharaoh decreed that every male infant born to an Israelite family should be murdered, no Egyptian organized a protest march. No Egyptian raised his or her voice against the slaughter. In fact, Hebrew families had to hide their infant sons out of fear they might be turned in to Pharaoh! Egyptians hardly lined up to offer shelter to Hebrew children. And this, despite the fact that Egyptians were renowned as a highly moral people!

Morals in Egypt

We know quite a bit about Egyptian views of right and wrong. The Egyptians believed that some forty-two "assessors" of the god Osiris questioned the deceased. To pass their examinations, chapter 125 of *The Book of the Dead* provides a list of "negative confessions" it recommends people memorize. These negative confessions—i.e., "I didn't do this or that"—provide a fascinating insight into ancient Egyptian ideas of right and wrong:

- I have not stolen.
- I have not plundered.
- I have not slain people.
- I have not said lies.
- I have not copulated with men.
- I have not copulated with the wife of another.
- I have not slandered.
- I have not caused terror.
- I have not sent forth my hand [i.e., done violence].
- I have not wronged.
- I have not done evil.
- I have not been arrogant.[2]

Glancing through this list, we can't help but appreciate the high moral standards of the Egyptian people. Yet the Egyptians' moral standards hardly were applied to their treatment of the Hebrews.

hide their sons
Exodus 2:3

The Book of the Dead
a book supposedly showing how to gain blessings after death

Not wronged the Israelites? Not done the Israelites violence? Not caused them terror? Of course the Egyptians wronged their Hebrew slaves. Of course they did them violence and caused them terror. The whole land of Egypt, not just Pharaoh, was guilty. And the punishment decreed by the Lord was death.

How Could They?

How could a moral people like the Egyptians treat their slaves as they did? The same way Hitler's Germany could treat twentieth-century Jews as they did. The same way some African tribal groups treat members of other tribes even as you read this chapter. What the Egyptians did and moderns all too often do is strip others of their humanity; redefine them as *untermenchen*, subhuman. Egyptian morality applied to the way Egyptians treated other Egyptians, not to how they treated "less than human" Hebrew slaves!

And so God judged them **guilty**. And the penalty was death.

How Can We?

Unless we're careful, we fall into the same trap and fail to apply standards fairly. A child molester is given a minimum sentence because he experienced **trauma** in his youth. A wife beater is excused because his mother failed to love him. We show so much compassion for the criminal that we ignore the **victim** completely! One of the demands of justice is that we stand with victims against those who have harmed them.

God took His stand alongside the oppressed Hebrew slaves. And the penalty He decreed for the Egyptians was the death of their first-born.

Getting Ready for the Big Event

Bad news for the Egyptians meant good news for the Hebrew slaves. A final judgment would win their release from Egypt. In fact, the morning after the angel of death visited the Egyptians, Pharaoh threatened to drive the Israelites out!

First, though, there were a few details to take care of:

- *Collect past wages* (Exodus 11:1–3). The Egyptians are now in awe of Moses. When an Israelite asks for gold or silver, the Egyptians gladly hand it over. The people won't leave Egypt emptyhanded!

- *Bring home a lamb* (Exodus 12:1–5). On the tenth of the month the head of every Hebrew family brings home a lamb. During the three days the lamb is there, the children especially grow fond of it.

- *Kill the lamb* (Exodus 12:6–10). On the fourteenth of the month the lamb is killed. Some of its blood is daubed on the doorframe, unmistakably identifying the building as the home of Hebrews. That night the lamb is roasted and eaten by the family. Any leftovers are burned.

- *Be ready to move out* (Exodus 12:11–13). The evening meal is to be eaten standing, wearing clothing suitable for travel. God's people are to be ready to leave as soon as the Lord strikes.

The Stroke of Midnight

On the set night, around midnight, the Lord passed through the land of Egypt. He saw the blood on the doorframe of the Israelites' houses and passed over them. But He visited the home of every Egyptian, from the greatest to the least, to "strike all the firstborn in the land of Egypt, both man and beast" (Exodus 12:12a NKJV).

This most terrible of the Exodus miracles was a judgment on the sins of the Egyptians. It was also a judgment "against all the gods of Egypt" (Exodus 12:12b NKJV).

key point

Not a Life-Giving Faith

The religion of Egypt focused on life. The many gods of Egypt were honored because it was thought that they guaranteed the Egyptians a good life both on earth and in the hereafter.

Egypt truly was a blessed land. Every year the Nile rose some thirty feet and overflowed its banks, depositing rich topsoil on fields a mile away. The sun warmed the land, and Egypt's fields produced such abundant crops that many Egyptians were freed from agricultural duties. This abundance allowed Egypt to maintain a standing army, a luxury other ancient nations could not afford. The abundance also allowed pharaohs to assign multiplied thousands to great building projects. No other ancient nation was able to produce so great and so many monuments to its peoples and its gods. For no other ancient people was life as pleasant or as secure.

The blessings experienced by the Egyptians led to an optimistic view of the afterlife. The Greeks and Romans gloomily looked forward to a colorless afterlife of wandering vast, empty plains. But tomb paintings show well-to-do Egyptians enjoying an afterlife much like the life they had on earth. They relax in their gardens, they net wild birds. They feast and drink beer. Surely the gods who blessed them here would welcome them into the great beyond.

But the plagues with which Yahweh struck Egypt exposed Egypt's deities as frauds and deceivers. Yahweh turned the life-bringing Nile to blood and the river's fish died. Yahweh turned daytime to darkest night, exposing the powerlessness of Ra, the sun god. Plague after plague exposed the impotence of individual deities, but the tenth plague was a judgment "against all the gods of Egypt," those demonic forces that promised the Egyptians everlasting life while leading them down the path to eternal death.

Anybody Listening?

God had told Moses that two of His purposes in striking Egypt such devastating blows were the execution of judgment against Egypt's deities and that "the Egyptians shall know that I am the LORD" (Exodus 7:5 NKJV). After the tenth plague there could no longer be any doubt about who the true God was. But were any of the Egyptians listening?

Meet Amenhotep IV

Less than a century after the Exodus, Amenhotep IV became pharaoh. In his fifth year he rejected the gods of Egypt and changed his name to Akhenaten, in honor of Aten, the one god, the sun, which was represented by a disc. Akhenaten placed a ban on Egypt's many gods. His attempt to introduce monotheism in Egypt failed, and Akhenaten is not even included on later king lists.[3]

Some speculate that Exodus miracles still echoed in Egypt in Akhenaten's time, and that the pharaoh's religion was a failed attempt to establish a relationship with Yahweh, despite Pharaoh's distorted notion of what the One God was truly like.

Few take this position, and at any rate Akhenaten's effort proved irrelevant. The Egyptians continued to worship their deities, and the demons behind the gods of Egypt continued to deceive that great land's people.

Pass the Passover, Please

EXODUS 12:14, 17 *So this day shall be to you a **memorial**; and you shall keep it as a feast to the LORD throughout your generations. You shall keep it as a feast by an everlasting **ordinance** . . . So you shall observe the Feast of Unleavened Bread, for on this same day I will have brought your armies out of the land of Egypt. Therefore you shall observe this day throughout your generations as an everlasting ordinance. (NKJV)*

There are some days that we remember. Our birthday. Our wedding day. (That's a day we'd better remember!) The day our first child was born. We remember these days because the events that took place on them are important to us.

The day the Israelites ate the first Passover meal—the very day the Lord passed over their homes but dealt death to Egyptian households—was another day the Israelites were to remember. Moses relayed God's command that on the anniversary of that first Passover every Hebrew household was to eat a commemorative meal as the culmination of seven sacred days, a week during which the Israelites would eat no bread made with yeast.

The significance of the Passover meal is underscored by activities that lead up to it. During the week leading up to the Passover meal, the family is to eat bread made without **leaven**. In fact, no yeast is to be allowed in the house during this week. A lamb is to be purchased ahead of time, and killed on the day of Passover. As on that first Passover, the lamb's blood is to be sprinkled on the doorframe, and the family is to stay inside until morning (Exodus 12:18–24). So Scripture says, "You shall observe this thing as an ordinance for you and your sons forever" (Exodus 12:24 NKJV).

G-d
Observant Jews today, like their fore-fathers, view "God" as too holy to speak or to write.

what others say

Maxie D. Dunnam

The Passover in the book of Exodus, according to the apostle Paul, was a type, a shadow of the great substance, our Lord Jesus Christ. Israel was saved by a lamb, the best and most perfect of its kind. The lamb was slain, and its blood was applied to their houses. Entering through blood-sprinkled doors, protected by the blood of the lamb, they then feasted on the lamb, which had been slain for them. See how clear the connection is between the Passover lamb and the "Lamb slain from the foundation of the world"?[4]

Table Talk

EXODUS 12:26–27 *And it shall be, when your children say to you, "What do you mean by this service?" that you shall say, "It is the Passover sacrifice of the LORD, who passed over the houses of the children of Israel in Egypt when He struck the Egyptians and delivered our households." (NKJV)*

Moses even recorded divine instruction on what is to be said when the family sits down for a Passover meal.

Today's Seder (Passover Meal) Service

What Happens	What Is Said
The Seder service begins with holding up a plate of *matza* (thin bread made without yeast) and announcing:	*This is the bread of affliction which our fathers ate in the land of Egypt. Let those who are in need come and celebrate the Passover.*
Traditionally the youngest person present then asks four questions:	*1. Why is this night different from all other nights?* *2. On all other nights we eat either leavened or unleavened bread. Why on this night do we eat only unleavened bread?* *3. On all other nights we eat all kinds of vegetables. Why on this night do we eat only bitter herbs?* *4. On all other nights we eat either sitting or reclining. Why on this night do we recline?*
After the questions are answered, the family pauses to remember the greatness of God's miracles of liberation.	*Slaves we were to Pharaoh in Egypt, and the Lord our **G-d** brought us out from there with a mighty hand and an outstretched arm. If the Holy One, Blessed be He, had not brought our fathers out of Egypt, then we and our children and our children's children would still be enslaved to Pharaoh in Egypt.*

Today's Seder (Passover Meal) Service (cont'd)

What Happens	What Is Said
A list of the ten plagues is then read from the **Haggadah**. As each plague is read aloud, a drop of wine is spilled from the participants' glasses. Finally the *Dayenu*, a song that praises the miracles God performed for the Jewish people from their liberation to the construction of the Temple in Jerusalem, is sung. This concludes the telling of the Passover story.[5]	Ten Plagues: 1. *The Nile turns to blood.* 2. *Frogs infest the land.* 3. *There's an infestation of gnats.* 4. *There's an infestation of "swarming insects."* 5. *A deadly disease strikes Egypt's livestock.* 6. *Everyone breaks out in painful boils.* 7. *A hailstorm destroys the early crops.* 8. *A cloud of locusts strips the land of growing things.* 9. *For three days there's absolute darkness.* 10. *Every firstborn Egyptian dies.*

an object
Joshua 4:1–7

Haggadah
a compilation of rabbinic texts read during Jewish holy days

Once More, with Meaning

The Seder service captures both the nature and the purpose of the Passover. In reciting "the Lord G-d brought *us* out from there," modern Jews gain identity with their ancestors. In a significant sense, through the Passover each generation is enabled to experience the deliverance God provided for His people.

It's a *Zikkaron*

EXODUS 12:14 *So this day shall be to you a memorial; and you shall keep it as a feast to the LORD throughout your generations. You shall keep it as a feast by an everlasting ordinance. (NKJV)*

The word translated "memorial" here is the Hebrew word *zikkaron*. At times *zikkaron* is also translated as "remembrance" or "reminder." Wherever it appears it has great significance. An object or an event that is a *zikkaron* is intended to be a door through which a believer enters to reexperience a work God performed for His people, and realize that God performed that work for *him*. When God performed mighty miracles to free the Hebrew slaves some 1,450 years before Christ, He didn't work those miracles for the Exodus generation alone; He performed those miracles for every one of their descendants as well. By participating in the *zikkaron* event of Passover, every Jew throughout history has been invited to sense how much God loves him or her, and how great is God's redeeming power.

the New Covenant
Jeremiah 31:31–34;
Hebrews 8

Calvary
Matthew 27:34–56;
Luke 23:26–49

sin's penalty
Romans 3:23;
Revelation 20:11–15

sin's power
Romans 8:9–11;
Ephesians 2:1–11

major religious revivals
2 Kings 23;
2 Chronicles 30; 35

Flash Forward

Flash forward over fifteen centuries and listen in as Jesus speaks to His disciples. They've just finished eating the Passover together. As His followers focus intently, Jesus breaks off pieces from a loaf of bread, offers a morsel to each disciple, and then says, "Take, eat. This is My body."

Then Jesus takes a cup of wine. He thanks His Father and extends the cup to His followers. "Drink from it, all of you." And as they drink He continues, "This is My blood of <u>the new covenant</u>, which is shed for many for the remission of sins." Luke tells us that Jesus added, "Do this in remembrance of Me" (Luke 22:19 NKJV). The apostle Paul understood the significance of the words *Do this in remembrance of Me*. In 1 Corinthians 11:24 and 25 (NKJV), he quotes Jesus as repeating "Do this in remembrance of Me" when offering both the bread and the wine.

Christian Communion, like the Passover, is a *zikkaron* event! As the bread and wine are passed, a door in time opens, and as we pass through we find ourselves standing at the foot of the cross. We see Christ's agony, we are stained by the blood He shed, and we realize, "Christ died for me!"

As God's Old Testament people stepped through the portal the Passover opened for them, they realized that God acted in Egypt to save each of them from bondage. In the same way, the Communion event opens the door for God's new covenant people—believing Jewish and Gentile Christians alike. In the Communion we go back in time to <u>Calvary</u>, and grasp afresh that God acted in Christ to save us from our bondage to <u>sin's penalty</u> and <u>power</u>.

Remember!

The Old Testament makes it clear that Israel all too often failed to keep Passover. Decade after decade passed during which no Hebrew ate a Passover meal. Yet this simple event, which God told Moses was to be faithfully observed each year, was a vital step in protecting against apostasy. It's a significant fact that every <u>major religious revival</u> during the years that a Jewish kingdom existed was marked by reinstituting the Passover.

To set aside time to remember what God has done, to realize afresh that He has acted for us, is one of the most significant ways a believer can remain strong in his or her faith.

apply it

The First One Is Mine

EXODUS 13:1–2, 14–15 *Then the LORD spoke to Moses, saying,* **"Consecrate** *to Me all the firstborn, whatever opens the womb among the children of Israel, both of man and beast . . . So it shall be, when your son asks you in time to come, saying, 'What is this?' that you shall say to him, 'By strength of hand the LORD brought us out of Egypt, out of the house of bondage. And it came to pass, when Pharaoh was stubborn about letting us go, that the LORD killed all the firstborn in the land of Egypt, both the first-born of man and the firstborn of beast. Therefore I sacrifice to the LORD all males that open the womb, but all the firstborn of my sons I* **redeem**.*'" (NKJV)*

Dedication of every firstborn male to the Lord was another reminder of deliverance from Egypt. As we continue tracing Moses's life and mission we'll see another, special way in which God's claim on the firstborn affects sacred history. But now, we need to pick up the story as told in Exodus 13:17–15:21.

what others say

Maxie D. Dunnam

In the Old Testament, "firstborn" (defined as that which first opens the womb) is most frequently used to designate the eldest son. His privileges and responsibilities include succession to the headship of the family and responsibility for the continuation and well-being of the family . . . In Israel, the first-born now had a special place—the firstborn was to be dedicated to God.[6]

Open Water

the big picture

Exodus 12:31–14:12

A disorganized mob of exslaves hurries out of Egypt. A great pillar of cloud bursting with fire moves ahead of them, showing them the way. The pillar leads them away from the well-worn trade route that runs along the Mediterranean shore. The

consecrate
dedicate, set aside for me

redeem
pay a price to buy back

Egyptians have built a line of forts along that route, and the flee-
ing slaves aren't ready for a fight. Instead, the pillar of fire leads
them into a trackless wilderness. Finally it stops before a wide
body of water, and Moses is given news that terrifies the
Israelites: Pharaoh is after them! He's changed his mind! With a
sea before them and their way blocked on either side, it seems
there's no escape. At the first sight of the pursuing army the
people panic.

The People Panic

EXODUS 14:10–12 *And when Pharaoh drew near, the children
of Israel lifted their eyes, and behold, the Egyptians marched
after them. So they were very afraid, and the children of Israel
cried out to the LORD. Then they said to Moses, "Because there
were no graves in Egypt, have you taken us away to die in the
wilderness? Why have you so dealt with us, to bring us up out of
Egypt? Is this not the word that we told you in Egypt, saying, 'Let
us alone that we may **serve the Egyptians**'? For it would have
been better for us to serve the Egyptians than that we should die
in the wilderness." (NKJV)*

On the one hand we can understand the fear that gripped the
Israelites. But on the other hand their conviction of doom is puzzling. They've just witnessed Egypt's pharaoh brought to his knees
by powerful acts of God. On their way out of Egypt they've been led
by a pillar of fire, more evidence that God is present with them. So
at the first sight of the dust rising behind them that marks Egyptian
pursuers, they simply give up?

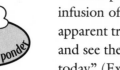

These people needed a backbone transplant—or at least a fresh
infusion of faith. This was in fact one reason God led Israel into an
apparent trap. Moses's response to the people's fear was, "Stand still,
and see the salvation of the LORD, which He will accomplish for you
today" (Exodus 14:13 NKJV).

Fear and Faith

All of us have experienced fear. Often fear is appropriate, and we
react in a healthy way. If we should wake up and find our house on
fire, we should feel fear. A healthy reaction to that fear would be to
grab our family members and hurry outside. If a dog growls at us

and bares its teeth, we should feel fear. A healthy reaction to that fear would be to move away from the dog rather than attempting to pet it. If we're hiking in snake country and hear a rattle coming from a nearby bush, we should feel fear. A healthy reaction to that fear would be to stop, look around carefully, and move away. Fear alerts us to danger, and a healthy reaction to fear is to act wisely in the situation.

take a boat
Mark 4:36

There are also unhealthy reactions to fear. At times fear paralyzes us and throws us into a panic. We become so filled with terror that we can't think clearly. When fear overcomes us we're all too likely to react unwisely.

The reaction of the Israelites at the sight of the Egyptian army is an example of this. In their panic, they couldn't think clearly. They anticipated the worst, and frantically accused Moses of trying to get them killed. They forgot all about Egyptian oppression and their anguished cries to God, and ragged on Moses for freeing them. Even with the fiery pillar filling the sky above them, they completely discounted God.

A Rocky Boat Ride

Centuries later, Jesus and His disciples <u>take a boat</u> to cross the Sea of Galilee. Exhausted from a full day of teaching and healing, Jesus falls asleep. A violent storm strikes; it is so violent that even the disciples who made their living fishing Galilee are terrified. Finally, convinced they're about to sink, the disciples rouse Jesus. Christ sees the situation, stands, and commands the winds to stop and the waters to be still. Instantly all is calm. Jesus looks at His companions in wonder. Why were they afraid? Wasn't He with them in the boat?

Fear, but Also Trust

PSALM 56:3–4
Whenever I am afraid,
I will trust in You.
In God (I will praise His word),
In God I have put my trust;
I will not fear.
What can flesh do to me? (NKJV)

In Psalm 56, David gives us a prescription to follow when we feel fear. The superscription to the psalm tells us that David wrote it commemorating a time when he was captured by the Philistines. He was afraid then, with good reason. As the killer of the Philistine champion Goliath, David was at the top of his enemies' list of "ten most wanted Israelites"!

Note the process:

- David feels fear, and acknowledges it.
- David consciously chooses to trust God.
- David recalls God's revelation of Himself in Scripture.
- David determines not to anticipate evil, for he knows God is greater than his enemies.

This is a prescription that neither the Israelites trapped beside the Red Sea nor Jesus's disciples terrified by the storm followed. Yet it's a prescription that can relieve terror and give us peace.

God was present in the fiery pillar in the sky. God was present in the Person of Jesus in the boat. And God, The One Who Is Always Present, is present with us today. Like David we can say, "Whenever I am afraid, I will trust in You"—and then experience an inner peace only God can give.

Moses Knew the Secret

The advice Moses gave the Israelites beautifully expresses his own response to the impending danger. Moses was only human, and the sight of Egypt's army on the horizon must have caused at least a twinge of fear. But Moses didn't panic. He recognized the enemy, but he also recognized the presence of God.

His words to the Israelites were, "Stand still, and see the salvation of the LORD, which He will accomplish for you today" (Exodus 14:13 NKJV). Moses's response in that stress-filled situation suggests another guideline we can follow to nurture a deeper relationship with God.

A healthy relationship with God is reflected in the expectation that He will act to deliver us in difficult and stressful situations.

key point

Not the Only Foolish Ones There

The panicked Israelites were foolish because they didn't expect God to act. But there were others there who were just as foolish, for a similar reason. Pharaoh and the Egyptian army that followed him were foolish because *they didn't expect God to act either*!

Like the Israelites, the Egyptians had seen God's miracle-working power. Since they were on the receiving end of the judgments, they had even more reason than the Israelites to have a healthy respect for the Lord. But instead of stopping to think, they rushed on headlong, actually expecting to recapture God's people. Not smart. Not smart at all.

Another Heart Hardening

EXODUS 14:3–4 *Pharaoh will say of the children of Israel, "They are bewildered by the land; the wilderness has closed them in." Then I will harden Pharaoh's heart, so that he will pursue them; and I will gain honor over Pharaoh and over all his army, that the Egyptians may know that I am the LORD." And they did so. (NKJV)*

In the last chapter, I suggested that verses telling us that God hardened Pharaoh's heart describe the response to God's miracles of a person whose heart was already hard. But with this verse, and possibly with similar statements in Exodus 10 and 11, something more is implied. Bible scholars call it "judicial hardening." What they mean is that by this point Pharaoh's heart was so hard that God determined to judge him. That judgment was to make it impossible for him to change. Simply put, Pharaoh had come so far down the wrong road that even if he had wanted to change—and he didn't— God wouldn't let him!

There's a parallel in Romans 1, where Paul describes how human beings and civilizations have heard God's voice in His creation and intentionally turned away. Rather than be thankful, humans "changed the glory of the incorruptible God into an image made like corruptible man—and birds and four-footed animals and creeping things" (Romans 1:23 NKJV). As Paul traces humanity's moral and spiritual decline, he says three times that God acted as judge:

- "Therefore God also gave them up . . ." (Romans 1:24 NKJV).
- "For this reason God gave them up . . ." (Romans 1:26 NKJV).
- "And even as they did not like to retain God in their knowledge, God gave them over . . ." (Romans 1:28 NKJV).

God gives us human beings freedom to make our own choices. But when those choices are constantly sinful and harden our hearts, there may come a time when it's too late to change. In his capacity as judge over all, God may judicially harden our hearts.

This is what was happening now to Pharaoh and his army. They were judicially blinded to the utter stupidity of further attacks on the people Yahweh loved.

More Miracles

Later that day Moses writes a song to commemorate God's victory over Pharaoh. His sister Miriam leads dancing, praising women, and shouts . . .

feared
respected, honored

believed
trusted

EXODUS 15:21
Sing to the LORD,
For He has triumphed gloriously!
The horse and its rider
He has thrown into the sea! (NKJV)

The Blame Game

EXODUS 15:22–24 *So Moses brought Israel from the Red Sea; then they went out into the Wilderness of Shur. And they went three days in the wilderness and found no water. Now when they came to Marah, they could not drink the waters of Marah, for they were bitter . . . And the people complained against Moses, saying, "What shall we drink?" (NKJV)*

As people age, they often experience a phenomenon known as "short-term memory loss." Here we have a prime example of an entire nation suffering short-term memory loss! It's hardly a month since God won their freedom by a final, terrible judgment against Egypt. It's just three days since the sea opened for the Israelites and then closed on the Egyptians!

key point

Three days earlier Scripture's comment was, "Thus Israel saw the great work which the LORD had done in Egypt; so the people **feared** the LORD, and **believed** the LORD and His servant Moses" (Exodus 14:31 NKJV).

Three days! Not only was their short-term memory gone, their faith had evaporated too!

Move On, Murmur On

Time after time as the Israelites journeyed deeper into the wilderness they faced similar challenges. They ran short of water. The food they'd carried from Egypt ran out. Each time something seemed to go wrong the Israelites reacted the same way:

- "The people complained against Moses"
  (Exodus 15:24 NKJV).

contended
argued, complained
bitterly

- "Then the whole congregation of the children of Israel complained against Moses and Aaron in the wilderness" (Exodus 16:2 NKJV).

- "Therefore the people **contended** with Moses" (Exodus 17:2 NKJV).

Exodus 15:22 through Exodus 18 relates the events that transpired on the Israelites' two-month journey from the Red Sea to Mount Sinai. Reading quickly through it, we garner the impression that the Israelites are a bunch of complainers. They gripe. They grumble. They "contend" with Moses. If you read other English versions, you'll see that they also murmur.

What we don't get from any English version is the significance of this reaction. The Hebrew phrase *lon 'al*, "grumble against," which occurs seven times in five verses in Exodus 16, describes an attitude of bitterness and hostility. The Hebrew verb *marah*, which depicts the people's words and actions in Exodus 15:22–24 and Exodus 16:1–8, describes these Israelites as *rebellious*. Their problem wasn't just a lack of trust. It wasn't simply that they whined a lot. These people bridled; they were totally unwilling to submit to God. Suddenly, unexpectedly, we see the same rebellious attitude in God's people that Egypt's pharaoh displayed!

---

what others say

J. Gerald Janzen

Just as the first flush of their belief in God's promised deliverance (4:31) gave way after further hardships to disbelief (6:9), so now the initial sweetness of the song in their mouths (15:1–2) gives way to bitterness. According to the NRSV, they "complained." That is not an adequate translation. In Job, in Psalms, and elsewhere, the Bible is full of entirely appropriate complaints. Here they do something the Bible always criticizes . . . This is not a loud outcry *to* God, but a rebellious muttering *about* God, "under their breath" plotting to pull out of the enterprise and head back to Egypt.[8]

Although the Israelites pointed their fingers at Moses and blamed him, their issue was with the Lord, not with Moses.

Moses Understood

EXODUS 16:7 *And in the morning you shall see the **glory** of the LORD; for He hears your complaints against the LORD. But what are we, that you complain against us?* (NKJV)

glory
splendor, revealed
power

Let's begin with "What are we?" The people were complaining to Moses, but their real problem was with the Lord. After all, Moses was simply following the lead of God's fiery-cloudy pillar!

Parents need to recognize this phenomenon. It's common enough, especially as we try to carry out our God-given responsibilities: establish bedtimes . . . assign chores . . . insist that homework be done . . . do all those things that God expects a responsible parent to do, and *wham!* You're barraged by sullen complaints and grumbling. It's hard not to feel overwhelmed. At such times, remember that your children's issue isn't with you, but with a God who expects them to "obey [their] parents in the Lord" (Ephesians 6:1 NKJV). Like Moses, we are to remain faithful to the Lord and not give up.

Moses Versus the Israelites

The Israelites were too hypocritical to acknowledge that their problem was with God. So they attacked Moses. It must have felt a lot safer to rail against Moses than to verbally attack Yahweh!

Moses took a totally different approach. He went directly to God. He laid his problems before the Lord, he expressed his frustrations, and he waited expectantly for the Lord to tell him what to do. The Israelites' approach showed a lack of respect and even contempt for Yahweh. Moses's direct approach honored the Lord, for it acknowledged His active involvement and His authority.

There's a vast difference between complaining *about* God and complaining *to* God. Which brings us to another guideline for a healthy relationship with the Lord:

A healthy relationship with God also calls for us to go to the Lord with our complaints, frustrations, and fears.

disobeyed God's commands
Exodus 16:19–20, 25–28

manna
a wafer-like food that appeared on the ground each morning

stone
execute by battering with heavy rocks

He Hears Your Complaints

Moses was well aware that the Lord heard the complaints of His people. I suspect Moses was also well aware of the fact that God knows how to deal with the rebellious. He certainly knew how to deal with Pharaoh.

But as we follow the story, we see something amazing. Each time the Israelites complain, God patiently provides for their needs!

- At Marah, the Israelites find water—but it's bitter, undrinkable. They "complain against Moses." Moses turns to the Lord, and is shown how to make the waters sweet (Exodus 15:22–27).
- In the Wilderness of Sin, they run out of food and "complain against Moses and Aaron." The next morning, the first of the **manna** that will miraculously feed the Israelites during their wilderness years appears on the ground. That evening a vast flock of quail provides meat (Exodus 16:2–13).
- At Rephidim, the people again had no water. They became so angry they were almost ready to **stone** Moses! God told Moses to strike a rocky outcrop, and water gushed out.

Talk About Ungrateful!

So, how did the Israelites respond to what we might call God's "nice treatment"? Instead of becoming more grateful and responsive, the Israelites got worse and worse. After the first incident the Lord challenged the Israelites to "diligently heed the voice of the LORD your God and do what is right in His sight." And He promised that then "I will put none of the diseases on you which I have brought on the Egyptians" (Exodus 15:26 NKJV).

In response, the Israelites persistently disobeyed God's commands. Each time supplies ran short they became more hostile and antagonistic. In the end, they even demanded that God prove to them that He was present (Exodus 17:7). The "nice treatment" wasn't working. Not, at any rate, if the goal was a change in rebellious people's attitudes.

Why the "Nice" Treatment?

The Bible tells us that God is a gracious God, who cares about people and is <u>kind to all</u>. But His "nice treatment" seemed to be making these Israelites worse!

kind to all
Matthew 5:44–45;
Romans 2:4

There's an important insight here for parents. Being too nice to our children, giving them whatever they want, failing to establish and enforce rules, isn't going to produce responsible, mature adults. The "nice treatment" doesn't work in raising children any better than it worked with the Israelites.

But God isn't going to keep on being nice. In the next chapters we'll look at the Law that God gave Israel through Moses. And after that we'll see how the Lord dealt with His rebellious people after standards were established, and the people had agreed to live by them.

As we study later experiences of Moses with the Israelites, we'll want to remember the Exodus 15:22–17:7 description of how the Israelites responded to God before He gave them His Law—and held Israel accountable.

The First Taste of War

EXODUS 17:8–16 *Now Amalek came and fought with Israel in Rephidim. And Moses said to Joshua, "Choose us some men and go out, fight with Amalek. Tomorrow I will stand on the top of the hill with the rod of God in my hand." So Joshua did as Moses said to him, and fought with Amalek. And Moses, Aaron, and Hur went up to the top of the hill. And so it was, when Moses held up his hand, that Israel prevailed; and when he let down his hand, Amalek prevailed. But Moses' hands became heavy; so they took a stone and put it under him, and he sat on it. And Aaron and Hur supported his hands, one on one side, and the other on the other side; and his hands were steady until the going down of the sun. So Joshua defeated Amalek and his people with the edge of the sword.*

Then the LORD said to Moses, "Write this for a memorial in the book and recount it in the hearing of Joshua, that I will utterly blot out the remembrance of Amalek from under heaven." And Moses built an altar and called its name, The-LORD-Is-My-Banner; for he said, "Because the LORD has sworn: the LORD will have war with Amalek from generation to generation." (NKJV)

go to

lighten his burden
Exodus 18:13–23

**applied to Israel's
military**
1 Samuel 22:7;
2 Samuel 18:1;
2 Kings 11:9–19

deteriorated
gotten worse and
worse

The Israelites won their skirmish with the Amalekites. So there would be no mistaking the Lord's involvement, the Israelites surged forward when Moses stretched out his arms in prayer, and they fell back when Moses's arms dropped. In the end, Aaron and a man named Hur had to support Moses's arms. By nightfall the Israelites had won.

Take a Load Off

Just before the Israelites reached Mount Sinai, Moses's father-in-law, Jethro, found him. Convinced by the miracles God had worked in Egypt, Jethro became a worshipper of the Lord. Jethro also suggested a way that Moses could <u>lighten his burden of leadership</u>. He divided the people into teams of ten. He then organized the tens into groups of fifty, the fifties into hundreds, and the hundreds into thousands. At each level one man was appointed leader, to teach and be responsible for those under him. The idea was that when problems arose that couldn't be solved among the ten, they would be taken to the next level, and so on. Moses would have to deal with only the most difficult cases.

While this structure was later <u>applied to Israel's military</u>, God would soon replace Jethro's invention with a very different social structure.

A Long, Long Way from Egypt

In the three months since leaving Egypt, the Israelites have come a long way geographically. They've come from the Nile delta region up the Sinai peninsula to its easternmost end, a journey of hundreds of miles. But Israel hasn't come far spiritually. In fact, their relationship with God has **deteriorated** from hesitant trust to a hostile rebellion. It's clear that something has to change. And change radically.

Chapter Wrap-Up

- When God strikes dead all Egypt's firstborn, Pharaoh is ready to drive the Israelites out of Egypt.

- A fiery-cloudy pillar leads the Israelites into an apparent trap beside the Reed Sea.

- Pharaoh pursues, but God parts the water so the Israelites can escape, and then closes it again to drown the Egyptian army.

- Initial praise by the Israelites is soon replaced by grumbling toward and criticism of Moses.

- God patiently meets every need of the Israelites. They respond by becoming more bitter and rebellious.

- Through it all, Moses demonstrates godly responses to both the danger and the Israelites' growing hostility.

Study Questions

1. What in Israel's experience suggests that God did not overreact in striking all the firstborn of Egypt?

2. What is special about the Passover meal to be eaten annually by the Israelites?

3. In what ways is Christian Communion like the Jewish Seder?

4. How is the hardening of Pharaoh's heart as he pursues the Israelites different from earlier hardenings?

5. Why did the Israelites panic when they saw Pharaoh's army approaching?

6. What miracles did God perform for His people at the Red Sea?

7. Why does the author suggest the Israelites suffered from "short-term memory loss"?

8. How would you contrast the behavior of the Israelites with the behavior of Moses in these chapters?

Chapter Highlights:
• Thunder Mountain
• God Has Big Plans
• Cutting Covenants
• A Bird's-Eye View of
  Mosaic Law
• Everybody Knows *That!*

Let's Get Started

Grumbling, complaining, resisting all the way, the mob of freed slaves has traversed the Sinai peninsula and arrived at the mountain where the Lord first <u>met with Moses</u>. They don't know it yet, but some big changes are in store.

The carrot is about to be replaced with a combination carrot-and-stick, and humankind is about to receive a bold new revelation.

God's appearance to Moses and His explanation of the significance of the name Yahweh defined the Lord as Always Present with His people. God's commitment to release Abraham's descendants from slavery displayed God's faithfulness. And the miracles God performed in Egypt made it clear that Yahweh is all-powerful, far above the counterfeits other nations worshipped as gods.

What God is about to reveal now is **His righteousness**. He will do it by establishing standards that have resonated for thirty-five hundred years, and even today shape our ideas of right and wrong.

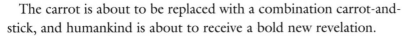

met with Moses
Exodus 3:12

His righteousness
God's total commitment to right moral behavior

Thunder Mountain

EXODUS 19:1 *In the third month after the children of Israel had gone out of the land of Egypt, on the same day, they came to the Wilderness of Sinai.* (NKJV)

It's one of the most desolate places on earth. Very little grows there. Scorching heat pounds down by day and radiates off after dark, leaving the nights chill and cold. It's hardly a place the Israelites would have chosen for a campout. Yet for the next twelve months they'll camp on these plains before the rugged peak that most scholars identify as a mountain known today as Jabal el Musa.

Why did God lead Israel to this place, and what does He intend to do here?

go to

human beings are spe-
cial
Genesis 1:26–28

chosen people
Deuteronomy 10:15;
Ezekiel 20:5;
John 15:16

God Has Big Plans for You!

EXODUS 19:5–6 *Now therefore, if you will indeed obey My voice and keep My covenant, then you shall be a special treasure to Me above all people; for all the earth is Mine. And you shall be to Me a kingdom of priests and a holy nation. (NKJV)*

We're not sure what the Israelites felt when Moses delivered this message from God. We can sense something of what they *should* have felt. Think about what the Lord is telling Israel.

- *You'll be My special treasure.* In the Genesis story of creation we're taught that <u>human beings are special</u>. Human beings are distinct from animals in that only humans, created in God's image and likeness, share those characteristics that make both Him and us persons: capacities like the ability to think and remember, to plan and to act, to love and to feel a wide range of emotions. Only humans have the ability to act on nature, and to sense a spiritual universe beyond the material.

Anyone who has pets knows that animals share some of these qualities. But animals are part of nature, equipped with instincts that enable them to live within the natural world. Only we humans share with God the full range of capabilities that mark us as persons.

When God tells Israel that they will be a special treasure "above all people," He reminds them and us that "all people" are special to Him. Yet He promises the Israelites that they will be more special than the rest. They truly will be His "<u>chosen people</u>."

- *You'll be a kingdom of priests.* In the ancient world priests were mediators. They served as a bridge between God and others. They approached God on behalf of others, offering sacrifices, bringing their requests, seeking forgiveness or aid. Priests also went to the people on God's behalf, giving them His message. As a "kingdom of priests" the Israelites were to become the bridge by which all humanity might approach the Lord, and also the bridge over which the Lord would reach out to humankind.

Centuries earlier God had promised Abraham, "In you all the families of the earth shall be blessed" (Genesis 12:3 NKJV). Through Moses the first step in keeping that promise is now revealed. The descendants of Abraham, the Israelites, are to become a kingdom of priests. Through Israel the Lord God will communicate His love to the world, and through them the world will have access to God.

- *You'll be a holy nation.* Here we need to remember that in Scripture the basic meaning of the word *holy* is "set apart for God's use." While God's holy people were and are called to live moral lives, morality is not primarily in view here. What is in view is the fact that God intends to set the Israelites apart to accomplish a special purpose through them.

go to

descendant of Abraham
Matthew 1:1;
Luke 3:23–34

> ### what others say
>
> **John L. Mackay**
>
> As the "holy"—that is, the "set apart"—nation they would be able to fulfill the function the Lord assigned them. Their "nation" would be unlike other nations which aim for the glory and dominance that characterize earthly politics. They would be a servant nation whose task was to mediate between the divine world and the ordinary world of mankind: That was the essence of priesthood.[1]

Israel would often stumble and fail to perform the function of a kingdom of priests. Yet through Moses and the prophets the Lord communicated His written Word for all peoples. And the Savior entered this world to live and die a Jew, one of God's chosen people, a <u>descendant of Abraham</u>.

Chosen! Chosen to be God's special people, chosen to become a kingdom of priests, a holy nation! What a burst of gratitude that announcement should have caused. And how utterly humbling.

key point

Flash Forward

Some fifteen hundred years pass. The moment comes; the Savior of the world is born! He teaches and heals, He dies on a cross; He rises to live again. His death and resurrection initiate yet another new revelation. As His followers spread the news that the Son of God has paid for sins by dying on a cross, they share a vision that Moses shared with the Israelites at Sinai.

Jesus's followers have been chosen by God to be a special people. As God's special people, Christians too are a kingdom of priests—bridges stretching between heaven and earth. They are a holy people, set aside to continue Christ's mission of bringing people to God.

What a burst of gratitude this announcement should cause us. And how humbling!

Chosen, Then and Now

Old Testament—Israelites	New Testament—Christians
You shall be a special treasure to Me. (Exodus 19:5 NKJV)	He chose us in Him before the foundation of the world. (Ephesians 1:4 NKJV)
You shall be to Me a kingdom of priests. (Exodus 19:6 NKJV)	You are a chosen generation, a royal priesthood, a holy nation, His own special people . . . (1 Peter 2:9 NKJV)
You shall be to Me . . . a holy nation. (Exodus 19:6 NKJV)	. . . that you may proclaim the praises of Him who called you out of darkness. (1 Peter 2:9 NKJV)

what others say

Wayne A. Grudem

So in verses 4 through 10 Peter says that God has bestowed on the church almost all the blessings promised Israel in the Old Testament. The dwelling place of God is no longer the Jerusalem temple, for Christians are the new "temple" of God. The priesthood able to offer acceptable sacrifices to God is no longer descended from Aaron, for Christians are now the true "royal priesthood" with access before God's throne (vv. 4–5, 9).[2]

I Do. Don't I?

EXODUS 19:8 *Then all the people answered together and said, "All that the LORD has spoken we will do." (NKJV)*

The Israelites' response to God's announcement of His purposes in choosing them reminds me of a very young couple eager to launch out on the sea of matrimony. They've had a rough courtship, but somehow they imagine that once they've said their vows, everything will change.

For the past two months the rebellious Israelites have bridled at everything God told them to do. Yet now they enthusiastically pledge, "All that the LORD has spoken we will do."

Fortunately, God is a gentleman. These people have no idea what they're getting into. And the Lord won't hold them to this initial, too-hasty commitment. But after His standards have been carefully explained, He'll ask them again.

That's one thing about the Mosaic Law that is unique. God didn't ask Abraham for a commitment when He gave Abraham <u>covenant promises</u>. But the covenant that God is about to make with the Israelites through Moses requires their agreement. More about that later.

go to

covenant promises
Genesis 12:1–3, 7

intercessory work
prayer on our behalf

<u>Thunder, and Then Some</u>

EXODUS 19:16 *Then it came to pass on the third day, in the morning, that there were thunderings and lightnings, and a thick cloud on the mountain; and the sound of the trumpet was very loud, so that all the people who were in the camp trembled. (NKJV)*

Much later, the writer of the New Testament book of Hebrews looks back on this scene and describes it graphically. Sinai was "the mountain that [may not] be touched and that burned with fire." It was shrouded with "blackness and darkness and tempest." "The sound of a trumpet and the voice of words" were so deafening "that those who heard it begged that the word should not be spoken to them anymore." The writer of Hebrews pictures it as "so terrifying" that even Moses cried, "I am exceedingly afraid and trembling" (Hebrews 12:18–21 NKJV).

key point

Certainly the sense of awe created by God's appearance on Mount Sinai left an indelible impression on the Israelites, an impression reflected in Psalm 68:33–35:

To Him who rides on the heaven of heavens, which were of old!
Indeed, He sends out His voice, a mighty voice.
Ascribe strength to God;
His excellence is over Israel,
And His strength is in the clouds.
O God, You are more awesome than Your holy places.
The God of Israel is He who gives strength and power to
   His people.
Blessed be God! (NKJV)

what others say

Peter Enns

Exodus 19 is a clear reminder that the God we meet with regularly by virtue of the **intercessory work** of the risen Christ and into whose presence we have confidence to come, is the

Creator of everything. He is fearful, threatening, unsettling, all-powerful, all-knowing. He is, to use the well-known expression of the beaver in C. S. Lewis's classic children's book *The Lion, the Witch and the Wardrobe*, not safe but good. He is both someone to be feared and the One who has traversed the universe to meet us where we are, in the form of a human being, born of a woman, who bore our sin in His own body and who loves us dearly. It is perhaps, in the end, a paradox well worth entertaining. We fear Him because He is good; we see His goodness because we fear Him.[3]

Definitely Convincing!

Centuries later, a group of **Pharisees** dismiss the testimony of a man Jesus miraculously healed, but confess, "We know that God spoke to Moses" (John 9:29 NKJV).

"Thunder mountain," shrouded in roiling black clouds, lit by constant flashes of lightning, left no doubt in anyone's mind. As Moses trudged up that mountain, everyone knew that he was going there to meet with Yahweh. And when he came down from the mountain, no one doubted that he carried with him the very Word of God.

Three things, then, in Exodus 19's prelude to the giving of the Law are particularly significant.

- God announces His choice of Israel as His chosen people, to be a holy nation and a kingdom of priests.
- God does not impose this role on the Israelites but gives them a choice.
- God's appearance on Mount Sinai is carefully crafted to awe the Israelites and establish beyond question that the Law Moses is about to deliver truly is Yahweh's.

key point

Cutting Covenants

I described the concept of "covenant" in an earlier chapter. If you recall, I said that a covenant is essentially an agreement between two or more parties. In Hebrew idiom you don't write down a covenant, you "cut" it. It's the kind of formal, binding agreement that's viewed as engraved in stone!

hierodule
concubine,
secondary wife

mina
a unit of weight,
about 1.2 pounds

Depending on the parties involved, covenants may be described differently. We'd probably call a covenant between businessmen a "contract." We'd call a covenant between nations a "treaty." We'd call a covenant between a ruler and his subjects a "national constitution." Yet in Old Testament times, they all went by the name "covenant."

Several common elements usually appeared in cutting a covenant. Covenants spelled out what each party to an agreement was expected to do. They spelled out the benefits each could expect from the relationship. And they usually spelled out what happened if one party failed to live up to what was agreed upon.

Here, for instance, is a marriage contract (a marriage covenant) executed in Assyria in the nineteenth century BC:[4]

> Laquipum has married Hatala, daughter of Enishru. In the country Laquipum may not marry another—in the City he may marry a **hierodule**. If within two years Hatala does not provide him with offspring, she herself will purchase a slave-woman, and later on, after she will have produced a child by him, he may then dispose of her by sale wheresoever he pleases. Should Laquipum choose to divorce her, he shall pay her five **minas** of silver; and should Hatala choose to divorce him, she must pay him five minas of silver. Witnesses: Masa, Ashurishtikal, Talia, Shupianika.

Note the elements to this contract.

Elements of the Marriage Covenant Between Laquipum and Hatala

Responsibilities	Laquipum is to have no other "country wife," though he may take a "city wife." Hatala is to produce offspring within two years, or purchase a female slave who will give Laquipum a child.
Benefits	Laquipum gets children and is permitted to have a secondary "city wife." Hatala gets to be the primary wife and is to be maintained in the country.
Penalties	If either divorces the other, he or she must pay five minas of silver.

As we move on in our look at Law, we'll see that the Mosaic Covenant incorporates the typical elements. It spells out the responsibilities of each party to the covenant and describes both benefits and penalties.

But when we look at other covenants cut between God and His people, we find a striking—and significant—difference.

The Abrahamic Covenant

"I will . . ." statements
Genesis 12:1–3, 7

formal covenant
Genesis 15:7–21

EXODUS 2:24 *So God heard their groaning, and God remembered His covenant with Abraham, with Isaac, and with Jacob.* (NKJV)

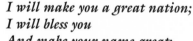

the big picture

Genesis 12–Exodus 1

Abraham is a pagan who worships the gods of his home city, Ur. The true God tells Abraham to leave Ur for an unknown land. At that time God makes a series of "I will . . ." statements, specifying what He intends to do for and through Abraham. God directs Abraham to Canaan. There God enters into a formal covenant ratifying the earlier "I will . . ." statements. Abraham dies, and the covenant promises are passed on to his son Isaac, then to his grandson Jacob, also known as Israel. Centuries later their descendants are slaves in Egypt. They cry out to God, and God remembers—determines to act on—His covenant with Abraham. Enter Moses.

Let's Make It Official

prophecy

GENESIS 15:18 *On the same day the LORD made a covenant with Abram . . .* (NKJV)

It's a few years after the Lord first spoke to Abraham and told him,

I will make you a great nation;
I will bless you
And make your name great;
And you shall be a blessing.
I will bless those who bless you,
And I will curse him who curses you;
And in you all the families of the earth shall be blessed . . .
To your descendants I will give this land.
(Genesis 12:2–3, 7 NKJV)

Despite the fact that Abraham and his wife remain childless, Abraham doesn't doubt the Lord. Even so, God intends to relieve any lingering doubts.

The Lord has Abraham assemble a heifer, a goat, a ram, a turtle-dove, and a pigeon. These animals are killed and cut in two, with the two halves separated to leave a pathway down the middle. Abraham knows what's happening. God is having him make preparations to cut a "covenant of blood," the most binding of all covenants!

solemnize
to make official, binding

what others say

Warren W. Wiersbe

God not only gave Abraham a promise, but He also confirmed that promise with an oath. When a witness takes an oath in court, he is confronted with the words "so help me God." We call on the Greater to witness for the lesser. None is greater than God, so He swore by Himself.[5]

Ronald Youngblood

The ceremony **solemnizing** the covenant with Abram was intended to confirm to Abram that what God had promised, He would surely fulfill . . . Significantly, covenants in the Bible were always solemnized by blood. There is no such thing as a biblical covenant without a blood sacrifice. This fact has supremely important implications for us as well, since our covenant relationship to Christ was sealed on Calvary with His own blood. We are reminded of His wounds when we hear His words at the Last Supper: "This cup is the new covenant in my blood" (1 Corinthians 11:25).[6]

But with One Big Difference

Typically, both parties to this kind of covenant pass between the animal halves, perhaps signifying they should be cut in two if either fails to live up to the promises being exchanged.

But then a strange thing happens. God causes Abraham to slip into a deep sleep, and only the Lord passes between the pieces! God has bound Himself by a binding oath to do exactly what He told Abraham earlier that He would do. And, because these commitments aren't contingent on what Abraham might or might not do, God has no way out!

God has transformed the normal covenant, cut between two parties, into a one-party commitment. What God has done is to transform His "I will . . ." statements into promises that He is committed to keep, no matter what Abraham does or does not do!

key point

go to

Davidic Covenant
Psalm 89:3–4

David's descendant will rule
2 Samuel 7:12–16

New Covenant
Jeremiah 31:31–34;
Hebrews 8:7–13

Looking back on this incident, the writer of the New Testament book of Hebrews says, "Thus God, determining to show more abundantly to the heirs of promise the immutability of His counsel, confirmed it by an oath, that by two immutable things, in which it is impossible for God to lie, we might have strong consolation" (Hebrews 6:17–18 NKJV).

God told Abraham, "I will . . ." But so there's no possibility of mistaking God's intentions, He "confirmed it by an oath." He entered into a legally binding contract with Abraham, and *He left Himself no way out!*

Three Promise Covenants

There are three great Bible covenants we can identify as "promise covenants." Each, like the covenant God cut with Abraham (the Abrahamic Covenant), spells out what God intends to do for and through Abraham's descendants.

key point

The second great promise covenant is called the <u>Davidic Covenant</u>. According to the Davidic Covenant, a <u>descendant of David will rule</u> forever and ever.

The third great promise covenant is called the <u>New Covenant</u>. This covenant gets its name from God's promise through Jeremiah to one day "make a new covenant with the house of Israel" (Jeremiah 31:31 NKJV). In it, God promises not only to forgive sins but to transform human hearts. This covenant was formally "cut" when Jesus died, and Christ's followers now relate to God through the New Covenant.

Linked Covenants

The three great promise covenants are intimately linked, as shown on the next page.

In essence, the second and third are expansions of the first, showing *how* God will accomplish what He promised Abraham.

The Link Between the Promise Covenants

The Abrahamic Covenant states what God will do:

> . . . in you all the families of the
> earth shall be blessed

The Davidic Covenant tells how God will bless:

> . . . through a descendant of David
> who will rule forever [Jesus]

The New Covenant shows more of how God will do it:

> . . . through forgiveness and inner
> transformation guaranteed by
> Jesus's death on Calvary

Each of these three promise covenants is unconditional. That is, nothing Abraham did or did not do can change God's commitment to accomplish what He promised. Nothing David did or did not do can affect God's commitment to accomplish His promises through the rule of a king descended from David. And nothing that any person does or does not do can affect God's commitment to provide forgiveness and inner transformation through His Son.

You and I can accept or reject the forgiveness God offers. But nothing we do changes the fact that God has provided salvation for us through Jesus, just as He promised.

So, Where Does the Mosaic Covenant Fit In?

EXODUS 19:5 *Now therefore, if you will indeed obey My voice and keep My covenant, then you shall be a special treasure to Me . . . (NKJV)*

Right away Exodus 19 makes it clear. The Mosaic Covenant *doesn't* fit in. It's not a promise covenant. It's not unconditional! God clearly says through Moses, "If you will indeed obey . . . then."

There is no "if . . . then" in the Abrahamic Covenant. There's no "if . . . then" in the Davidic Covenant. There's no "if . . . then" in the New Covenant.

And so we're told right from the start that this Law Covenant given through Moses is different from the three great promise covenants.

A Bird's-Eye View of Mosaic Law

Scholars were well aware of the wide-ranging application of covenants in Old Testament times. And then a University of Michigan professor named George Mendenhall noticed parallels between the biblical Law Covenant and a special covenant in use by the **Hittites**. It's called a "Hittite suzerainty covenant," and it is essentially a constitution. The suzerainty covenant was prepared by the ruler to clearly define his relationship with his subjects. After Mendenhall's initial observation it quickly became clear that what we call Mosaic Law, the Mosaic Covenant, or the Law Covenant, is essentially a suzerainty covenant.

All the elements of a suzerainty treaty are found right here in Exodus where the Law is first introduced:

Mosaic Law as a Suzerainty Treaty Between God and Israel

Hittite Suzerainty Treaty	Parallels in Exodus
Preamble, identifying the author and giving his titles.	"I am the LORD your God, who brought you out of the land of Egypt, out of the house of bondage" (20:2 NKJV).
Historical prologue, recounting deeds of the king for his people.	"You have seen what I did to the Egyptians, and how I bore you on eagles' wings and brought you to Myself" (19:4 NKJV).
Stipulations, laying out principles on which the relationship is to be based.	The Ten Commandments (20:2–17), based on case law rulings (21:1–23:19)
Pronouncement of blessings and *curses* linked to keeping, breaking the covenant stipulations.	"Behold, I send an Angel before you to keep you . . . Do not provoke Him, for He will not pardon your transgressions . . . Obey His voice and do all that I speak" (23:20–22 NKJV).
Oath of acceptance of the vassals.	"So Moses came and told the people all the words of the LORD and all the judgments. And all the people answered with one voice and said, 'All the words which the LORD has said we will do'" (24:3 NKJV).

The parallels between the Hittite suzerainty treaty and this first recounting of God's words to Israel help us understand just what's happening here. Yahweh is presenting Himself to the Israelites as their king. He has delivered them and now He intends to rule this "kingdom of priests." In the Old Testament books of Exodus, Leviticus, and Deuteronomy, the Lord will continue to spell out covenant stipulations—just what God expects from His people—in more detail. He will also spell out in much greater detail the blessings that obedient generations will experience, and the curses—the punishments—that will fall on the disobedient.

In promising, "All the words which the LORD has said we will do," the Israelites acknowledged God as their king, and committed themselves to obey Him.

Here, and Deuteronomy Too

If anyone doubted the reflection of the Hittite suzerainty treaty in Exodus, its even more detailed application in the structure of the Old Testament book of Deuteronomy is too obvious to mistake.

- Deuteronomy 1:6–3:29 provides the historical prologue, introducing the relationship the ruler (Yahweh) has with His subjects (the Israelites).

- Deuteronomy 5:1–11:32 specifies the basic stipulations, the general principles that are to govern the relationship between Yahweh and His people.

- Deuteronomy 12:1–26:19 provides detailed stipulations, giving specific regulations that are to be followed.

- Deuteronomy 27:1–26 contains the oath of acceptance by the subjects, also called the "document clause" to the treaty.

- Deuteronomy 28:1–14 lays out blessings that Yahweh as King will provide for His obedient people.

- Deuteronomy 28:15–68 lays out curses that Yahweh as King will bring upon the Israelites if they are disobedient.

- Deuteronomy 29:1–20:10 reviews and summarizes the treaty.

The Hittite suzerainty treaty would have been familiar to Moses, brought up as a prince of Egypt. And there is no doubt that the Law

**the Ten
Commandments**
Exodus 20:1–17;
Deuteronomy
5:6–21

**books containing
God's law**
primarily Exodus,
Leviticus, and
Deuteronomy

of Moses, adopting the form of the suzerainty treaty, has little in common with the great promise covenants of Scripture.

Another Bird's-Eye View

It's important to understand the nature of Mosaic Law as a constitution spelling out the relationship between King Yahweh and His Israelite subjects. Yet there are other ways to classify the contents of these **books containing God's law**. Fly with another bird, and you might notice different types of stipulations (rules). Among the types of laws or rulings that we find in stipulation passages are:

- Abstract moral principles
- Rulings on specific moral behaviors
- Rulings on nonmoral behaviors

Abstract Moral Principles

The clearest example of abstract moral principles is the most familiar to us, the Ten Commandments. These lead the way in Mosaic Law, being found immediately after the historical prologue. Principles such as "You shall have no other gods before Me" (Exodus 20:3 NKJV), and "You shall not covet" (Exodus 20:17 NKJV) state broad ideals. They don't deal with specific situations, but call for us to reason from the general principle, in order to apply the principle in a variety of life situations.

In stating abstract moral principles, Mosaic Law introduces an element not found in other ancient law codes. We'll look more closely at the Ten Commandments in our next chapter.

Rulings on Specific Moral Behaviors

The Law of Moses is hardly the world's first law code. Older law codes have been found in Mesopotamia and Egypt, as well as on other continents. Those other ancient law codes adopt the same "case-by-case law" approach we see in Exodus 21–23. "Case-by-case law" deals with *specific behaviors*, not general principles. Typically, ancient law codes dealt with issues that we would call moral issues.

The codes regulated sexual behavior; they identified violations of property rights; they defined the rights of a victim of violence; and so on and so forth. Usually, each case described a behavior and specified appropriate punishment. Some people are surprised to find how closely biblical and other ancient law codes reflect a common morality.

key point

Nonmoral Behavior

Many of the stipulations (rulings) found in Mosaic Law have no relationship to what we call morality. For instance, Leviticus 11 goes into detail on what an Israelite can and cannot eat. It's all right to eat beef or goat meat, because these animals both have divided hooves and chew the cud. On the other hand, an Israelite couldn't eat camel, because while it chews the cud it doesn't have divided hooves (11:3–4). It's all right to eat sea creatures that have fins and scales. But shrimp and lobster are out.

There are a number of rules like this that are morally neutral, but which the Israelites are to abide by.

Why the morally neutral rules? God told the Israelites that they were to be a holy people. Remember, again, "holy" in the most basic Old Testament sense means "set apart for God's use." And to be "set apart" means to be different from that which is common or ordinary.

Many if not most of the nonmoral rulings in the Old Testament have the primary purpose of reminding the Israelites that they are different from the pagan peoples around them. They are not to be like other nations, and everything about them is to testify that they belong to God.

something to ponder

Three Kinds of Laws

Abstract Moral Principles Exodus 20:3–17	Specific Moral Behaviors Exodus 21–23	Nonmoral Behaviors Various texts
No other gods No carved images No taking God's name in vain Keep the Sabbath Honor parents Don't murder Don't commit adultery Don't steal Don't bear false witness Don't covet	He who kidnaps a man and sells him, or if he is found in his hand, shall surely be put to death. (21:16 NKJV) If a man opens a pit . . . and does not cover it, and an ox . . . falls in it, the owner of the pit shall make it good. (21:33–34 NKJV) You shall not circulate a false report . . . Nor shall you testify in a dispute so as to . . . pervert justice. (23:1–2 NKJV) If a man entices a virgin who is not betrothed, and lies with her, he shall surely pay the bride-price for her to be his wife. (22:16 NKJV)	The gecko, the monitor lizard . . . these are unclean to you among all that creep. Whoever touches them when they are dead shall be unclean until evening. (Leviticus 11:30–31 NKJV) If a woman has conceived, and borne a male child, then she shall be unclean seven days. (Leviticus 12:2 NKJV) Tell them to make tassels on the corners of their garments . . . and to put a blue thread in the tassels. (Numbers 15:38 NKJV) You shall not plow with an ox and a donkey together. (Deuteronomy 22:10 NKJV)

We'll look more closely at the various kinds of stipulations (laws or rulings) found in Mosaic Law in coming chapters. But let's go back to something I wrote a bit ago; namely, that some people are surprised to find how closely biblical and other ancient law codes reflect a common morality.

But Everybody Knows *That*!

EXODUS 21:1 *Now these are the judgments which you shall set before them. (NKJV)*

Read through the "judgments" in Exodus 21–23 and it's clear that most of the cases Moses deals with raise moral issues and show a concern for doing the right thing. There's nothing surprising about this. We expect it of Scripture.

What we may not expect is that the other law codes of the ancient world deal with the same kinds of issues, and seem just as concerned with doing the right thing. Here, for instance, are some of the 282 rulings from the Code of Hammurabi, a case-by-case law code that his records say he published in the second year of his reign, 1726 BC:

seignior
also spelled "seigneur," a man of rank or authority

4. If a **seignior** came forward with false testimony in a case concerning grain or money, he shall bear the penalty of that case.

14. If a seignior has stolen the young son of another seignior, he shall be put to death.

46. If a seignior has let his field to a tenant, and later Adad [a deity] has inundated the field or a flood has ravaged it, the tenant and the owner of the field shall divide proportionately the grain which is produced in the field.

117. If an obligation came due against a seignior and he sold (the services of) his wife, his son, or his daughter, or he has been bound over to service, they shall work in the house of their purchaser for three years, with their freedom reestablished in the fourth year.

129. If the wife of a seignior has been caught while lying with another man, they shall bind them and throw them into the water. If the husband of the woman wishes to spare his wife, then the king in turn may spare his subject.

150. If a seignior, upon presenting a field, orchard, house, or goods to his wife, left a sealed document with her, her children may not enter a claim against her after (the death of) her husband, since the mother may give her inheritance to that son of hers whom she likes, (but) she may not give it to an outsider.

229. If a builder constructed a house for a seignior, but did not make his work strong, with the result that the house which he built collapsed and so has caused the death of the owner of the house, that builder shall be put to death.[8]

Hammurabi's code prescribes the death penalty much more than the Law of Moses. But in its dealing with issues case by case, and its concern for doing right by all involved, its moral roots are obvious.

Compare, Comparison Proves

The fact that the moral vision seen in Mosaic Law often seems found in the law codes of other ancient peoples is even more clear when we compare specific biblical rulings with rulings found in other law codes.[9]

Comparison of Mosaic Code with Other Codes of Law

The Ur-Nammu Code 2100 BC	The Mosaic Code 1400 BC
If the daughter of a citizen, with her parents' knowledge, walks about the city and is raped, then the rapist, if he swears an oath that he did not know she was a free-born woman, shall not be charged. (Article 8)	If a young woman who is a virgin is betrothed to a husband, and a man finds her in the city and lies with her, then you shall bring them both out to the gate of that city, and you shall stone them to death with stones, the young woman because she did not cry out in the city, and the man because he humbled his neighbor's wife. (Deuteronomy 22:23–24 NKJV)
The Hittite Code 1400 BC	**The Mosaic Code 1400 BC**
If a citizen, who is married to a woman who is also a citizen, sexually abuses his wife's daughter, the sentence is death. If a citizen sexually abuses his mother-in-law or his sister-in-law, the sentence is death. (Article 195)	None of you shall approach anyone who is near of kin to him, to uncover his nakedness [abuse sexually]: I am the LORD . . . The nakedness of your father's wife's daughter, begotten by your father—she is your sister—you shall not uncover her nakedness. (Leviticus 18:6, 11 NKJV)
The Middle Assyrian Code 1190 BC	**The Mosaic Code 1400 BC**
If either a man or a woman prepares magical potions or objects and is caught with them in his or her possession, then the sentence, following due process, is death. (Article 47)	You shall not permit a sorceress to live. (Exodus 22:18 NKJV) A man or a woman who is a medium, or who has familiar spirits, shall surely be put to death. (Leviticus 20:27 NKJV)

something to ponder

There are differences between other ancient codes and the biblical code. The Ur-Nammu and the Hittite codes treat people of different social classes differently; Scripture has one law for all. Yet the similarities are too clear to dismiss. All the ancient codes are concerned with the same issues: protection of the vulnerable, fairness in business and in treatment of family members, responsibility for economic losses, regulation of sexual practices, etc. Evidently, ancient peoples had a relatively clear-cut concept of right and wrong.

Remember the "negative confessions" prescribed in the Egyptian *Book of the Dead* that we looked at in an earlier chapter? "I haven't stolen"? "I haven't gossiped"? "I haven't copulated with men"? "I haven't stirred up strife"? Descending in direct line from the Old Kingdom period (c. 2680–2180 BC), these "confessions" reflect an Egyptian moral vision that predates even the oldest of the Mesopotamian law codes.

Comparison Proves . . . What?

Some, comparing various rulings in the Mosaic Law with case-by-case law rulings in other ancient law codes, have jumped to the conclusion that Moses *depended on* the older law codes. That is, Moses copied from what already existed in his culture. The next jump is to conclude that there is no necessity to involve "God" in morality at all!

The trouble with this rather wild leap is that a strong sense of morality, a clear awareness of right and wrong, shows up in the records of *all* ancient civilizations. Concern with right and wrong is reflected in the civilizations of China and India. It's found in South and North America long before people on those continents ever even heard of Moses, much less Hammurabi.

If Moses got his sense of morality from Egypt or the Hittites, where did the Egyptians get it? If China had no contact with the ancient Middle East, how does it happen that nations in both areas clearly show a similar awareness of the moral issues their cultures must address? The answer to this question is found—surprise!—in Scripture.

The Real Root of Moral Awareness

ROMANS 2:14–15 *When Gentiles, who do not have the law, by nature do the things in the law, these, although not having the law, are a law to themselves, who show the work of the law written in their hearts, their conscience also bearing witness . . .* (NKJV)

In this chapter of Romans, the apostle Paul is arguing that all human beings are separated from God and under His wrath. His Jewish readers didn't buy the argument. After all, the Jews were given the Law by God Himself. They *know* right from wrong. Gentiles, on the other hand, who are without the benefit of Mosaic Law, certainly are doomed.

Paul's response is to point out that it isn't "the hearers of the law" whom God counts as righteous. You have to *do* the law—something Paul will soon demonstrate is impossible for human beings.

First, though, Paul goes back to the issue raised by his Jewish readers. They're assuming that Mosaic Law is the *only* standard of right and wrong human beings can appeal to. And they're dead wrong.

Paul says that when the Gentiles (who don't have Mosaic Law) "by nature do the things in the law," they "show the work of the law written in their hearts." That is, *God created humans moral beings, with an innate awareness of right and wrong.* The proof of this is that humans have a conscience that either accuses or excuses when a person does something he judges to be wrong.

The Uninformed Conscience

While everyone has a conscience and makes judgments about right and wrong, those judgments aren't always correct. The Ur-Nammu code said rape of a "free-born" young woman is wrong, *unless* the rapist is unaware of her social standing. Most of us would agree that rape is wrong. But we'd want the standard to apply to all young women, not just the social elite.

What is unique about the Law of Moses is that, as the giver is God, the moral standards established are intended to inform the conscience. That is, Mosaic Law resolves the debate of whose notions of right and wrong are best, and provides an authoritative standard by which to judge what is truly right, and what is truly wrong.

Mosaic Law is intended to *inform*—to shape, to instruct—the consciences of God's people:

Good Golly, Miss Molly

What I've been saying in this chapter probably seems complicated. But it can be boiled down to a few rather easy-to-understand statements.

- Human beings were created as moral beings. This is shown by our consciences, which label our actions as "right" or "wrong" even when we don't particularly want them to!

- Human cultures agree on what the moral issues are. Every culture has rules governing sexual expression, the treatment of other persons, and so on.

That's why ancient law codes are so similar. Everyone agrees on the issues that should be governed by a common understanding of right and wrong. But human beings' ideas of right and wrong are flawed, and too often our consciences are uninformed. Mosaic Law is intended to instruct the conscience; to teach us what is truly right, and truly wrong. And it is this, the establishment for the Israelites of a reliable standard revealed by God Himself, that made Mosaic Law so special.

key point

One More Thing

Earlier I noted that ancient codes are in the form of *case-by-case law*. That is, they look at specific situations and tell us how to deal with them. Yet the very first stipulation clause in Exodus 20 presents the Ten Commandments—a statement of general principles. And such statements of general principle just aren't found in other ancient law codes!

In the next chapter we'll look closely at the Ten Commandments, and see if we can discover why they play such a central role in fulfilling the mission to which Moses was called by God.

Chapter Wrap-Up

- At Sinai, God announced that if the Israelites would obey Him they would be His special people, a kingdom of priests, and set apart for His purposes.

- The Lord then outlined the terms of their relationship with Him, in the form of a Hittite suzerainty covenant.

- This, the Mosaic Covenant, or Law Covenant, is a conditional covenant rather than an unconditional, promise covenant like the Abrahamic, Davidic, and New Covenants of the Old Testament.

- Like other ancient law codes, Mosaic Law contains case-by-case law, descriptions of specific behaviors. But Mosaic Law also includes general principles (the Ten Commandments) and prescribes specific behaviors that have no moral roots.

- Similarities between Mosaic Law and other ancient law codes demonstrate the fact that God created humans moral beings. Specific content may differ, but all cultures agree on the issues (like property rights, sexual behavior), which are moral in nature.

Study Questions

1. According to Exodus 19:5–6, what did God intend for Israel?

2. Why does the author call Mount Sinai "thunder mountain"?

3. Describe a "covenant."

4. What three biblical covenants does the author describe as "promise covenants"? How are they related?

5. How do we know the Mosaic Covenant (the Law of Moses) is not a promise covenant?

6. What is the significance of Mosaic Law taking the form of a Hittite suzerainty covenant?

7. What three types of laws or rulings are found in Old Testament law?

8. Which of the three types are found in other ancient law codes? Which are not?

9. Can you explain the close parallels between OT laws and law codes of other peoples?

Chapter Highlights:
• Claim to Fame
• Four for Me
• No Other Gods
• Six for You
• Fast Break!

Chapter 6
The Big Ten

Let's Get Started

As the Israelites tremble at the base of Thunder Mountain, Moses goes up into the storm to meet with the Lord. There God will personally engrave His Ten Commandments on stone tablets. On the surface, these commandments appear simple. Yet the more we examine them, the more profound and significant each becomes.

But while Moses communes with God on the top of Mount Sinai, something is happening on the plains below that will shake Moses to the core.

review the Ten Commandments
Deuteronomy
5:6–21

Israel's Claim to Fame

DEUTERONOMY 4:7–8 *For what great nation is there that has God so near to it, as the LORD our God is to us, for whatever reason we may call upon Him? And what great nation is there that has such statutes and righteous judgments as are in all this law which I set before you this day? (NKJV)*

the big picture

Deuteronomy 4–6

It's forty years later. Moses is speaking to the children of the men and women who camped on the plains below Mount Sinai. He's about to review the Ten Commandments and expand on the Law's other rulings. But Moses begins by stating the Israelites' claim to fame. First, Yahweh, The One Who Is Always Present, is available to be called on. No other people have "God so near." Second, Israel possesses God's law. Other nations have laws that incorporate a moral vision, but none have "such statutes and righteous judgments as are in all this law."

These two things set Israel apart from all other peoples: their God, and their Law.

go to

Sermon on the Mount
Matthew 5:1–7:27

Flash Forward

Jesus is giving His <u>Sermon on the Mount</u>. As He speaks, Jesus makes a bold claim. "Do not think that I came to destroy the Law or the Prophets. I did not come to destroy but to fulfill" (Matthew 5:17 NKJV).

Every listener understands what Jesus means. It's the dream of every first-century rabbi to "fulfill" the Law, by which He means "give a full and accurate explanation of the true meaning of God's law."

what others say

J. C. Ryle

These verses deserve the closest attention of all readers of the Bible. A right understanding of the doctrines they contain lies at the very root of Christiantiy. The Lord Jesus here explains more fully the meaning of His words, "I have not come to abolish them but to fulfill them" (verse 17). He teaches us that His gospel makes much of the Law, and exalts its authority; He shows us that the Law, as expounded upon by Him, was a far more spiritual and heart-searching rule than most of the Jews supposed; and He proves this by selecting three commandments out of ten as example of what He means.[1]

Jesus goes on to do what He promised. Selecting specific commandments, Jesus *shifts the focus from outward behaviors to inward attitudes.*

- "You have heard that it was said to those of old, 'You shall not murder . . .' [the forbidden behavior]. But I say to you that whoever is angry with his brother without a cause shall be in danger of the judgment" [the attitude—anger, hostility—that leads to murder] (Matthew 5:21–22 NKJV).

- "You have heard that it was said to those of old, 'You shall not commit adultery . . .' [the forbidden behavior]. But I say to you that whoever looks at a woman to lust for her [the attitude, lust, that leads to adultery] has already committed adultery with her in his heart" (Matthew 5:27–28 NKJV).

A Closer Look at the Big Ten

The Ten Commandments can be broken down into two categories. The first four commandments are about relating to God, and the last six are about relating to other people. Most are stated as negatives: "Do not" do this or that.

The Ten Commandments

Commandments About Relationship with God	Commandments About Relationship with Each Other
1. No other gods before Me (Exodus 20:3)	5. Honor father and mother (Exodus 20:12)
2. Do not make carved images (Exodus 20:4)	6. You shall not murder (Exodus 20:13)
3. Do not take God's name in vain (Exodus 20:7)	7. You shall not commit adultery (Exodus 20:14)
4. Keep the Sabbath (Exodus 20:8)	8. You shall not steal (Exodus 20:15)
	9. You shall not bear false witness (Exodus 20:16)
	10. You shall not covet (Exodus 20:17)

apply it

Jesus's teaching in His Sermon on the Mount gives us the key to analyzing the original Ten Commandments. We are, of course, to understand the behavioral boundary each commandment establishes, the moral line we are not to cross, the sins we must not commit.

But to truly understand the Ten Commandments, we need to look deeper. We need to identify *internal* boundaries. We need to discern the harmful attitudes that lead to sinful behavior. And we need to discern the positive attitudes we're called to maintain.

That's our task in this chapter. We're going to look *into* the Ten Commandments, to discover the deeper lessons God teaches His people in each one.

Four for Me

The first four commandments concern the believer's relationship with the Lord. Each has powerful, positive messages for us today.

No Other Gods Before Me

EXODUS 20:3 *You shall have no other gods before Me. (NKJV)*

In Old Testament times, challengers to Yahweh's position as God of Israel were easy to recognize. Every nation had its own deities. These gods and goddesses were local deities, part of the material universe and not above it. They shared vices as well as virtues with their human worshippers. The gods were supposed to control agriculture, and worship of the major deities often involved performing sexual acts that were supposed to stimulate the gods to copulate and thus fertilize the earth. It is unthinkable that Yahweh should be confused with the gods of surrounding peoples. Yet again and again Israel would turn away from the God of the Bible to worship pagan deities.

In Our Day

Rhonda thinks of God as a stickler for keeping the rules. If she does, He will be good to her. If she meets seven "conditions" for answered prayer, He'll come through. If not—if she messes up even one—God won't listen.

Stacy thinks of God as a kindly grandfather. He may mildly disapprove of some of her choices, but He dotes on her too much to even think of rebuking her. He dotes on everyone, really, and if a person is sincere, he or she can believe whatever he or she wishes and it will turn out all right in the end.

Ken's God wears a perpetual frown on His face. However hard Ken works to please God, it's never enough. No wonder Ken feels guilty all the time.

It's harder to recognize the "other gods" that people worship today. It was easier when they came in pagan guise, in the shape of wood or stone figures. Today, not even contemporary pagans think

of God in history's grosser terms. But the distorted views that moderns have of what God is like are just as much "other gods" as the jackal-headed deity of the Egyptians or the multi-breasted clay model of Ashtoreth of the Canaanites.

a jealous God
cares deeply, is
fiercely committed
to His people

It's significant that the Ten Commandments are introduced with the announcement, "I am the LORD your God, who brought you out of the land of Egypt, out of the house of bondage" (Exodus 20:2 NKJV). We worship a God who has acted in history, and *who has revealed Himself to us.* Our God has defined Himself by His actions, and explained Himself in the Bible. Every other deity is a human invention.

The external boundary the first commandment established for Israel was intended to keep God's people from worshipping pagan deities. The internal boundary it implies is more subtle. It's a boundary we must take seriously as we seek to develop our own understanding of God. Simply put, *We are to reject every idea about God that is not rooted in His self-revelation in Scripture.*

The very first step in anyone's relationship with God is to come to know God as He really is. And the only way to do this is to search God's Word to understand God on His own terms.

apply it

No Graven Images

EXODUS 20:4–5 *You shall not make for yourself a carved image—any likeness of anything that is in heaven above, or that is in the earth beneath, or that is in the water under the earth; you shall not bow down to them nor serve them. For I, the LORD your God, am **a jealous God**. (NKJV)*

In the ancient world, deities were represented by idols. Worshippers of the Canaanite god Baal bowed down before metal images of a bull, representing the god's supposed strength. They didn't think the bull was Baal. Instead, they pictured an invisible Baal standing on the back of their idol. But they still felt the need for something material to represent their god. They still needed to *see* something.

The boundary that the second commandment established for Israel is simple. *There is to be no material representation of the invisible God.* No idol for Israel, because it isn't possible for anything material to represent God.

In Our Day

Sarah's excited. A TV minister has promised that if she gives to his ministry, God will repay her a hundred times over. If she'll just show her faith by sending in $77, God will send her $7,700!

Later she shares the news with the wife of an attorney whose house she cleans. The wife has often told Sarah how thankful she is for her beautiful home. "My husband faithfully takes time to serve the Lord and help others," she'll say. "He deserves the house God has given us. I'm thankful I can see how good God is as I look around each day."

Sarah and the attorney's wife are both committed Christians. Neither has any idea she's crossing a boundary established in the second commandment.

The external boundary stated in the second commandment is clear: Don't worship idols. The internal boundary is less obvious, but still clear. *Nothing material is to represent God to me.*

Whether or not Sarah receives her $7,700 dollars has nothing to do with the faithfulness of God or His presence with her. The fact that the attorney's wife lives in a beautiful house instead of a two-room apartment isn't evidence that God loves her. Oh, we should be thankful for material blessings. But we're not to take poverty as a sign of God's disapproval, or plenty as a sign of His favor. Simply put, we can never gauge any person's relationship with God by what he or she does or doesn't possess.

apply it

How can we tell if we honor the inner boundary established in the second commandment? Paul, who has known both poverty and prosperity, and experienced times when he's been hungry and times when he's been full, tells us: "I have learned in whatever state I am, to be content" (Philippians 4:11 NKJV). And, as Paul tells Timothy, "Godliness with contentment is great gain" (1 Timothy 6:6 NKJV).

Do Not Take God's Name in Vain

EXODUS 20:7 *You shall not take the name of the LORD your God in vain, for the LORD will not hold him guiltless who takes His name in vain.* (NKJV)

The Hebrew word translated "in vain" in the third commandment is *sawe'*. It occurs fifty-three times in the Old Testament, in each occurrence describing something that's without substance, something *unreal*. This commandment isn't really about swearing, although we often take it that way. It's about acting as though God were unreal, or didn't count.

Flash Forward

Hananiah, who claims to be a prophet, interrupts the warning Jeremiah is giving to the people of Jerusalem. Shouting loudly that he has a message from God, Hananiah contradicts Jeremiah. He says that the Lord is about to break the power of the king of Babylon. He promises in God's name that the Jewish captives there will return home.

After Jeremiah leaves, the Lord sends him back with a message for Hananiah:

Hear now, Hananiah, the LORD has not sent you, but you make this people trust in a lie. Therefore thus says the LORD: "Behold, I will cast you from the face of the earth. This year you shall die, because you have taught rebellion against the LORD." (Jeremiah 28:15–16 NKJV)

Two months later, Hananiah is dead.

Both Hananiah and Jeremiah announced, "Thus says the LORD of hosts, the God of Israel" (Jeremiah 28:2, 14 NKJV). But God had not spoken to Hananiah, and He *had* spoken to Jeremiah. So why would Hananiah wrap the mantle of divine authority around his words? Simply because to Hananiah, "God" wasn't real enough to count. Hananiah wanted to please the crowd by taking a popular, patriotic stand. What "God" thought about it was irrelevant.

go to

pray in Jesus's name
John 16:23

In Our Day

Before you apply the third commandment exclusively to non-Christians who use "Jesus" and "God" as curse words, look a little more closely at Exodus 20:7. The text says, "*You* shall not take the name of the Lord *your* God in vain" (NKJV). The commandment is addressed to God's Old Testament people, not to the pagans of ancient nations or the unbelievers of our day. And the message of the third commandment to believers is, *Never act as if the "Lord your God" is irrelevant to your life.*

Are you employed? The Lord, The One Who Is Always Present, is relevant to your work.

As you married? The Lord, The One Who Is Always Present, is relevant to your marriage.

Are you in school? The Lord, The One Who Is Always Present, is relevant to your studies.

key point

In Bible times, a name was more than a label. The name of a person or thing was linked to its essence. When Jesus told His disciples to <u>pray in His name</u>, He wasn't talking about an "add-on" phrase. To pray in Jesus's name means to identify fully with Christ's motives and purposes, and to count so completely on The One Who Is Present that we pray with confidence.

Israel understood the third commandment as an external boundary that was not to be crossed. Hananiah crossed it when he spoke in the name of the Lord even though God had not spoken to him.

Today, the third commandment is an inner boundary you and I are to set up in our hearts, to keep us close to God. It is a boundary that enables us to remember at all times, in every circumstance, that the Lord is real, and that the Lord is with us.

Keep the Sabbath

Exodus 20:8–10 *Remember the Sabbath day, to keep it holy. Six days you shall labor and do all your work, but the seventh day is the Sabbath of the Lord your God. In it you shall do no work: you, nor your son, nor your daughter, nor your male servant, nor your female servant, nor your cattle, nor your stranger who is within your gates. (NKJV)*

The fourth commandment seems to be the simplest of the first four. Just take each seventh day off. Stop work and rest.

The problem that later generations of Jews faced was to define "work." After many intense discussions, the following examples of a person engaging in prohibited Sabbath activities emerged:

significance lost
Matthew 12:1–12;
Mark 2:22–26;
Luke 6:1–9, 14:1–5

(1) he who sows, (2) plows, (3) reaps, (4) binds sheaves, (5) threshes, (6) winnows, (7) selects (sorts fit and unfit produce), (8) grinds, (9) sifts, (10) kneads, (11) bakes; (12) he who shears wool, (13) washes it, (14) beats it, (15) dyes it, (16) spins, (17) weaves, (18) makes two loops, (19) weaves two threads, (20) separates two threads, (21) ties, (22) unties, (23) sews two stitches, (24) tears in order to sew two stitches; (25) he who traps a deer, (26) slaughters it, (27) flays it, (28) salts it, (29) cures its hide, (30) scrapes it, and (31) cuts it up; (32) he who writes two letters, (33) erases two letters in order to write two letters; (34) he who builds; (35) he who tears down; (36) he who puts out a fire; (37) he who kindles a fire; (38) he who hits with a hammer; (39) he who transports an object from one domain to another.

The prohibition of each of these behaviors led to further debate. What constitutes plowing? If a person spits and moves the earth, is it plowing? (The ruling was yes.)

The rabbis' intent was good. They wanted to guard against the most unintentional violation of the fourth commandment. But the end result was to become so bogged down in details and minutiae that by Jesus's time the true <u>significance of the commandment was lost</u>.

<u>In Our Day</u>

Today, discussions about keeping Sunday, the first day of the week that Christians celebrate rather than Saturday, the seventh, often deteriorate into arguments about what we should and shouldn't do Sunday afternoon. When I was growing up my parents wouldn't play cards on Sunday, something they enjoyed every other day. A few purists may even insist the preacher not rush home after his sermon to watch an NFL game.

But the more we debate behaviors, the more likely we are to miss the inner boundary the fourth commandment establishes. Three Old Testament passages help us understand that inner boundary, for they remind us that the Sabbath is explicitly linked with God's greatest acts.

- *Genesis 1 links the Sabbath to Creation.* God's people were given the Sabbath "for in six days the LORD made the heavens and the earth, the sea, and all that is in them, and rested the seventh day" (Exodus 20:11 NKJV). The Sabbath was a day that reminded Israel of Creation and that the Lord God was, and is, the Source of all that exists.

- *Deuteronomy 5:15 links the Sabbath to release from Egypt.* "And remember that you were a slave in the land of Egypt, and the LORD your God brought you out from there by a mighty hand and by an outstretched arm; therefore the LORD your God commanded you to keep the Sabbath day" (5:15 NKJV).

- *Exodus 31 links the Sabbath to Israel's covenant relationship with God.* "Surely My Sabbaths you shall keep, for it is a sign between Me and you throughout your generations, that you may know that I am the LORD who sanctifies you" (31:13 NKJV).

Simply put, the Sabbath was a day on which the Israelites were to remember all God had done for them.

The inner boundary that the Sabbath day set is a boundary that we need to establish for ourselves if we're to strengthen our relationship with God. *We are to take time away from "work" and the cares of this life to focus our attention on God.* As the three passages above clearly teach, we are to contemplate the wonder of who God is and all that He has done for us. Our God is the Source of all that is. He is the One who has won our release from bondage to sin. He is the One who has loved us and set us apart to be His own.

Whatever day we keep, if we are to live by the fourth commandment, we must take time to contemplate and worship Him.

Six for You

The first four commandments are all about personal relationship with the Lord. The final six commandments are about our relationships with other people.

Honor Father and Mother

EXODUS 20:12 *Honor your father and your mother, that your days may be long upon the land which the LORD your God is giving you. (NKJV)*

The primary application of this commandment up to the time of Christ was one of financial support of parents in their old age. Proverb 3:9 says "Honor the LORD with your possessions" (NKJV). Surely this was also a major way children should honor their parents.

Another way that children were to honor parents was to show them respect, to "hear the instruction of your father, and do not forsake the law of your mother" (Proverbs 1:8 NKJV). Old Testament law even had a provision where parents could bring a totally rebellious child to the congregation for stoning (Deuteronomy 21:18–21). A child who would not obey parents would never submit to God, and was a danger to the whole community.

apply it

In Our Day

key point

The New Testament agrees that providing financial support for aged parents is one way in which we are to honor them (Mark 7:10–13; 1 Timothy 5:8). But the command to honor parents also implies listening to, respecting, and obeying them (Ephesians 6:1–3). Honoring is a matter of a fundamental attitude toward mothers and fathers.

As a child, Richard lived with his mother and stepfather. They ran a neighborhood bar, and after school Richard was expected to show up and work. He wasn't paid, except with a cuff to the ear if he was not quick enough to obey one of his stepdad's shouted demands. Supper was whatever sandwich Richard could make when he had a moment. Looking back, Richard can't remember hearing a kind or loving word from either parent.

Today Richard honors his mother by visiting her, shopping for her, getting her medicine, and taking her to the doctor. But he can't help feeling bitter inside as he remembers the way she mistreated him, and her sharp tongue still dissects him today. His stomach churns every time she calls, and he becomes more and more tense and irritable as the time for a visit draws near.

Sis grew up in a "Christian" home. Mom and Dad went to church regularly, and even sang in the choir. But both were alcoholics. Although Sis was never molested by her father, she can remember how frightened she was as a teenager to take a shower. Her dad had adjusted the lock on the bathroom door so he could open it and peek in at her whenever he wanted.

What was worse, of course, was that when Mom and Dad got drunk they fought. Dad, who had a physically taxing job in construction, would often beat Mom when that happened. Sis can remember clearing up blood streaks from the floor after her dad dragged her mom through the house. Sis can also remember her mother shouting at her dad and cursing him after he'd visited a prostitute and given Mom syphilis. By the time Sis was in junior high school she was rushing home after school to prepare supper. She knew that if her mom and dad ate early they'd be less likely to get drunk. If she didn't make supper and feed them, they'd get drunk for sure. Sis would have to run to her room, cover her ears, and try to keep out the sound of the shouts and blows that were sure to follow.

Today Sis realizes that her mother did the best she could. She wasn't a caring person. But Mom did instill in her daughter traits Sis appreciates. She expected Sis to do well in school. And Sis did. She expected Sis to work hard. And Sis does. She expected Sis to be responsible and truthful. And Sis is.

Sis long ago confronted her parents and has come to realize that they simply did not understand how they hurt her. They were too caught up in their own twisted lives to be able to step back, to understand, or even to have compassion. Sometimes Sis wonders what it would have been like to grow up in that "ideal" Christian home we read about. But Sis knows that many of her most important qualities grew out of the pain and frustration of her childhood and teen years. And she is truly thankful to God, and to Mom and Dad.

There's a fascinating promise attached to this commandment: "Honor your father and your mother, *that your days may be long upon the land which the LORD your God is giving you*" (Exodus 20:12 NKJV, emphasis added). Honoring our parents benefits *us*. The commandment is not so much for the benefit of our mothers and fathers as for ours!

Looking at Richard and Sis, who are real people (although these are not their real names), we can see how honoring parents benefits children. Sis has found the grace to see her parents as weak and fallible human beings, sinners who, as sinners do, have hurt both themselves and those they love. How tragic that Richards's mom is still the bitter, negative person that he remembers from childhood. How tragic that Sis's mom and dad never knew the joy of a truly loving union or the peace that comes with mutual respect. When we look at our parents this way, we not only find it in our hearts to understand, but to have compassion as well.

apply it

Richard, while honoring his mother outwardly, constantly crosses the inner boundary established by the fifth commandment. He dwells on past hurts and is vulnerable to new ones. He doesn't, and can't seem to, love his mother or feel compassion for her. Somehow he's never opened his heart to God or asked the Holy Spirit to free him from his bondage to the past by enabling him to forgive, and to love.

God has established a new boundary in Sis's heart as she relates to her parents. She will no longer cross over that boundary to feel bitter toward them. And as she lives within the framework of what truly is meant by honoring parents, she continually finds her heart softened toward her mom and dad. Today she reaches out to them with compassion and love that have brought healing—to her.

No Murder

EXODUS 20:13 *You shall not murder. (NKJV)*

Much of the debate over capital punishment hinges on an earlier mistranslation of the sixth commandment. The King James Version reads, "Thou shalt not kill." The New King James Version rightly translates, "You shall not murder."

The listing of the Ten Commandments in Exodus 20 is immediately followed in chapters 21–23 with rulings on a series of very specific cases. What if a person is gored by a neighbor's ox? What if a fire breaks out and burns a neighbor's field? What if someone is injured in a fight?

key point

At first it seems strange. Why move from the most profound and basic principles of morality to such, if you will, little things? One answer is that such case-by-case law illustrates application of the principles. In a sense, much of the case-by-case law in Exodus and later in Deuteronomy illustrates how the principles in the Ten Commandments are to be applied.

We see this clearly in the case of this sixth commandment. We're not to raise our hand in hostility against another and cause his death (Exodus 21:20). Nor are we to testify falsely against another person to do him harm (Exodus 23:1).

Old Testament case-by-case law even illustrates how "You shall not murder" can be turned into a positive command. A person who digs a pit is to cover it, lest even an animal fall in and be hurt (Exodus 21:33–34). And Deuteronomy 22:8 says, "When you build a new house, then you shall make a parapet for your roof, that you may not bring guilt of bloodshed on your household if anyone falls from it"

(NKJV). Clearly, the command not to murder implies actively seeking to protect the life and welfare of others.

In Our Day

Remember how Jesus dissected this commandment in His Sermon on the Mount? "You have heard that it was said to those of old . . . but I say to you . . ."? In this series of illustrations, Jesus went on to shift attention from an external boundary to an internal one. In dealing with this commandment Jesus acknowledged the external boundary, and warned that whoever crosses it "will be in danger of the judgment" (Matthew 5:21 NKJV). But then He went on to address the real issue.

The real issue raised in the sixth commandment is the hostility that wells up within us and leads progressively to more and more **belligerent acts**. According to Jesus, even a person saying "Raca! [You fool!]" to his brother "shall be in danger of hell fire" (Matthew 5:22 NKJV). The person who truly keeps the commandment isn't the one who feels hostility but stops short of murder. The person who keeps this commandment is the one *who is not hostile*!

But there's more. Just as Old Testament case-by-case law has both negative (don't murder) and positive (protect others' lives) aspects, so Jesus's teaching on the sixth commandment has negative and positive aspects. The negative (don't be hostile) finds positive expression in Christ's next words:

> I say to you, love your enemies, bless those who curse you, do good to those who hate you, and pray for those who spitefully use you and persecute you, that you may be sons of your Father in heaven; for He makes His sun rise on the evil and on the good, and sends rain on the just and on the unjust. (Matthew 5:44–45 NKJV)

There's no way that we can help a surge of hostility when we suffer real or imagined injuries. There's no way we have the capacity to love those who have shown themselves to be our enemies. But as we commit ourselves to live by God's Word, and as we rely completely on the Holy Spirit to do in our hearts what we cannot, He will work. Our hearts will be changed, and we will <u>be enabled</u> to live the life that God calls us to know.

go to

be enabled
Romans 8:1–11;
Ephesians 2:1–3

belligerent acts
hostile, war-like acts

apply it

go to

relationships
Leviticus 18

sex within marriage
Genesis 1:27;
1 Corinthians 7:1–5

spiritual adultery
Jeremiah 3:1–9;
Ezekiel 23:1–45;
Hosea 4

No Adultery

Exodus 20:14 *You shall not commit adultery. (NKJV)*

This is the second of the commandments that Jesus used to illustrate the real message of the Law. The behavior it prohibited is clear enough. And if it weren't, case-by-case law lists <u>relationship after relationship</u> that is not to be violated sexually. The consistent testimony of Scripture is that <u>sex within marriage is good</u>, but any sex outside of that context is wrong.

Later Old Testament prophets adopted marriage as a metaphor for Israel's relationship with God, and described the Israelites' abandonment of God for pagan idols as <u>spiritual adultery</u>. At its heart, marriage is about commitment. Sexual union symbolizes and reaffirms that commitment. Adultery is the violation of the deepest of human trusts; it is the repudiation of a commitment that, once made, is to be reaffirmed daily by caring for and sharing oneself with our spouse.

In Our Day

This is the second of the Ten Commandments that Jesus analyzed in his Sermon on the Mount. Christ pointed out that the commandment against adultery also condemned the lustful look. While "You shall not commit adultery" helps me define the nature of my relationship with my wife, it also helps me define the nature of my relationship with others.

The book of Proverbs gives this insightful advice:

Proverbs 6:25–26
Do not lust after her beauty in your heart,
Nor let her allure you with her eyelids.
For by means of a harlot
A man is reduced to a crust of bread. (NKJV)

The prostitute is using her customer, treating him as her next dinner rather than valuing him as a person. In the same way, a man's lust turns a woman into a sex object, and robs her of her value as a human being.

Ads in magazines and on TV typically rely on presenting women as sex objects. One recent ad has a couple of girls commenting on the buns of men that walk by. Another has women in an office running to the window to ogle a construction worker taking a soft-drink break. With the Internet, pornography has expanded to become an even bigger business. In every case, women or men are presented as objects of the playful lusts of the opposite sex.

case-by-case laws
Exodus 22:1, 3, 5

When we dress to attract others sexually, we cheapen ourselves and our value, and cross a boundary established in the seventh commandment. As 1 Peter 3:3–4 says, "Do no let your adornment be merely outward—arranging the hair, wearing gold, or putting on fine apparel—rather let it be the hidden person of the heart, with the incorruptible beauty of a gentle and quiet spirit, which is very precious in the sight of God" (NKJV). We are far too valuable to present ourselves to others as if we were mere objects for them to use, whether with their eyes or in an act of adultery.

The message of the seventh commandment is that I must learn to see other persons as God does, as individuals who are to be valued for themselves. Jesus said that He "did not come to be served, but to serve, and to give His life a ransom for many" (Matthew 20:28 NKJV). When we see others through Jesus's eyes, as persons to be loved and served rather than exploited, we'll begin to experience the real meaning of the seventh commandment.

Don't Steal

EXODUS 20:15 *You shall not steal. (NKJV)*

A number of <u>case-by-case laws</u> in the Old Testament explore the practical application of this commandment. We get the impression that the way stealing violates another person is of major concern. In each case the remedy for theft is to restore what's been stolen, plus an extra percentage. If a stolen animal has been slaughtered, the thief repays the victim four or five animals for the one taken. If the stolen animal is recovered alive, the thief repays double.

In our society, stealing is viewed as a crime against society and the criminal is jailed. In Old Testament law, stealing is viewed as a crime against the victim and the remedy is not punishment but actions the criminal must take to make his victim whole. The criminal must restore what was taken, doubled or even more.

The Creation story reminds us that God made Adam from the dust of the earth, and breathed the breath of life into his body (Genesis 2:7). Human beings are material *and* spiritual beings. As material, we live in the physical universe and, to a significant extent, are defined here by our possessions. Walk into my garage and you'll see a wall filled with fishing poles. There are far more than I can use on any one fishing trip. But the rods say something about me as a person. I have large rods for shark fishing, medium rods for bass, ultralight rods for panfish. I wouldn't be terribly upset if someone stole my car. It's insured. But if someone took my fishing poles I'd be upset. These objects are closely linked with my sense of who I am.

I'd even want my own fishing rods back. This is the one I used to catch my first shark; that one I carried on a hike into the Rocky Mountains to fish for native trout. Give me back the rod you stole, and hand me another new one, and my sense of being violated is reduced. But fail to recover my special rod and it will take at least five more like it to help me heal.

In Our Day

Doesn't what I've been saying about the eighth commandment conflict with what I wrote about the second? Remember, that's the one that insists nothing material represent God to us. The answer is no, the two don't conflict. Not at all. The second commandment emphasizes the fact that nothing in this world can represent God or affect my relationship with Him. The eighth commandment recognizes the fact that we humans are called to live our lives in a material universe, and that what happens in this universe can and does impact our relationship with one another.

Not only that, but the way we value and use material possessions speaks powerfully about our relationship with the Lord. In his first letter to Timothy, the apostle Paul warns, "The love of money is a root of all kinds of evil" (1 Timothy 6:10 NKJV). We will always experience tension between material and spiritual motivations. The thief loves money, and is willing to violate others to gain it. The believer is to love others, and be willing to use his money for their benefit.

The commandment "You shall not steal" seems so straightforward on the surface. The behavior it requires is "Don't take what doesn't belong to you." But if we look deeper, and see how the Old Testament applies the commandment in dealing with the crime of stealing, we see that the eighth commandment is saying something far more profound.

God guards our right to private property because, as individuals who live in a material world, to some extent our temporal identity is defined by the things we possess. Even more important, God guards our right to private property because as individuals who are also spiritual, having private property creates the opportunity for us to choose between living a secular life or a life set apart to God.

The decisions of those who choose to live a secular life reflect the tragic fact that they ascribe ultimate value to material possessions. The daily decisions made by those whose hearts are in tune with God and who are dedicated to Him and to others will reflect this commitment too.

step forward
Leviticus 5:1

Don't Bear False Witness

EXODUS 20:16 *You shall not bear false witness against your neighbor. (NKJV)*

The Old Testament legal system was very different from our own. OT law presupposes no local or national police force. All of God's people were expected to take personal responsibility to maintain the harmony of their community. In cases where civil or criminal disputes arose, matters were dealt with by local elders, who knew the character and reputation of those involved and who knew the witnesses. Only when a case was too difficult to resolve was the matter taken to a central court composed of a panel of priests.

Several things were necessary for this system to work. It was necessary to have godly local elders who couldn't be bribed and who wouldn't show partiality. It was also necessary for anyone in the community who had knowledge to <u>step forward</u> and testify and tell what they knew. Several instructions in Exodus 23:1–3, 6–8 that illustrate application of the ninth commandment make it clear how crucial this was.

- You shall not circulate a false report. Do not put your hand with the wicked to be an unrighteous witness. (23:1 NKJV)

- You shall not follow a crowd to do evil; nor shall you testify in a dispute so as to turn aside after many to pervert justice. (23:2 NKJV)

- You shall not show partiality to a poor man in his dispute. (23:3 NKJV)

- You shall not pervert the judgment of your poor in his dispute. (23:6 NKJV)

- Keep yourself far from a false matter; do not kill the innocent and righteous. For I will not justify the wicked. (23:7 NKJV)

- And you shall take no bribe, for a bribe blinds the discerning and perverts the words of the righteous. (23:8 NKJV)

Old Testament law guarded against false witness by requiring the testimony of two or more persons, each speaking from personal knowledge, before a case could even be heard. And if a witness was found to have testified falsely, that person was to receive the penalty the accused would have suffered if found guilty (Deuteronomy 19:15–20).

But what is "false witness"? In Exodus 20:16, the Hebrew word for "false" is *seqer*, a term that means "groundless." Thus, a false witness is anyone who makes a groundless accusation.

In Deuteronomy 5:20, where this commandment is repeated, the word translated false is *sawe'*, which means "empty" or "vain." Here the false witness is described as presenting testimony that is insubstantial or unreal.

Whatever the intent of the false witness, to harm, to go along with the crowd, to make himself look good, or simply to repeat a rumor, this commandment forbids charging another person with *anything* without substantial grounds. *Simply put, a witness must have personal and direct knowledge of anything to which he testifies.* Otherwise, he must keep silent, and not speak out.

key point

In Our Day

The boundary behavior that's forbidden in the Old Testament is expressed in the New Testament's injunctions <u>against gossip</u>. Yet as we look at the New Testament more closely, we see an inner boundary as well as the behavioral boundary expressed there. It's particularly clear in Romans 14. There Paul urges believers to welcome one another, but "not to disputes over doubtful things" (Romans 14:1 NKJV).

What Paul means by "doubtful" is any matter of personal conviction on which Scripture fails to speak **definitively**. Murder and adultery are not doubtful things. God's "you shall not" makes that unmistakably clear. But what about all those things on which Christians differ and the Bible is silent?

What about whether or not to <u>eat meat</u>? What about <u>what day to keep</u>, and how to keep it? Should a man hunt deer? Should a person pray for healing and refuse to see a doctor? Should a Christian tithe, or give more, or less? Whom should you marry? Should a Christian homeschool, or not? Is it "Christian" to see a psychiatrist? Should someone take another course of chemotherapy after the cancer has returned, or trust God to take her home if it's time? Should a person who doesn't speak in tongues be an elder? The list is endless.

And the list should be endless. While the behavioral boundaries established by the Ten Commandments and other clear commands of Scripture are to be honored within the Christian community, in all other areas we are to extend to each other the *freedom to live without being judged*!

This is the point made in Romans 14: "Who are you to judge another's servant?" Paul asks in verse 4 (NKJV). And "to this end Christ died and rose and lived again, that He might be Lord of both the dead and the living" (Romans 14:9 NKJV).

Jesus is Lord. Jesus Christ alone is qualified to judge the choices we make regarding doubtful things.

The ninth commandment teaches us not to bear false witness by speaking groundless words. When your friend Esther whispers that just possibly Carol may be the source of the rumor that's going around, it's clear that Esther is gossiping, groundlessly accusing Carol of something she may not have done. But when we criticize a

against gossip
Romans 1:29;
2 Corinthians 12:20;
1 Timothy 5:13

eat meat
Romans 14:6;
1 Corinthians 8:8–13

what day to keep
Romans 14:6

definitively
clearly, unmistakably

go to

intrinsically wrong
Proverbs 6:25;
Deuteronomy 7:25

person for the way he or she exercises freedom in Christ, we are doing the same thing! Whatever the crowd says, whatever our personal convictions may be, we have no right to judge another of Jesus's servants in any "doubtful thing." When we consciously resist our tendency to judge another's motives or spirituality, we maintain an essential boundary in our hearts.

No Coveting

EXODUS 20:17 *You shall not covet your neighbor's house; you shall not covet your neighbor's wife, nor his male servant, nor his female servant, nor his ox, nor his donkey, nor anything that is your neighbor's.* (NKJV)

When we read this commandment, we immediately notice that it's different from the others. Except for this and the first commandment, the rest establish a clear behavioral boundary. All those "don'ts" prohibit actions we and others can see.

But you and I can't "see" coveting. We can covet another's ox without ever stealing it. We can covet his wife without committing adultery with her. Coveting is something that happens *inside* us.

key point

The Hebrew word translated "covet" is *hamad*, and it simply means to take pleasure in or find desirable. It's perfectly fine for me to take pleasure in my own house, or find my own wife desirable. Of course, there are things I shouldn't desire because they are <u>intrinsically wrong</u>, like a prostitute or the gold overlay of an idol. But covetousness is different. Covetousness isn't a desire for something evil. It's a desire for something good—but something that belongs to my neighbor.

In Our Day

I noted above that the first and tenth commandments are alike in that neither spells out a behavior. They are also linked, for a person who is free from covetousness has *learned to understand himself in relationship to God.*

The New Testament's teaching on **spiritual gifts** illustrates what I mean. First Corinthians 12 tells us that the Holy Spirit distributes spiritual gifts "to each one individually as He wills" (verse 11 NKJV). God is the One who chooses which gifts we each receive. In essence, the Holy Spirit's gifts define who we are and how we are to function among God's people. What's more, the same passage teaches that each gift, each believer, is <u>just as important</u>.

If I sit in the pew and think, *I wish I could sing like that*, or *I wish I could preach*, I'm coveting another's gift. Even more, I'm rejecting the person God created me to be.

Take Mellisa, a teen who feels her nose is too big and wishes it were like Kristi's. Mellisa is not simply coveting; she is failing to appreciate the fact that God fashioned her to be herself, a special person with her own worth and her own contribution to make to others.

Here we see the link between the first commandment and the tenth, the only two that do not establish clear behavioral boundaries. The first says I'm to have no other gods before the Lord. I'm to purify my understanding of who God is, and come to know Him as He has revealed Himself in Scripture. Loving. Wise. Just. And as the Lord—The One Who Is Always Present, always active and sovereign in our lives.

If I truly know and honor God as He is, then I must acknowledge that He has shaped me and my circumstances for His own good and loving purposes. And I simply cannot covet anything my brother has, for I take delight in being "me" and in fulfilling the purposes God had in mind in making me as I am.

go to

just as important
1 Corinthians
12:12–25

spiritual gifts
special abilities God gives that enable us to serve other believers

apply it

The Ten Commandments

#	The Commandment	Behavior Boundary for Israel	Lesson for Us Today
1	Have no other gods before Me (Exodus 20:3).	Reject pagan concepts of God.	Develop accurate God concept from Scripture.
2	Do not make carved images (20:4).	Do not worship or rely on idols.	Let no material thing stand for God or serve as evidence of His favor/disfavor.
3	Do not take God's name in vain (20:7).	Do not claim to speak for God when you do not.	Remember at all times and in every circumstance that God is real and present.

The Ten Commandments (cont'd)

#	The Commandment	Behavior Boundary for Israel	Lesson for Us Today
4	Keep the Sabbath day (20:8).	Do no work on the Sabbath.	Set aside time away from the cares of this life to focus attention on the Lord.
5	Honor your father and mother (20:12).	Support parents in their old age.	View parents with love, understanding, compassion, and forgiveness.
6	You shall not murder (20:13).	Do not kill another for personal reasons.	Identify hostile feelings as sin. Love enemies.
7	You shall not commit adultery (20:14).	Reserve sexual activity for marriage.	Be loyal to spouse in word and deed. View all other members of opposite sex as persons of value, not as sex objects.
8	You shall not steal (20:15).	Do not take any possessions of others.	Use private property in a godly way, guided by commitment to God's values.
9	You shall not bear false witness (20:16).	Tell only the truth in court cases.	Do not criticize or judge another's motives or in any matters left to the individual conscience.
10	You shall not covet (20:17).	Don't desire what belongs to others.	Accept yourself and your circumstances as God's gifts, and use every opportunity to serve.

Fast Break!

the big picture

Exodus 19–32

Moses is on the mountain with God. On the plains below, the people come to Aaron and demand he make an idol they can worship. Aaron takes the people's gold earrings and casts an idol in the shape of a young bull. Early in the morning the people gather and worship before the idol, breaking the first and second commandments. At the top of the mountain the Lord tells Moses what's happening. Moses pleads with God, but when Moses goes down to the plains and sees what's happening for himself, he is shaken to his core. Moses throws down the stone tablets containing the Ten Commandments. The tablets shatter. Burning with fury, Moses demands that every worshipper be executed—immediately!

How long can Moses stand to lead such a rebellious people? And how long will the Lord put up with them?

Chapter Wrap-Up

- Ancient Israel was distinct from other nations in that its God was near and its commandments were righteous.
- Jesus demonstrated that the Old Testament's commandments and rulings are about more than behavior. Correctly understood, they are about the heart, our inner attitudes and motivations.
- Following this principle, we can understand the deeper meaning of the four commandments that govern our relationship with God.
- Following this principle, we can also understand the deeper meaning of the six commandments that govern our relationship with other people.
- Tragically, an incident that took place while Moses was on Mount Sinai with the Lord illustrates humankind's failure to live even by the behavioral demands of God's law.

Study Questions

1. What were Israel's two "claims to fame"?

2. How did Jesus analyze the commandments against murder and adultery?

3. List as many of the Ten Commandments as you can recall.

4. How many commandments concern our relationship with God?

5. How many commandments concern our relationships with other people?

6. Next to each commandment you listed, describe the behavior it prohibits. Then describe the inner boundary it establishes.

Chapter Highlights:
• Calf and Consequences
• Block Heads
• Not on Our Own
• Goodness, Gracious
• Moses Unveiled

Chapter 7
Moses Moments

Let's Get Started

Moses is concentrating on his mission as lawgiver. He's communicated God's Ten Commandments. He's provided a number of case-by-case rulings for the Israelites. And the Israelites have enthusiastically agreed that Yahweh is King and they will obey Him. Now Moses is back on the mountaintop, receiving further instructions from God.

But something is happening at the base of Mount Sinai that will bring Moses to his knees. The prayers he addresses to the Lord will reveal much about Moses the man, and lead us to rethink our own relationship with God.

go to

revelation in nature
Psalm 19;
Romans 1:19–21

idolatry
Romans 1:22–25

immorality
Romans 1:26–32

Calf and Consequences

EXODUS 32:1–4 *Now when the people saw that Moses delayed coming down from the mountain, the people gathered together to Aaron, and said to him, "Come, make us gods that shall go before us" . . . And Aaron said to them, "Break off the golden earrings . . ." And he received the gold from their hand, and he fashioned it with an engraving tool, and made a molded calf. Then they said, "This is your god, O Israel, that brought you out of the land of Egypt!"* (NKJV)

The Israelites weren't aware of it, but they were following a pattern long engrained in the human race. Peering back before recorded history, the apostle Paul describes humankind's reaction to God's <u>revelation of Himself in nature</u>: "For the wrath of God is revealed from heaven against all ungodliness and unrighteousness of men, who suppress the truth . . . because, although they knew God, they did not glorify Him as God, nor were [they] thankful" (Romans 1:18, 21 NKJV).

That pattern of suppressing known truth about God had hurtled humanity toward <u>idolatry</u> and <u>immorality</u>. Now that pattern is repeated by the Israelites, who agitate for an idol to worship. The God of miracles, whose voice thundered from Sinai, is too terrifying

key point

living waters
constantly flowing
waters

cisterns
receptacles for stor-
ing rainwater hewn
in rock

for comfort. A god made from their own golden earrings is no
threat. Nor could such a god make rules for them. They would make
their own rules, and seek to satisfy the universal need for Someone
Greater by pretending the idol had delivered them from Egypt!

In demanding an idol, the Israelites shattered the first and second
of Yahweh's commandments, "No other gods before Me" and "No
carved images."

Block Heads

ISAIAH 44:16–17, 19
He burns half of it in the fire;
With this half he eats meat;
He roasts a roast, and is satisfied.
He even warms himself and says,
"Ah! I am warm,
I have seen the fire."
And the rest of it he makes into a god,
His carved image.
He falls down before it and worships it,
Prays to it and says,
"Deliver me, for you are my god!" . . .
And no one considers in his heart,
Nor is there knowledge nor understanding to say, . . .
"Shall I fall down before a block of wood?" (NKJV)

key point

Worshipping idols has to be one of the absolute stupidest things a
human being can do. Hundreds of years after Moses's time, the
prophet Isaiah ridicules idol worshippers. He pictures a man who has
just cut down a tree.

Not Just Stupid. Insulting!

History shows that the Israelites remained terribly vulnerable to
idolatry. Through the prophet Jeremiah the Lord laments, "My people have committed two evils: They have forsaken Me, the fountain
of **living waters**, and hewn themselves **cisterns**—broken cisterns
that can hold no water" (Jeremiah 2:13 NKJV).

It was bad enough to turn from the Lord. But then to commit the ultimate insult of turning to useless idols! It was the same as spitting in Yahweh's face.

That's what has happened here. The Israelites have not just disobeyed Yahweh. They have credited a *thing*, a hunk of hammered gold, with the miracles that Yahweh performed to free them.

No wonder God's anger burned.

stiff-necked
rebellious, stubborn

mediator
a person who represents another's interests

what others say

Maxie D. Dunnam

God had laid His life on the line for these people, rescued them from slavery and death in Egypt, delivered them time and time again, guided them, miraculously fed them, saved them from death by thirst. God had identified with them, had made them His people. Now, here they are, still rebellious, seduced by idolatry, responsive to the gracious acts of love constantly coming their way. What a description for a stiff-necked people! Is it any wonder that God was ready to allow His wrath to burn hot and consume them? Yes, it's tough to be God.[1]

Burning Hot Anger

EXODUS 32:9–10 *And the LORD said to Moses, "I have seen this people, and indeed it is a **stiff-necked** people! Now therefore, let Me alone, that My wrath may burn hot against them and I may consume them. And I will make of you a great nation."* (NKJV)

what others say

Peter Enns

To understand the intensity of God's reaction, we must keep this broad perspective in mind. We must look at the degree to which God has revealed Himself in the preceding chapters, not just to Moses but to the people. In a manner of speaking, God has been pouring His heart out. He handpicked a man to act as deliverer and **mediator**. He opened up the powers of heaven against the Egyptians. He brought heaven to earth for them in the form of the Law and the Tabernacle. Yet, no sooner does He do these things than the *people*, not God, become fickle. This is a story not only of the people's rebellion against God, but of their rejection of something God has been planning and working out since the time of Abraham. It is a rejection of God Himself![2]

provided Aaron
Exodus 4:14–16

Moses knew something of God's anger. When God first appeared to him, Moses had tried again and again to avoid being sent to Egypt. Finally, the text tells us, "The anger of the LORD was kindled against Moses" (Exodus 4:14 NKJV). But that anger was nothing compared to the burning hot wrath that Moses sensed now. Then Yahweh had simply <u>provided Aaron</u> to be Moses's spokesman. Now the Lord seemed intent on destroying the people He had just rescued from slavery!

We're not told whether this revelation of God's anger shocked Moses. But the idea that God can feel intense anger troubles some. If we're to enter into the spirit of the first commandment, we need to explore this issue and let what we find in Scripture clarify our concept of who our God truly is.

Anger in the Old Testament

Several Hebrew words express aspects of anger. While any can be translated "anger," "wrath," or "fury," there are distinctive emphases. Like many words in Hebrew, they tend to describe physical reactions, not abstract concepts.

Hebrew Words for Anger

Hebrew Words	Their Meaning
Ka'as and 'ap	A strong emotional reaction in which nostrils flare. These most common Hebrew words for anger are frequently used to describe God's reaction when His people break the Law of Moses.
Hemah and haron	These words mean "burning." They are often used with other terms for anger and emphasize the intensity of the emotional reaction as blood pressure rises and the face turns red.
Qasap and qesep	Typically translated "wrath." These are the strongest of the words describing anger. They emphasize the damage done to a relationship by the one whose action caused the reaction.
'ebrah	Emphasizes the fierceness of the anger. It's often used to portray human anger as an implacable fury.

Any of these terms may be used to describe human anger or divine anger. None indicate whether the anger described is justified or unjustified. The words simply tell us that a strong emotion exists, without indicating whether that emotion is right or wrong.

However, when we study the situations that give rise to the emotion and the actions of the person who is angry, and pay attention to biblical evaluations of anger, it's clear that the Old Testament distinguishes between human anger and the anger or wrath of God.

persecuted
1 Samuel 20:34

jealous anger
1 Samuel 18:18

Angry People

Most people think of anger as a negative emotion. Yet anger is something we all feel at times. Before we condemn that emotion, there are several questions we need to ask:

justified
right, a correct and
godly response

1. What makes people angry?

2. How do people express anger?

3. How are people to deal with anger?

What makes people angry? Check out the following situations, and see if you think becoming angry is justified in any of them. I suspect that most people would feel getting angry is an appropriate reaction in at least one of these situations.

- A neighbor's child cuts across your flower bed on his way home from school.
- Another neighbor regularly and brutally beats his dog.
- A third neighbor plays loud music after 10:00 p.m.

Later, in Exodus 32, we'll see Moses become angry when he sees the idol worship for himself. King Saul's son, Jonathan, became angry when his jealous father persecuted the future king, David. In each case the anger was **justified**, for injustice and betrayal are violations of God's standards in any relationship.

In contrast, the jealousy stimulated Saul's anger at David, and that was completely unjustified: David had done nothing against Saul.

We can understand how walking through a flower bed or playing music late at night might make a person angry, but we can't say these irritations *justify* anger. Yet we would be out of touch with God's values if we failed to become angry at the mistreatment of an animal or another person.

If we become angry at the same injustices that cause God's anger, that emotion is justified. If we become angry when another person

sinful actions
Genesis 49:6–7;
Psalm 37:8–9;
Proverbs 29:22

simply irritates us or pricks our pride, that anger can't be considered justified or right.

How do we express our anger? Psalm 4:4 says, "Be angry, and do not sin" (NKJV). Anger itself isn't a sin. But all too often anger leads to <u>sinful actions</u>.

How do we deal with our anger? In Psalm 37:8, David advises us not to let anger fester. He tells us, "Cease from anger, and forsake wrath; do not fret—it only causes harm" (NKJV). In this same psalm, David suggests positive steps we can take. "Trust in the LORD, and do good" (37:3 NKJV) reminds us that we can turn any situation over to the Lord and be free to concentrate on doing good. Continuing with his advice, David says,

> *Depart from evil, and do good;*
> *And dwell forevermore.*
> *For the LORD loves justice,*
> *And does not forsake His saints;*
> *They are preserved forever. (Psalm 37:27–28 NKJV)*

David concludes with this promise:

> *The salvation of the righteous is from the LORD;*
> *He is their strength in the time of trouble.*
> *And the LORD shall help them and deliver them;*
> *He shall deliver them from the wicked,*
> *And save them,*
> *Because they trust in Him. (Psalm 37:39–40 NKJV)*

This prescription doesn't imply that we're to do nothing when a situation causes justifiable anger. We are to take a stand against injustices. It does mean that not even justifiable anger excuses our losing control and striking back. There will be a right way to respond in every situation, and we're to be committed to "do good."

An Angry God

One reason we react against the idea of an angry God is that we imagine His anger is the same as ours. We know from experience that when we're angry we tend to lose control. And the idea of God losing control and lashing out is frightening. So it's only fair to pose the three questions we asked about human anger of God's anger:

1. What makes God angry?

2. How does God express His anger?

3. How does God deal with His anger?

reflection of His
Genesis 1:26

idolatry
Exodus 32:7–12;
Numbers 25:3;
Deuteronomy
11:16–17

moral judge
Psalm 50:6;
Isaiah 33:22

What makes God angry? The same Old Testament words used to describe an angry human are used to describe our angry God. God is a person, and our emotional makeup is a <u>reflection of His</u>. He feels love, disappointment, compassion, and yes, anger. But there are significant differences between God's anger and our own.

The first difference is that God's anger is *righteous*. That is, God's anger is directed against sin. The second difference is that God's actions even when angry always promote what is good. The third difference is that God's anger is never out of control.

- *God's anger is always directed against sin.* In the case-by-case law that Moses had already given the Israelites, the Lord warned of His anger. God said, "You shall neither mistreat a stranger nor oppress him . . . You shall not afflict any widow or fatherless child. If you afflict them in any way, and they cry at all to Me, I will surely hear their cry; and My wrath will become hot" (Exodus 22:21–24 NKJV). Any act by God's covenant people that harmed others or violated their covenant relationship with God was cause for justifiable anger (Deuteronomy 29:23–28). <u>Idolatry</u> was a particularly harmful sin, for it was a rejection of the covenant relationship itself and would bring terrible judgments on the whole community (Deuteronomy 28:15–68). God's anger is never petty, but is a reaction to sins committed by or against the covenant community.

- *God's actions promote what is good.* Scripture views God's anger in a positive rather than a negative light. God's anger is directed against sin, and has positive results. As <u>moral judge</u> of the universe, God takes responsibility to uphold His standards by punishing the wicked, and this is good. As God of the covenant the Lord judges those who harm His people, and He disciplines and corrects His own. And this too is good. In every case when God acts in anger the outcome is intended for good.

- *God's anger is never out of control.* Exodus 34:6–7 provides a context for God's anger. It describes the Lord as: "merciful and gracious, longsuffering, and abounding in goodness and truth, keeping mercy for thousands, forgiving iniquity and transgression and sin, by no means clearing the guilty . . ." (NKJV). We fear anger because it can cause us to lose control. God's anger is never so great that it cancels out His goodness, mercy, or grace. Even motivated partly by anger, God's every act is also an expression of His goodness, mercy, and love.

How does God express His anger? God expresses His anger in perfectly balanced acts of judgment. Yet even when God would be perfectly justified in punishing, He often chooses to forgive instead. As another psalmist put it,

PSALM 85:2–3
You have forgiven the iniquity of Your people;
You have covered all their sin.
You have taken away all Your wrath;
You have turned from the fierceness of Your anger. (NKJV)

How does God deal with His anger? God expresses it appropriately, in judgment and in mercy.

Back on Sinai

The Lord has just informed Moses how angry He is with the Israelites. Yahweh has said, "Let Me alone, that My wrath may burn hot against them and I may consume them," and has offered to "make of you a great nation" (Exodus 32:10 NKJV). There is no more stunning insight into the relationship between Yahweh and Moses than "Let Me alone, that My wrath may burn hot against them."

One afternoon in the Arab quarter in Jerusalem I watched an argument develop between a man unloading a truck and a bystander. As their voices grew louder, person after person stopped to listen. Everyone had a comment to make, and soon a crowd had gathered, with everyone shouting and gesturing. In our Western society, most

people would have glanced at the angry men and hurried on. In that culture everyone was expected to intervene to see that the arguing pair didn't come to blows. There, no one was willing to leave the two alone.

In the next chapter of Exodus, Scripture comments that "the LORD spoke to Moses face to face, as a man speaks to his friend" (Exodus 33:11 NKJV). In saying "Let Me alone," Yahweh was inviting Moses to take the role of a friend and restrain the full expression of His anger!

And Moses did.

Moses's Plea

EXODUS 32:11–13 *Then Moses pleaded with the LORD his God, and said: "LORD, why does Your wrath burn hot against Your people whom You have brought out of the land of Egypt with great power and with a mighty hand? Why should the Egyptians speak, and say, 'He brought them out to harm them, to kill them in the mountains, and to consume them from the face of the earth'? . . . Remember Abraham, Isaac, and Israel, Your servants, to whom You swore by Your own self, and said to them, 'I will multiply your descendants as the stars of heaven; and all this land that I have spoken of I give to your descendants, and they shall inherit it forever." (NKJV)*

Moses didn't plead for the Israelites, or try to minimize their offense. What Moses was concerned about was God's reputation! It was unthinkable that pagan nations should have a reason to scoff at Yahweh, or that the Lord should act in any way that was inconsistent with His character.

Moses was concerned for the glory of God, and so he pleaded with God to act in a way that would bring Him praise.

In this incident we see another guideline for maintaining a healthy relationship with God. Let us approach God in prayer confidently, *and in every prayer make the glory of God our primary concern.* Moses was interceding for the people he led. But his ultimate concern was for the glory of God.

go to

orgy
Exodus 32:18, 29;
32:6

punished
Exodus 32:33

orgy
mass, unrestrained
sex

A healthy relationship with God is expressed in prayers whose primary concern is the glory and reputation of our God.

The Rest of the Story

the big picture

Exodus 32:19–35

Moses reaches camp and sees a crowd of Israelites worshipping the calf idol and engaging in a mass **orgy**. Moses burns with fury. He throws down the stone tablets on which God engraved the Ten Commandments. They shatter. A cringing Aaron makes excuses. Moses ignores him, and calls for those who are on the Lord's side to rally to him. The Levites respond. On Moses's order, they attack the worshippers, killing some three thousand. Moses begs the Lord to forgive His sinning people. God will never forgive those who actually participated in the worship, but He will bring the others to the Promised Land. Yet the whole community is responsible for what has happened, and they will be <u>punished</u>.

Not on Our Own, Please

EXODUS 33:1–3 *Then the LORD said to Moses, "Depart and go up from here, you and the people whom you have brought out of the land of Egypt, to the land of which I swore to Abraham . . . And I will send My Angel before you, and I will drive out the Canaanite . . . for I will not go up in your midst, lest I consume you on the way, for you are a stiffnecked people." (NKJV)*

These words shocked Moses. Even the people were shaken. Ever since leaving Egypt the fiery-cloudy pillar that was the mark of God's presence had led them, and had floated over the Israelites' tents when they camped. The people had ignored the cloud when they demanded an idol to worship. But now that the Lord threatened to withdraw His presence, they were afraid.

Earlier we saw that Israel had two claims to fame: "What great nation is there that has God so near to it . . . ?" and "What great nation is there that has such statutes and righteous judgments . . . ?" (Deuteronomy 4:7–8 NKJV). If God were to withdraw, what hope would they have? So the people stripped off their jewelry as a sign of repentance and mourning (Exodus 33:4).

Moses pitched his tent well outside the Israelite camp and called it the "tent of meeting." God had abandoned the Israelite camp, but when Moses went into his tent the fiery-cloudy pillar settled to the ground, and the Lord talked with Moses. The awed Israelites observed from a distance. Moses was meeting with God, but no one knew what was being said.

go to

bring cares to God
Philippians 4:6;
1 Peter 5:7

Moses's Second Plea

EXODUS 33:13–16 *"Now therefore, I pray, if I have found grace in Your sight, show me now Your way, that I may know You and that I may find grace in Your sight. And consider that this nation is Your people." And He said, "My Presence will go with you, and I will give you rest." Then he said to Him, "If Your Presence does not go with us, do not bring us up from here. For how then will it be known that Your people and I have found grace in Your sight, except You go with us? So we shall be separate, Your people and I, from all the people who are upon the face of the earth." (NKJV)*

First Things First

Moses's first concern was that Yahweh "show me now Your way, that I may know You." It's fascinating how seldom this concern drives us to prayer. Visit any church prayer meeting, or ask anyone about the last thing he prayed for, and you're almost sure to find that prayer for healing, a new job, or some other material benefit tops the lists. There's nothing wrong with any of these prayers. God is a heavenly Father, and He wants us to <u>bring all our cares</u> to Him. Yet how pleasing to God it must be if our first concern in prayer mirrors that of Moses: that we may be shown God's way, that we may know Him.

apply it

This is the focus of several of the apostle Paul's prayers for his converts. Paul realizes that if God's people come to truly know Him, the rest of life will fall into place. Life takes on perspective only as we grow to know the Lord better and better.

go to

glorious in
righteousness
Psalm 66:2

Prayers for God-Seekers

Scripture Reference	Prayer
From Colossians 1:9–10	I ask to be filled with the knowledge of Your will in all wisdom and spiritual understanding; that I may walk worthy of You, fully pleasing You, being fruitful in every good work and increasing in the knowledge of You.
From Ephesians 1:17–20	Father, give me the spirit of wisdom and revelation that I may know You. May the eyes of my understanding be enlightened, that I may know what is the hope of Your calling, the riches of the glory of Your inheritance in the saints, and the exceeding greatness of Your power toward us who believe, according to the working of Your mighty power, which You worked in Christ when You raised Him from the dead.
From Ephesians 3:17–19	Lord, may Christ dwell in my heart through faith, that being rooted and grounded in love, I may be able to comprehend with all the saints the width and length and depth and height—to know the love of Christ which passes knowledge, that I may be filled with all the fullness of God.

Request Granted

EXODUS 33:17 *So the LORD said to Moses, "I will also do this thing that you have spoken; for you have found grace in My sight, and I know you by name." (NKJV)*

God would continue to teach Moses His ways, and Moses would come to know the Lord better and better. God would also grant Moses's request for the Israelites. He would go with them, all the way.

Goodness, Gracious

EXODUS 33:18–20 *And he said, "Please, show me Your glory." Then He said, "I will make all My goodness pass before you, and I will proclaim the name of the LORD before you. I will be gracious to whom I will be gracious, and I will have compassion on whom I will have compassion." But He said, "You cannot see My face; for no man shall see Me, and live." (NKJV)*

This is Moses's third prayer. It is the boldest plea of all, for Moses asks for a vision of God as He really is, in His essential splendor. This is a request that God cannot grant, and for good reason.

Show Me Your Glory

The word translated "glory" is closely linked to the idea of social reputation. To be glorious means to be deserving of respect or honor. A "glorious kingdom" is one whose wealth and power are impressive. To say that God is <u>glorious in righteousness</u> or <u>glorious in faithfulness</u> means that God's righteousness and faithfulness are impressive, and that He is to be respected and honored for them. But in asking the Lord to "show me Your glory," Moses is taking us a step further. Moses isn't asking to be shown that which gained God His reputation. He is asking God to unveil His very self; to disclose all that He is to His servant.

This is something that is simply impossible for God to do. No mortal is capable of grasping the totality of God. To be exposed to such a revelation would be more than a human could stand. It would quite literally kill Moses.

Using imagery that Moses could understand, the Lord told Moses He would reveal as much of Himself as Moses could comprehend. He would place Moses in a cleft in one of Sinai's rocky sides, cover Moses while His full glory passed by, and then take His hand away so Moses could see His back. Moses would have to be satisfied with this.

glorious in faithfulness
Psalm 79:9

vision of Jesus
Revelation 1:10–17

Fast-Forward

Nearly fifteen hundred years pass. Jesus is born. He lives a perfect life. He teaches, He heals. He is crucified and rises again. The apostle John, telling the story of Jesus, writes, "And the Word became flesh and dwelt among us, and we beheld His glory, the glory as of the only begotten of the Father, full of grace and truth" (John 1:14 NKJV). In Jesus, God reveals Himself more fully than at any time in history past.

When John is an old man, exiled to an island in the Mediterranean Sea, he is given a <u>vision of Jesus</u> that stuns him. John says, "When I saw Him, I fell at His feet as dead" (Revelation 1:17 NKJV). The glory of God revealed in the man Jesus was not the full glory of God, and even John's vision of the glorified Jesus falls short of complete revelation. Only in our own resurrection will we be able to see our God in all His glory, for Scripture promises, "We shall be like Him, for we shall see Him as He is" (1 John 3:2 NKJV).

go to

psalmists celebrate
Psalms 25:6; 86:5;
135:3

prophets affirm
Jeremiah 24:6;
Nahum 1:7

Jesus reminds us
Matthew 5:44–45

Welcome Back, Moses

EXODUS 33:19 *Then He said, "I will make all My goodness pass before you, and I will proclaim the name of the LORD before you. I will be gracious to whom I will be gracious, and I will have compassion on whom I will have compassion." (NKJV)*

God promised to show Moses His back even though Moses would not be able to see His face. What in this passage represents the "back" of God? And what does God's display of His "back" to Moses teach us? The answer is found in two revelatory announcements by God.

- *The significance of "name."* We've noted this before. In the Old Testament world, the "name" of a person or thing was intended to express something of the essence of the person or thing named. When God says "I will proclaim the name of the LORD before you," He's saying, "I'm going to tell you something really important about Me."

- *The name itself.* Earlier, the Lord had revealed the name Yahweh to Moses, and explained its meaning. As Yahweh, the I AM, He is The One Who Is Always Present. Now God reveals a different name: "I will be gracious to whom I will be gracious, and I will have compassion on whom I will have compassion." This name tells us that God has chosen to be gracious and compassionate. He is under no obligation to care about human beings. He is under no obligation to treat humans kindly. Yet, despite the fact that humanity has rebelled against Him and continually sins, God has chosen to be gracious and compassionate.

- *The significance of the name.* In saying, "I will make all My goodness pass before you," the Lord sums up the significance of His name. Simply put, God is good. It is the goodness of God that is the "back" He showed to Moses. If Moses wants to know God as He truly is, it is the fact that God is good that he must always keep in mind.

Scripture has much to say about the goodness of God. The psalmists celebrate it. The prophets affirm it. Jesus reminds us that the Lord is good to all, believer and unbeliever alike. It is the essential goodness of God that has moved Him to be compassionate and gracious.

If we are to truly know God, we too must always keep in mind that the Lord is good.

There are a number of ways to approach knowledge of God. Some theologians, like Calvin, build their systems on a foundation of God's sovereignty. Others, like Luther, take love as their starting point. Wesleyans tend to emphasize the freedom God grants to human beings to make their own responsible choices. Each of these theological schools presents important truths about who God is and what He is like.

But Moses wasn't trying to develop a theology. Moses was simply a man who yearned to know God in a deeper, more personal way. And God's advice to Moses was to focus on the one thing about God that would bring everything else into perspective. God is good. And because God is good, He is gracious and compassionate.

Proclaim the Name

EXODUS 34:5–8 *Now the LORD descended in the cloud and stood with him there, and proclaimed the name of the LORD. And the LORD passed before him and proclaimed, "The LORD, the LORD God, merciful and gracious, longsuffering, and abounding in goodness and truth, keeping mercy for thousands, forgiving iniquity and transgression and sin, by no means clearing the guilty, visiting the iniquity of the fathers upon the children and the children's children to the third and the fourth generation." So Moses made haste and bowed his head toward the earth, and worshiped.* (NKJV)

When the moment arrived for this fresh revelation, God expanded on the theme of His goodness. It's as if He handed Moses a jeweler's loupe, used to examine every facet of a precious gem, and invited him to look closely at facet after facet of His "abounding [overflowing, endless]" goodness. These are the facets the Lord emphasized:

- *We see God's goodness in His mercy.* In mercy God reaches down to us without considering whether we deserve His aid.

- *We see God's goodness in His grace.* In grace God is moved by our desperate need to exercise His power to help us.

- *We see God's goodness in His longsuffering.* In longsuffering God waits patiently for us to respond to His love, holding back punishments that we deserve.

- *We see God's goodness in its abundance.* God's goodness keeps on overflowing.

- *We see God's goodness in its harmony with "truth."* God's goodness is established, faithful, ever reliable, something we can count on.

- *We see God's goodness in His forgiveness of sins.* God does not simply forgive our sins of falling short of perfection. God forgives sins rooted in our rebellious nature and our callous disregard of others.

- *We see God's goodness in His unwillingness to "clear the guilty."* In His goodness God doesn't overlook justice. He is forgiving, yet at the same time fulfills His responsibility to act as moral judge of His universe.

- *We see God's goodness in the moral order He established for human society.*

The last statement in this proclamation by Yahweh of His goodness is often misunderstood. The text states that God "[visits] the iniquity of the fathers upon the children and the children's children to the third and the fourth generation" (Exodus 34:7 NKJV). This does not mean that God punishes children for their parents' sins. It does mean that God has fashioned a moral universe whose orderliness mirrors the orderliness of the material universe. In each universe, effect follows cause in a predictable way. Drop a rock, and it will fall. Commit iniquity—deviate from God's moral standards or twist them—and there will be consequences that impact not just you but your children and your children's children. And yet God intervenes within the framework of the predictable moral universe, not to punish, but to show His patience, His mercy, His grace, and His willingness to forgive.

Don't Miss God's Grace

The writer of the book of Hebrews warns readers who are discouraged and are losing heart because of difficult times. He tells them to be careful "lest anyone fall short of the grace of God; lest any root of bitterness springing up cause trouble" (Hebrews 12:15 NKJV). The phrase "fall short of" here means to miss, or to fail to see. It's so easy when things are difficult to focus on our problems and to lose sight of **God's grace** and His goodness.

It would have been easy for Moses to lose sight of God's grace. The people he led were hostile and rebellious. He'd just discovered that his brother Aaron was totally unreliable. Even God had threatened to abandon the Israelites, lest they anger Him so much He destroys them.

Imagine that God now hands Moses a pair of blue-tinted sunglasses. When Moses puts them on, nothing in the Israelites' camp will have changed. But to Moses everything will be tinted blue. This, in effect, is exactly what God does. God hands Moses a pair of goodness-tinted sunglasses. As Moses looks around, his people will still be hostile and rebellious. His brother will still be unreliable. But now everything will be tinted by his awareness of God's goodness. And in this fresh vision of the goodness of God, Moses will gain perspective and find the strength to go on.

And so we've come again to one of those guidelines for maintaining a healthy relationship with God. To maintain a healthy relationship with God, *let the awareness that God is good provide perspective.*

A healthy relationship with God is nurtured by keeping His goodness in view when we face difficult times.

Moses Unveiled

EXODUS 34:29–35 *Now it was so, when Moses came down from Mount Sinai (and the two tablets of the Testimony were in Moses' hand when he came down from the mountain), that Moses did not know that the skin of his face shone while he talked with Him. So when Aaron and all the children of Israel saw Moses, behold, the skin of his face shone, and they were afraid to come near him . . . And when Moses had finished speaking with them, he put a veil on his face. But whenever Moses went in before the LORD to speak with Him, he would take the veil off until he came out . . . And whenever the children of Israel saw the face of Moses, that the skin of Moses' face shone, then Moses would put the veil on his face again, until he went in to speak with Him. (NKJV)*

Moses's prayers have been answered. God has restrained His anger and promised to remain with the Israelites. Moses has come to know God better through Yahweh's revelation of His goodness. Moses has been up on Mount Sinai once again. There God wrote the Ten Commandments on new stone tablets, and gave Moses further instructions for the Israelites. When Moses returns, his face shines brightly, awing the Israelites and even his brother Aaron.

This reception must have been a welcome change. Rather than complain to Moses, the Israelites are "afraid to come near him" (Exodus 34:30 NKJV). They stand back in awe, and listen respectfully to whatever message Moses has for them. What must have been even more encouraging was that whenever the Lord joined Moses in the "tabernacle of meeting" (Exodus 33:7 NKJV), the glow on his face was renewed. At last Moses experienced some relief from the constant nagging of the unhappy Israelites. That shining face truly was a godsend!

What's significant here, however, is Moses's use of a veil to cover his face. He removed the veil when he spoke with the Lord. He kept the veil off when leaving the Lord's presence until he had delivered Yahweh's message. Then he quickly put the veil over his face again. The text of Exodus doesn't explain Moses's motive, but centuries later the apostle Paul does.

Help! The Splendor's Fading!

> 2 CORINTHIANS 3:13 *Moses . . . put a veil over his face so that the children of Israel could not look steadily at the end of what was passing away.* (NKJV)

The NIV clarifies Paul's point. Moses put on a veil "to keep the Israelites from gazing at [his face] while the radiance was fading away." It was being in the presence of God that made Moses's face shine brilliantly. But when Moses left God's presence, the glow gradually faded. And Moses didn't want the Israelites to see that special glow fade!

We can understand and sympathize with Moses. It was his shining face that awed the people. It was his shining face that kept them away from him. Why in the world would Moses want to return to being an "ordinary" man that the people would challenge, complain to, and mutter about? It was so much easier to remain at a distance, to act like some legendary figure rather than a flesh-and-blood, vulnerable human being.

It may well be that Moses needed to maintain this distance, and that God intended the visible evidence of Moses's time with God to provide it. But the apostle Paul reminds us that in this, at least, Moses set an example we are *not* to follow. That verse I quoted above begins, "Unlike Moses . . ." and later Paul concludes, "We all, with unveiled face, beholding as in a mirror the glory of the Lord, are being transformed into the same image from glory to glory, just as by the Spirit of the Lord" (2 Corinthians 3:18 NKJV).

Let Them See . . . Jesus

What is Paul teaching? Simply that Moses used the veil to *maintain distance between himself and the people he led*. In contrast, Christians are to remove the masks we wear to hide ourselves from others. We want them to know us as we are, despite our many flaws and imperfections. Why? Because while the shine that was evidence of Moses's presence with God faded, something very different is happening within Christians today. God the Holy Spirit is progressively, gradually **transforming** us from within. The mark of God's presence in the Christian life isn't the supposed "goodness" we wear on our sleeve. The mark of God's presence is our transformation toward Christ's likeness, "from glory to glory," which is the work of God's Holy Spirit.

If we are to reveal Christ to others, we need to let them see us as we are now, warts and all, so they can also see the difference that Jesus is making in our lives.

Moses Moments

The Old Testament books that tell of Moses and his mission often seem dense with information. But every now and then there's a pause for narrative, for story. And it's in these story portions that we gain a sense of Moses the man of God.

The Law that God gave through Moses was central to the lives of generations of Israelites. That Law has been a key to the Jews' preservation as a people through some four thousand tragedy-packed years. What's more, if we're to understand the Old Testament and, indeed, the New Testament, we need to learn about Mosaic Law. At the same time, the Moses moments, when we're given glimpses of the man and of his relationship with God, are both important and refreshing. Those Moses moments can teach us how we, too, can truly be friends of God.

Chapter Wrap-Up

- While Moses is on Sinai receiving instructions from God, the Israelites turn to idolatry and credit a calf idol with freeing them from Egypt.
- God is angry enough to destroy the whole people, but Moses pleads with God to remember His covenant promise and His own reputation.
- When Moses returns to the base of the mountain he can hardly restrain his own anger. On Moses's orders some three thousand worshippers are executed.
- Moses pleads with God to stay with His people, and also to show Moses His glory.
- God promises to remain with Israel. Then the Lord reveals Himself to Moses as God—as much of a revelation as His servant can handle.
- Now, whenever Moses meets with God his face shines, awing the people. But as soon as Moses delivers God's message he covers his face with a veil so the worshippers will not see the glow fading away.

Study Questions

1. What commandments did the Israelites break by demanding Aaron make a calf idol?

2. What was God's reaction to the Israelites' idolatry?

3. In what ways is God's anger different from human anger?

4. Exodus 32–34 describes three special prayers offered by Moses. What are they?

5. How did God answer Moses's plea to be shown God's glory?

6. This chapter introduced two guidelines for maintaining a healthy relationship with God. What are they?

7. How does the apostle Paul explain Moses's use of a veil for his face? How does Paul apply this to Christians today?

Chapter 8
Torah, Torah

Chapter Highlights:
• Book by Book
• Follow My Instructions
• About a Worship Center
• Spiritual Realities
• The Sum of the Parts

Let's Get Started

Our Moses moment has passed. In this chapter we're back exploring Moses's mission of laying down a law for God's Old Testament people.

Unfortunately, that phrase "laying down a law" is confusing. When you see "law" in an Old Testament passage, you probably assume it's referring to the Ten Commandments or some specific set of rules. But that's not all that "law" refers to.

The Hebrew word translated "law" is *torah*. It's true that the Ten Commandments are *torah*. It's also true that every Old Testament moral rule is *torah*. The nonmoral rules that governed life in Israel are *torah* too. But the whole book of Exodus is *torah*. So are the other four books of Moses. The description of the tent where Israel worshipped the Lord is *torah*. The priesthood is *torah*. The sacrifices and offerings are *torah*. The worship calendar that gave structure to the Israelites' year is *torah*. In short, God's entire revelation through Moses, and any part or the whole, is *torah*!

So, to understand the Law of Moses, we have to redefine our concept of "law" to match the concept of *torah*.

other four books of Moses
Genesis, Leviticus, Numbers, and Deuteronomy

Torah, Book by Book

Moses is credited with writing the first five books of the Old Testament. Together these five books contain the "Law of Moses."

In these five books we find two primary types of literature. One type is narrative, or story. The other is instruction, or teaching. While at times the two intermingle, generally the two types of literature are separated. The following chart shows the balance of narrative and instruction in these five books.

Ten Commandments
Exodus 20

case-by-case law
Exodus 21–23

Narrative and Instruction in the Five Books of Moses

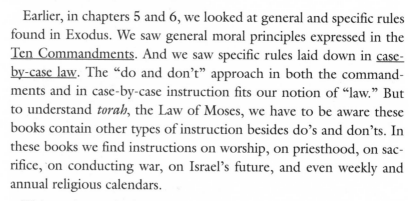

	Genesis	Exodus	Leviticus		Numbers	Deuteronomy
Narrative	1–50	1–19			11–27	1–4
		32–40			31–33	30–36
Instruction		20–31	1–27		1–10	5–29
					28–30	
					34–36	

It's important to remember that as far as the Bible is concerned, both the stories and the instruction in these five books are *torah*, the authoritative revelation from God given to and through Moses.

Follow My Instructions

Earlier, in chapters 5 and 6, we looked at general and specific rules found in Exodus. We saw general moral principles expressed in the Ten Commandments. And we saw specific rules laid down in case-by-case law. The "do and don't" approach in both the command-ments and in case-by-case instruction fits our notion of "law." But to understand *torah*, the Law of Moses, we have to be aware these books contain other types of instruction besides do's and don'ts. In these books we find instructions on worship, on priesthood, on sac-rifice, on conducting war, on Israel's future, and even weekly and annual religious calendars.

We're going to look at each of these types of instruction now. As we do, you'll want to open your Bible to sample one or more of the chapters dealing with each type.

Follow My "Do and Don't" Instructions

Moses's "do and don't" instructions deal with both moral and nonmoral issues. There are distinct differences between these two kinds of "do and don't" instructions.

Moral issues. Moral issues focus on either our relationship with God or our relationship with other persons. General principles gov-erning these interpersonal relationships are set down in the Ten Commandments. But general principles are also found at times in passages giving case-by-case instruction. For instance, Leviticus 19:18 states, "You shall not take vengeance, nor bear any grudge against the children of your people" (NKJV). This is a specific case of "don't." But then the verse goes on to state a general principle: "You shall love your neighbor as yourself" (19:18 NKJV).

Oftentimes, moral case-by-case laws apply or expand on one of the Ten Commandments. For instance, we mustn't understand the commandment "Don't commit adultery" to permit sex with *anyone but* another person's spouse. To make sure there's no misunderstanding on this point, Leviticus 18 lists case after case in which sexual activity is forbidden.

Another distinctive of the Old Testament's moral do's and don'ts relates to violations. If a person violates the commandment against stealing, for example, that person must compensate his victim, plus pay him an additional amount (Exodus 22:1). And because the person who steals disobeys God, his or her sin must be covered by a blood sacrifice (Leviticus 16:30; 17:11).

what others say

R. A. Barclay

The Law of the book of Leviticus is severe for these "breaches of faith." It requires restoration of the property plus one-fifth in addition to the offering, which is also strictly valued in cash (4:15; 6:6). Thus restoration and propitiation (making right with God) are combined in the sin offerings and the guilt offerings. Religion and morality are joined together in a single practice. Every human action is done in the sight of God. The sacrifices underline man's duty to God and his obligation to his neighbor.[1]

To Sample Moral Do's and Don'ts, Read . . .

Chapter in the Bible	Moral Guides Concerning . . .
Exodus 21	Servants, violence
Exodus 22	Property
Exodus 23	Personal responsibility, violence
Leviticus 18	Sexual practices
Leviticus 19	Neighbors
Numbers 35	Murder, cities of refuge (Deuteronomy 19)
Deuteronomy 5	The Ten Commandments
Deuteronomy 11	Loving God
Deuteronomy 15	The poor

neither right nor wrong
Romans 14:14–17;
1 Corinthians 8:8;
Colossians 2:20–23

evening
evening was considered the beginning of a new day by the Jews

Nonmoral issues. Many case-by-case rules and commands have no moral basis. These commands—such as don't eat pork—proscribe activities that are <u>neither right nor wrong</u> *in themselves.* Usually such Old Testament rules are intended simply to remind God's covenant people that they are different from other peoples, set apart to God for His own purposes.

It's easy to find examples of nonmoral commands and rules. Earlier we noted that the Israelites were to attach tassels to their clothing that contained a blue thread. The command in Exodus 23:19 not to boil a young goat in its mother's milk—the ruling that has led modern Orthodox Jews to avoid serving milk and meat dishes at the same meal, and even to keep two separate sets of tableware—is another "don't" command dealing with an issue that is neither right nor wrong *in itself.*

Torah governing nonmoral issues are usually classified as "ceremonial laws" or "ritual laws." While breaking a ceremonial law isn't an offense against another person, breaking any law is an offense against God. The penalty for violating a ceremonial law was to immediately become ceremonially "unclean."

"Clean" and "unclean" are important concepts in the Law of Moses. A person who had not violated ceremonial law was considered "clean"—that is, in a state of ritual purity. The "clean" person could participate fully in Israel's worship and in the life of the community. However, if a person violated a ceremonial law, he or she became "unclean." Until the state of ritual purity was restored, that person *could not* participate in worship or in the life of the community.

key point

For some offenses against a ceremonial law, the state of purity could be restored by time alone. For others, time plus washing with water were required. Leviticus 11:39 rules that "if any animal which you may eat dies, he who touches its carcass shall be unclean until **evening**" (NKJV). The next verse states that if anyone eats of the animal who died rather than being killed, he "shall wash his clothes and be unclean until evening" (Leviticus 11:40 NKJV). Quite often the cure for uncleanness is this combination of water and time.

In other instances time and blood sacrifice were required. For instance, a woman who bore a girl child was ritually unclean for eighty days, after which she brought an animal or bird to a priest to be offered as a blood sacrifice. After the required time passed and the blood sacrifice was offered, she became ritually clean again (Leviticus 12:5–8). In this case the woman hadn't violated a ceremonial law. She simply became unclean by bearing her child.

It's important to understand that when cleanness or uncleanness is at issue, it's ritual rather than a moral matter. It wasn't wrong for the woman to have sex with her husband or produce a child. No moral "do" was left undone, and no moral "don't" had been committed. The fact that both time and blood sacrifice were required for her to become ritually clean again is simply one of those many reminders built into Mosaic Law to keep the Israelites conscious of the fact that Yahweh is involved in every aspect of their lives. And to remind them that as His chosen people, they were to be different from all others.

sanctuary
a place set aside for worship

tabernacle
a tent, a portable worship center

To Sample Ceremonial Do's and Don'ts, Read . . .

Chapter in the Bible	Moral Guidelines Concerning . . .
Leviticus 11	Foods
Leviticus 12	Childbirth
Leviticus 13	Infectious diseases
Leviticus 14	Mold in houses
Leviticus 15	Bodily discharges
Deuteronomy 22	Mixed moral/nonmoral laws
Deuteronomy 26	Mixed moral/nonmoral laws

Follow My Instructions About a Worship Center

EXODUS 25:8–9, 40 *And let them make Me a **sanctuary**, that I may dwell among them. According to all that I show you, that is, the pattern of the **tabernacle** and the pattern of all its furnishings, just so you shall make it . . . And see to it that you make them according to the pattern which was shown you on the mountain. (NKJV)*

Moses was on Mount Sinai when God spoke these words. Down below, the people, who had committed themselves to obey Yahweh's commandments, were about to break the first two by worshipping an idol. The fact that the instructions concerning the Tabernacle were given before the Israelites actually worshipped their golden calf is significant.

Why the Tabernacle?

When Yahweh laid down His "do and don't" instructions, He was fully aware the Israelites would soon sin. And that they would keep on sinning. The Tabernacle was more than a visible symbol of God's presence with His people. It was a stage on which the drama of **redemption** would be played out again and again. Through the design of this worship center and its furnishings, and through what was to happen there, God would teach His sinning people about salvation and forgiveness, and would prepare the way for the coming Savior.

It was necessary that the Tabernacle follow exactly the pattern God provided. Every detail must accurately reflect spiritual truths concerning God's plan for humankind's ultimate salvation.

The Tabernacle and Its Furnishings Represent Spiritual Realities

- *A continuous wall* enclosed the Tabernacle that prevented access from any direction but one. Other religions do not lead worshippers to the God of the Bible.

- *A single door* allowed access, indicating that there was and forever would be only one way to approach God. Later Jesus would announce, "I am the door. If anyone enters by Me, he will be saved" (John 10:9 NKJV).

- *A bronze altar for sacrifice* (Exodus 27:1–8) stood immediately inside this one door. Sinners were required to sacrifice an animal before approaching the tent symbolizing God's presence. "For the life of the flesh is in the blood, and I have given it to you upon the altar to make **atonement** for your souls" (Leviticus 17:11 NKJV). These sacrifices foreshadowed the sacrifice of Christ on the cross, where His blood won us eternal salvation (Hebrews 10:11–19).

- *The interior of the Tabernacle* was divided into two rooms. The innermost room and its furnishings symbolized heaven and the real presence of God. The outermost room and its furnishings symbolized worship of God by believers during their time on earth.

- *The golden table in the outmost room* (Exodus 25:23–30) held loaves of bread, symbolizing God's provision. Later Jesus presented Himself as the Bread of Life, who sustains those who trust in Him (John 6).

- *A seven-branched lampstand filled with oil* (Exodus 25:31–40) provided the only light in the outermost room. It symbolized revelation, which provides the only light by which we can see God. The lamps were to be kept burning permanently (Exodus 27:20–21).

- *An altar for burning a special incense* (Exodus 30:1–9), which represented the prayers of God's people.

- *A gold-covered chest—the Ark of the Covenant—*(Exodus 25:10–21) that contained the stone tablets on which God engraved the Ten Commandments, rested in the innermost room. Its solid-gold top, featuring the figures of two angels whose gaze focused on its center, was called the mercy seat. There on the Day of Atonement (Leviticus 16) the high priest sprinkled blood that atoned for all the sins of Israel for the past year. It was there, where the blood was sprinkled, that God and man met (Exodus 25:22). One day Jesus, our High Priest, would enter heaven with His own blood, and through His sacrifice enable those who believe to be forever reunited with the Lord God (Hebrews 9:23–28).

- *A thick woven curtain (veil) separated the innermost and outer rooms* of the Tabernacle (Exodus 26:31–33). Only the high priest could pass beyond the curtain, and only once each year, to sprinkle blood on the mercy seat. The curtain symbolized the fact that full access to God was not yet possible. The New Testament tells us that when Christ died this curtain was <u>torn from top to bottom</u>. Through Christ believers can now "come boldly to the throne of grace, that we may obtain mercy and find grace to help in time of need" (Hebrews 4:16 NKJV).

torn from top to bottom
Matthew 27:51;
Mark 15:38

Tabernacle Teachings

go to

blood sacrifice
Genesis 3:21;
Leviticus 17:11;
Hebrews 9:13–14

Christ's blood
Hebrews 9:23–28

law
the *torah*, the whole
system given
through Moses to
the Israelites includ-
ing do's and don'ts,
the Tabernacle, sac-
rifices, etc.

sanctified
set apart through
faith in Jesus as
God's own

tribe
Descendants of
each of the twelve
sons of Jacob/Israel
formed a tribe.
There were also sev-
eral family lines
within each tribe.

HEBREWS 10:1 *For the **law**, having a shadow of the good things to come, and not the very image of the things, can never with these same sacrifices, which they offer continually year by year, make those who approach perfect. (NKJV)*

I suggested earlier that the Tabernacle was essentially a stage on which the drama of redemption was played out again and again. Each day the priest officiating there offered blood sacrifices. Each year the high priest entered the innermost room of the Tabernacle with sacrificial blood. The first lesson the drama taught was that sinful human beings could only approach God through blood sacrifice. Sin merits death, and if the sinner is to go free, a substitute must die. The second lesson the drama taught was that the blood of bulls and goats was not enough. If animal sacrifices had won God's forgiveness, there would have been no need to repeat them endlessly.

And then Jesus came. In His death on the cross, human beings were shown the reality that had cast its shadow throughout Israel's history. Calvary was the true altar, Christ's blood the true sacrifice. In dying He took our place, and by His "one offering He has perfected forever those who are being **sanctified**" (Hebrews 10:14 NKJV).

To Find Out More About the Tabernacle, Read . . .

Bible Reference	About the Tabernacle
Exodus 25:1–22	The Ark and Mercy Seat
Exodus 25:23–30	The Table
Exodus 25:31–38	The Lampstand
Exodus 26:1–30	The Tabernacle Itself
Exodus 26:31–34	The Innermost Room
Exodus 26:35–37	The Outer Room
Exodus 27:1–8	The Bronze Altar for Sacrifice
Exodus 30:1–9	The Altar for Burning Incense

Follow My Instructions About a Priesthood

Another vital element of Moses's *torah* was the priesthood. Old Testament law required that only descendants of Aaron serve as priests. Other families from the **tribe** of Levi were set aside to transport and care for the Tabernacle.

The priests served as mediators between God and His Old Testament people. They offered the necessary sacrifices for sin, and they were <u>responsible to teach</u> God's people how to be holy according to Moses's *torah*.

responsible to teach
Leviticus 10:11;
2 Chronicles 17:9

determine ritually clean and unclean
Leviticus 13–14

what others say

R. A. Barclay

The book of Leviticus gives prominence to the priest and to what he does at the sacrifice. Indeed, worship through sacrifice is only done properly by the recognized priesthood. Aaron and his sons are specially appointed for this task by Moses.[2]

The priests also <u>determined who was ritually clean and who was unclean</u> under the Law. Specific directions told the priests how to conduct their ministries, and priests were held to a higher standard of holiness than were other Israelites.

There was also a high priest. The high priest had two special religious functions. On the Day of Atonement he entered the innermost room of the Tabernacle and sprinkled the mercy seat with the blood that atoned for the Israelites' sins of the past year (Leviticus 16). The high priest also wore a vestlike garment that contained the Urim and Thummin, objects that were used to determine God's will for the people (Exodus 28:30). The high priest served for life, and only after his death could another high priest be appointed from Aaron's descendants.

The New Testament presents Jesus as the Christian's High Priest. He entered heaven itself with His own blood, obtaining eternal— not just annual—forgiveness of sins for believers (Hebrews 9:24–26). And, through the Holy Spirit, Jesus teaches and guides His people today (John 16:13).

key point

To Find Out More About the Jewish Priesthood, Read . . .

Bible Reference	About the Priesthood
Exodus 28	The High Priest's Garments
Exodus 29	Ordination of the Priests
Leviticus 8	Instructions to the Priests Concerning Sacrifice
Leviticus 9	Instructions to the Priests Concerning Sacrifice
Leviticus 13	Instructions Concerning Uncleanness

Bible Reference	About the Priesthood
Leviticus 14	Instructions Concerning Cleansing of Uncleanness
Leviticus 21	Special Regulations for Priests
Leviticus 22	Special Regulations for Priests

Follow My Instructions About Sacrifice

The primary ministry given the priests was to offer the sacrifices required by *torah*. The majority of these were blood sacrifices that required the death of a ceremonially clean animal such as a bull, sheep, or lamb. Any act that made a person guilty of failing to keep any of God's regulations required a blood sacrifice.

There are distinctive differences between the sacrifices offered in pagan cultures and the sacrifices called for in the Law of Moses. In general the sacrifices offered by pagans were viewed as payments (bribes) offered either to placate an angry deity or to win the deity's favor so he or she would grant the worshipper's request. Mosaic Law acknowledges the reality of sin and the fact that sin requires punishment. But the theme of substitution that is woven so tightly into Moses's *torah* is lacking in pagan systems.

The following chart, adapted from the author's *Bible Reader's Companion* (Chariot-Victor) summarizes different kinds of sacrifice called for in Mosaic Law. In addition to the sacrifices offered by individuals, the priests also offered daily sacrifices and special sacrifices during the religious holidays (Numbers 28–29).

Sacrifices Brought by Individual Israelites

Name	Contents	Practice	Significance
Burnt sacrifice Leviticus 1; 6:8–13	Bull, ram, goat, male dove or pigeon—without defect.	Offerer lays hands on the sacrifice's head, kills it, cuts it up, and washes the pieces. The priest pours the blood on the altar, burns the body.	The sacrifice is voluntary and indicates complete surrender to God.
Grain offering Leviticus 2; 6:14–23	Grain, flour, or bread, with olive oil. No yeast must be present.	The food is prepared by the offerer. The priest burns a handful. He keeps the rest to eat.	The sacrifice is voluntary and accompanies most burnt offerings. It symbolizes devotion to God.

Sacrifices Brought by Individual Israelites (cont'd)

Name	Contents	Practice	Significance
Peace offering Leviticus 3; 7:11–36	Any unblemished clean animal from herd or flock.	Offerer lays hands on the head of the sacrifice. He kills it. The priest throws the blood on the altar. Part of the meat is eaten by the offerer and his family.	The meal eaten after this voluntary offering symbolizes fellowship with God and expresses thanks for His blessings.
Sin offering Leviticus 4; 5:13; 6:24–30; 12:6–8; 14:12–14	The animal sacrificed depends on status and position. The very poor may offer fine grain.	Offerer lays hands on the head of the sacrifice. He kills it. The priest pours the blood on the altar. The best of the meat is burned. The priest gets the rest.	This offering is for sin or ritual uncleanness. The hands on the head signify the union of the offerer with the sacrifice, that the animal's death is in place of his own.
Guilt offering Leviticus 5:14–6:7; 7:1–6; 14:12–18	A valuable lamb or ram without defect.	Offerer makes restitution to the person harmed first. He then lays hands on head, kills the animal. Priest pours the blood on ground. Best parts burned; rest for priest.	This sacrifice was required when an Israelite violated another's rights, and when healed of an uncleaness.

go to

only unintentional sins
Leviticus 4:1, 13, 22; 5:1, 15, 17

The Sacrifice of the Day of Atonement

LEVITICUS 16:30 *For on that day the priest shall make atonement for you, to cleanse you, that you may be clean from all your sins before the LORD. (NKJV)*

A unique thing about the sacrifices brought by individuals was that they only cleansed the worshipper <u>from unintentional sins</u>. There was no access through these sacrifices to forgiveness for knowing and willful sins. Only the sacrifice that was offered by the high priest on the Day of Atonement made Israelites "clean from all your sins before the LORD."

key point

expiation
covering of the sin,
cleansing,
restoration

what others say

Allen P. Ross

Sacrifices brought **expiation**. Every animal sacrifice had some sanctifying function because of the blood (Lev. 17:11). But some sacrifices were specifically legislated for those times that the need for expiation was more acutely felt. When people became defiled in one way or another, they needed to find cleansing and consecration for readmission into the presence of God. And when people sinned, they needed to renew the benefits of God's grace. Thus, people needing purification were able to bring specific sacrifices to maintain their covenantal relationship with God. In expiatory sacrifices no incense was added because these were not times of joy but times of spiritual need. And no covenantal meal was involved since union with God had been interrupted. The blood of these sacrifices was put to special use—atonement.[3]

To Find Out More About Sacrifices in the Old Testament, Read . . .

Bible Reference	About Sacrifices
Leviticus 1	Burnt Sacrifice
Leviticus 2	Grain Offerings
Leviticus 3	Peace Offerings
Leviticus 4	Sin Offerings
Leviticus 5	Guilt Offerings
Leviticus 16	The Sacrifice of the Day of Atonement
Numbers 28	National Sacrifices
Numbers 29	National Sacrifices

Follow My Instructions About the Calendar

key point

The *torah* of Moses departed from patterns found in other cultures in the design of a calendar that governed Israelite worship. Every seventh day was set aside as a day of rest. The Romans might have a ten-day week, but the tenth day was hardly a day of rest. In addition a number of annual festivals celebrated historic events. The week set aside in preparation for Passover recalled the miracles Yahweh performed in releasing His people from their bondage in Egypt (Exodus 12). Other festivals reminded the Israelites of God's goodness in the past and in their present.

While other peoples held religious festivals, the nature and the function of Israel's festivals further set Israel apart, and called God's people to trust and rely on Him fully.

In a totally unique invention, God gave the people and the land rest each seventh year, during which time no crops were to be planted (Leviticus 25:2–7). And every fiftieth year, the Jubilee, the ancestral lands of each family were to be restored (Leviticus 25:8–38).

To Find Out More About Israel's Calendar, Read . . .

Bible Reference	About Israel's Calendar
Exodus 12	Passover
Leviticus 23	Religious Festivals
Leviticus 24	Daily Worship
Leviticus 25	Year of Jubilee
Numbers 9	Passover
Numbers 28	Offerings at Religious Festivals
Numbers 29	Offerings at Religious Festivals
Deuteronomy 16	Concerning Festivals

The Sum of the Parts

HEBREWS 7:12 *For the priesthood being changed, of necessity there is also a change of the law.* (NKJV)

In the book of Hebrews the writer points out that Jesus is the Christian's High Priest. But Jesus came from the tribe of Judah, not the tribe of Levi. This involved a radical change in the priesthood, and the writer of Hebrews argues that such a change means "of necessity there is also a change of the law."

The reason is that Old Testament *torah* is a *unified system*, not a construction of isolated parts. Every element is linked to every other element.

The Law established do's and don'ts. When a person violated one of God's moral or even ritual rulings, he sinned. That sin created a barrier between the sinner and a holy God. The remedy was to remove the barrier. Violations of ritual do's and don'ts might be removed by time and washing with water, although many ritual violations required blood sacrifice. But only blood sacrifice could cover a worshipper's failure to be holy, even if that failure was uninten-

the one sacrifice
Leviticus 16:29–34

God appointed Jesus
Hebrews 7:17–22

tional. So the Law had to incorporate sacrifice. And the Law had to establish a priesthood to offer those sacrifices, and especially a high priest who could offer <u>the one sacrifice</u> that covered the past year's accumulated sins. The Law also had to provide a place where those sacrifices could be offered and humans could approach God to worship and to pray. And that place had to accurately reflect spiritual realities in its construction and furnishing.

Again and again we see how tightly every aspect of Yahweh's instructions to Moses are woven together to fashion a whole that is far more than the sum of its individual parts.

Perhaps the closest analogy is our solar system. Each of the planets rotates on its own orbit around our sun. Balanced centrifugal and gravitational forces maintain the delicate balance. If even one of the planets that make up our solar system were to be removed, the balance would be destroyed. Planet after planet would either plunge into the sun or wander off into empty space.

Just as the solar system can exist only as a balanced whole, so the Law of Moses had to function as a whole. There is no way the *torah* system could be maintained unless each part functioned just as it was designed to function.

That's why the writer of Hebrews says that when <u>God appointed Jesus</u> our High Priest, "of necessity" the *torah* system itself changed, and was done away with!

Not Under Law, but Under Grace

ROMANS 6:14 *For sin shall not have dominion over you, for you are not under law but under grace.* (NKJV)

These words, written by the apostle Paul, tend to confuse and frighten moderns. That's because today when we read "law" we think only of Scripture's moral do's and don'ts. We jump to the conclusion that Paul is implying that the standards of righteousness established in Scripture no longer apply.

key point

We couldn't be further from the truth! What Paul is teaching is that the *law system*, the *torah* of the Old Testament, has been replaced by a *grace system*. We no longer relate to God through the system established in the Old Testament. We relate to God through the new system established by Jesus's death, resurrection, and continuing presence in heaven at the very throne of God.

The Law as a System

Each element in the Law—the whole *torah*, not just its do's and don'ts—had a specific function:

- The do's and don'ts established external standards of right and wrong for God's people.

- The sacrifices provided a temporary covering for the sins God's people committed, giving them access to God for prayer and worship.

- The priest mediated between humans and God, offering the sacrifices that provided temporary covering, and teaching God's rules for holy living.

- The Tabernacle symbolized God's presence, and its furnishings taught critical truths about relationship with God.

In saying we "are not under law but under grace" (Romans 6:14 NKJV), the apostle Paul is simply saying that *this entire system* has been replaced by a *grace system*.

to bring to perfec-
tion, to complete its
mission of reuniting
human beings with
God

Why Get Rid of Old Testament Law?

HEBREWS 7:18–19 *On the one hand there is an annulling of the former commandment because of its weakness and unprofitableness, for the law made nothing **perfect**; on the other hand, there is the bringing in of a better hope, through which we draw near to God. (NKJV)*

What the writer of Hebrews is saying is that God canceled the Law (remember, "Law" is the whole *torah* system, not standards of right and wrong) simply because the Law didn't *work*! The Law was unable to provide a salvation that fully reunited sinful human beings with a holy God.

key point

The apostle Paul teaches that "what the law could not do . . . God did by sending His own Son" (Romans 8:3 NKJV). The Law system didn't work. So Jesus stepped in to do for us what no human being could do for himself.

Comparing Law and Grace

When we compare the law and grace systems, we note something important. Each system deals with the *same issues*. They just deal with them in different ways.

- *Both are concerned with right and wrong.* Grace is just as concerned with righteousness as Law is. The difference is that Law is external. It provides us with the standards, but it has no power to enable us to do what we know is right. Grace, on the other hand, reaches into the human heart and provides an <u>inner transformation</u>, enabling us to actually live good and righteous lives.

- *Both rely on priests as mediators.* But the priests who function under Law died and were replaced. We now have Jesus as our High Priest, and because Jesus "continues forever," He is "able to save to the uttermost those who come to God through Him, since He always lives to make intercession for them" (Hebrews 7:24–25 NKJV).

- *Both deal with sin by blood sacrifice.* But the animal sacrifices of the Law provided only a temporary covering. Jesus's blood provides full and complete forgiveness for believers, both believers of <u>the Old Testament era</u> and our own. (Hebrews 9:14; Ephesians 1:7).

- *Both provide access to God for prayer and worship.* The Law provided limited access to God, for Old Testament believers were prevented from entering His presence by the veil that hung between the outer and inner rooms of the Tabernacle. Today, through Jesus, we are invited into the very <u>throne room of God</u>, where we are guaranteed that He will hear our prayers.

In Old Testament law, we have patterns and shadows that represent spiritual realities. In Christ we have the realities themselves. We are no longer under Law because a new system, grace, has replaced the law system that was always <u>intended to be temporary</u> and left in place only until the Savior arrived.

inner transformation
Hebrews 8:9–10;
Romans 8:3–4

the Old Testament era
Hebrews 9:15;
Romans 3:24–25

throne room of God
Hebrews 4:14–16

intended to be temporary
Hebrews 8:7–9;
Galatians 3:15–25

<u>Then Why the Law?</u>

The Law of Moses conferred a number of blessings on the people of Israel. It served as a revelation of the nature of Yahweh, who was shown to be righteous and good, and who expected goodness from His people.

The Law of Moses also defined the consequences of right and wrong behavior. For those generations of Israelites who remained faithful to the Lord and sought to live by His law, there were multiplied blessings (Deuteronomy 28:1–14). For generations who turned from Yahweh to idols, there were terrible punishments and troubles that were intended to turn God's people back to Him (Deuteronomy 28:15–68). This statement of consequences provided a basis for the actions God would take in the future. No generation of Israelites would be able to plead ignorance, either to what God's standards were or the punishments that would follow violation of His law.

And the Law of Moses prepared the way for the Savior. On the Tabernacle stage, the drama of redemption—with its sinners, its priests, its sacrifices, and its access to God in prayer and worship—was acted out again and again. Surely only willful blindness would keep God's people from recognizing their Savior when He came.

Chapter Wrap-Up

- The word translated "law" in English is the Hebrew word *torah*. The basic meaning of *torah* is "instruction."
- All five books of Moses, which contain narrative and instructional elements, are also called *torah*.
- Thus, Mosaic Law is more than standards of right and wrong, or do's and don'ts.
- Additional elements in Mosaic Law include instructions concerning the Tabernacle, the priesthood, sacrifices, a calendar structuring the year, etc.
- The Old Testament religious system, *torah*, or Mosaic Law, was replaced with a new system through and after the death of Jesus. Thus Christians are "not under law, but under grace."

Study Questions

1. Which book of Moses is nearly all narrative?

2. Which book of Moses is nearly all instruction?

3. What three kinds of "do and don't" instructions are found in Moses's *torah*?

4. What other matters are covered in instructions given in Moses's *torah*?

5. What confusion does our translation of *torah* as "law" create?

6. What does Paul mean when he says we are not under law but under grace?

7. How would you answer a person who fears that not being "under law" provides a license to sin?

8. What issues do both law and grace deal with? How do they compare with and differ from each other on these issues?

Chapter 9
On the Road Again

Chapter Highlights:
• Get Ready
• Get Set
• Go!
• Same Old, Same Old
• Rebellion in the Ranks

Let's Get Started

Moses and the Israelites camped beneath Mount Sinai for over a year. God finished giving Moses the *torah* that was to govern His people's lives—the whole *torah*, with its moral and ceremonial do's and don'ts, its Tabernacle, its priesthood, its sacrifices, and its religious holidays.

It's likely that during that year the Lord also revealed the true story of Creation and of Adam and Eve and the Great Flood, events that Moses recorded in the book of Genesis.

With these vital revelations given and the *torah* lifestyle laid out, it was time to get on the road again. After all, it was a relatively short journey from Sinai to the borders of the Promised Land, where Israel's destiny lay.

Get Ready

NUMBERS 1:2–3 *Take a census of all the congregation of the children of Israel, by their families, by their fathers' houses, according to the number of names, every male individually, from twenty years old and above—all who are able to go to war in Israel. (NKJV)*

The Israelites had exited Egypt as an unruly mob. Before they moved on to Canaan, it was necessary for them to get organized. A census of men of military age was taken by **tribe** and **family**. Each tribe was given a **standard** to follow. Each was assigned a place in the <u>marching order</u>, and a place to set up its tents when the people <u>camped</u>.

The Tabernacle rested in the center of the Israelite camp, with the families of the tribe of Levi (the Levites) camped around it. Each of the other tribes was assigned a place to the east, west, north, or south of the Tabernacle. Whenever the Israelites moved, the Levites

go to

standard
Numbers 1:52; 2:2

marching order, camp
Numbers 2:1–34

tribe
Israelite tribes were made of the descendants of the sons of Jacob, later known as Israel.

family
Israelite families were made up of descendants of leading men of the tribes.

standard
an identifying banner, flag

led by Zebulon
Numbers 2:7–9

inspired by God
2 Timothy 3:16;
2 Peter 1:21

took down and transported the Tabernacle, and each tribe then moved out in its turn, <u>led by the tribe of Zebulon</u>.

How Many Thousands?

Numbers 1:46 lists the number of men of military age in each tribe, and gives us a total of 603,550. If we estimate the number of women and children consistent with this number of men, the total number of Israelites who escaped from Egypt would be somewhere between two and six million!

Critics have long argued that this number is totally unrealistic. Archaeologists have estimated that the total population of Egypt in the second millennium BC was only about three million persons. And there is no evidence of a sudden depopulation of the land near any of the suggested dates for the Exodus. Critics have also pointed out that known armies of Moses's time averaged between five and six thousand men. An army of over half a million would easily have overwhelmed any force that might have come against them.

Some have suggested that the problem lies in a misunderstanding by men who copied Moses's original documents. The Hebrew word *elef*, which normally means "thousand," may also mean "units." In Judges, *elef* is rendered "families," but never "thousands." If we assume that early copyists misunderstood the intent here, Numbers 1:37 would not state that the tribe of Benjamin contributed 35,400 men, but that Benjamin consisted of 35 units, which contributed 400 men of military age.

If we apply this to the summary statement in 1:46, where *'alifim* (the plural of *elef*) occurs twice and the copyists apparently added the two numbers together, the text would indicate that the Israelite camp contained 589 units, which contributed a total of 5,550 men of military age.

Aha! Another "Error" in Scripture!

Let's not leap to the conclusion that this theory means Christians must abandon their cherished belief in the reliability of Scripture. The belief that <u>all Scripture is inspired by God</u> and thus without error relates to the original documents as penned by the writer. What is being questioned here is not whether Moses made a mistake in setting down the census numbers. The question is *whether or not later copyists misunderstood Moses's use of the word* elef, and so amended the text to give us a distorted idea of how many Hebrews actually left Egypt.

Such an "error" would not be a mistake in Scripture but a mistake made by those who later copied the original documents.

So, How Many?

We can look through all the figures given in the books of Moses and conclude that the alternative numbers are correct. Or we can look through all the figures and conclude that the 603,550 is the right number. The fact is that we don't—and probably never will—know. But that's all right.

Whether the Israelites fled Egypt by the thousands or millions, it took an act of God to win their release. Whether there were thousands or millions on the journey to Sinai, the Lord was able to protect them and to provide the food they needed. Whether thousands or millions were about to set out for the promised land of Canaan, it would take God's active intervention to bring them safely home.

One More Census to Take

NUMBERS 3:14–15 *Then the LORD spoke to Moses in the Wilderness of Sinai, saying: "Number the children of Levi by their fathers' houses, by their families; you shall number every male from a month old and above." (NKJV)*

Every Israelite tribe except that of Levi was included in the first census, which determined the number of men of military age. The Levites were a special case. The Lord claimed members of this tribe

assist priests
Numbers 4

assist in the Temple
1 Chronicles 23–26

age twenty-five
Numbers 8:24

the firstborn of Egypt
Exodus 12:29–30

sanctified
set apart

and set them aside to serve at the Tabernacle and to <u>assist the sons of Aaron</u> who were Israel's priests. Centuries later, when a temple was constructed in the Promised Land, the Levites served God and <u>assisted the priests</u> there.

As a tribe set apart to serve God, the Levites were exempt from military duty. And, unlike men of the other tribes who were considered soldiers at age twenty, the Levites began to serve at the Tabernacle when they reached <u>age twenty-five</u>, and retired when they reached age fifty.

When the male Levites a month of age and older had been counted, Moses counted the number of firstborn sons who had been spared when the Lord struck <u>the firstborn of Egypt</u>. The numbers nearly matched and the Lord explained, "I Myself have taken the Levities from among the children of Israel instead of every firstborn . . . because all the firstborn are Mine. On the day that I struck all the firstborn in the land of Egypt, I **sanctified** to Myself all the firstborn in Israel" (Numbers 3:12–13 NKJV).

Moses then assigned each Levite family duties to perform at the Tabernacle and its own place to set up tents when the Israelites camped (Numbers 3:14–4:49).

With the census taken, and each tribe and family assigned its own place in camp and on the road, the Israelites were nearly ready to move out.

Get Set

Under God's direction, Moses had taken the practical steps necessary to organize the Israelites for their journey to Canaan. Now God instructs Moses on even more significant preparations. Yes, organization was important. But even more important was preparation of the hearts of God's people.

While some of the instructions given in chapters 5 through 9 of Numbers may seem strange, each is related to the heart preparation of the people of God.

Themes in Numbers 5–9

Theme	Where You Can Find It
Prepare by getting right with God.	Numbers 5:1-10
Prepare by sensing the jealousy of God.	Numbers 5:11-31
Prepare by consecrating yourself totally to the Lord.	Numbers 6:1-21
Prepare by focusing on worship.	Numbers 7:1–8:26
Prepare by recalling what God has done for you.	Numbers 9:1-14

leper
a person with an infectious skin disease

Prepare by Getting Right with God

NUMBERS 5:1–2 *And the LORD spoke to Moses, saying: "Command the children of Israel that they put out of the camp every **leper**, everyone who has a discharge, and whoever becomes defiled by a corpse." (NKJV)*

When this had been done, the Lord told Moses that those who had committed sins against others must now make restitution and offer the required sacrifices (5:6–8). Only when the camp was ritually cleansed and each individual had dealt with sins that created barriers between himself and others and himself and the Lord would the Israelites be ready to set out on their journey.

what others say

Preston A. Taylor

God gave a command to Moses to "put out of the camp every leper, everyone with an issue, and whosoever is defiled by the dead." A person in any of those categories became ceremonially unclean. Hence, anyone suffering from any of those types of sin was expelled from Israel's camp. Since God dwells in the midst of His people, we need to keep sin out of our lives. God is holy. He does not allow sin in His presence . . . Since God is holy, He wants His people to be holy and put away sin.[2]

However well designed any Christian organization may be, it can only reach its goals if its members are right with God.

Prepare by Sensing the Jealousy of God

NUMBERS 5:11–12, 14 *And the LORD spoke to Moses, saying, "Speak to the children of Israel, and say to them: . . . If the spirit of jealousy comes upon him and he becomes jealous of his wife . . ."' (NKJV)*

go to

bring them back
Hosea 11:14

The passage recognizes that a man may be jealous of a perfectly innocent wife as well as of one who has "defiled herself." In either case, the husband was to bring his wife to a priest with an offering. The priest then prepared a drink of water containing dust from the Tabernacle floor. After writing down the penalty for unfaithfulness, the priest scraped the ink into the water too, and the woman drank it. If she was innocent, nothing would happen to her; but if she was guilty, "her belly will swell [and] her thigh will rot" (5:27 NKJV).

It seems strange to find these instructions inserted here . . . until we remember that the Lord has told Moses, "The LORD, whose name is Jealous, is a jealous God" (Exodus 34:14 NKJV). God is fiercely committed to His people. They, in turn, must be just as committed to Him. While human jealousy necessarily distorts our understanding of God's jealousy, we at least realize that a jealous husband cares that his wife is faithful. He is far from indifferent! An innocent wife should not have to bear the burden of her husband's suspicions, nor should the husband have to bear the torment of uncertainty. Knowing the truth might hurt, but it would hurt less than the doubt and uncertainty.

If Israel should be unfaithful to the Lord it would hurt Him too. But the Lord knows the truth, and knows how to deal with His straying people. Israel would suffer consequences for unfaithfulness, but God would continue to care. In the end He would bring them back to Himself.

By giving Israel instructions on how to deal with jealousy, the Lord reminded His people how intensely He cares for His own. This knowledge was important for them, for the opposite of jealousy is indifference. Should God ever become indifferent to us, we truly would be doomed.

something to ponder

what others say

Christopher J. H. Wright

The fire of Yahweh as a jealous God is the fire of an exclusive commitment to the people that demands an exclusive commitment in return . . . It was the fire of God's jealousy that protected the strength of God's mercy and covenant faithfulness to this people.[3]

Prepare by Consecrating Yourself Totally to the Lord

NUMBERS 6:1–2 *Then the LORD spoke to Moses, saying, "Speak to the children of Israel, and say to them: 'When either a man or woman consecrates an offering to take the vow of a Nazirite, to separate himself to the LORD . . .'" (NKJV)*

Every Israelite as a member of the chosen people was considered set apart as God's own. But here provision is made for those who wish to dedicate themselves even more completely to the Lord. Such a person could go to a priest with an offering and commit to live as a Nazirite for a specified period of time.

During the days of his or her vow, the Nazirite drank or ate nothing that came from the grapevine, and let his or her hair grow. If a near relative died, the Nazirite wasn't to go near the body or otherwise make himself ritually unclean. When the vow was fulfilled, the Nazirite brought an animal sacrifice and specified offerings plus gave freewill offerings at the Tabernacle. He also shaved his head and burned the hair on the altar.

Again, it seems a strange place to introduce the Nazirite vow . . . until we realize these instructions constitute an invitation to the Israelites to voluntarily draw nearer to the Lord. Those about to undertake the journey to Canaan would need to be wholly committed to Him.

Get Ready to Be Blessed!

NUMBERS 6:22–23 *And the LORD spoke to Moses, saying: "Speak to Aaron and his sons, saying, 'This is the way you shall bless the children of Israel.'" (NKJV)*

People who have gotten right with God, who have acknowledged the fierce love God has for them, and who have consecrated themselves wholly to the Lord, truly can expect His blessing. And so at this point the Lord instructs the priests on how they are to bless the people.

The blessing that follows gives us insight into what constituted God's best for His Old Testament people.

go to

animal offerings
Numbers 7:15–17

presented to the Lord
Numbers 8:21

Passover
Exodus 12

the First Temple Period
from about 963 BC to 586 BC

BCE
Before Common Era, used by some in place of BC

NUMBERS 6:24–26
The LORD bless you and keep you;
The LORD make His face shine upon you,
And be gracious to you;
The LORD lift up His countenance upon you,
And give you peace. (NKJV)

Today we'd probably say, "May God love you and fill you with His peace."

> **what others say**
>
> **Dennis T. Olson**
>
> The importance of the Aaronic or priestly blessing in ancient Israel has been confirmed by recent archaeological findings from **the First Temple period** in Jerusalem. Two silver cylinders were discovered in burial caves dating from 600 **BCE**; the blessing from Numbers 6 was written on the two silver scrolls. These are the earliest known fragments of any biblical texts . . . This archaeological discovery confirms the antiquity and prominence of the priestly blessing from Numbers 6 in the religious life of Israel.[4]

Prepare by Focusing on Worship

NUMBERS 7:1 *Now it came to pass, when Moses had finished setting up the tabernacle, that he anointed it and consecrated it and all its furnishings . . . (NKJV)*

Now the whole community gathered around the Tabernacle for an extended time of worship. Each day for twelve days a leader from one of the twelve tribes brought silver and gold, with animals for the various offerings. After this the Levites were ceremonially cleansed by shaving the whole bodies and sprinkling with water, and the sacrifice of young bulls as sin offerings. The Levites were officially presented to the Lord to serve at the Tabernacle.

Prepare by Recalling What God Has Done for You

NUMBERS 9:1–2 *Now the LORD spoke to Moses in the Wilderness of Sinai, in the first month of the second year after they had come out of the land of Egypt, saying: "Let the children of Israel keep the Passover at its appointed time." (NKJV)*

This would be the first Passover celebrated outside of Egypt, and within days of its celebration the people would set out for Canaan.

We've seen that Passover was one the *zikkaron* events that annually called God's people to reexperience what the Lord did for His people. How significant this first Passover outside of Egypt must have been, as the Israelites recalled their still-vivid memories of the devastating miracles that God worked to free them from slavery!

Remembering what God has done for us is one of the best ways to prepare for fresh challenges. Surely the God who has delivered will continue to work on our behalf.

within days
Numbers 9:11;
10:11

---

what others say

James Philip

Keeping the Passover was a reminder to Israel of the standard under which they were to advance, and the principle by which they were to walk. Their lives were to be rightly related to the redemption that God had wrought. In the New Testament this speaks to us in the language of Christ: "If anyone desires to come after Me, let him deny himself, and take up his cross, and follow Me" (Matt. 16:24).[5]

Go!

NUMBERS 10:11–12 *Now it came to pass on the twentieth day of the second month, in the second year, that the cloud was taken up from above the tabernacle of the Testimony. And the children of Israel set out . . . (NKJV)*

God had done all that He could to prepare the Israelites for their journey. The camp had been organized, and Moses had directed activities intended to prepare the people spiritually.

Even more significantly, the Lord Himself would visibly lead His people. Moses describes the daily schedule:

NUMBERS 9:15–22 *Now on the day that the tabernacle was raised up, the cloud covered the tabernacle, the tent of the Testimony; from evening until morning it was above the tabernacle like the appearance of fire. So it was always: the cloud covered it by day, and the appearance of fire by night. Whenever the cloud was taken up from above the tabernacle, after that the children of Israel would journey; and in the place where the cloud settled, there the children of Israel would pitch their tents.*

At the command of the LORD the children of Israel would journey, and at the command of the LORD they would camp; as long as the cloud stayed above the tabernacle they remained encamped . . . Whether it was two days, a month, or a year that the cloud remained above the tabernacle, the children of Israel would remain encamped and not journey; but when it was taken up, they would journey. (NKJV)

key point

There was not, could not possibly be, any question of the Lord's active presence with His people on their journey, for the fiery-cloudy pillar led them. Nor could there be any question that God Himself was directing their path. The Israelites were on the road again. And God was with them.

Same Old, Same Old

Moses provides accounts of two journeys. The first, described in Exodus 15–18, catalogs events on the trip from the Red Sea to Mount Sinai. The second, described in Numbers 10 and following, catalogs events on the journey from Mount Sinai toward Canaan, the land promised to Abraham's descendants. Events that took place on these two journeys are eerily similar, yet with major differences.

Complaints, Complaints

EXODUS 15:24 *And the people complained against Moses . . . (NKJV)*

Three days after leaving the Red Sea the people complain when they find no drinkable water (Exodus 15:22–23). Even though they are led by the fiery-cloudy pillar that marks God's presence, they direct their complaints "against Moses" (Exodus 15:24). Moses goes to the Lord, who shows him how to sweeten the waters. God then encourages the Israelites to listen to the Lord and do what's right in His eyes (Exodus 15:26–27).

Three days after leaving Sinai, even though they are again led by the fiery-cloudy pillar, the people again complain (Numbers 11:1). This time there is no apparent cause. And this time their Lord's anger is aroused, so that "the fire of the LORD burned among them" (Numbers 11:1 NKJV). Now the Israelites cry out "to Moses." Moses prays, and the fire is quenched (Numbers 11:2).

It's clear that the Israelites have experienced no change of heart. Even though they've made <u>a commitment</u> to worship and obey the Lord, and even though time was given before leaving Sinai for <u>spiritual preparation</u>, the people seem just as negative and rebellious as ever. God has provided opportunities for a change of heart, but the people clearly haven't taken advantage of them.

There is, however, a significant change in God's response to the Israelites. No longer is their mutinous attitude overlooked. Instead, when the people complain, "the fire of the LORD" burns among them.

go to

a commitment
Exodus 24:3

spiritual preparation
Numbers 5–9

Talk About Difficult Kids!

It's fascinating to note that Scripture depicts the Exodus era as Israel's childhood. Speaking through the prophet Hosea, the Lord laments these early years:

HOSEA 11:1–4
When Israel was a child, I loved him,
And out of Egypt I called My son . . .
They sacrificed to the Baals,
And burned incense to carved images.

I taught Ephraim to walk,
Taking them by their arms;
But they did not know that I healed them.
I drew them with gentle cords,
With bands of love,
And I was to them as those who take the yoke from their neck.
I stooped and fed them. (NKJV)

prophecy

go to

providing quail
Exodus 10:13;
Numbers 11:31

manna
a food left with each
morning's dew that
Scripture describes
as "like white corian-
der seed, and the
taste of it was like
wafers made with
honey" (Exodus
16:31 NKJV)

All this God did for His people, and they responded with endless complaints and hardened defiant insubordination.

Now, as any father who loves an unruly child, God set out to discipline and correct His children. The boundaries of right and wrong behavior had been established, and would be enforced. Only if the Israelites learned to trust God and respond to His guidance would they be able to experience the blessings God had promised their forefathers.

From Sinai onward we'll observe God's commitment to discipline the unruly and rebellious. Finally, in the next generation, we'll see the results of the painful, but necessary, disciplining of God's people.

What, Manna Again?

EXODUS 16:2 *Then the whole congregation of the children of Israel complained against Moses and Aaron in the wilderness.* *(NKJV)*

Shortly after the first incident on the road from the Red Sea to Mount Sinai the Israelites ran out of food. Again they directed their complaint against Moses, this time accusing him of having "brought us out into this wilderness to kill this whole assembly with hunger" (Exodus 16:3 NKJV). The Lord told Moses to promise the Israelites both bread (Exodus 16:4–6) and meat (Exodus 16:12–13). From that day onward the Lord had faithfully supplied His people with the **manna**.

Not long after the first incident on the road from Sinai to Canaan the Israelites again complain about food. This time the reason isn't hunger. It's craving for something more than the manna God has been supplying. They fanaticize over the fish and vegetables they ate in Egypt. Soon everyone is "weeping . . . everyone at the door of his tent," and complaining, "Who will give us meat to eat?" (Numbers 11:10, 4 NKJV).

This ingratitude arouses the anger of the Lord, and the text tells us that "Moses also was displeased" (Numbers 11:10 NKJV).

In each case, God responds by providing quail for the Israelites to eat. But this time the quail come with a plague! "While the meat was still between their teeth, before it was chewed, the wrath of the LORD was aroused against the people, and the LORD struck the people with a very great plague" (Numbers 11:33 NKJV). From Sinai on, God's grace will be expressed in discipline.

Before Sinai God had not disciplined Israel. The result had been <u>increasing rebelliousness</u>. After Sinai God disciplines His people for *the same actions that He had overlooked earlier*. Why the difference?

Check at That Intersection!

Suppose on Monday you come to a place where two roads cross. Without slowing down or even looking you speed on through the intersection. That's foolish, because there might be cars approaching the same intersection on the other road.

On Tuesday you approach the same intersection. But overnight, stop signs have been put up at each corner. Without slowing down, you speed on through the intersection. What you did Tuesday is still foolish. But now it's also against the law, and you can be arrested.

At Sinai, God spelled out what He expected of His people and they agreed to obey Him. What Israel did on the road to Sinai was foolish and harmful. What Israel did on the road *after* Sinai was foolish and harmful, but now it was also <u>breaking the law</u>! And God disciplines lawbreakers.

It's important in thinking about this analogy to remember that the reason the government puts up stop signs and enforces driving laws is for the benefit of drivers. In the same way, when God disciplined the Israelites it was for the benefit of the whole people. Only if Israel learned to trust God and to obey Him could the people experience the good things God had prepared for them.

When God **disciplines** us it's with the same intent. He is seeking to teach us to trust and obey Him, that we might experience His best. Like Israel, we can choose to respond to God's discipline or we can harden our hearts against Him. As we go on in our study we'll discover the choice the Israelites made, and the consequences of that choice.

Kill Me Now!

NUMBERS 11:11, 15 *So Moses said to the LORD, "Why have You afflicted Your servant? And why have I not found favor in*

increasing rebelliousness
Exodus 15:24; 16:3, 7; 17:2, 4

breaking the law
1 John 3:4

disciplines
corrects, punishes, instructs

to know God better
Exodus 33:13

Your sight, that You have laid the burden of all these people on me? . . . If You treat me like this, please kill me here and now—if I have found favor in Your sight—and do not let me see my wretchedness!" (NKJV)

The complaints of God's disgruntled people were too much for Moses. The event that triggered God's anger "displeased" Moses, and triggered his own feelings of frustration. It was just too much. "I am not able to bear all these people alone, because the burden is too heavy for me" (Numbers 11:14 NKJV).

We can empathize with Moses. I suspect most of us have times we feel so overwhelmed that we dread facing another day. Moses's "I can't take it anymore" response echoes in many a believer's heart.

Two things are striking about God's response to Moses. First, the Lord doesn't criticize Moses, either for feeling the way he does or for speaking out so honestly. Second, God responds in an utterly practical way: by relieving Moses of some of his burden.

Telling It Like It Is

Some are quick to criticize Moses for his outburst. It's hardly "spiritual" enough for them. Shouldn't Moses take comfort in the fact that God is with him? What does he mean, he bears the burden of the Israelites "alone"? Don't Moses's feelings reveal he's not trusting God enough?

The fact is that Moses does and has been trusting God. Not only that, he's been seeking to obey God and <u>to know Him better</u>. But Moses is a human being, and we humans are imperfect at best. Moses experiences stress just as every human does. Moses can become discouraged, just as every human will. Events can even push Moses near to despair, as events now have. *What is special about Moses is that he trusts God enough to be totally honest with Him.* Moses doesn't pretend.

The self-proclaimed "spiritual" among us pretend that an intimate relationship with God rules out every human emotion. But they aren't being honest with themselves, with others, or with the Lord. Here Moses acknowledges his human frailty and appeals to the Lord for help, a far more spiritual approach to life than that of always wearing a happy face.

A "Spiritual" Solution

Then
Exodus 18:13–27

NUMBERS 11:16 *So the LORD said to Moses: "Gather to Me seventy men of the elders of Israel, whom you know to be the elders of the people and officers over them; bring them to the tabernacle of meeting, that they may stand there with you." (NKJV)*

Moses has shared his feelings of being overwhelmed and of carrying the burden of the Israelites alone. This event too has a parallel in the journey from the Red Sea to Sinai. <u>Then</u> Moses's father-in-law, Jethro, observed Moses acting as a judge to decide issues raised by the Israelites. Jethro warned that both Moses and the people "will surely wear yourselves out" (Exodus 18:18 NKJV). Jethro advised Moses to do something to relieve the burden.

And Jethro had a solution. Moses followed Jethro's advice and organized the people into groups of tens, fifties, one hundreds, and one thousands. The theory was that when an issue couldn't be resolved on one level, it would be taken to the next, with only the most difficult issues being brought to Moses. Moses followed Jethro's advice, but the rest of Scripture suggests that this system didn't work. In later times we see this system applied only in organizing Israel's military units.

In Numbers we see that God had a different solution. In taking the census described in Numbers 1 and 2, and in readying Israel for their journey, the nation was organized by tribes, families, and *elefs* (intra-family units). Apparently Jethro's approach was abandoned as unworkable.

Now, as God responds to ease Moses's burden, He does it not by setting up a new organizational structure but in an entirely different way. He tells Moses to select seventy men who are already **elders of the people** and says, "I will take of the Spirit that is upon you and will put the same upon them; and they shall bear the burden of the people with you, that you may not bear it yourself alone" (Numbers 11:17 NKJV).

What Moses needed was not a better way to organize but the support of those who shared his own love for God and concern for God's people.

elders of the people
leaders of Israel's tribes and families

R. K. Harrison

God did not remove some of the Spirit on Moses and distribute it to the seventy. The Lord gave the seventy the same Spirit, that they might have his same concern for the people and for God's glory.[7]

It's fascinating to me that so many of those who write books on church leadership rush back to Exodus 18 to buttress a hierarchical approach to church structure, never noting that there is no evidence the Exodus 18 system ever worked. How foolish to ignore the God-given solution in Numbers 11 in favor of a solution suggested by Jethro, a mere human, and a recently converted pagan human at that.

What Moses needed was to know that he was not alone; that there were others too who cared. The fact that the seventy prophesied when the Spirit came upon them reassured Moses that he was not alone. The fact that they "never did so again" (Numbers 11:25 NKJV) was protection against the possibility that the Israelites might try to force one or more of the seventy into a role that God intended for Moses alone.

Mentor On, Moses!

Moses was far from perfect. But that is one of the reasons why Moses is such a capable mentor for you and me. He was a very human individual who nevertheless deeply desired and struggled to maintain an intimate, growing relationship with God.

As the incident discussed above reminds us, one aspect of maintaining a close relationship with the Lord is being totally honest with Him, expressing our feelings and needs in the expectation that God cares for us, and that He will respond to meet our needs.

apply it

From this incident, and from Moses, we learn that a healthy relationship with God is promoted by a free and honest expression of our feelings and our needs to the Lord.

Rebellion in the Ranks

go to

prophetess and worship leader
Exodus 15:20

commissioned him
Exodus 3:7–10

NUMBERS 12:1–2 *Then Miriam and Aaron spoke against Moses because of the Ethiopian woman whom he had married . . . So they said, "Has the LORD indeed spoken only through Moses? Has He not spoken through us also?" And the LORD heard it.* (NKJV)

If Moses had been an arrogant man, one who prided himself on leading Israel, we might understand the attempts by Moses's brother and sister, Aaron and Miriam, to push their way into the limelight. But, as the next verse notes, Moses was "very humble, more than all men who were on the face of the earth" (Numbers 12:3 NKJV).

Moses had never shown any envy of Aaron's exaltation as Israel's high priest. He had apparently fully approved of Miriam's gifting as a prophetess and as women's worship leader. It's clear from the only criticism that the brother and sister could muster—that Moses had married an Ethiopian woman—that the two could find no real flaw in Moses's character or in his leadership. What also comes through clearly is that Aaron and Miriam envied their brother his position and whatever respect the people had for him. They wanted Moses to move over so they could climb up beside him and be acknowledged as his equal, if not his superior.

It's fascinating that this is the same attitude displayed by a being identified in Isaiah 14 as "Lucifer, son of the morning." Like Aaron and Miriam, this being, whom many Bible scholars believe is none other than Satan, wasn't satisfied with the high position God had given him. Instead he decided, "I will ascend into heaven, I will exalt my throne above the stars of God" (Isaiah 14:12–13 NKJV).

something to ponder

If Bible scholars are correct in identifying Lucifer as Satan, the passage describes the entry of sin into the material and spiritual universe. And it identifies the root of sin as a creature's desire to assert his own will over the will of the Creator.

God had chosen Moses and commissioned him to deliver Israel. Aaron and Miriam had their own roles to play in the grand deliverance. But they had not been chosen as Israel's deliverer or as Israel's lawgiver.

Humble's the Word

NUMBERS 12:3 *Now the man Moses was very humble. (NKJV)*

In this passage, Moses stands in stark contrast to his brother and sister. They are motivated by greed for a higher position; by an unseemly passion to be honored by men. Their insatiability drives them to attack Moses, apparently believing that if they can cut him down it will raise their own standing with the people.

What a contrast with Moses, who never asked for the position he was given, and who has just begged the Lord to let him die because leadership is such a burden. It's no wonder that someone—possibly a scribe who later copied Moses's words—interjected the comment on Moses's humility. Anyone who understands that leadership is serving others, not a chance to shine brighter than others, will discover that caring deeply for others *is* a burden, and will be humbled by the role God has given him or her.

key point

The concept of humility is an important one in the Bible. In the Old Testament, the word has both positive and strongly negative connotations. Hebrew words linked with humility suggest being bowed down or oppressed. In passages where the words are used negatively, humility tends to be viewed as submission; as a loss of strength or power or reputation, stripped from the individual by another. In passages where the word is used positively, as here, the submission is self-chosen.

A passage that helps us see the positive aspect of humility is described in the reaction of King Josiah: A lost book of the Law was found, and the king realized how far God's people had strayed from following the Lord. God told the distraught ruler, "'Because your heart was tender, and you humbled yourself before the LORD when you heard what I spoke against this place and against its inhabitants . . . and you tore your clothes and wept before Me, I also have heard you,' says the LORD" (2 Kings 22:19 NKJV).

A truly humble person has a tender heart that eagerly responds to God's Word. A humble person gladly *chooses* to submit to God's will. Neither Miriam nor Aaron was satisfied with the place God had chosen for them, and demanded more. Because they were unwilling to submit to God's will, the Lord would humble them in the sight of all the people.

God Steps In

go to

ritually unclean
Leviticus 13

NUMBERS 12:4 *Suddenly the* LORD *said to Moses, Aaron, and Miriam, "Come out, you three, to the tabernacle of meeting!" So the three came out. (NKJV)*

The first thing the Lord did was to confirm the special relationship that He had with Moses. God might speak to prophets in visions and dreams, but God spoke to Moses "face to face, even plainly." Aaron and Miriam knew this, and yet dared to "speak against My servant Moses" (Numbers 12:8 NKJV).

After this rebuke the Lord withdrew . . . and "Miriam became leprous, as white as snow" (Numbers 12:10 NKJV). Stunned and horrified, Aaron begged Moses to pray for Miriam's healing. God did heal her leprosy, but not until she had been forced to live outside the camp for seven days.

For seven days the entire people waited, with everyone fully aware of Miriam's condition. How ashamed Miriam must have felt as she finally reentered the Israelite camp. It may well be that the apostle James was thinking of this incident as he quoted Proverbs 3:34, "God resists the proud, but gives grace to the humble," and went on to advise, "Humble yourselves in the sight of the Lord, and He will lift you up" (James 4:6, 10 NKJV).

Moses and his siblings remind us of the importance of cheerfully submitting to the will of God, rather than greedily demanding something He does not intend for us. A truly healthy relationship with God is marked by the humble submission of our will to His, which introduces one more guideline.

apply it

A healthy relationship with God is marked by a humble and selfless submission of our will to His.

Sexist? Not Really?

Some have gone so far as to accuse Scripture of sexism here because Miriam was struck with leprosy and Aaron was not. The fact is that their sex had nothing to do with it. Aaron was Israel's high priest. Leprosy would have made Aaron <u>ritually unclean</u>, and a high priest who was defiled by ritual uncleanness could not serve

(Leviticus 21). If Aaron had been struck with leprosy, Israel would have had no high priest to represent the people before the Lord or to offer the sacrifice of the Day of Atonement. This was the reason, and the only reason, that Aaron was spared while Miriam was not.

<u>Chapter Wrap-Up</u>

- The Israelites' camp is organized for traveling from Sinai to the Promised Land.

- Teachings and events provide opportunities for the Israelites' spiritual preparation for the journey.

- The Israelites set out with God guiding by the pillar of cloud and fire that has accompanied them since Egypt.

- Immediately the Israelites begin complaining, and God responds by disciplining them. As they continue to complain, God continues to discipline.

- Moses appeals to the Lord for help with bearing his burden. The Lord gives His Spirit to seventy elders of the people.

- Aaron and Miriam challenge Moses's leadership, and are rebuked by the Lord.

Study Questions

1. What options are there for explaining the large numbers of Israelites in the first census?

2. How were the Israelites organized for travel and for camping?

3. Why weren't the Levites numbered in the initial census?

4. What opportunities did God provide for spiritual preparation of the Israelites' hearts?

5. In what way(s) were the Israelites' reactions on the journey from Sinai like their reactions on the journey to Sinai from the Red Sea?

6. In what way(s) were God's responses to the Israelites' ingratitude different on the journey from Sinai from His responses to similar situations on the journey to Sinai from the Red Sea?

7. Compare and contrast Aaron and Miriam with Moses.

Chapter 10
The Choice

Let's Get Started

It was only some two hundred miles from Mount Sinai to the southern tip of Canaan. Nearing the Promised Land, the Israelites camped outside its borders, at Kadesh-Barnea in the wilderness of Paran. From this staging area it would be easy to strike at the Canaanites and other peoples inhabiting the land God promised to give to Abraham's descendants.

Moses sent out scouts, selecting one from each tribe, to look over the land the Israelites were about to invade. They all returned safely. But forty more wilderness years would pass before God's people actually began the conquest.

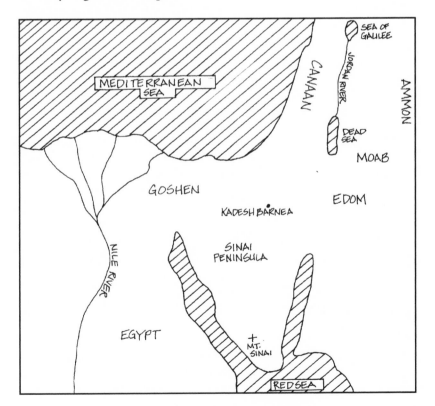

The Exodus Map

strongholds
fortified cities

But We *See* the Giants

NUMBERS 13:1–2 *And the LORD spoke to Moses, saying, "Send men to spy out the land of Canaan, which I am giving to the children of Israel; from each tribe of their fathers you shall send a man, every one a leader among them." (NKJV)*

God's motive in sending men into Canaan ahead of the people is suggested in the criteria Moses was to use to select them. Each one was to be a leader in one of the twelve tribes. These were men of influence, men whose opinions counted.

The twelve were to spend forty days traveling through the land, with the specific assignment to "see what the land is like: whether the people who dwell in it are strong or weak, few or many; whether the land they dwell in is good or bad; whether the cities they inhabit are like camps or **strongholds**; whether the land is rich or poor; and whether there are forests there or not" (Numbers 13:18–20 NKJV).

In today's business world we'd call their mission one of risk/benefit assessment. They were to look things over and balance the benefits of taking over the land against the risk of facing the Canaanites in battle. However, the true purpose of the mission was not for the Israelite leaders to assess the land, but for the Lord to assess the people's faith!

A Mixed Report

NUMBERS 13:27–28 *We went to the land where you sent us. It truly flows with milk and honey . . . Nevertheless the people who dwell in the land are strong. (NKJV)*

A traveler on a train ride in 1917 looked out the widow at the dry, barren landscape of the land then called Palestine and ridiculed Scripture's description of Canaan as a land "which flows with milk and honey" (Numbers 14:8 NKJV). Mile after mile, all that could be seen was dry desert, broken only by sparse bushes and the occasional Bedouin caring for a flock of scraggly sheep. But that was before hundreds of thousands of Jews returned to their ancient homeland, drilled wells to irrigate the fields, and planted forests to help hold the water that fell now and then from the sky. Today, wherever the land has been irrigated, the desert produces abundant crops and the landscape greens.

Studies of climate have shown that in the middle of the second millennium BC, Canaan was a fertile land indeed. Forests covered the now denuded hills; streams ran in fertile valleys and produced the kind of rich crops described in Numbers 13. In the day when the Israelite spies even brought back samples of the produce, a single bunch of grapes was so heavy <u>it took two men to carry it</u> tied to a pole! The reward was there; Canaan was a prosperous land. Its fields were cleared of stones and planted in vegetables and grain, and there were vast acres of olive trees and vineyards nurtured by the people of the land.

two men
Numbers 13:23

Two of the men sent to scout the land, Caleb and Joshua, agreed that "the people who dwell in the land are strong; the cities are fortified and very large" (Numbers 13:28 NKJV). But Caleb wasn't impressed. He enthusiastically urged the Israelites, "Let us go up at once and take possession, for we are well able to overcome it" (Numbers 13:30 NKJV).

Able? Not Poor Little Ol' Us!

NUMBERS 13:31–33 *But the men who had gone up with him said, "We are not able to go up against the people, for they are stronger than we." And they gave the children of Israel a bad report . . . saying, "The land through which we have gone as spies is a land that devours its inhabitants, and all the people whom we saw in it are men of great stature. There we saw the giants . . . We were like grasshoppers in our own sight, and so we were in their sight." (NKJV)*

These two different reactions are revealing. Faith sees the reward, and urges, "Let us go up at once." Unbelief sees the giants, and says, "We are not able."

Yet this was the land of which the Lord announced, "I am giving to the children of Israel." The people of the land might be strong, and the Israelites weak, but there could be no doubt about the outcome. It was the Lord who would provide the victory and who would *give* the land to the Israelites.

key point

Now it was up to the people to choose whose advice to take. They could follow the example of Caleb and Joshua, trust God, and forge ahead. Or they could follow the advice of the other ten scouts and fix their eyes on the giants.

What you and I fix our eyes on when we face challenges in life largely determines how we respond. Do we only see the giants, or do we acknowledge the giants, yet fix our eyes on the Lord?

Preston A. Taylor

The unbelieving Decision Makers overlook what God has done and what He does today, as well as what He will do tomorrow. They forgot about the deliverance from the hand of Pharaoh, the Red Sea experience, the provisions along the way, and the presence of God with them in those years. They overlooked all of that . . . What makes the difference between success and defeat? Some see grasshoppers and others see God.[1]

R. K. Harrison

The Israelites reacted to the reconnaissance report in panic, unmindful of God's delivering and sustaining power during the journey from Egypt to Kadish. Even worse was the fact that they were rebelling against God and defying His purpose, which was that the Israelites were to occupy the land of Canaan. Although they were ceremonially holy, they were not possessed of strong individual faith . . . As with the majority of people who do not trust in the Lord's mighty power, the Israelites became consumed with fear and worry, which are the antitheses of faith.[2]

This was the choice the Israelites faced. What they chose would set them on the road to blessing, or the road to disaster.

No, No! We Won't Go!

NUMBERS 14:1–4 *So all the congregation lifted up their voices and cried, and the people wept that night. And all the children of Israel complained against Moses and Aaron, and the whole congregation said to them, "If only we had died in the land of Egypt! Or if only we had died in this wilderness! Why has the LORD brought us to this land to fall by the sword, that our wives and children should become victims? Would it not be better for us to return to Egypt?" So they said to one another, "Let us select a leader and return to Egypt."* (NKJV)

This reaction horrified Moses and Aaron. What contempt for the Lord the people were displaying! They had challenged His power ("we are not able"), and now they were questioning His motives! The people were in open rebellion! The two faithful scouts tried desperately to reason with the people.

- It's an exceedingly good land! (14:7)
- If the Lord delights in us He will bring us into the land. (14:8)
- Don't rebel against the Lord. (14:9)
- Don't fear the people of the land; they have no protection. (14:9)
- The Lord is with us! Don't fear! (14:9)

But nothing they said reached the panicked people. Instead of listening, the Israelites shouted, "Stone them!" (14:10). But before the Israelites could act, blazing light burst from the Tabernacle and the murderous crowd fell back. The "glory of the LORD appeared in the tabernacle of meeting before all the children of Israel" (14:10 NKJV).

What's Wrong with the Israelites?

NUMBERS 14:11 *Then the LORD said to Moses: "How long will these people reject Me? And how long will they not believe Me, with all the signs which I have performed among them?"* (NKJV)

At Sinai, <u>God had promised</u> to be an enemy to Israel's enemies, and to cut off the peoples who lived in Canaan before them. At the same time God warned them not to provoke Him, for He would not pardon such sin (Exodus 23:21). Now the Lord was provoked indeed!

God had promised
Exodus 23:22–23

signs
miracles, with a special focus on their evidence of God's presence and power

what others say

George Coats

Here for the first time, the murmuring is followed by the move to return to Egypt. The murmuring tradition therefore involves not simply an expression of a wish that the Exodus had not occurred or a challenge of Moses' authority in executing the Exodus, but now an overt move to reverse the Exodus. Yahweh is the God "who brought Israel out of Egypt." The murmuring results in a rejection of this deity and a move to elect a new leader to take the people back to Egypt.[3]

key point

synagogue
Jewish house of worship, representative in the first century of the whole *torah* system

In later years, God's people would look back at these events and shake their heads in amazement.

PSALM 78:40–43
How often they provoked Him in the wilderness,
And grieved Him in the desert!
Yes, again and again they tempted God,
And limited the Holy One of Israel.
They did not remember His power:
The day when He redeemed them from the enemy,
When He worked His signs in Egypt,
And His wonders in the field of Zoan. (NKJV)

The Israelites didn't lack for evidence of God's power. They simply ignored the evidence. But again, why? Another psalm provides an answer:

PSALM 106:24–25
Then they despised the pleasant land;
They did not believe His word,
But complained in their tents,
And did not heed the voice of the LORD. (NKJV)

Flash Forward

the big picture

Hebrews 1:1–4:11

First-century Jews who have converted to Christianity are suffering persecution in Jerusalem. Under intense pressure they consider returning to the **synagogue**. In a powerful letter, an unknown Christian urges them to stand fast in their commitment to Jesus. The writer looks back to the events described in Numbers 14 and warns his contemporaries against hardening their hearts, "lest anyone fall according to the same example of disobedience" (Hebrews 4:11 NKJV). And why did they disobey? They knew what God wanted. But they did not obey "because of unbelief."

A Word About Faith and Unbelief

Words like *faith* and *belief* are rather slippery. They have so many different shades of meaning. "Sure, I believe in Jesus" can mean little more than "I agree that there once was a person named Jesus." Even "I believe Jesus is the Son of God" can be a fact statement rather than a faith statement.

The apostle James points this out in a letter to first-century Christians. "You believe that there is one God," he says to his readers. Good for you! And then he adds, "Even the demons believe—and tremble!" (James 2:19 NKJV).

What James is pointing out so effectively is that there's a great gap between belief on an "it's a fact" level, and belief on a faith level. Fact-level belief agrees that something is true. Faith-level belief responds to that truth with trust.

key point

The Israelites who rebelled on the border of Canaan knew for a certainty God exists. They had overwhelming evidence of His existence and of His power. Like the demons who know God exists, they knew beyond doubt that God is real. But these Israelites had never gone beyond a fact-level belief. Simply put, they knew God was real, but they didn't trust God enough to obey His Word.

James contemptuously dismisses that kind of faith, saying that a "faith without [good] works is dead" (2:20 NKJV).

Dead Faith

what others say

David P. Nystrom

James goes on to say that faith without deeds is dead. By this he means, of course, that such a faith fails to accomplish the end of true faith. That kind of faith may have a type of power, but it is not the power proper to faith. As Ropes notes, the contrast is not so much between faith and deeds (although this stands in the background) but between dead, useless faith and living faith. Faith alone without works is as dead as a body without breath. Deeds are not something extra to be added to faith; they are an expression of true faith.[4]

It's as if James leads us into a funeral home and invites us to look into caskets arranged along a corridor. As he walks with us he points to one corpse after another and says, "Look at them. No (good) works. They're dead."

When we get outside James says, "Now do you understand?" We shake our heads, so James explains. "True faith, faith on a trust level, always produces (good) works. Look at Abraham. How do we know his faith was a real, trust-level belief in God? We know because when God told him to do something, he did it! You can always tell trust-level belief by how a person responds to God's commands. A person with that kind of belief will obey the Lord. The truth is, a mere fact-level belief that fails to respond to God's Word is nothing but unbelief in disguise!"

That was the problem with the Exodus generation. They had only a fact-level belief in God, and that kind of "belief" simply doesn't count.

apply it

I fear that thousands of people who go to church every Sunday have only a fact-level belief in Jesus. They know He is the Son of God. They agree that He died for our sins and rose again. But mere fact-level belief is still nothing more than unbelief in disguise. Faith saves only when fact-level belief is transformed by trusting ourselves fully to the Lord. When we come to a trust-level belief in God we'll know it by our growing commitment to respond obediently to the Lord and His Word.

The good works that grow out of trust-level belief in God don't contribute to our salvation. But they do provide evidence that our faith in God is a living rather than a dead faith.

Back to Kadesh-Barnea

PSALM 106:24–25 *They did not believe His word, but complained in their tents, and did not heed the voice of the LORD. (NKJV)*

something to ponder

There could no longer be any question about the spiritual condition of the Israelites. They were totally unwilling to trust God or to obey Him. There was now no way that God could bring this rebellious people into the Promised Land.

An Offer Moses Can Refuse

NUMBERS 14:12 *I will strike them with the pestilence and disinherit them, and I will make of you a nation greater and mightier than they. (NKJV)*

This is the second time that Yahweh has been angry enough to threaten to disinherit the Israelites. The first time was after Israel's worship of the golden calf (Exodus 32:7–9). Strikingly, the Lord sees Israel's current refusal to attack Canaan as as great a rejection of Him as the earlier idolatry. In each case the Lord offers to simply wipe out the Israelites and start all over again with Moses and his family.

But here, as on Mount Sinai, Moses refuses God's offer. Instead Moses pleads with the Lord to spare the Israelites.

kill me now
Numbers 11:15

Moses's response is fascinating in view of his plea shortly before to "kill me now." The burden of leading the people was so great that Moses pleaded for his own death. But now, when the Lord offers to kill the people who had driven Moses to despair, Moses intercedes for them! While Moses's responses may seem inconsistent, when we compare the two prayers Moses offers we realize just how consistent Moses is. In each case, Moses's concern is for the reputation of Yahweh as well as for the benefit of the people.

Moses's Two Prayers for Israel

Exodus 32:10–14	Numbers 14:12–23
"Let Me alone, that My wrath may burn hot against them and I may consume them. And I will make of you a great nation" (32:10 NKJV).	"I will strike them with the pestilence and disinherit them, and I will make of you a nation greater and mightier than they" (14:12 NKJV).
"LORD, why does Your wrath burn hot against Your people whom You have brought out of the land of Egypt with great power and with a mighty hand? Why should the Egyptians speak, and say, 'He brought them out to harm them, to kill them in the mountains, and to consume them from the face of the earth'? Turn from Your fierce wrath, and relent from this harm to Your people" (32:11–12 NKJV).	"Then the Egyptians will hear it, for by Your might You brought these people up from among them, and they will tell it to the inhabitants of this land. They have heard that You, LORD, are among these people; that You, LORD, are seen face to face and Your cloud stands above them, and You go before them in a pillar of cloud by day and in a pillar of fire by night. Now if You kill these people as one man, then the nations which have heard of Your fame will speak, saying, 'Because the Lord was not able to bring this people to the land which He swore to give them, therefore He killed them in the wilderness'" (14:13–16 NKJV).
"Remember Abraham, Isaac, and Israel, Your servants, to whom You swore by Your own self, and said to them, 'I will multiply your descendants as the stars of heaven; and all this land that I have spoken of I give to your descendants, and they shall inherit it forever'" (32:13 NKJV).	"And now, I pray, let the power of my Lord be great, just as You have spoken, saying, 'The LORD is longsuffering and abundant in mercy, forgiving iniquity and transgression; but He by no means clears the guilty, visiting the iniquity of the fathers on the children to the third and fourth generation.' Pardon the iniquity of this people, I pray, according to the greatness of Your mercy, just as You have forgiven this people, from Egypt even until now" (14:17–19 NKJV).
"So the LORD relented from the harm which He said He would do to His people" (32:14 NKJV).	Then the LORD said: "I have pardoned, according to your word; but truly, as I live, all the earth shall be filled with the glory of the LORD—because all these men who have seen My glory and the signs which I did in Egypt and in the wilderness, and have put Me to the test now these ten times, and have not heeded My voice, they certainly shall not see the land of which I swore to their fathers, nor shall any of those who rejected Me see it" (14:20–23 NKJV).

Alike, Yet Different

These two situations are alike, and yet different in significant ways. In each the Israelites show utter contempt for God, pushing Him almost beyond endurance. In each case Moses intercedes for the Israelites, winning them a reprieve. In each situation both God and Moses behave consistently. The Lord is angered by the gross sins of the people He has rescued. And Moses's primary concern continues to be the glory—the reputation—of God.

key point

In the Exodus incident, Moses appeals to God's faithfulness to the covenant promises He made to Abraham, Isaac, and Israel. In the Numbers incident, Moses appeals to God's character as the Lord Himself has revealed it. In each incident Moses begs God to do nothing that would open Himself up to criticism by mere humans.

This consistency is one of Moses's most attractive qualities. Although Moses has been driven to near despair by the Israelites, the thing that continues to matter most is that everyone who hears the name of the Lord honor Him. Moses forgets himself, and seeks only to glorify God.

In this, Moses challenges you and me to, in the words of the apostle Paul, "let this mind be in you which was also in Christ Jesus" (Philippians 2:5 NKJV). Like Jesus, Moses abandons all "selfish ambition," and is willing to make himself "of no reputation" (2:3, 7 NKJV). Like Jesus, Moses is willing to be a mere servant, and to humble himself to the point of death (Philippians 2:8). Moses could not be tempted by God's offer to "make of you a nation greater and mightier than they" (Numbers 14:12 NKJV). God's glory, and not any personal benefit, has become Moses's sole concern.

apply it

Clearly, a healthy relationship with God is maintained by consistently setting aside every selfish ambition and making it our sole concern to glorify our Lord.

God's Responses

In Exodus, God responds to Moses's appeal to remain faithful to His covenant promises. God responds by withdrawing the threatened punishment. In Numbers, God responds to Moses's appeal that the Lord remain true to His character. God tells Moses, "I have pardoned, according to your word" (Numbers 14:20 NKJV). God will do just as Moses has asked. He will not destroy the nation.

But in quoting God's earlier revelation of Himself, Moses has opened a new door. Moses's appeal is based on God's revelation that "the LORD is longsuffering and abundant in mercy, forgiving iniquity and transgression; but He by no means clears the guilty" (Numbers 14:18 NKJV). God will show mercy. But in this case He will also glorify Himself by demonstrating that He is not one who takes sin lightly. Now God will "by no means clear the guilty"!

The Forty-Year Sentence

NUMBERS 14:28–35 *Say to them, "As I live," says the LORD, "just as you have spoken in My hearing, so I will do to you: The carcasses of you who have complained against Me shall fall in this wilderness, all of you who were numbered, according to your entire number, from twenty years old and above. Except for Caleb the son of Jephunneh and Joshua the son of Nun, you shall by no means enter the land which I swore I would make you dwell in. But your little ones, whom you said would be victims, I will bring in, and they shall know the land which you have despised . . . According to the number of the days in which you spied out the land, forty days, for each day you shall bear your guilt one year, namely forty years, and you shall know My rejection. I the LORD have spoken this. I will surely do so to all this evil congregation who are gathered together against Me. In this wilderness they shall be consumed, and there they shall die." (NKJV)*

go to

God's earlier
revelation
Exodus 34:6–7

The Smart Guide to the Bible

As if to underline God's verdict against the Israelites, the ten scouts who "brought the evil report about the land" died immediately (Numbers 14:37 NKJV).

God's rest
Hebrews 3:7–4:13

Fast-Forward Again

When the writer of the New Testament letter to the Hebrews urged them to think about the Exodus generation, he was making two important points:

1. The first important point was that what God communicates to us must be "mixed with faith" (Hebrews 4:2 NKJV). We are to listen to what God says, but not as if His words were merely facts to be believed. What God says is to be understood as truth, to be trusted and acted on.

Anything less than a trust in God that is expressed in responsive obedience is nothing but unbelief in disguise.

The people Moses led had a fact-level belief in God. But when challenged to trust and obey Him, their underlying unbelief was displayed.

2. The second major point was that trusting and obeying God is the only way to blessing. The Israelites whose unbelief drove them to disobey God were in turn driven into the wilderness, to wander for forty years until the last of them died. During that forty-year exile their children did learn to trust the Lord, and they were the ones who entered the Promised Land and experienced God's rest.

God's Rest

The writer of Hebrews makes much of the idea of "God's rest." He views Israel's conquest of Canaan and subsequent settling down there as a powerful illustration of a rest that God offers to all His people.

When the Israelites had conquered Canaan they settled down there in homes they hadn't built. They farmed fields that had already been cleared of stones. They plucked olives from trees that had already matured. They gathered figs from trees they hadn't planted and harvested grapes from vines that someone else had pruned and cared for. Theirs, at least initially, was a life without stress, a life of external and inner peace.

This experience of those who conquered Canaan is an illustration of what God has in store for all believers, not just in heaven, but here and now. And so the writer of Hebrews urges these early Christians—Christians who are undergoing persecution—to respond to God's voice and experience rest, now.

The inspired writer's point is a simple yet profound one. God still speaks to His people as He spoke to Israel in the desert. He may speak through His Word, or His Spirit may speak through circumstances or the wise counsel of another believer. But when we hear God's voice and recognize it, we must respond with a true faith and be obedient. What God says to us may be unwelcome. We may see giants ranged against us, but whatever the circumstances, we are to trust God and to obey Him.

When we do, we enter into God's rest. We stop relying on ourselves and rely completely on Him. As we trust and obey God we find that He gives us peace despite the dangers, and relieves our stress despite our fears.

God knows the way through the wilderness. God is able to lead us into our own Promised Land. All we need to do—all we can do—is trust and obey.

Two Roads Diverged in a Yellow Wood

The words above, from "The Road Not Taken" by Robert Frost, open one of the best-known works of any American poet. Perhaps they are so well-known because they are so true. Every day we come to places where two paths diverge.

Numbers 14 recounts what happened when the Israelites came to Kadesh-Barnea, where two paths diverged. One was the path of unbelief. The other was the path of complete trust in the Lord. The Israelites chose the path that is traveled by all too many. And that path led into the wilderness, where for forty years the people traveled in circles until the last of that generation died.

How important that you and I choose the path less traveled, the path of utter trust in God that leads to our Promised Land, and to rest.

Too Little, Too Late

NUMBERS 14:39–40 *Then Moses told these words to all the children of Israel, and the people mourned greatly. And they rose early in the morning and went up to the top of the mountain, saying, "Here we are, and we will go up to the place which the LORD has promised, for we have sinned!" (NKJV)*

God's sudden appearance and Moses's pronouncement of his sentence shook the Israelites. They "mourned greatly," and professed themselves ready to obey God at last. "Here we are, and we will go up!"

But it is clear that their "repentance" and the confession that "we have sinned" hardly reflected a change of heart. What they were sorry about was the penalty God imposed, not their rebelliousness. We know this, for if they had experienced a true change of heart they would have submitted to God and humbly turned back into the wilderness.

What they did was to again display their willfulness, trying to mask it as obedience. Moses warned that they were once again violating God's command, and that an attack couldn't succeed. The people refused to listen. They headed up into the hills of Canaan, and "then the Amalekites and the Canaanites who dwelt in that mountain came down and attacked them, and drove them back" (Numbers 14:45 NKJV).

presumptuously
knowingly, openly
defiant

what others say

R. Dennis Cole

Sometimes the consequences of sin and rebellion are irreversible, and one must endure the experience of God's judgment before a new course of action brings blessings. Sometimes those consequences endure for a lifetime, but even in those settings we must continue in faith so that our lives reflect redemption rather than further reproach.[9]

Finally the Israelites followed Moses and the fiery-cloudy pillar back into the desert.

Not If, When

NUMBERS 15:1–2 *And the LORD spoke to Moses, saying, "Speak to the children of Israel, and say to them: 'When you have come into the land you are to inhabit, which I am giving to you . . .'"* (NKJV)

The whole of chapter 15 of Numbers is filled with instructions on how the Israelites are to live when they finally enter the land God has promised them. There is no "if" about it. The first Exodus generation has failed utterly, and is destined to die in the wilderness. But there will be another generation. God will fulfill His purpose in them.

Remember the Exodus Generation

NUMBERS 15:30–31 *But the person who does anything **presumptuously**, whether he is native-born or a stranger, that one brings reproach on the LORD, and he shall be cut off from among his people. Because he has despised the word of the LORD, and has broken His commandment, that person shall be completely cut off; his guilt shall be upon him.* (NKJV)

Much of chapter 15 is given to discussing how to deal with unintentional sins, and with a reminder that there is a real difference between such sins and what Scripture calls presumptuous or defiant sins. This is the one great lesson Israel would take from the first Exodus generation's refusal to obey God.

When reading these verses, we need to remember the word in Hebrews that traces the defiant response to unbelief (Hebrews 3:19). The Israelites had plenty of contact with God, but they had no personal, faith-based relationship with Him. Today, if you have trusted Christ as Savior, sins you may commit knowingly won't lead to your rejection by God.

persistent
repeated, frequent

But if you find that your life is marked by **persistent**, knowing disobedience to the will of God, you might be wise to look deeply into your heart. It's possible, and even likely, that what you've imagined is your faith in Jesus is nothing more than fact-level belief, and not a saving trust in the Savior at all.

<u>Chapter Wrap-Up</u>

- When scouts spy out Canaan, they find a prosperous and lush land inhabited by powerful peoples.

- The scouts' report emphasizes the size and strength of the Canaanites, and causes panic among the Israelites.

- The terrified Israelites refuse to obey God and enter Canaan. Instead, they threaten to kill Moses and Aaron and return to Egypt.

- Moses pleads with the Lord to spare the Israelites. God does so, but He sentences Israel to forty years of wandering in the desert. During those years every Israelite over age twenty, except for two faithful spies, will die.

- Despite this generation's refusal to trust God, the Lord will give Israel the land as He promised. But it will be the first generation's children that gain the blessing, and even then only after their parents have died.

Study Questions

1. What impressed the spies who spent forty days scouting the land of Canaan?

2. What was the response of the Israelites to the spies' report?

3. How did the Lord react to the Israelites' response?

4. Compare and contrast Moses's two prayers, at this time and after the incident of the golden calf.

5. Compare and contrast God's answers to Moses's two prayers, and explain any differences.

6. How was the length of time the Israelites were sentenced to wander in the desert determined?

7. What distinction does the author draw between fact-level belief and true faith in God? How can we tell if our belief in God is truly trust in Him rather than a "dead" faith that is in fact unbelief?

Chapter 11
The Next Forty Years

Chapter Highlights:
- Aaron's the Man!
- Blessing and Curse
- You Too, Moses?
- Look, and Live
- War Clouds Gather

Let's Get Started

The Israelites have made their choice, and there's no going back. For the next four decades God's people will travel in circles in the desert lands south of Canaan, until all in that first Exodus generation have died.

Some will die natural deaths. But continuing rebelliousness will cause many to be struck dead suddenly, and unexpectedly. The lesson of God's severe judgments on His people in their wilderness wanderings won't be lost on the next generation.

During these years both Miriam and Aaron will die. And Moses will make a tragic mistake that will disqualify him from ever setting foot in the Promised Land.

three Levite leaders
Numbers 16:1

Some Folks Never Learn

> NUMBERS 16:3 *They gathered together against Moses and Aaron, and said to them, "You take too much upon yourselves, for all the congregation is holy, every one of them, and the LORD is among them. Why then do you exalt yourselves above the assembly of the LORD?" (NKJV)*

We have some sense of the timing of various events that took place before the rebellion at the border of Canaan. Now, as the Israelites traverse the wilderness with no destination in mind, we have no clue as to the length of time between the events described in the book of Numbers. Yet the weary, seemingly endless days are interrupted by outbursts which make it clear that God was right in sentencing the first Exodus generation to death. Time after time they insistently demand their own way, unwilling to submit to the Lord.

The first incident Moses records is an attack on Moses fomented by <u>three Levite leaders</u> with the support of a respected Reubenite. The four assemble a group of 250 other leaders, "representatives of the congregation, men of renown" (Numbers 16:2 NKJV), and confront Moses.

already a leader
Numbers 16:2

Moses had taught
Exodus 19:6

Hiding Behind Theology

Clearly this attack on Moses is motivated by envy and jealousy. Everyone who joined in the rebellion was <u>already a leader</u>. Not one would have considered an ordinary Israelite *his* equal. Yet they condemn Moses for "exalting himself" over them.

Typically when a church comes close to a split the underlying reason is interpersonal conflict. We can usually tell when this is the case by the way the two sides characterize each other. When attacks become personal and accusations start flying, the reason for the conflict seldom has valid theological roots. Yet, like Korah and his followers, both sides in a modern conflict tend to appeal to theology to justify their behavior.

Korah appealed to an important truth that <u>Moses himself had taught</u>. All the Israelites *were* holy, in the sense of having been set apart to God. In this sense Moses was no different—and no better—than any other Israelite. What Korah said was true, but far from the whole truth.

There's Holy and Then There's Holy

The Hebrew word translated "holy," *qadas*, is also translated "sacred." We saw earlier that persons, places, times, and objects that are designated "holy" or "sacred" are special. They are set apart by God, and for God.

God had chosen Israel and set this people apart as His own special possession. This choice of the Israelites definitely marked them as holy—but only in the sense of being set apart by and for God.

key point

There is also a moral dimension to holiness. When giving Israel *torah* commands, the Lord told Moses to say to the people, "You shall be holy, for I the LORD your God am holy" (Leviticus 19:2 NKJV). The commands that follow deal with issues such as idolatry, theft, lying, fraud, slander, and so on. And they include the command to love one's neighbor as oneself (Leviticus 19:18). Clearly a people who are set apart by God and for God are to adopt a lifestyle that reflects Yahweh's own commitment to what is right.

This is the first irony in the claim of Korah and his followers. Their claim that all Israel is "holy" stands in utter contrast to the people's *unholy* behavior. The Israelites have been quick to <u>turn from God to idolatry</u>. They have consistently slandered Moses, and have rejected God's authority, <u>refusing again and again to obey</u> Him.

Korah's appeal to theology was utterly hypocritical, for the leader's behavior shows that the Israelites actually care nothing about honoring the Lord.

go to

turn from God to idolatry
Exodus 32

refusing to obey
Leviticus 10:13;
Numbers 11:1–2,
10–11; 14:11

There's Truth and Then There's Truth

In court a witness is pledged to tell "the truth, the whole truth, and nothing but the truth." Korah starts off with a truth, follows with an implied half-truth, and then lies in his effort to discredit Moses.

- "All God's people are holy." True.
- "All God's people are equal." Implied half-truth.
- "You and Aaron have exalted yourselves." Lie.

Today, too, all God's people are holy, in the sense that each true believer belongs to the Lord. And all Christian are equal, in the sense that each of us has at least one spiritual gift given to us by the Holy Spirit (1 Corinthians 12:7). But all Christians do not have the same gift, nor the same calling. Just as God commissioned Moses to lead Israel, so Scripture tells us that God chooses some apostles, some prophets, some pastors and teachers (Ephesians 4:11). Moses and Aaron had hardly exalted themselves. It was God who gave each his position.

There's one last distortion in Korah's challenge. He claimed that Moses and Aaron had exalted themselves "above the assembly" (Numbers 16:3 NKJV).

Remember in a previous chapter how we discussed Moses's humility? Moses understood that he had not been called by God to be *over* the Israelites, but to serve them, just as Christ "did not come to be served, but to serve, and to give His life a ransom for many" (Matthew 20:28 NKJV).

Korah's attack on Moses revealed how little he understood of God, and how little he understood of leadership. When men like Korah assume leadership, God's people truly are in trouble.

censers
containers in which
incense was burned
as an offering to the
Lord

Never Satisfied

NUMBERS 16:9–10 *Is it a small thing to you that the God of Israel has separated you from the congregation of Israel, to bring you near to Himself, to do the work of the tabernacle of the LORD, and to stand before the congregation to serve them . . . ? And are you seeking the priesthood also? (NKJV)*

Moses "fell on his face" in prayer (Numbers 16:4 NKJV), and then he responded. He told Korah and his followers to take **censers** and appear at the Tabernacle the next day. But before they left, Moses confronted the ambitious Korah and his fellow Levites.

> **what others say**
>
> **R. K. Harrison**
>
> Moses discerned correctly the real motive for Korah's rebellion. Korah wanted a popular election to be held for the office of high priest with himself as a candidate. In his view he was the only suitable person for that exalted function. To set Korah's position in Israel in proper perspective, Moses pointed out the great privilege of his having been called to serve God in the ministry of the sanctuary. Moses evidently perceived that this status did not satisfy Korah's ambitions, however, and for this reason he questioned him directly on the matter of his desire to be high priest in Israel, without receiving any apparent rebuttal.[1]

key point

Korah and the rest of the Levites had been given such a great blessing. Yet rather than praise God for the privilege, they were gripped by a great discontent, complained, and wanted more.

Hiding Out Among the People

The two leading Levites who had stirred up this rebellion with Korah were Dathan and Abiram. While Korah boldly led his 250 men to openly confront Moses, these two stayed back by their tents. Like so many who foment discontent in the church today, they hid among the people; they were glad to stir up trouble but unwilling to take a public stand. When Moses called for them to come out they refused (Numbers 16:12). But from the supposed safety of relative anonymity they continued to attack Moses, accusing him of dragging them out of a land of milk and honey—Egypt!—to kill them in the wilderness.

Judgment Day Comes Early

The next morning Korah and his 250 appeared before the Tabernacle. Moses warned the people to get away from the tents of Korah, Dathan, and Abiram, and announced:

NUMBERS 16:28–30 *By this you shall know that the LORD has sent me to do all these works, for I have not done them of my own will. If these men die naturally like all men, or if they are visited by the common fate of all men, then the LORD has not sent me. But if the LORD creates a new thing, and the earth opens its mouth and swallows them up with all that belongs to them, and they go down alive into the pit, then you will understand that these men have rejected the LORD. (NKJV)*

what others say

R. K. Harrison

In an attempt to understand the purely physical mechanics of the engulfing of the confederates, Hort suggests that the camp was pitched on a *kewir*. This is an area of land with a fairly solid crust overlying marshlike terrain and occurs in an area stretching from the Arabah to the Red Sea. Although such an area might well have been a physical concomitant of the miraculous incident, it would in no way detract from the supernatural cause of death but would even enhance it, since this was specifically an act of divine judgment and not merely a seismic phenomenon.[2]

Moses no sooner finished speaking than the earth did open and the households and goods of all the men who were with Korah tumbled into a yawning chasm, which then closed over them. At the same moment "a fire came out from the LORD and consumed the two hundred and fifty men who were offering incense" (Numbers 16:35 NKJV).

Another *Zikkaron*

At God's command the censers carried by the 250 were gathered up and hammered into metal plates, to be used as a covering for the altar. There they functioned as a memorial—a *zikkaron*. Whenever any offering was burned on the altar of sacrifice the metal plates

Day of Atonement
Leviticus 16

recalled the judgment of Korah and served as a warning that only descendants of Aaron were qualified to fulfill priestly duties.

Aaron's the Man!

In our earlier look at the *torah* we traced the link between the different elements of the Old Testament worship system. God gave Israel moral and ceremonial rules to follow. But Israel sinned and violated these laws laid down by God. So God gave Israel a priesthood to represent them and to offer the blood sacrifices that covered their sins. While the sacrifices of ordinary priests served only to cover unintentional sins, the sacrifice offered by the high priest the <u>Day of Atonement</u> cleansed the people from all sins. With sins atoned for, the people could approach the Lord and worship Him at the Tabernacle.

What happened the day after God judged Korah and his followers illustrates how badly this people needed the services of their high priest.

One Man Stands Between Life and Death

NUMBERS 16:41–42 *On the next day all the congregation of the children of Israel complained against Moses and Aaron, saying, "You have killed the people of the LORD." Now it happened, when the congregation had gathered against Moses and Aaron, that they turned toward the tabernacle of meeting; and suddenly the cloud covered it, and the glory of the LORD appeared. (NKJV)*

Once again the Lord was angry enough to wipe out the entire people, and in fact a deadly plague struck at that moment. Moses told Aaron to quickly take a censer for burning incense and "make atonement for them; for wrath has gone out from the LORD. The plague has begun" (Numbers 14:46 NKJV). Aaron did as Moses commanded and ran into the crowd. The text tells us that Aaron "stood between the dead and the living; so the plague was stopped" (14:48 NKJV).

This incident provides one of the clearest pictures of the ministry of the high priest. The high priest of Israel stood between sinful

Israelites and the death-dealing wrath of God. Aaron, Israel's high priest, was the one and only man who could save God's people from the consequences of their sin.

Jesus, He's the Man

The New Testament book of Hebrews presents Jesus Christ as the Christian's High Priest. Like the high priests of the *torah* era, Jesus offers a sacrifice that <u>atones for sin and protects us from the wrath of God</u>. Just as only the high priest could enter the inner room of the Tabernacle on the Day of Atonement with <u>the one sacrifice</u> that covered all the sins Israel had committed the previous year, only Jesus, who sacrificed Himself for us on the cross, could <u>pay for all our sins</u> past, present, and future.

The Scriptures tell us that "all have sinned and fall short of the glory of God" (Romans 3:23 NKJV). God's Word also states that "the wages of sin is death" (Romans 6:23 NKJV). Thank God that through Jesus's blood we have "the forgiveness of sins" (Colossians 1:14 NKJV).

The image of Aaron running to stand between the Israelites and the death-dealing wrath of God is a strikingly vivid picture of what Jesus has done for all who believe in Him.

atones and protects
John 3:16–18;
Romans 5:9

the one sacrifice
Leviticus 16

pay for all our sins
Hebrews 9:23–29;
10:11–14

Two High Priesthoods

Old Testament High Priests	Jesus as Our High Priest
Appointed by God (Numbers 40:13)	Appointed by God (Psalm 110:4)
Offered sacrifices for sins (Leviticus 16)	Offered Himself as a sacrifice (Hebrews 7:27)
Sacrifices had to be repeated (Leviticus 16)	His one sacrifice won eternal redemption (Hebrews 9:12)
Offered the blood of animals (Leviticus 16)	Offered His own blood (Hebrews 9:12)
Sacrifices gave only temporary covering of sins (Hebrews 10:1)	His sacrifice "put away sin" completely (Hebrews 9:26 NKJV)

One High Priest and Only One

NUMBERS 17:1–3 *And the LORD spoke to Moses, saying: "Speak to the children of Israel, and get from them a rod from each father's house, all their leaders according to their fathers' houses—twelve rods. Write each man's name on his rod. And you shall write Aaron's name on the rod of Levi." (NKJV)*

That night Moses placed the rods in the Tabernacle, and when they were collected the next morning the rod of Levi had sprouted and produced buds, blossoms, and ripe almonds! Moses showed the rods to all the children of Israel and then returned Aaron's rod to the Tabernacle. Aaron's rod that budded was to be "kept as a sign against the rebels" (Numbers 17:10 NKJV).

There could be only one high priest in Israel. Only one individual could offer the annual sacrifice that covered the people's sins and provided access to the Lord.

Flash Forward

It's the night before the Crucifixion, and Jesus is sharing a Passover meal with His disciples. When the meal is over, Christ gathers them around and encourages the troubled men. Soon He will return to the Father and prepare heavenly homes for all His followers. As the conversation continues, Jesus makes this statement: "I am the way, the truth, and the life. No one comes to the Father except through Me" (John 14:6 NKJV).

Good News!

After the Resurrection, this statement galvanized Jesus's followers. Quickly they spread the news that the Jesus who died on a cross outside Jerusalem was the Son of God, and had offered Himself as a sacrifice for sins. Gladly they proclaimed the good news: "There is no other name under heaven given among men by which we must be saved" (Acts 4:12 NKJV), and "Believe on the Lord Jesus Christ, and you will be saved" (Acts 16:31 NKJV).

Christ had opened the way to God for all humanity.

One Way, and Only One

Too many today waver and speak hopefully that perhaps God will welcome followers of other paths. Would God refuse forgiveness just because others might call Him by another name, such as Allah? And what about God's Old Testament people? Surely Jews who reject the idea that Jesus is the promised Messiah won't be turned away?

To all who offer such false hope, Christ's own words provide a definitive answer. "No one comes to the Father except through Me." The testimony of Scripture is clear.

The Lord turned away Korah, who sought to force his way into the priesthood, for only Aaron's descendants were qualified to serve as high priests. And only the high priest was qualified to offer the one sacrifice that covered Israel's sins.

Just so, the Lord will <u>turn away</u> those who seek to force their way into heaven by taking a different route than trust in Jesus and in the blood He shed to win our salvation.

turn away
John 3:36

what others say

Steve Hill

The Bible says, "For God so loved the world that He gave His only begotten Son, that whoever believes in Him should not perish but have everlasting life." Many people—even clergy—believe the scope of God's grace extends beyond the Christian community. Basically, they argue that a just and merciful God would never condemn anyone simply because he did not profess faith in Jesus Christ. I assure you, there is only one way to heaven, and that's through our Savior, Jesus Christ. One Savior, one way. *His* way.[3]

A Blessing and a Curse

NUMBERS 18:1–2 *Then the LORD said to Aaron: "You and your sons and your father's house with you shall bear the iniquity related to the sanctuary, and you and your sons with you shall bear the iniquity associated with your priesthood. Also bring with you your brethren of the tribe of Levi, the tribe of your father, that they may be joined with you and serve you while you and your sons are with you before the tabernacle of witness."* (NKJV)

the big picture

Leviticus 8–10; Numbers 18–19

Aaron and his offspring have been confirmed as Israel's sole priests, and the Levites have been confirmed in their temple ministries. Numbers 18 and 19 go into detail on the duties and privileges of the service they provide for the people. It is a privilege to serve God and His people. But such service is also a heavy burden for the priests to bear.

go to

Miriam's death and burial
Numbers 20:1

Oops! You Too, Moses?

So far we've seen glimpses of Moses's human frailties, but at the same time we've no doubt that he is a great man. Moses truly loves God and serves Him faithfully. But Moses isn't perfect, as events following the <u>death and burial of Miriam</u> are about to reveal.

> **NUMBERS 20:2–8** *Now there was no water for the congregation; so they gathered together against Moses and Aaron. And the people contended with Moses and spoke, saying: "If only we had died when our brethren died before the LORD! Why have you brought up the assembly of the LORD into this wilderness, that we and our animals should die here? And why have you made us come up out of Egypt, to bring us to this evil place?" . . . So Moses and Aaron went from the presence of the assembly to the door of the tabernacle of meeting, and they fell on their faces. And the glory of the LORD appeared to them.*
>
> *Then the LORD spoke to Moses, saying, "Take the rod; you and your brother Aaron gather the congregation together. Speak to the rock before their eyes, and it will yield its water; thus you shall bring water for them out of the rock, and give drink to the congregation and their animals." (NKJV)*

We can perhaps imagine how frustrated Moses must have felt. Here the Israelites are *again*. They're raising the same old complaints. They're making the same old charges. They're whining and criticizing and blaming Moses. And all Moses has done is obey the Lord's commands. All Moses has done is follow the supernatural cloud of fire that everyone knows has led the Israelites from place to place.

Moses must have been about ready to tear his hair out! We can sense his frustration in the following words, which Moses spoke to the congregation: "Hear now, you rebels! Must we bring water for you out of this rock?" (Numbers 20:10 NKJV).

We can also sense frustration in what Moses did afterward. "Then Moses lifted his hand and struck the rock twice with his rod; and water came out abundantly, and the congregation and their animals drank" (Numbers 20:11 NKJV).

No Excuses

NUMBERS 20:12 *Then the LORD spoke to Moses and Aaron: "Because you did not believe Me, to hallow Me in the eyes of the children of Israel, therefore you shall not bring this assembly into the land which I have given them." (NKJV)*

key point

Moses's failure to obey and simply speak to the rock was at heart unbelief. He had not done what God told him to do. Now Moses would not be permitted to enter the Promised Land.

what others say

Dennis T. Olson

Moses and Aaron disobeyed God's commands, arrogating to themselves God's power and honor, and not trusting in God's power to fulfill God's promises. This later sin of not trusting in God is explicitly stated in 20:12. The same Hebrew phrase characterized the sin of the Israelites in the spy story in Numbers 14:11; the Israelites did not trust in God's power to do what God promised, namely, to bring them into the Promised Land. Not only is the verb the same, "did not trust [believe in]," but the punishment in both Numbers 14 and 20 is the same: The Israelites and now also their leaders, Moses and Aaron, will die outside the Promised Land. Thus, the sin involved in both cases is likely to be similar—a public failure to trust God to fulfill God's word.[4]

R. Dennis Cole

Yahweh's specific charge is *you have not trusted in me to hold me as holy before the eyes of the children of Israel.* To trust in Yahweh means basically to find that He is worthy of reliance. In Num. 14, . . . *lo'he'emin* describes the rebellion of the Israelites, who, in spite of the many signs Yahweh had done in their midst, refused to rely on Him to fulfill His further promises. Here Moses and Aaron succumb to the same sin; they have refused by their actions to rely on God.[5]

Too Harsh? Not Really

Some might feel God overreacted to what seems a minor failure on Moses's part. But there are at least two reasons to view what Moses did as a serious infraction.

The first reason is that Moses was Israel's lawgiver, the one who set the standard for Israel's behavior. No matter how frustrated he

Jesus alone
Acts 4:12

might become, he must not allow himself to set a bad example for Israel. In this same vein the apostle James warns his readers, "My brethren, let not many of you become teachers, knowing that we shall receive a stricter judgment. For we all stumble in many things" (James 3:1–2 NKJV). Moses had stumbled indeed, and if God's judgment was stricter than it might have been for someone else, it was appropriate for Moses.

But there is an even more significant reason why Moses's action was a serious rather than a minor infraction.

The Real Reason Why?

Looking back on the Exodus years, the apostle Paul points out that "all these things happened to them as examples, and they were written for our admonition" (1 Corinthians 10:11 NKJV). What Paul is saying is that the events recorded by Moses have symbolic spiritual significance. They are more significant than they seem. These events portray spiritual realities that impact every era of sacred history.

We've just suggested that Aaron's dash into the Israelite camp to stand between the dead and the living has just this kind of significance. His action not only provides a vivid image of the role of a high priest. It also foreshadows the high priestly work of <u>Jesus, who alone</u> stands between sinners and the wrath of God.

What then is the spiritual significance of the rock and of Moses's action? The answer is found in this same chapter of 1 Corinthians. There Paul tells us that "all drank the same spiritual drink. For they drank of that spiritual Rock that followed them, and that Rock was Christ" (1 Corinthians 10:4 NKJV).

Paul is telling us that the rock of Numbers 20 is the same rock mentioned in Exodus 17:5–7. The Israelites had run out of water shortly after leaving the Red Sea, and at that time God told Moses to strike the rock with his rod. When Moses did, water gushed out, providing for the needs of God's people.

Whether the Israelites had circled back to that same place or whether the rock literally followed them, it was essentially the same rock. And that Rock represented Jesus Christ and His ability to provide for all the needs of His people.

So why was what Moses did so serious? Moses *struck the rock again*. And this distorted the truth that God intended to convey when He told Moses simply to <u>speak to the rock</u>.

Isaiah 53:4–6 tells us that the Messiah, Jesus, is to be "stricken, smitten by God, and afflicted." But the prophet adds that "He was wounded for our transgressions . . . and the LORD has laid on Him the iniquity of us all" (NKJV). The book of Hebrews makes much of the sufficiency of Jesus's one sacrifice of Himself. It says,

> HEBREWS 9:25–28 *Not that He should offer Himself often, as the high priest enters the Most Holy Place every year with blood of another—He then would have had to suffer often since the foundation of the world; but now, once at the end of the ages, He has appeared to put away sin by the sacrifice of Himself . . . So Christ was offered once to bear the sins of many. (NKJV)*

The Savior suffered a single blow, and it was enough. From that moment on through all of time, Christ would provide all that His people required.

This is the spiritual reality that Moses was to illustrate by simply speaking to the rock. Instead Moses struck the rock again, and in so doing distorted the truth God intended to communicate. It was for the serious offense of distorting God's truth that Moses was condemned to die before the Israelites entered the Promised Land.

Not long after this event Aaron died and was buried. Like Moses, Aaron would not be permitted to enter Canaan. Aaron's high priestly garments were removed and put on his son, Eleazar, the new high priest (Numbers 20:24–29).

Look, and Live

> NUMBERS 21:5–9 *And the people spoke against God and against Moses: "Why have you brought us up out of Egypt to die in the wilderness? For there is no food and no water, and our soul loathes this **worthless bread**." So the LORD sent fiery serpents among the people, and they bit the people; and many of the people of Israel died.*
>
> *Therefore the people came to Moses, and said, "We have sinned, for we have spoken against the LORD and against you; pray to the LORD that He take away the serpents from us." So Moses prayed for the people. Then the LORD said to Moses, "Make a*

speak to the rock
Numbers 20:8

worthless bread
The contemptuous reference is to the manna that God supplied for His people.

key point

comes at night
John 3:2

replace Israel's heart
of stone
Jeremiah 24:7;
32:39;
Ezekiel 11:19

eternal death
Matthew 25:46;
Revelation 20:10,
14–15

the Sanhedrin
the supreme reli-
gious and civil court
in first-century
Judaism

fiery serpent, and set it on a pole; and it shall be that everyone who is bitten, when he looks at it, shall live." So Moses made a bronze serpent, and put it on a pole; and so it was, if a serpent had bitten anyone, when he looked at the bronze serpent, he lived. (NKJV)

Flash Forward

It's early in Jesus's public ministry. The miracles of healing He has performed have the nation buzzing, and the religious leaders are growing suspicious. One of them, a man named Nicodemus who serves on **the Sanhedrin**, <u>comes to Jesus at night</u> to feel Him out. During their conversation Jesus tells Nicodemus that human beings must be "born again" to enter the kingdom of God.

The phrase "born again" puzzles Nicodemus. Jesus expresses surprise that one of Israel's religious leaders wouldn't understand, for the Old Testament makes frequent references to a future time when God would <u>replace Israel's heart of stone</u> with a living, responsive heart. Still puzzled, Nicodemus asks, "How can these things be?"

Jesus responds, "As Moses lifted up the serpent in the wilderness, even so must the Son of Man be lifted up, that whoever believes in Him should not perish but have eternal life" (John 3:14–15 NKJV).

The Heart of the Gospel

Strangely, the incident of the bronze serpent reveals the living heart of the gospel. We can see that clearly today, some two thousand years after Calvary.

- *Then.* The issue was one of life or death. There was no natural cure for the poison injected by the serpent's bite. But Moses raised a pole topped by a bronze serpent in the center of the camp. Whoever had been bitten was invited to come and simply look at the bronze serpent, and was promised that he or she would live. Those who trusted God's promise responded in faith, and they did live.

- *Now.* The issue is one of life or death. The poison of sin courses through the veins of every human being and brings <u>eternal death</u>. There is no natural cure for sin; nothing a human being does can cancel sin's death-dealing power. But

God lifted up His own Son on an executioner's cross, and invites sinners to look to Him for salvation. God promises that all who do will be given eternal life. Today those who trust God's promise respond in faith, and they are given <u>eternal life</u>.

Both *then* and *now* all we need to do, all we can do, is to believe God's promise of life and look to that which He has raised up as an object of faith.

go to

eternal life
John 3:16–18;
Ephesians 2:8–9

substitutionary atonement
Romans 5:8;
2 Corinthians 5:21;
Galatians 3:13

sanctification
becoming holy in our daily living

substitutionary atonement
Jesus died in our place, to pay for our sins that we might be forgiven and made right with God.

---

what others say

Preston A. Taylor

When Israel cried to Moses, God told Moses to make a serpent of brass and put it on a pole so the people might live. That serpent was a symbol of sin that has been judged. Romans 8:3 says, "Christ was made in the likeness of sin . . ." Again, "He became sin for us" (2 Co. 5:21). Christ took our judgment of sin and death (Deut. 21:23; Gal. 3:13; Rom. 8:1). That serpent "on the pole" symbolizes Christ, who said, "If I be lifted up . . ." That "shining serpent" could be seen anytime, any place, by all. The Redeemer gives immediate healing. The bitten Hebrews saw the serpent and were healed in that instant. The one who believes in Jesus is saved in a moment. **Sanctification** is a long process. However, salvation is instantaneous.[6]

James Philip

The provision God made for Israel illustrates the great gospel provision for sin. The significance of the uplifted bronze serpent is that bronze speaks of sin judged . . . and, as Matthew Henry puts it, "That which cured was shaped in the likeness of that which wounded." As Israel was given this symbol of **substitutionary atonement**—their sin, represented by the bronze serpent, was cursed and cancelled, and it was this they were bidden to look upon—so also Christ, for our sakes, and for our healing, was made in the likeness of sinful flesh, and made sin for us, and was lifted up from the earth, when He bore in His own body the judgment of a holy God upon sin. And, since judgment cannot come where judgment has already been, we are bidden to look upon the uplifted Christ for our salvation. As the old hymn puts it, "There is life for a look at the Crucified One."[7]

go to

various judgments
Numbers 14:37, 43;
16:27–33, 35,
46–48; 21:5–6

tracing the journey
Numbers 21:10–19

King's Highway
one of three major
trade routes in the
ancient Middle East

Flash Forward

Jesus continued to explain this truth to Nicodemus, using words that are among the most familiar in the Bible.

> JOHN 3:16–18 *For God so loved the world that He gave His only begotten Son, that whoever believes in Him should not perish but have everlasting life. For God did not send His Son into the world to condemn the world, but that the world through Him might be saved. He who believes in Him is not condemned; but he who does not believe is condemned already, because he has not believed in the name of the only begotten Son of God. (NKJV)*

The gospel invitation remains the same: Believe God and accept His invitation.

Look, and live.

War Clouds Gather

By now Israel has served most of its forty-year sentence. A majority of the adults who left Egypt have now either died natural deaths or been killed in <u>various judgments</u> on the continually rebelling Israelites. After <u>tracing their journey</u>, Moses places the Israelites in the country of Moab, on the **King's Highway** near the boarders of the Amorite kingdom.

> NUMBERS 21:21–23 *Then Israel sent messengers to Sihon king of the Amorites, saying, "Let me pass through your land. We will not turn aside into fields or vineyards; we will not drink water from wells. We will go by the King's Highway until we have passed through your territory." But Sihon would not allow Israel to pass through his territory. So Sihon gathered all his people together and went out against Israel . . . and fought against Israel. (NKJV)*

the big picture

Numbers 21–35

Sihon's failure to trust the Israelites led to a devastating war. The Israelites either killed or drove out the Amorites and occupied their territory. When the ruler of neighboring Bashan gathered an army to fight the Israelites, the Israelites occupied that land as well.

But occupying lands outside of Canaan was not Moses's goal. The Israelites continued to push toward the Promised Land, and they camped across the river Jordan from the city of Jericho, a walled city that was the key to breaking into Palestine's central highlands.

A Preview of Coming Attractions

The Moabites were terrified of Israel. Desperate, Balak, the king of Moab, sent for one of the most curious characters to be found in the Old Testament. The man is named Balaam, and like Moses he's a prophet. In fact, we might even call him the anti-Moses!

Chapter Wrap-Up

- Korah, a Levite, leads a challenge to Moses's and Aaron's leadership. The rebels and their families are killed when the earth opens and swallows them.

- The next day the Israelites accuse Moses of killing the rebels. Only Aaron's intervention stops a deadly plague from wiping out all the people.

- A miracle budding of Aaron's staff confirms it: He and his descendants alone are to serve as priests in Israel.

- Moses fails to obey God, distorting a vital spiritual truth the Lord intended to teach. His punishment: Moses will not enter Canaan with the Israelites.

- Moses erects a serpent-topped pole that heals those bitten by deadly snakes.

- The Israelites are forced to fight the Amorites. Victorious, they occupy their land.

Study Questions

1. What motivated those who joined Korah's rebellion? What charge did they bring against Moses and Aaron?

2. What miraculous judgments ended the rebellion?

3. What is the spiritual significance of Aaron's interposing himself and stopping a plague that was killing the Israelites?

4. What is the spiritual significance of God's command to Moses to speak to the rock to bring forth water?

5. What New Testament passage provides the principle we can use to better understand the significance of many events of the Exodus period?

6. What is the spiritual significance of Moses's raising up a serpent-topped pole when serpents were killing the Israelites? In what New Testament passage is this event referred to?

Chapter Highlights:
• Go See the Seer
• My Servants
• Couldn't Do It
• Cashing In
• Moses Versus Balaam

Getting Started

With most of the first Exodus generation dead and buried in the wilderness, Israel has again been moving toward the Promised Land. On the journey they were attacked by the Amorites. The new generation fought back, defeated the Amorite nation, and have now occupied Amorite lands east of the Jordan River.

This victory has terrified the neighboring Moabites and Midianites. The king of Moab is convinced he'd lose to Israel in battle. So he's decided to call for supernatural aid! He's about to send for someone he's convinced can help, a man called Balaam.

the River
the Euphrates

Go See the Seer

NUMBERS 22:2–6 *Now Balak the son of Zippor saw all that Israel had done to the Amorites. And Moab was exceedingly afraid of the people because they were many, and Moab was sick with dread because of the children of Israel . . . Then he sent messengers to Balaam the son of Beor at Pethor, which is near* **the River** *in the land of the sons of his people, to call him, saying: "Look, a people has come from Egypt. See, they cover the face of the earth, and are settling next to me! Therefore please come at once, curse this people for me, for they are too mighty for me. Perhaps I shall be able to defeat them and drive them out of the land, for I know that he whom you bless is blessed, and he whom you curse is cursed." (NKJV)*

Who Is This Guy?

what others say

Dennis T. Olson

The first character is Balaam, a professional seer or prophet who travels about and curses military enemies for money. He is a kind of unattached hired gun, a mercenary, but his only weapons are words that have the power to curse or bless.[1]

go to

last will and testament
Genesis 27

blessing as a prayer
Numbers 6:24–26

**God source of all
blessing**
Genesis 12;
Psalm 5:2;
Deuteronomy
11:26–28

**consequences of
disobedience**
Deuteronomy 28:20

key point

It's clear that Balaam established quite a reputation before the Israelites ever approached Canaan. He was known to possess supernatural powers. When Balaam blessed people they were blessed, and when he cursed people they stayed cursed.

- *The power to bless.* It was common in Old Testament times for the heads of households to bless their children. In some cases this blessing served as a <u>last will and testament</u>. Or when the head of a household or a family pronounced a blessing on a child or subordinate in God's name, the blessing might <u>serve as a prayer</u>, which all expected to be answered, for God is recognized as the <u>source of all blessing</u>.

But in the pagan world, a blessing was also viewed as possessing supernatural power. According to the *Theological Wordbook of the Old Testament*, to bless means "to endue with power for success, prosperity, fecundity, longevity, etc."[2] King Balak was convinced that Balaam possessed this supernatural power.

- *The power to curse.* Like bless, "curse" has several meanings. One Hebrew word translated "curse," *'alah*, generally indicates a solemn warning. Another Hebrew word, *'arar*, goes beyond the idea of warning to define <u>consequences of disobeying God</u>. In other cases, a "curse" is an announcement of the consequences of disobedience, as in Genesis 3, where God explains what now must follow Adam and Eve's sin.

But to curse can mean far more. In the ancient world curses were viewed as magic tools that a person with occult powers could use to harm an enemy. The concept is that a curse binds or limits an individual or people, making them vulnerable. This meaning of "to curse" is definitely intended where the Hebrew term *'qabab* appears, as it does eight times in the story of Balaam.

There is no doubt that Balak intended to call on supernatural powers to paralyze Israel, so the Moabites and their Midianite allies could drive them away.

Such was Balaam's reputation for using magic to supernaturally bless and to supernaturally curse, that he was the natural one for King Balak to enlist.

R. Dennis Cole

Ancient Near East texts recount the power of priests and prophets to discern, intervene, and even manipulate the will of the gods through means of augury, special sacrificial rituals, and oral pronouncement of blessing or cursing . . . The power to curse one's enemies via ritual and oral pronouncement would be an invaluable gift whereby the upper hand could be gained on the divine level and military victory achieved in the human sphere.[3]

R. K. Harrison

That Balaam was a real person and not a legendary figure has been made evident additionally by the discovery at Deir 'Alla in modern Jordan of an Aramaic prophet text. Its author is described as "Balaam son of Beor" and is spoken of as a seer of the gods whose specialty was that of a professional **imprecator** who imposed curses upon others. This material was recovered from what seemed to be a sanctuary or a shrine and testifies to the high esteem that Balaam claimed in antiquity.[4]

imprecator
a person who curses others

occult
having to do with the supernatural

pass through fire
be burned as an offering to an idol

spiritist
A person who serves as a channel through which a "spirit" speaks.

What About the Occult?

We know without doubt that the people of Canaan were deeply involved in **occult** practices. In Deuteronomy, Moses forbids the Israelites to engage in any of them, saying:

DEUTERONOMY 18:9–14 *When you come into the land which the LORD your God is giving you, you shall not learn to follow the abominations of those nations. There shall not be found among you anyone who makes his son or his daughter* ***pass through the fire****, or one who practices witchcraft, or a sooth-sayer, or one who interprets omens, or a sorcerer, or one who con-jures spells, or a medium, or a* ***spiritist****, or one who calls up the dead. For all who do these things are an abomination to the LORD, and because of these abominations the LORD your God drives them out before you. You shall be blameless before the LORD your God. For these nations which you will dispossess lis-tened to soothsayers and diviners; but as for you, the LORD your God has not appointed such for you. (NKJV)*

go to

sacrificing to demons
Leviticus 17:7;
Deuteronomy 32:17

demonic influence or
possession
Matthew 8:29–33;
9:33;
Luke 13:10–16

what others say

Christopher J. H. Wright

The list of practices here is comprehensive and not at all out-of-date, since all these forms of occult, magic, and spiritism are still widespread today. And we must assume that, given the consistency of God, they are just as *detestable to the Lord* now as they were then. That they should be put in the same "detestable" category as child-sacrifice is an interesting window on biblical values. God knows there are more things that destroy human life and dignity than physical fire. The same severe moral assessment of the occult is implied in the statement that *because of these practices, the Lord your God will drive out those nations* (v.12), which is a reminder of the moral context in which the OT sets the conquest.[5]

The existence of such occult practices in every civilization is evidence of humankind's sense of need for some supernatural source of information about the future, or some way to influence events. The problem with the occult is that such practices may actually tap real supernatural powers . . . powers that are demonic and evil. The Old Testament makes it clear that when pagans sacrificed to idols they were in fact <u>sacrificing to demons</u>!

When Christians today go to a palm reader or spiritist, or seek guidance from a horoscope or Ouija board, they violate the clear command of Scripture to avoid the occult. One reason for this prohibition is that Christians are to live by faith and be led by God's Holy Spirit. The other reason is that such dabbling in the occult may open a person up to <u>demonic influence or possession</u>. Evil spirits do exist, and God's people are to have nothing to do with them.

what others say

David F. Payne

It would plainly be an exaggeration to suggest that the average horoscope page in a magazine encourages immorality. Most often their recommendations are obviously innocent enough. But divination shaded into what we might call black magic, and it sought to manipulate gods and unseen powers—often enough to cause the hurt of other human beings. At their worst, occult practices are undoubtedly demonic and downright evil.[6]

Back to Balaam

Relying on Scripture's description of Balaam's reputation, it seems clear that this seer—for this is how those with the power to bless and curse were <u>identified in ancient times</u>—truly was in contact with the spirit world, and possessed supernatural powers. Balak certainly was convinced. "I know that he whom you bless is blessed, and he whom you curse is cursed" (Numbers 22:6 NKJV).

go to

identified in ancient times
1 Samuel 9:9;
2 Samuel 15:27

> NUMBERS 22:7 *So the elders of Moab and the elders of Midian departed with the diviner's fee in their hand, and they came to Balaam and spoke to him the words of Balak. (NKJV)*

God Intervenes

> NUMBERS 22:9–12 *Then God came to Balaam and said, "Who are these men with you?" . . . And God said to Balaam, "You shall not go with them; you shall not curse the people, for they are blessed." (NKJV)*

Some have assumed because Balaam told Balak's representatives that he would have to wait to see what God told him, that the Lord was the source of Balaam's power. They express doubt that God would actually speak to a pagan, especially one who was linked with demons. We'll see later that Balaam was hardly on God's side, even though he speaks of Yahweh as "my God" (Numbers 22:18 NKJV).

God had a specific, simple, and unmistakably clear message for Balaam. "You shall not go with them." So when Balaam reported to Balak's ambassadors the next morning, he told them, "Go back to your land, for the LORD has refused to give me permission to go with you" (Numbers 22:13 NKJV). Disappointed, the ambassadors returned to Balak with the bad news.

That should have settled it. But Balak didn't give up.

Take This Blank Check. Please!

> NUMBERS 22:15–17 *Then Balak again sent princes, more numerous and more honorable than they. And they came to Balaam and said to him, "Thus says Balak the son of Zippor: 'Please let nothing hinder you from coming to me; for I will cer-*

tainly honor you greatly, and I will do whatever you say to me. Therefore please come, curse this people for me.'" (NKJV)

Balak was offering Balaam a blank check and saying, "Fill in any amount you want."

There's no doubt this offer got to Balaam. His next words suggest that his eyes lit up as he imagined the "house full of silver and gold" that he might demand from the desperate ruler (Numbers 22:18 NKJV). There was only one problem. God had given Balaam that specific, simple, and unmistakably clear message: "Don't go."

God's Way or My Way?

key point

Christians today often find themselves facing Balaam's dilemma. There's something they want badly. They ask God for guidance and sense His answer. But they don't like the answer. Their desire for what God denies is so intense that they keep on asking, begging the Lord to change His mind.

- Lord, let me marry this person.
- Lord, I've just got to move on. Don't make me stay here.
- Lord, I can't go *there*. Please, somewhere else. Anywhere else!

Sometimes we want our own way so badly that the Lord releases us. We marry the person we think we love; we move on when we should have waited; or we refuse to step out in faith and follow. When we choose our way over God's way, we discover there is a vast difference between God's best and what God permits.

This is a difference that Balaam is about to experience. Balaam desperately wanted to go with Balak's ambassadors and fill his house with silver and gold. In essence he asked God to change His mind. Balaam told Balak's representatives to wait, hoping that God would have more to say and would permit Balaam to go.

That night God came to Balaam again and told him, "If the men come to call you, rise and go with them; but only the word which I speak to you—that shall you do" (Numbers 22:20 NKJV).

Not Your Will but My Will

NUMBERS 22:21–22 *So Balaam rose in the morning, saddled his donkey, and went with the princes of Moab. Then God's anger was aroused because he went, and the Angel of the LORD took His stand in the way as an adversary against him.* (NKJV)

Song lyrics sum up Balaam's spiritual condition: "Do what you wanna do. Go where you wanna go." He had been totally unwilling to do what God commanded. So God gave Balaam permission to do what he intended to do all along. Balaam would do what he wanted to do, and go where he wanted to go.

That's the thing about continuing to pray for leading when we already know God's will. Such prayers are rebellion in disguise. They are an implicit challenge to God's right to direct our lives. They are the opposite of Jesus's prayer in Gethsemane, "Nevertheless, not what I will, but what You will" (Mark 14:36 NKJV).

By going, Balaam was spitting in God's face, loudly announcing, "Not what You will, Lord, but what I will."

The result was that God's *anger was aroused*. Balaam was in real danger of dying then and there!

Will the Real Donkey Please Stand Up?

Events now take a ridiculous twist. As God's Angel is about to strike Balaam, the donkey he's riding on suddenly shies and turns off the path. Balaam strikes the donkey and jerks the bit to turn her back on the path. A few yards farther on, the path leads between stone walls enclosing two vineyards. Again the donkey sees the Angel ready to strike. This time she moves so close to one of the walls that Balaam's foot is bruised. Balaam clubs her again with his staff. Farther on, the path narrows even more. Now there's no room for the donkey to squeeze to one side. So she simply lies down. Furious, Balaam clubs his donkey again.

At this point God gives the donkey the ability to speak, and she challenges her master. In all the years he's ridden her, has the donkey ever done anything like this before? Balaam admits she hasn't. And then the Lord opens Balaam's eyes and he sees the Angel of the Lord standing there with a drawn sword.

we're warned
1 Corinthians
12:7–11

effectiveness of ministry
Philippians 1:15–18

The real donkey in this story isn't the beast of burden, but Balaam. Balaam, who failed to see any significance in the strange behavior of his donkey. Balaam, who imagined that he could show disrespect for God with impunity. Balaam, who assumed that he could go his own way without suffering any adverse consequences. The real donkey is Balaam, who is blind to such spiritual realities, and blind to the danger of going his own way.

If Donkeys Can Talk

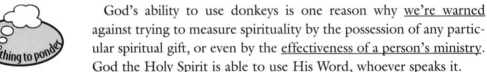

The young daughter of a friend of ours thinks she's in love with an older man. She's a committed Christian; he's training to be in ministry. Despite serious character flaws this young man is an enthusiastic witness and has won several to Christ. He's also a gifted speaker, whose sermons have impressed many. Somehow the young woman, like many others, views his gifts as proof that he's a mature and truly spiritual individual. She's apparently never stopped to consider that God is able to cause even donkeys to speak.

God's ability to use donkeys is one reason why <u>we're warned</u> against trying to measure spirituality by the possession of any particular spiritual gift, or even by the <u>effectiveness of a person's ministry</u>. God the Holy Spirit is able to use His Word, whoever speaks it.

When the New Testament gives qualifications for spiritual leadership, it doesn't tell us to look closely at a person's gift or to count the number of people who have been converted. Instead we're told to look closely at the potential leader's character. Spiritual maturity is measured by evidence of one's growth in Christlikeness, displayed in a blameless, temperate, sober-minded character. It is the person who is marked by good behavior, who isn't greedy for money or violent or quarrelsome or covetous and who thus displays integrity, whom we can trust and follow (1 Timothy 3:1–7).

Somehow our friend's daughter can't seem to see the significance of the lies her love has told her parents, of his indifference to a young daughter of his whom he has never supported, or his failure to work to pay his bills. She only sees the apparent effect of his witnessing and his ability to speak convincingly. She utterly fails to consider the fact that God is able to work even through donkeys.

What Do You Mean, "If"?

NUMBERS 22:31–34 *Then the LORD opened Balaam's eyes, and he saw the Angel of the LORD standing in the way with His drawn sword in His hand; and he bowed his head and fell flat on his face . . . And Balaam said to the Angel of the LORD, "I have sinned, for I did not know You stood in the way against me. Now therefore, if it displeases You, I will turn back."* (NKJV)

Two things in Balaam's words to the Angel of the Lord stand out. The seer confesses, "I have sinned, for I did not know You stood in the way against me." But the sin Balaam should have confessed was his sin in not bowing to God's will at the beginning, when God told him, "You shall not go with them" (Numbers 22:12 NKJV).

The second thing that stands out is Balaam's hypocritical offer, "If it displeases You, I will turn back."

What does he mean, "if"? There was no "if" about it, and Balaam certainly knew it. The moment the Lord told Balaam, "You shall not go with them," Balaam knew that going with the men would displease the Lord. His sin was that he didn't care whether God was displeased or not. He was greedy for gain, and eager to go anyway.

Of course, with the sword-wielding Angel standing before him now, there was nothing else Balaam could do but offer to go back. Yet the "if" tells us that Balaam still hoped he might go and gain a fortune.

---

what others say

James Philip

Perhaps the chief lesson here, however (and which the New Testament writers take up in their application) is the character study it gives us of Balaam himself. It is a remarkable picture of the battle that went on in his own heart—a battle for integrity of character, a battle which he eventually lost, if we interpret the last stage of the story aright. Thus, within the battle to harm and hurt Israel, there was also this hidden battle for the soul of a man.[7]

apply it

One Lesson Learned

go to

ruled out the occult
Deuteronomy
18:9–14

NUMBERS 22:35 *Then the Angel of the LORD said to Balaam, "Go with the men, but only the word that I speak to you, that shall you speak." So Balaam went with the princes of Balak.* (NKJV)

The appearance of the Angel of the Lord and Balaam's brush with death seem to have reached the seer. God has made it very clear to Balaam that he has no more leeway. He must say what God tells him to say, whatever his employer expects.

When Baalam reaches Balak the first thing he does is make sure that Balak understands this point. He'll take the king's money. But he won't promise results. "The word that God puts in my mouth, that I must speak" (Numbers 22:38 NKJV). The last thing Balaam wants to do is to face the Angel of the Lord again!

apply it

When God <u>ruled out any contact with practitioners of the occult</u> for Israel, He was not implying that His people wouldn't need special supernatural guidance. What the Lord was saying was that believers are not to seek such guidance from occult, or demonic, sources.

Specific Versus General Guidance

Through Moses, God provided Israel with *general guidance*. That is, God provided rules and principles that defined for His people how they were to live. There was no need for special guidance as to whether or not to commit adultery. There was no need for special guidance as to whether it was acceptable to steal in a particular situation. There was no need for special guidance for a person called to testify in a court case to know whether or not he should tell the truth. God's *torah* was clear on such points.

But the written word provided *only* general guidance. There would always be situations in which God's people had to make decisions where no ruling or principle of *torah* applied.

Flash Forward

David and his men are exiles, pursued by King Saul. Saul intends to kill David and his followers. When a band of Philistines attack the Israelite town of Keilah, David doesn't know what to do. Should he go help his fellow countrymen? Or should he keep on hiding from Saul? The written Scriptures are no help here. David needs a specific word from the Lord to guide him. So David inquires of God, and God answers: "Go and attack the Philistines, and save Keilah" (1 Samuel 23:2 NKJV). David attacks and saves the city.

But King Saul hears that David is at Keilah and calls out his army. Again David faces a decision where the general guidance provided in Scripture doesn't help. So again David inquires of the Lord: "Will Saul come down?" And the Lord tells David, "He will come down." Now David has another question: "Will the men of Keilah deliver me and my men into the hand of Saul?" Again the Lord answers, "They will deliver you" (1 Samuel 23:11–12 NKJV).

Now that David knows what will happen, he knows what to do. David takes his six hundred men and escapes into the wilderness. When Saul learns David has left the city, Saul calls off his expedition.

the Urim and the Thummim
Exodus 28:30;
Leviticus 8:8;
Numbers 27:21

Inquiring of God

In the incident described above, David needed a supernatural source that could provide specific guidance. He could reason out what was *likely* to happen. But David really needed to know. There was no way that David could obtain specific guidance for his situation from the Scriptures. David had to get answers directly from God.

It was this kind of situation that drove pagans to occult practices. With such practices ruled out, what could a person like David do?

Old Testament *torah* did provide one way that a person might get specific guidance from the Lord. This was by "inquiring of the Lord" through <u>the Urim and the Thummim</u>. The Urim and Thummim were two objects, possibly stones, that were placed in a pocket in the ephod, or vest, worn by the high priest. When a person came to the high priest to ask God a specific question, the high priest reached into the ephod and drew out one of the two stones. The stone he chose provided a "yes" or "no" answer to the question

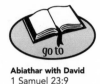

Abiathar with David
1 Samuel 23:9

posed. As at that time a priest named Abiathar had the ephod, and <u>Abiathar was with David</u>, David could use the Urim and Thummim to get specific guidance from the Lord.

While the Urim and Thummim could meet the need for specific guidance in difficult situations, there were limitations:

1. *A person had to have access to the high priest.* There was only one high priest in Israel, and not everyone had access to him. A king might call for the high priest and inquire about a matter of national interest, but the average person couldn't seek guidance for his or her personal situation.

2. *The Urim and Thummim gave only "yes" or "no" answers.* A person had to ask the right questions in the right way. It was possible or even likely that important information wouldn't be communicated simply because the one inquiring didn't ask the right questions.

3. *A person had to seek guidance.* All too often in Israel's history, rulers and others didn't want to know God's will. They wanted to go their own way, and so failed to inquire of the Lord. The Urim and Thummim did not provide God with a channel through which He could take the initiative in giving specific guidance to His people.

For all these reasons, while the Urim and Thummin were available to provide specific guidance for those willing and able to inquire of God, they failed to meet all of Israel's or God's need for a channel of special communication.

<u>Enter Stage Right: The Prophet</u>

God had forbidden His people to seek guidance through the occult sources used by pagan nations. But there would be times when His people would need the kind of specific guidance that the written word simply could not provide.

In the Deuteronomy passage that forbids occult practices, the Lord goes on to explain how He Himself will provide the special guidance His people will need:

DEUTERONOMY 18:14–19 *For these nations which you will dispossess listened to soothsayers and diviners; but as for you, the LORD your God has not appointed such for you. The LORD your God will raise up for you a **Prophet** like me from your midst, from your brethren. Him you shall hear . . . "I will raise up for them a Prophet like you from among their brethren, and will put My words in His mouth, and He shall speak to them all that I command Him. And it shall be that whoever will not hear My words, which He speaks in My name, I will require it of him."* (NKJV)

prophet
a person through whom God speaks

interpreting
correctly discerning the meaning

new revelation
previously unknown information, truth

God's people will have no need to look to demonic occult sources. God promises to "raise up" for them "a Prophet like" Moses. Like Moses, the prophet will be God's spokesperson, and God will "put My words in His mouth." Through the prophet, God will take the initiative and provide the special guidance His people need. Between the Word, which provides general guidance, and the Prophet, who provides special guidance, every need of God's Old Testament people for guidance will be met!

key point

The Law of Double Reference

Those who study Scripture have noticed that special rules, or principles, apply to **interpreting** different types of biblical literature. One of the rules for the interpretation of predictive prophecy is called the "law of double reference." That is, a single biblical prediction may provide information about more than one event.

Deuteronomy 18:14–19 is a good example. As the capitalized pronouns, He, Him, and His, in this passage indicate, the translators believe that Moses is speaking primarily of Jesus, the Messiah and Son of God. Jesus was "like Moses" in that He appeared with a **new revelation** from the Lord that forever reshaped the way God's people would live in harmony with Him.

prophecy

But this passage also refers to all those prophets that God would send Israel until the Prophet appeared. Throughout Israel's history, God would raise up men and women, put His words in their mouths, and through them speak to Israel. The prophets would speak with the full authority of God; their words would be the very Word of God. And Israel was required to hear, to obey, the words of the prophets God sent.

Prophets, the True and the False

DEUTERONOMY 18:20 *But the prophet who presumes to speak a word in My name, which I have not commanded him to speak, or who speaks in the name of other gods, that prophet shall die.* (NKJV)

God's promise of prophets posed a problem. How could the Israelites tell the difference between someone who was really speaking God's words, and someone who was making His message up? In Deuteronomy the Lord provides four tests that a true prophet must meet:

prophecy

1. "If there arises among you a prophet or a dreamer of dreams, and he gives you a sign or a wonder, and the sign or the wonder comes to pass, of which he spoke to you, saying, 'Let us go after other gods' . . . you shall not listen to the words of that prophet or that dreamer of dreams" (Deuteronomy 13:1–3 NKJV). The first test of a prophet is that his teaching must not contradict the written Word. Even if a person works miracles or accurately predicts the future, he is not a true prophet unless his teaching is in complete harmony with Scripture.

2. "God will raise up for you a Prophet like me from your midst, from your brethren" (Deuteronomy 18:15 NKJV). God would never entrust His Word to a pagan. Only an Israelite could be a true prophet.

3. "The prophet who presumes to speak a word in My name, which I have not commanded him to speak, or who speaks in the name of other gods, that prophet shall die" (Deuteronomy 18:20 NKJV). The true prophet will speak in the name of Yahweh. That is, he will claim that he is delivering Yahweh's message, not a message from some other deity.

4. "When a prophet speaks in the name of the LORD, if the thing does not happen or come to pass, that is the thing which the LORD has not spoken; the prophet has spoken it presumptuously; you shall not be afraid of him" (Deuteronomy 18:22 NKJV). God promises to authenticate the true prophet by the simple fact that what he or she says will happen, does happen.

Flash Forward

God sends the prophet Isaiah to King Ahaz of the southern Hebrew kingdom, Judah. The king is terrified because the Syrians and the northern Hebrew kingdom, Israel, have forged an alliance against him. Isaiah (7:14) tells the king not to worry, and tells him to ask God for a sign authenticating this good news. Ahab refuses to ask for a sign. Isaiah then utters a famous messianic prophecy: One day a virgin will bear a child, who will be Immanuel, God with us.

go to

predictions Isaiah made
Isaiah 37:5–7;
38:1–8

But this prophecy was fulfilled some seven hundred years later in the birth of Jesus. It could hardly authenticate Isaiah as a true prophet.

So Isaiah points to the infant in his arms, his son, Shear-Jashub. Isaiah says that before the child is weaned, the two kingdoms Ahaz fears will be crushed by the Assyrians. Two years later the power of the Syrians and Israel has been broken. Isaiah's prophecy has come true. Events have again provided proof that Isaiah was a true prophet of God.

Near Term, Far Term

In the story above from Isaiah chapter 7, the prophet Isaiah made two predictions. The first, concerning the virgin birth, lay over seven hundred years in the future. It could hardly authenticate him as a true prophet to his contemporaries. So Isaiah also uttered another prediction, one that was fulfilled within two years. This prophecy, and <u>other predictions Isaiah made</u> that were fulfilled quickly, made it clear to everyone that Isaiah spoke the words of God.

key point

Prophets typically gave "near-term" predictions, which would be fulfilled quickly. Many also made "far-term" predictions, which were to be fulfilled in the distant future. The fulfillment of the near-term predictions proved to the prophets' contemporaries that they truly did speak for the Lord. And the fulfillment of dozens of far-term predictions provides evidence that the Scriptures the prophets penned are indeed the very Word of God.

What About Today?

I've pointed out that Scripture provides *general guidance* for believers, but that often we feel the need for *specific supernatural*

go to

lives in believers
1 Corinthians 12:7, 13;
Romans 8:9

supernatural guidance
Acts 13:2–3; 20:22
Romans 8:14

committed to obey
John 7:17

guidance for difficult choices. In the days when Israel related to God through the *torah*, the need for specific guidance was met through the Urim and Thummim, and also through prophets whom God raised up.

Today we no longer live under the *torah* system. We Christians rely on God's Word for *general guidance* on how to please God. But do we have a source we can turn to for *specific guidance* in situations that simply aren't covered in the written Word?

The answer is yes! And that source is God the Holy Spirit, who <u>lives within every true believer</u>. The Holy Spirit who is present in us provides specific <u>supernatural guidance</u> when we rely on Him and are <u>committed to do God's will</u>.

Today you and I have direct access to the One who knows the best choice we are to make in every circumstance, God Himself! What an insult it would be if we looked to some occult source for the guidance that God the Spirit is eager and able to provide. And what an affirmation of confidence in God's faithfulness to rely constantly on His leading.

He Tried, but He Couldn't Do It

Back on the plains of Moab, Balaam is ready to lay a curse on the Israelites. He has Balak build seven altars, and the two offer a bull and a ram on each. Balaam goes to a desolate height overlooking the Israelite camp to meet with Lord. But when Balaam returns he has no curse, but a blessing!

> **NUMBERS 23:8, 10**
> *How shall I curse whom God has not cursed?*
> *And how shall I denounce whom the LORD has not denounced? . . .*
> *Let me die the death of the righteous,*
> *And let my end be like his! (NKJV)*

Balak screams at Balaam, "What have you done to me? I took you to curse my enemies, and look, you have blessed them bountifully!" (Numbers 23:11 NKJV).

Balak suggests they try again. This time they move to another vantage point, and build seven more altars and offer fourteen more sacrifices. This is in fact a second attempt to use sorcery against the Israelites by manipulating God (Numbers 24:1). Again Balaam meets with God, and returns with a blessing!

latter days
a phrase that often
refers to events at
history's end

NUMBERS 23:23–24
For there is no sorcery against Jacob,
Nor any divination against Israel.
It now must be said of Jacob
And of Israel, "Oh, what God has done!"
Look, a people rises like a lioness,
And lifts itself up like a lion;
It shall not lie down until it devours the prey,
And drinks the blood of the slain. (NKJV)

Balak is near distraction. In frustration he tells Balaam, If you can't curse them, at least don't bless them! But Balaam is bound to report what God says to him.

Balaam tries again, this time without relying on sorcery. But the response is the same.

NUMBERS 24:8–9
God brings him out of Egypt;
He has strength like a wild ox;
He shall consume the nations, his enemies;
He shall break their bones
And pierce them with his arrows . . .
Blessed is he who blesses you,
And cursed is he who curses you. (NKJV)

Now Balak is really angry: "I called you to curse my enemies, and look, you have bountifully blessed them these three times! Now therefore, flee to your place. I said I would greatly honor you, but in fact, the LORD has kept you back from honor" (Numbers 24:10–11 NKJV).

But Balaam has the last word. In a powerful prophecy of the second coming of Jesus, Balaam predicts the ultimate triumph of God's people in the **"latter days"** (Numbers 24:15–24).

prophecy

It would seem that Balaam has done all he can. The text simply tells us that Balak and Balaam then separated, and returned home.

It's only later that we learn the rest of the story!

Cashing In

We have to put together the rest of the story from brief comments embedded in later chapters of Numbers. All we know from the next chapter of Numbers is what's happening in the Israelite camp. And that's bad enough!

harlotry
physical adultery
and spiritual adultery, i.e., the worship
of pagan gods

Baal of Peor
"Baal" means "lord"
or "god." "Peor" is
a place-name. The
phrase means the
god who owns or
rules at Peor.

Idolatry!

NUMBERS 25:1–3 *Now Israel remained in Acacia Grove, and the people began to commit **harlotry** with the women of Moab. They invited the people to the sacrifices of their gods, and the people ate and bowed down to their gods. So Israel was joined to **Baal of Peor**, and the anger of the LORD was aroused against Israel. (NKJV)*

In modern espionage novels it's called a "honey pot." An intelligence service sets out to gain control over a potential source of information by trapping him in illicit sex. In this first recorded use of this strategy, the Moabites set up a camp filled with beautiful women next to the Israelites. As the women make it clear they're available, Israelites begin to visit the Moabite camp. Blinded by lust, the Israelite men soon find themselves taking part in idolatry and in the sexual orgies associated with pagan worship. As we might expect, "the anger of the LORD was aroused against Israel."

It's here that we stop and wonder. Where did the Moabites get the idea of setting out the honey pot?

Numbers 31 provides the answer. The chapter describes a war between Israel and the Midianites. One of the casualties of that war is none other than Balaam (31:8). When the Israelite army returns with a number of women captives, Moses is upset. "Look," he says, "these women caused the children of Israel, *through the counsel of Balaam*, to trespass against the LORD in the incident of Peor . . . Now therefore, . . . kill every woman who has known a man intimately" (Numbers 31:16–17 NKJV, emphasis added).

The honey pot was Balaam's idea!

If Balaam couldn't curse Israel himself, he reasoned that perhaps he could manipulate the Lord into cursing them for him! Balaam knew that the Lord is righteous, and punishes sin. And so Balaam recommended that Balak and his allies seduce the Israelites sexually, and then spiritually. Balaam supposed that if the Israelites were unfaithful to the Lord, the Lord would destroy them. And Balaam would earn his house full of silver and gold!

It seems that Balaam went home a wealthy man. He had found a way to cash in. But his ill-gotten gain did him no good. In fact, Balaam's advice led directly to the war in which he was killed, as the Lord told Moses to "harass the Midianites, and attack them; for they

key point

harassed you with their schemes by which they seduced you in the matter of Peor" (Numbers 25:17–18 NKJV).

Back in the Israelite Camp

Balaam was correct in believing that the Lord would be angered by His people's idolatry. But rather than strike out at the whole nation, the Lord told Moses, "Take all the leaders of the people and hang the offenders before the LORD, out in the sun, that the fierce anger of the LORD may turn away from Israel" (Numbers 25:4 NKJV). But before the Lord's command could be carried out, twenty-four thousand died in a plague (Numbers 25:9).

With that twenty-four thousand, the last of the first generation of Israelites fell. Of those who had left Egypt as adults, only Moses, Joshua, and Caleb remained alive.

The plot Balaam had hatched to force God to curse the Israelites had instead purified the nation by ridding it of the last of the rebellious generation.

The new generation was nearly ready to enter, and to conquer, Canaan.

Moses Versus Balaam

The New Testament comments on both Moses and Balaam. Moses is commended as a person who was "faithful in all [God's] house" (Hebrews 3:5 NKJV), and Moses won a place in Hebrews 11's gallery of Heroes of the Faith.

Balaam, on the other hand, is condemned, and three New Testament books warn believers against adopting his ways:

- *2 Peter 2:15* Peter warns Christians against contemporary false prophets, who have "forsaken the right way and gone astray, following the way of Balaam the son of Beor, who loved the wages of unrighteousness" (NKJV). The "way of Balaam" is marked by using religion to seek wealth. One test for false prophets in today's church is their attitude toward money. The greater love they display for material riches, the less we should trust their teachings.

- *Jude 8, 11* The book of Jude also warns against false prophets, and describes them as those who "defile the flesh, [and] reject authority," saying that they "have run greedily in the error of Balaam for profit" (NKJV). The *error of Balaam* was to choose wealth over obedience.

- *Revelation 2:14* Jesus speaks of those "who hold the doctrine of Balaam, who taught Balak to put a stumbling block before the children of Israel, to eat things sacrificed to idols, and to commit sexual immorality" (Revelation 2:14 NKJV). The *doctrine of Balaam* is the sanctioning of immorality by religion. For instance, those today who reject the authority of Scripture and permit the ordination of homosexuals practice the doctrine of Balaam.

key point

what others say

William Barclay

In this story Balaam did not do what Balak wanted him to do, but his unholy desire to do it is printed across the whole narrative. Balaam already emerges as a most detestable character. In Numbers 25 there emerges the second story. In it, Israel is seduced into the worship of Baal with evil and dreadful and repulsive moral consequences. As we read later (Numbers 31:8, 16), it was Balaam who was responsible for that seduction, and he perished miserably because he taught others to sin.

Out of this composite story Balaam stands for two things. (a) He stands for the covetous man, who was prepared to sin in order to gain reward. (b) He stands for the evil man, who was guilty of the greatest of all sins—the sin of teaching others to sin . . . To sin for the sake of gain is bad; but to rob someone else of his or her innocence, and to teach another to sin, is the most sinful of sins.[8]

What a vast difference between the two men, Moses and Balaam.

The Anti-Moses?

In almost every respect, Balaam is the opposite of Moses. Moses was commissioned by God for his mission. Balaam was warned by God not to go on his mission. Moses was reluctant to go. Balaam was eager to go. Moses's desire was to know and obey God. Balaam's desire was to gain wealth even if it meant disobeying God.

Moses sought to protect Israel. Balaam sought to destroy Israel. Moses was committed to accomplishing God's purposes. Balaam plotted to thwart God's purposes. Moses submitted to God's will. Balaam rejected and tried to subvert God's will. Moses's goal was the glory of God. Balaam's goal was to gain worldly wealth.

We could go on. But what is important is to see that each choice made by Moses and each choice made by Balaam reflect each individual's most basic commitment. Moses was committed to God. Balaam was committed to worldly wealth. Everything each did grew out of his most basic commitment.

The question we need to ask ourselves is a simple one: Am I more like Moses, committed to God and eager to glorify Him? Or am I more like Balaam, committed to this world's treasures and eager to gain them for myself?

Chapter Wrap-Up

- Threatened by Israel, the King of Moab tries to enlist the services of Balaam, a man with occult powers, to curse Israel.

- Although it's clear that God does not want Balaam to accept King Balak's commission, Balaam goes anyway.

- The reliance of the pagan world for supernatural help on practitioners of the occult is forbidden to Israel. Instead God provides specific guidance (in contrast to general guidance) through the Urim and Thummim and through His prophets.

- Balaam tries to curse Israel, but is forced to bless the nation instead.

- In an effort to earn a reward, Balaam counsels Balak to trick the Israelites into sexual sin and idolatry. The plot succeeds.

- But rather than destroy Israel, only the guilty Israelites are executed and the last of the first Exodus generation perishes. A new generation is about ready to conquer Canaan!

Study Questions

1. What does "curse" mean in the Old Testament? What does "curse" mean in this story?

2. What clues are there in this story to Balaam's motivation?

3. What difference does the author suggest between *general guidance* and *specific guidance*? Where was Israel not to turn for specific guidance? Where could Israel turn for specific guidance? Where are Christians today to look for specific guidance?

4. When Balaam was unable to curse Israel, what did he do in an effort to get money from Balak?

5. What were Balaam's assumptions in offering this counsel? How were his assumptions correct? How were they wrong?

6. What three things about Balaam does the New Testament warn us of?

7. How many contrasts between Balaam and Moses can you think of?

Chapter 13
Look Both Ways

Chapter Highlights:
- We Want a Recount
- The Logic of Lots
- Be Prepared
- Total War
- And Now, Introducing . . .

Let's Get Started

To the **Canaanites**, the vast Israelite camp must have seemed like the darkest of storm clouds, gathered just across the river Jordan. The invaders had already conquered the Amorites and Moabites and would soon crush the Midianites. How would the disorganized city-states of Canaan ever withstand their assault?

Canaanites
the peoples who lived in Canaan, the Promised Land

In the camp, Moses was readying the Israelites for the invasion. There were preparations to make. And there was a final challenge to set before the people. As the days grew shorter for the man who had led the Israelites for forty long years, it must have seemed there was simply too much to do.

We Want a Recount

NUMBERS 26:1–2 *And it came to pass, after the plague, that the LORD spoke to Moses and Eleazar the son of Aaron the priest, saying: "Take a census of all the congregation of the children of Israel from twenty years old and above, by their fathers' houses, all who are able to go to war in Israel." (NKJV)*

Just before the Israelites set out from Sinai, some forty years earlier, the Lord had ordered a census. When every male of military age had been counted, the final count was 603,550. The recount, during which every man over age twenty was counted, showed that "among these there was not a man of those who were numbered by Moses and Aaron the priest when they numbered the children of Israel in the Wilderness of Sinai" except for Caleb and Joshua (Numbers 26:64 NKJV). Yet there had hardly been a change in the strength of Israel's forces. The second census revealed that there were now 601,730 men available to fight.

At the same time there was a truly significant difference between those numbered in the first census and in the second. Moses identifies the difference in the preface to his final restatement of God's law, in Deuteronomy 4:4: "You who held fast to the LORD your God are

go to

given cities
Joshua 21

alive today, every one of you" (NKJV). Unlike the first Exodus generation that was characterized by rebelliousness, this generation is characterized by its commitment to God.

A Tribe-by-Tribe Census

Tribe	The First Census	The Second Census
Reuben	46,500	43,700
Simeon	59,300	22,200
Gad	45,650	40,500
Judah	74,600	76,500
Issachar	54,400	64,300
Zebulun	57,400	60,500
Ephraim	40,500	32,500
Manasseh	32,200	52,700
Benjamin	35,400	45,600
Dan	62,700	64,400
Ashur	41,500	53,400
Napthali	53,400	45,400

The change in tribal numbers would prove to be important, for when Canaan was conquered the amount of land each tribe received was determined on the basis of this second census (Numbers 26:54).

Count the Levites Again Too

There was also a recount of each Levite family. The first census revealed 22,000 male Levites over a month old. The second census counted 23,000. While the Levites would be given no tribal lands, they would be <u>given cities</u> scattered through the territory of the other tribes.

What About Us Girls?

NUMBERS 27:1–4 *Then came the daughters of Zelophehad . . . saying: "Our father died in the wilderness . . . and he had no sons. Why should the name of our father be removed from among his family because he had no son? Give us a possession among our father's brothers." (NKJV)*

The census had numbered the men of Israel, and land in Canaan would be distributed according to male heads of families. This was typical of all ancient civilizations, where ancestry was traced through fathers. But a delegation of women came to Moses with a problem.

When Moses brought their case to the Lord, the Lord told him that "the daughters of Zelophehad speak what is right" (Numbers 27:7 NKJV). Inheritance tradition in Israel was modified so daughters could inherit if a man had no sons. Later, this was further modified. Land originally allotted to a tribe or family was to remain in that family forever. So a daughter who inherited land must marry within her own tribe (Numbers 36:1–9).

While sons inherited the land from their fathers, it was the duty of the eldest son to provide for his mother as long as she lived, and also to care for any sisters and arrange for their marriages.

God is giving to you
Exodus 20:12;
Numbers 13:2; 15:2;
Deuteronomy 1:20;
3:20: 4:21, 40

> ### what others say
>
> **James Philip**
>
> It is remarkable to find this piece of humanitarian legislation at such an early date, when the rights of minorities, let alone minorities of women, were so little recognized or noticed, and it emphasizes once again how advanced the Mosaic code really was. But it does something far greater: It underlines the reality of the fatherly care of God for all those who have been hardly used by life, those whom misfortune has buffeted, who are the poor of the land, who tend to be forgotten in the mad whirl of life, who have few to care for them and fewer still to plead their cause.[1]

The Logic of Lots

NUMBERS 33:54 *And you shall divide the land by lot as an inheritance among your families; to the larger you shall give a larger inheritance, and to the smaller you shall give a smaller inheritance; there everyone's inheritance shall be whatever falls to him by lot. (NKJV)*

This verse gives us the reason why it was so important to take the second census. It also explains why resolving potential problems, like the one posed by the daughters of Zelophehad, was so important. Again and again God had spoken of Canaan as "the land which I am giving to you" or as the land "which the LORD your <u>God is giving to you</u>."

go to

determining God's will
Leviticus 16:8;
1 Samuel 14:42

To emphasize the fact that the land truly was God's gift, the Lord would do more than simply provide military victory. God Himself would *distribute the land by lot.* Today, rather than saying "casting lots," we would probably say "throwing dice" or "drawing straws." Casting lots was normally a game of chance.

In certain circumstances, casting lots was used as a means of <u>determining God's will</u>, for Proverbs 16:33 notes that "the lot is cast into the lap, but its every decision is from the LORD" (NKJV).

In distributing the land of Canaan each tribe would receive its territory according to how the lots fell. Each extended family would be given its land within tribal territory by lot. And each household would be assigned its land with the family territory by lot.

The result of using this process was that each household in Israel realized that its land had been specially chosen for it by God Himself. The plot where the house stood and its surrounding fields truly were gifts, given by God personally. Those precious gifts of God were to be handed down from one generation to the next, and were never to change hands (Numbers 36:9).

> **what others say**
>
> **R. Dennis Cole**
>
> The land belonged to the Lord, and it was His to grant to whom He desired. By His love, grace, and mercy He had promised and was now presenting the gift of the land to His people Israel. The distribution of the land among the tribes was to be proportionate, based on the size of the tribe through the casting of lots. Lots were cast with the confidence in the providence of God to apportion justly and fairly among the tribal components of the people of the land.[2]

Flash Forward

From the window of his palace, King Ahab of Israel can see a nearby vineyard. *What a great place for a garden*, he thinks. So the king contacts the owner, Naboth, with an offer Ahab is sure Naboth won't refuse. He'll pay cash for the vineyard, or he'll trade Naboth an even better vineyard for it. Naboth is shocked, and his answer is a resounding no. "The LORD forbid that I should give the inheritance of my fathers to you!" (1 Kings 21:3 NKJV). That vineyard had been a gift to his family, specially chosen and given by the Lord.

Ahab doesn't take the refusal well. He goes home and sulks. When his wife, Jezebel, asks what's wrong, Ahab explains. Jezebel shakes her head. What a wimp! She arranges to have Naboth accused of blasphemy, and Naboth is stoned to death. She then tells Ahab, "Go ahead, take the vineyard. Naboth's gone." Ahab cheers up and rushes off to have the vines torn out so he can plant his vegetables. What Ahab doesn't know is that one day in the place where Naboth's blood had been shed, dogs would lick the blood of the king (1 Kings 21).

vows
commitments made to God above and beyond what the law required

This Land Is My Land

Before the Israelites set foot in Canaan, the Lord defined its boundaries (Numbers 34:1–12). Israel did not occupy most of the Promised Land until the time of King David. But one day it would all belong to the descendants of the second Exodus generation.

God truly would give the land of Canaan to the Israelites. Soon the Lord would personally distribute a parcel of land to each household. From the time of the conquest onward, the godly in Israel would honor the Lord for the land they called "my land," deeply aware that the land on which they lived was really "His land."

Be Prepared

There were other preparations to be made before the invasion of Canaan could take place. Moses's replacement must be appointed. The duty the nation owed to God needed to be reemphasized. The matter of **vows** needed clarification. And there was unfinished business with the Midianites. Then, too, there was the shocking request of the Reubenites and Gadites to be considered. There was also a need to select "cities of refuge," something we'll consider in the next chapter. It seems that even in Moses's time, "housekeeping items"— the drudgery of taking care of details—simply couldn't be avoided. Yet each detail was important, and Moses wasn't a man to leave matters to others.

key point

Moses's Replacement

NUMBERS 27:15–17 *Then Moses spoke to the LORD, saying: "Let the LORD, the God of the spirits of all flesh, set a man over the congregation, who may go out before them and go in before them, who may lead them out and bring them in, that the congregation of the LORD may not be like sheep which have no shepherd." (NKJV)*

God's answer was to select Joshua, "a man in whom is the Spirit" (Numbers 27:18 NKJV), and appoint him as the next leader. And to ease the transition, Moses was told to "give some of your authority to him, that all the congregation of the children of Israel may be obedient" (Numbers 27:20 NKJV).

There is nothing more difficult than to follow a legend. And Moses truly was a legend in his own time. Moses was the only leader the surviving Israelites had known. It would be difficult for the people who were used to obeying Moses to give Joshua the same allegiance. Three things, however, would make the transition easier:

- Joshua had long been Moses's right-hand man (Exodus 24:13) as well as Israel's military leader (Exodus 17:13).

- Moses would publicly appoint Joshua in front of the entire congregation (Numbers 27:22).

- Moses would give up some of his authority immediately (27:20).

In addition, when Moses was gone and Israel was ready to enter Canaan, God Himself would confirm the appointment by performing a Moses-like miracle (Joshua 3).

key point

It must have been difficult for Moses to let go. It's difficult for anyone to turn his or her life-work over to another. But Moses remained obedient, and "he laid his hands on [Joshua] and inaugurated him, just as the LORD commanded" (Numbers 27:23 NKJV).

what others say

Dennis T. Olson

Although Joshua is not simply a carbon copy of Moses, an essential continuity of leadership exists between them. This continuity is expressed through the laying of hands by Moses on the new leader, Joshua. The ceremony of placing the hands upon another signified the transfer of the power of authority, blessing, or sin from one to another. The one upon whose head hands are placed becomes a representative or substitute for the other.[3]

The Duty to God Reemphasized

> NUMBERS 28:1–2 *Now the LORD spoke to Moses, saying, "Command the children of Israel, and say to them, 'My offering, My food for My offerings made by fire as a sweet aroma to Me, you shall be careful to offer to Me at their appointed time.'"* (NKJV)

Sacrifices offered regularly at the Tabernacle were essential reminders of the duty Israel owed the Lord to worship Him. Moses goes into great detail listing the daily offerings, the Sabbath offerings, and the offerings associated with special religious holidays (Numbers 28:1–29:40).

Each festival on the religious calendar had special significance and reminded God's people of what the Lord had done for them.

Israel's Religious Calendar

Month	Date	Festival Significance
April (*Nisan*)	14–21	Passover: Remembrance of deliverance from Egypt
May (*Iyar*)		
June (*Sivan*)	6	Pentecost: A harvest feast of thanksgiving
July (*Tammuz*)		
August (*Ab*)		
September (*Elul*)		
October (*Tishri*)	1–2	Trumpets: Rosh Hashanah, beginning of the civil year
	10	Day of Forgiveness of all sins; Atonement
	15–21	Tabernacles: Remembrance of the wilderness years on the way to Canaan
November (*Machesevan*)		
December (*Kislev*)	25	Hanukkah: A festival added in the 200s BC to celebrate a restoration of temple worship
January (*Tebeth*)		
February (*Shebat*)		
March (*Adar*)	14	Purim: A festival added in the 500s BC to recall deliverance under Queen Esther

The Making of Vows Clarified

> NUMBERS 30:2 *If a man makes a vow to the LORD, or swears an oath to bind himself by some agreement, he shall not break his word; he shall do according to all that proceeds out of his mouth.* (NKJV)

go to

widow or divorced
woman
Numbers 30:9

judge
an individual who
served as military,
political, and judicial
leader of one or
more of Israel's
tribes

monarchy
a nation led by a
hereditary king

vengeance
repayment for a
serious wrong

Earlier we saw that individuals who wished to express special devotion to the Lord could make a vow to live as a Nazirite. But individuals could pledge special gifts to the Lord without becoming Nazirites. Whether the pledge was a lamb or half of next year's crop, once made, the vow was binding. There was no going back.

There was, however, a special rule governing the vows of women. An unmarried woman's vow was subject to veto by her father, while a married woman's vow was subject to veto by her husband. The reason for this was simply that in Israel, as in other ancient cultures, the father or husband was responsible for the well-being of the entire family. It was his responsibility to determine whether the thing the woman pledged might threaten the family economically, and so he was given the right to confirm or void the woman's vow. This provision was not a gender issue but an economic issue. A widow or divorced woman, who was responsible for herself and her household, could make any vow she chose.

Flash Forward

A woman named Hannah is sobbing uncontrollably outside the Tabernacle. She is childless, and desperately wants to give her husband a son. Especially as her husband's other wife has children and constantly mocks Hannah. Bowing there, she begs the Lord for a male child, and pledges, "If You will indeed look on the affliction of Your maidservant and remember me . . . then I will give him to the LORD all the days of his life" (1 Samuel 1:11 NKJV). God did answer Hannah's prayer, and her husband, Elkanah, agreed that when the child was weaned Hannah could present him to the Lord (1:22–23).

The boy, Samuel, grew up at the temple as an apprentice to the high priest, Eli. God spoke to Samuel as a child, and he became a prophet and Israel's last **judge**, who guided the transition of Israel from leadership by judges to the **monarchy**.

Unfinished Business with the Midianites

NUMBERS 31:1–2 *And the LORD spoke to Moses, saying: "Take* ***vengeance*** *on the Midianites for the children of Israel. Afterward you shall be gathered to your people." (NKJV)*

It had been Midianites who set up the "honey pot" at Peor that enticed so many Israelites into adultery and idolatry. Thousands had been killed in the plague that followed. So before Moses's work was finished, there was a score to settle with Midian.

honey pot at Peor
Numbers 25:1–2

what others say

R. Dennis Cole

Holy war had as its purpose the eradication of all impure elements from the geographical region or ethnic territory placed under the ban. Coming on the heels of an idolatrous and adulterous affair at Baal Peor involving Israelite and non-Israelite participants, a cleansing of the congregation was in order.[4]

Chapter 31 of Numbers records the story of that brief war, during which the Midianites were crushed and the seer Balaam was killed. But when the army returned to camp, Moses discovered that the Israelites had returned with many captives, including women who had been involved in the plot to turn the Lord against Israel. Moses ordered the execution of the adult women and any male captives, sparing only young girls who had never "known a man intimately" (Numbers 31:17 NKJV).

The Midianite war established a number of precedents. Soldiers who had killed in battle or touched a dead body were to remain outside the camp. On the seventh day they were to wash themselves and their equipment, and be ritually clean. Other precedents involved keeping only metal objects as plunder, and dividing captured animals equally between the congregation and the men who had done the fighting. One of every fifty of the soldier's share was to be set aside for the Lord.

key point

When a count of the soldiers who'd gone into battle was taken, the officers discovered "not a man of us is missing" (Numbers 31:49 NKJV).

A Shocking Request

NUMBERS 32:1–5 *Now the children of Reuben and the children of Gad had a very great multitude of livestock; and when they saw the land of Jazer and the land of Gilead, that indeed the region was a place for livestock, the children of Gad and the*

at Kadesh-Barnea
Numbers 14

cut them off
Hebrew idiom
for "kill" or
"exterminate"

*children of Reuben came and spoke to Moses, . . . "The country
which the LORD defeated before the congregation of Israel, is a
land for livestock, and your servants have livestock . . . Let this
land be given to your servants as a possession. Do not take us
over the Jordan." (NKJV)*

Moses was shocked! It seemed to him that these two tribes were
acting just as their fathers had at Kadesh-Barnea when they had
refused to enter Canaan! That rebellion forced Israel back into the
desert for forty years. Shaken and angry, Moses cried, "And look!
You have risen in your fathers' place, a brood of sinful men, to
increase still more the fierce anger of the LORD against Israel"
(Numbers 32:14 NKJV).

The leaders of the two tribes were quick to reassure Moses. They
weren't rebelling. They would battle for Canaan along with the
other tribes. In fact, they would be the first to engage the enemy. All
they wanted was to build cities for their little ones and folds for their
flocks and leave them on the conquered lands. "But your servants
will cross over, every man armed for war, before the LORD to battle,
just as my lord says" (Numbers 32:27 NKJV).

There's no record in the text that Moses inquired to see what the
Lord thought of the two tribes' proposal. All the Numbers text tells
us is that "Moses gave to the children of Gad, to the children of
Reuben, and to half the tribe of Manasseh the son of Joseph, the
kingdom of Sihon king of the Amorites and the kingdom of Og king
of Bashan" (32:33 NKJV).

Total War

Biblical descriptions of the war for Canaan trouble many. As in the
war against the Midianites, the Israelites waged total war: war that
led to the slaughter of men, women, and children. What seems even
more disturbing is that this was done at the direct command of
Moses and of the Lord!

- *Exodus 23:23–24:* "For My Angel will go before you and
  bring you in to the Amorites and the Hittites and the
  Perizzites and the Canaanites and the Hivites and the
  Jebusites; and I will **cut them off**. You shall not bow down
  to their gods, nor serve them, nor do according to their
  works; but you shall utterly overthrow them" (NKJV).

- *Numbers 31:17:* "Now therefore, kill every male among the little ones, and kill every woman who has known a man intimately" (NKJV).

- *Deuteronomy 3:3, 6:* "So the LORD our God also delivered into our hands Og king of Bashan, with all his people, and we attacked him until he had no survivors remaining . . . And we utterly destroyed them, as we did to Sihon king of Heshbon, utterly destroying the men, women, and children of every city" (NKJV).

- *Deuteronomy 7:2:* "When the LORD your God delivers them over to you, you shall conquer them and utterly destroy them. You shall make no covenant with them nor show mercy to them" (NKJV).

- *Deuteronomy 20:16–17:* "But of the cities of these peoples which the LORD your God gives you as an inheritance, you shall let nothing that breathes remain alive, but you shall utterly destroy them: the Hittite and the Amorite and the Canaanite and the Perizzite and the Hivite and the Jebusite, just as the LORD your God has commanded you" (NKJV).

promises He's made
Genesis 12:1–3, 7

Here's a Hint

One of the most fascinating phrases in the Old Testament is found in Genesis 15. God has just cut the most binding of Old Testament covenants, guaranteeing that He will keep the covenant <u>promises He's made</u> to Abraham. As Abraham, in a "deep sleep," observes, the Lord gives Abraham a glimpse of the future. He tells Abraham that his descendants will be strangers in a land that is not theirs for four hundred years, and will become slaves there. But God will judge that nation, and Abraham's descendants will come out "with great possessions." God also promises that Abraham's offspring will then return to the Promised Land, and adds this curious phrase: "for the iniquity of the Amorites is not yet complete" (Genesis 15:16 NKJV).

This phrase, almost casually added by the Lord, provides a hint as to why Israel was to wage total war in Canaan. Even in the time of Abraham, the people of Canaan were remarkable for their iniquity. But their iniquity was "not yet complete." That is, the people of Canaan were not yet *completely* evil. But during the four hundred

Prophecy

go to

Midianite "honey pot"
Numbers 25

occult practices
Deuteronomy
18:11–14

burning children alive
Deuteronomy 18:10

years between the time of Abraham and the Exodus, Canaanite civilization would become utterly corrupt.

We've seen indications of this already. We've seen it in Balaam's advice to Balak, and in the <u>Midianite "honey pot"</u> set out to corrupt Israel sexually and spiritually. We've seen it in the description of the <u>occult practices</u> common in Canaan that the Lord forbids His people. We've seen it in the reference to the pagan practice of <u>burning their children alive</u> as sacrifices to placate some demon god or to gain a favor. We see it just as clearly in the hymns to the grossly immoral Canaanite deities uncovered by archaeologists, and the grossly immoral practices of their worshippers.

Clearly, God intended to use the Israelites as an instrument of divine judgment. And just as clearly, God delayed freeing His own people until the sins of the Canaanites were so deeply imbedded in their culture that He could no longer withhold the punishment they deserved!

---

what others say

J. Vernon McGee

All these nations were to be put out of the land and utterly destroyed because of their abominations. Now don't say that God had not been patient with them. Way back in Genesis 15:16 God had told Abraham that his descendants would not come back into the land until the fourth generation, "for the iniquity of the Amorites is not yet full." God gave these people 430 years to see whether they would turn to God and turn from their sins. Friends, how much more time do you want God to give them? Do you know of any other landlord who will give his tenant that long to pay his rent? God gave them a time of mercy that lasted 430 years. Then the cup of iniquity was full, and the judgment of God fell upon them. So let us not have a false kind of pity for these nations. Rather, let us learn from these events. God is a God of mercy and of love in the Old Testament as well as He is in the New Testament.[5]

Let God Explain

DEUTERONOMY 7:2, 4 *You shall make no covenant with them nor show mercy to them . . . For they will turn your sons away from following Me, to serve other gods. (NKJV)*

While Genesis 15 invites us to see the total war waged against the Canaanites as God's judgment, the Lord provides an even more compelling motive. If the peoples of Canaan were allowed to live, they would surely corrupt the morals and the religion of Israel! This explanation is repeated as frequently as the command to utterly destroy.

Shema
Israel's confession of faith that the Lord is One, not many gods

- *Deuteronomy 7:16:* "Also you shall destroy all the peoples whom the LORD your God delivers over to you; your eye shall have no pity on them; nor shall you serve their gods, for that will be a snare to you" (NKJV).

- *Deuteronomy 12:29–30:* "When the LORD your God cuts off from before you the nations which you go to dispossess, and you displace them and dwell in their land, take heed to yourself that you are not ensnared to follow them, after they are destroyed from before you, and that you do not inquire after their gods" (NKJV).

- *Deuteronomy 20:17–18:* "You shall utterly destroy them . . . just as the LORD your God has commanded you, lest they teach you to do according to all their abominations which they have done for their gods, and you sin against the LORD your God" (NKJV).

God commanded the Israelites to utterly destroy the Canaanites in order to protect His people from moral and spiritual corruption.

---

what others say

Christopher J. H. Wright

The moral justification for the destruction of the Canaanites will be expressed in terms of the wickedness of their society . . . The polytheism of many altars and idols cannot coexist with the God of the **Shema**. Together the stone pillar and wooden image would have represented the male and female element in the fertility cult. The moral factor in the condemnation is beneath the surface but not completely absent; it is in a different but unmistakable form.[6]

Fast-Forward

JUDGES 2:1–2, 11–13 *"I led you up from Egypt and brought you to the land of which I swore to your fathers; and I said, 'I will never break My covenant with you. And you shall make no covenant with the inhabitants of this land; you shall tear down their altars.' But you have not obeyed My voice" . . . Then the*

go to

moral judge
Psalms 7:8; 75:2;
Ezekiel 7:3, 8;
2 Timothy 4:8

Baals
the male deities of
the Canaanites

Ashtoreths
the female deities of
the Canaanites

*children of Israel did evil in the sight of the LORD, and served the **Baals**; and they forsook the LORD God of their fathers, who had brought them out of the land of Egypt; and they followed other gods from among the gods of the people who were all around them, and they bowed down to them; and they provoked the LORD to anger. They forsook the LORD and served Baal and the **Ashtoreths**. (NKJV)*

Israel has conquered Canaan and defeated the Canaanites. But rather than utterly destroy the peoples of the land, the Israelites let some remain alive. It's now a generation later, and the people have gathered at Bochim. Suddenly the Angel of the Lord appears, and confronts them.

---

what others say

J. A. Thompson

The religion was polytheistic, and highly sensuous, with a strong emphasis on fertility rites. In the temples of the Canaanites there were male and female prostitutes ("sacred" men and women) and all sorts of sexual excesses were practiced. It was believed that in some way these rites caused the crops and the herds to prosper. Baal was the god who cared for the rain and the growth of the crops and the flocks. The goddess Asherah, the goddess of passion and the consort of Baal, was the inspiration of every form of passion whether in love or in war.[7]

Israel's failure to obey God and utterly destroy the peoples of Canaan proved disastrous. For nearly a thousand years the Israelites would stubbornly turn from the Lord again and again to practice idolatry.

Think Again

Those who express horror that God could call for the extermination of the Canaanites need to stop and think again. The very Scriptures that contain reference to the utter destruction of these pagan peoples make the reason for the command clear.

First, the destruction of Canaanite civilization was a divine judgment on a culture that had become utterly corrupt. Let's never forget that God is the <u>moral judge</u> of the universe, and that He will

key point

judge sin. The fact that the Lord intended to use Israel as His instrument of judgment doesn't make His verdict of death any less just.

Second, God called Israel to be a holy nation. The Lord was fully aware of the danger the Canaanites represented to His people. By calling for the utter destruction of that civilization, God intended to protect His people from a very real danger. Israel's failure to obey the command to wage total war led directly to apostasy and to centuries of suffering.

God's call for Israel to wage total war in Canaan, and to utterly destroy the Canaanites, was both **just** and loving. The sins of the Canaanites brought this judgment upon them. And God's command was an expression of His love for and commitment to His chosen people.

just
the right thing to do

Rules of Engagement

Those who loudly decry the treatment God prescribed for the Canaanites typically overlook the reasons Scripture states for the divine command. They also fail to note that Scripture provides two sets of rules of engagement governing warfare. One set of rules governed war with people within the borders of Canaan. The other set of rules governed war with peoples who lived outside Canaan's borders.

While the rules of engagement for war within Canaan call for extermination of the enemy, the rules of engagement for war with peoples outside Canaan are exceptionally humane. These rules are established in Deuteronomy 20. We can summarize them as follows:

- *Deuteronomy 20:1–4:* Before battle the army is to be encouraged by a priest who reminds them that "the LORD your God . . . goes with you, to fight for you against your enemies" (NKJV).

- *Deuteronomy 20:5–7:* Men who have just purchased land or are newly married are exempt from service and are to be sent home.

- *Deuteronomy 20:8–9:* Men who are fainthearted or fearful are to be sent home lest their fear infect the rest of the army.

- *Deuteronomy 20:10–11:* Before any city is attacked it must be given the opportunity to surrender. If the city does surren-

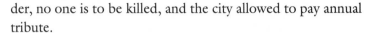

der, no one is to be killed, and the city allowed to pay annual tribute.

- *Deuteronomy 20:12–15:* If the city resists and the people make war, the city is to be besieged. When the city is taken the men are to be killed but the women, little ones, and livestock are to be spared.

- *Deuteronomy 20:19–20:* No fruit trees are to be cut down during a siege. Only trees that aren't used for food can be cut down, "for the tree of the field is man's food" (verse 19 NKJV).

There is a significant difference, then, between the total war that the Israelites were to wage against the peoples of Canaan and the humane war they were to wage against peoples who lived outside the Promised Land. It was necessary to utterly destroy the Canaanites, both as a divine judgment on their civilization and as a protection for God's own people. In all other wars the Israelites were to act as humanely as possible, indeed, far more humanely than other peoples of ancient times.

And Now, Introducing . . .

DEUTERONOMY 1:1 *These are the words which Moses spoke to all Israel on this side of the Jordan in the wilderness, in the plain opposite Suph.* (NKJV)

Preparations for the invasion of Canaan are complete. The census, which will provide the basis for distribution of the land, has been taken. Joshua has been appointed to succeed Moses. The importance of worship has been emphasized. The Midianites have been punished for their attempt to corrupt Israel. And the Reubenites and Gadites have been assigned land east of the Jordan River.

Now Moses gathers all the people together and launches into what will be his final message to them. It's a message that takes up the bulk of the book of **Deuteronomy**, a book that we noted earlier follows the pattern of a Hittite suzerainty treaty. The first four chapters of Deuteronomy are introduction, which in a suzerainty treaty served as a historical prologue.

It's a good idea to take time to read these four chapters before continuing in our study.

Remember What's Gone On

In his review of history, Moses traces events on the journey from Egypt up to the then-present time. Several themes are given repeated emphasis:

- *The rebelliousness of the Israelites.* Again and again Moses points to the rebellious acts of the first Exodus generation. It's clear from his review of history that no merit of the people has brought them to the borders of the Promised Land. It was "because [the Lord] loved **your fathers**, therefore He chose their descendants after them; and He brought you out of Egypt with His Presence, with His mighty power" (Deuteronomy 4:37 NKJV). The events of the journey establish the fact that "(. . . the LORD your God is a merciful God), He will not forsake you nor destroy you, nor forget the covenant of your fathers which He swore to them" (Deuteronomy 4:31 NKJV).

- *This importance of obeying God.* The disobedience of the first Exodus generation forced the Lord to wait until the rebels had all died before He could fulfill His promise. Obedience is the key to blessing. So Moses exhorts the new generation, "Now, O Israel, listen to the statutes and the judgments which I teach you to observe, that you may live, and go in and possess the land which the LORD God of your fathers is giving you" (Deuteronomy 4:1 NKJV). The lessons of their experience on the journey are to take root in their hearts. "Only take heed to yourself, and diligently keep yourself, lest you forget the things your eyes have seen, and lest they depart from your heart all the days of your life. And teach them to your children and your grandchildren" (Deuteronomy 4:9 NKJV).

- *The critical role of Moses himself.* As Moses reviews the journey to the Promised Land, he can't leave himself out. Moses's role was simply too critical to ignore. It was Moses who <u>gave and explained God's *torah*</u>. It was Moses who <u>exhorted the people to obey</u>. It was <u>Moses who prayed</u> for God's straying people. In reminding the people of all that has transpired, there's no way Moses can leave himself out.

gave God's torah
Deuteronomy 1:5, 16; 4:5, 14, 44

exhorted obedience
Deuteronomy 1:20–21, 29; 4:9, 15–19, 23

Moses who prayed
Deuteronomy 3:23

your fathers
Abraham, Isaac and Jacob (Israel)

key point

In a significant sense Moses has been the **mediator** of the relationship God has established with this generation. And the *torah* the Lord gave Israel through Moses will show each succeeding generation how to maintain a healthy personal relationship with the Lord until the *torah* age comes to an end.

Moses's Feet of Clay

Throughout our study we've focused on Moses's many strengths and on what we can learn from him about deepening our own relationship with God. Yet Moses, like every human being, has his own weaknesses and flaws.

We saw some of them when we first met Moses as a young man, driven by the dream of delivering his people, who looked both ways and then killed an Egyptian overseer who was mistreating an Israelite slave. Yet forty years as a shepherd in the Sinai humbled Moses, preparing him to be used by God in carrying out the deliverance he'd once dreamed of. As we've traced his experiences in Egypt and in the wilderness, we've learned much from Moses about nurturing a healthy personal relationship with the Lord. Moses is a man we've come to admire, a man from whom we expect only the best.

In one sense that's the problem with every human mentor. There are godly men and women from whom we can learn. Yet let's not suppose that our mentors are perfect, or let our faith be shaken when they prove as weak and fallible as we are. The fact is that even Moses had feet of clay.

Moses's Fatal Flaw

Three times in the four-chapter review of Israel's journey from Egypt to Canaan Moses says something that simply is not true.

- *Deuteronomy 1:37:* "The LORD was also angry with me for your sakes, saying, 'Even you shall not go in there'" (NKJV).

- *Deuteronomy 3:23–26:* "Then I pleaded with the LORD at that time, saying: 'O Lord GOD, You have begun to show Your servant Your greatness and Your mighty hand, for what god is there in heaven or on earth who can do anything like Your works and Your mighty deeds? I pray, let me cross over and see the good land beyond the Jordan, those pleasant mountains, and Lebanon.' But the LORD was angry with me on your account, and would not listen to me. So the LORD said to me: 'Enough of that! Speak no more to Me of this matter'" (NKJV).

- *Deuteronomy 4:20–22:* "But the LORD has taken you and brought you out of the iron furnace, out of Egypt, to be His people, an inheritance, as you are this day. Furthermore the LORD was angry with me for your sakes, and swore that I would not cross over the Jordan, and that I would not enter the good land which the LORD your God is giving you as an inheritance. But I must die in this land, I must not cross over the Jordan; but you shall cross over and possess that good land" (NKJV).

In each of these quotes we can sense Moses's longing to see Canaan for himself; to set foot on its rich earth, to breathe in the fragrance of its fields. Not to be allowed to enter the land is the greatest disappointment of Moses's life.

Yet in each of these quotes we sense something else. Each time Moses returns to this theme he tells the Israelites, "The LORD was angry with me for your sakes," or "The LORD was angry with me on your account." And this simply isn't true.

key point

Let's go back and look at the record. The story begins when the Israelites find themselves without water and complain to Moses. Totally frustrated, Moses looks to the Lord.

NUMBERS 20:7–12 *Then the LORD spoke to Moses, saying, "Take the rod; you and your brother Aaron gather the congregation together. Speak to the rock before their eyes, and it will yield its water; thus you shall bring water for them out of the rock, and give drink to the congregation and their animals." So Moses took the rod from before the LORD as He commanded him. And Moses and Aaron gathered the assembly together before the rock; and he said to them, "Hear now, you rebels! Must we bring water for you out of this rock?" Then Moses lifted his hand and struck the rock twice with his rod; and water came out abundantly, and the congregation and their animals drank.*

Then the LORD spoke to Moses and Aaron, "Because you did not believe Me, to hallow Me in the eyes of the children of Israel, therefore you shall not bring this assembly into the land which I have given them." (NKJV)

fashioned leaves
together
Genesis 3:7

deal with sin through
confession
1 John 1:9; 2;
James 5:16;
2 Corinthians 3:18

God wasn't angry with Moses "on your account." God was angry because Moses struck the rock rather than spoke to it. It was "because you did not believe Me, to hallow Me in the eyes of the children of Israel" that Moses was not allowed to enter Canaan. The Lord was angry with Moses *on his own account*!

What a Lesson Lost

Moses, for all his greatness, was a fallible human being, vulnerable as we all are to all sorts of temptations. Somehow Moses, although a humble man, could not bear to be honest about his one great failure. Rather than openly admit that God refused to let him enter Canaan because of his own sin, Moses tries to shift the blame to the people.

What an opportunity Moses lost to communicate a vital truth. Even the greatest of men must constantly focus on remaining obedient to God's Word. If Moses can fall, so can any man. And if Moses is punished for this single infraction, Israel surely will be disciplined if the people depart from God's way.

We can understand the feeling of shame that kept Moses from being totally honest. Like Adam and Eve, who frantically fashioned leaves together in an attempt to cover their nakedness, Moses did not want his weaknesses exposed. Yet the reality is that we all are weak; we all have failings, and we all must rely on the forgiving grace of God.

In his attempt to shift blame from himself to the Israelites, Moses distorted this most basic of spiritual realities. Rather than set for Israel an example of how to deal with sin and shame through confession, Moses set for Israel the worst example of all.

Yet Moses's flaw does provide us with another guideline to help us in nurturing our own relationship with God. A healthy relationship with God is best communicated when we are honest about our own weaknesses and our total dependence on His forgiving grace.

Chapter Wrap-Up

- With the first Exodus generation all dead, Moses orders a census of the new generation.

- Moses deals with details of preparing this new generation for the coming invasion of Canaan.

- Moses's command to exterminate the Midianites raises the question of Israel's total war against the Canaanites.

- Scripture provides two reasons why God commanded that the Canaanite peoples be utterly destroyed.

- Scripture also provides different rules of engagement for Israel's wars with people living outside the Promised Land.

- Moses launches into his final sermon, recorded in Deuteronomy, with a review of events along the journey from Egypt to the then-present time.

Study Questions

1. What did the census of the new generation of Israelites reveal?

2. What details did Moses deal with before the Israelites were ready to invade Canaan?

3. What two reasons were there for God's command to utterly destroy the peoples who lived in Canaan?

4. What are some differences between the rules for war with the Canaanites and rules for war with peoples living outside of Canaan?

5. What does Moses emphasize in Deuteronomy 1–4's review of Israel's travels from Egypt to the border of Canaan?

Chapter 14
The Real "Great Society"

Let's Get Started

Moses has led the Israelites to the verge of the Promised Land. Soon he must leave them. But Moses has a few things to say before he dies. He gathers the people together for a series of three farewell sermons, contained in the Old Testament book of Deuteronomy. Moses's introductory sermon reviews what God has done for the Israelites, and urges them to give Yahweh their complete allegiance.

It's appropriate that Moses's second sermon should be a powerful restatement of God's *torah*. While there are no radical changes in *torah* content, there is a subtle shift in emphasis. In the book of Deuteronomy, Moses spells out King Yahweh's motives in giving Israel His law, and presents a vision of the truly Great Society that will emerge . . . if only Israel returns God's love and keeps God's law.

Deuteronomy: That's Powerful Preachin'!

   I. Moses's First Sermon: What God Has Done 1:1–4:40

       1. Reflect on God's Goodness 1:1–3:29

       2. Respond to Him Gladly 4:1–40

  II. Moses's Second Sermon: Life Under *Torah* 5:1–28:68

       1. Principles of a *Torah* Lifestyle 5:1–11:32

       2. Details of a *Torah* Lifestyle 12:1–26:19

       3. Ratification of the *Torah* Covenant 27:1–26

       4. *Torah* Blessings and Cursings 28:1–68

 III. Moses's Third Sermon: A Call to Commitment 29:1–30:20

       1. Exhortation to Commit 29:1–15

       2. Warnings 29:16–29

       3. Forgiveness Assured 30:1–10

       4. Appeal to Choose Life 30:11–20

 IV. The Last Days of Moses 31:1–34:12

go to

wrath of God
Romans 1:18;
Ephesians 2:3

atoning sacrifices
sacrifices that cover
sins and permit the
sinner to approach
God

Another Look at the Law

One of the wonders of the *torah* Moses delivered to Israel is that we can look at it from so many different angles:

- *Torah is a set of rules and regulations* that God's people are to follow. The rules include both moral principles (such as the Ten Commandments) and moral precepts (specific rules governing behavior), as well as nonmoral precepts (specific rules dealing with ritual cleanness and uncleanness). While it's possible to compare the moral precepts of Old Testament law with the law codes of other ancient peoples, God's *torah* is unique in its statement of the principles on which the precepts rest, and on the integration of nonmoral precepts within the overall law.

- *Torah is a suzerainty treaty governing relationships* between Yahweh as ruler and the Israelites as His people. Each element of the Hittite treaty that defined relationships between Hittite kings and their subjects is reflected in the initial statement of the *torah* covenant in Exodus, and particularly in the structure of the book of Deuteronomy. Even today, in the *bar mitzvah* and *bat mitzvah* ceremonies, where a child becomes a "son of the law" or "daughter of the law," Jewish young people entering adulthood personally agree to the Lord's right to govern them and their behavior.

- *Torah is a total religious system designed to provide access to God.* No individual can perfectly keep the principles and precepts of *torah*. Everyone sins, and sinners are under the wrath of God. So *torah* provides for a priesthood to represent the sinner before God, and **atoning sacrifices** for the priests to offer. The *torah* also provides a worship center (the Tabernacle) where an individual may come to worship the Lord and seek His help. It provides a worship calendar that organizes each week and establishes annual holidays to keep God's people mindful of Him. *Torah* is a tightly woven religious system in which each part depends on and reflects the others.

Each of these aspects of the Law that God established through Moses is important if we're to understand the Old Testament and grasp the significance of Moses's mission. But if we're to truly grasp what a wonderful gift *torah* was, we need to look at the Law in yet another way. We need to see Moses's *torah* as a gift of love that laid out the blueprint for a just and moral society.

redemptively
in a saving way

The Law and Love

DEUTERONOMY 7:7–8 *The LORD did not set His love on you nor choose you because you were more in number than any other people, for you were the least of all peoples; but because the LORD loves you, and because He would keep the oath which He swore to your fathers, the LORD has brought you out with a mighty hand, and redeemed you from the house of bondage, from the hand of Pharaoh king of Egypt. (NKJV)*

This is the first thing we need to understand if we're to understand the moral principles and precepts of the *torah*. The Lord's motive in all His dealings with Israel is simply "because the LORD loves you." Love moved God to call Abraham and give him wonderful covenant promises. Love motivated God to intervene in Egypt. And love led the Lord to give the Israelites the whole *torah*, including the moral rules and regulations imbedded in it.

what others say

Raymond Brown

Some of those people who stood in the plains of Moab might be tempted to say, "Yes, I am convinced that God proved His love for our parents, but how can we be sure He loves us?" Here Moses says that He acted **redemptively** in the past not only because He loved their fathers but because *He chose their descendants after them* (37, see also 5:3) . . . God's love is not confined to any one particular generation. He loves the descendants as well as the forefathers; He loves us as much as He loved them.[1]

God's love is expressed in specific statements in the *torah*. It is also expressed in the benefits that the Law conferred on Israel. First and foremost was the benefit of knowing God better, for His moral character shines through the laws He gave to His people. But there are other benefits as well, benefits that could be claimed by being obedient.

key point

Obedience Brings Divine Blessing

Moses intensely desires that each generation keep Yahweh's law. After all, God gave the Law so He might "bless you and multiply you." If Israel obeys the Law, God "will also bless the fruit of your womb and the fruit of your land, your grain and your new wine and your oil, the increase of your cattle and the offspring of your flock, in the land of which He swore to your fathers to give you" (Deuteronomy 7:13 NKJV).

In this statement, God commits Himself to actively bless the nation of Israel when His people love and obey Him. Thus Moses continues to exhort the new generation, saying:

DEUTERONOMY 11:13–15 *And it shall be that if you earnestly obey My commandments which I command you today, to love the Lord your God and serve Him with all your heart and with all your soul, then I will give you the rain for your land in its season, the early rain and the latter rain, that you may gather in your grain, your new wine, and your oil. And I will send grass in your fields for your livestock, that you may eat and be filled. (NKJV)*

This promise directly connects the gift of Law to God's love. God loved His people and gave them the Law that He might act to bless the generations that were faithful to Him and that obeyed His law.

God the Spoilsport?

One of the most peculiar notions people have is that Scripture's moral code puts a damper on life. If only we were left to ourselves, many suppose, we could enjoy all those things we're not supposed to do!

It's true that many of Scripture's "don'ts" prohibit actions that provide momentary pleasure. But it's simply not true that if we were to reject God's standards or replace them with standards of our own—something that happens all too frequently these days—we'd find our lives greatly improved.

The fact is that Scripture's moral **imperatives** define a way of life designed to bring human beings joy and fulfillment. The moral "don'ts" of Scripture are boldly posted signs that warn us away from actions that in the end harm us and others. There are long-term consequences to sin—and living by any set of standards other than God's standards is sin—that far outweigh sin's momentary pleasures.

For instance, casual sex does more than expose us to sexually transmitted diseases like AIDS. Promiscuous sex cheapens an experience that has the capacity within marriage to deepen intimacy and strengthen the bond between husband and wife. When sexuality is no longer deemed sacred, and is treated as recreation, each partner surrenders something significant and gradually loses the capacity to experience intimacy.

consequences
Romans 3:23;
Galatians 6:7–8

The morality defined in the Old Testament *torah* and reaffirmed in the New Testament Epistles truly is a good gift. Living moral lives benefits human beings in significant ways, while living immoral lives robs us of much that is truly good.

This is another reason to view the *torah* as a gift of love. *Torah's* moral precepts are shaped to fit the human heart, offering personal fulfillment to those who choose to live God's way, and warning of the empty life to which those who reject God's way doom themselves.

A Great Society Too?

There's also another intimate link between God's love and His law. If the people of God had chosen to live by God's rules, society itself would have been transformed in wonderful ways. The evils that pervert justice, and the institutions that produce poverty, would all be swept away.

This theme is emphasized in an earlier passage in Deuteronomy. There Moses comments,

> DEUTERONOMY 4:6–8 *Therefore be careful to observe them; for this is your wisdom and your understanding in the sight of the peoples who will hear all these statutes, and say, "Surely this great nation is a wise and understanding people." For what great nation is there that has God so near to it, as the LORD our God is to us, for whatever reason we may call upon Him? And what great nation is there that has such statutes and righteous judgments as are in all this law which I set before you this day? (NKJV)*

key point

what others say

Christopher J. H. Wright

By suddenly introducing the nations as observers and commentators, the text opens up the whole significance of Israel's law to a much wider horizon. The nations will *hear about all these decrees*, that is, they will notice and inquire and take an interest in the phenomenon of Israel as a society, with all the social, economic, legal, political, and religious dimensions of the Torah. And that social system will lead them to the conclusion that Israel as a people qualify as a *great nation*, regarded as *wise and understanding*.[2]

God's revelation that the gift of *torah* regulations is rooted in His love is confirmed by the benefits that obeying the Law confirms:

- God acted to bless His people when they loved Him and obeyed His *torah*.

- *Torah's* moral do's and don'ts continue to point the way to a life of joy and fulfillment for individuals.

- And, as we have seen, *torah* laid the foundation for a just, moral society in which every individual has an opportunity to achieve his or her full potential.

To catch a vision of what life under the Law was intended to be like for God's people, we're going to look at several of those foundational issues, such as eradicating poverty. We'll see how the foundational issues are dealt with, and how the problems of poverty and criminal justice are resolved in the *torah*. While it is impossible to simply impose the *torah* approach on our own society, principles imbedded in the Old Testament should be considered whenever moderns explore social reform.

apply it

How *Torah* Deals with Poverty

DEUTERONOMY 15:3–5 *You shall give up your claim to what is owed by your brother, except when there may be no poor among you; for the LORD will greatly bless you in the land which the LORD your God is giving you to possess as an inheritance—only if you carefully obey the voice of the LORD your God, to observe with care all these commandments which I command you today. (NKJV)*

This is one of the most stunning of the prospects that Moses holds out to God's people. There may be a day "when there may be no poor among you"!

The eradication of poverty is one of the great unfulfilled dreams of humankind; the dream of a day when social justice has been established and those suffering under the oppression of poverty are released from its terrible burden. For poverty truly has a devastating impact on human beings.

The Impact of Poverty

That dream of eradicating poverty was alive in Old Testament times as well as in our own. The Scripture shows an acute awareness of the causes of poverty and of its devastating impact. This awareness is reflected in Hebrew words translated "poor" and "poverty":

- *Dal* and *Dallah*. These two words, normally translated "poor" and "poorest," describe both a person's financial situation and social position. A poor person lacks material resources, especially in contrast to the wealthy. A poor person also is ranked among a society's lowest classes, again in contrast to the wealthy.

- *'ant*. This word generally represents financial distress. Derived from the root *'anah*, which means "to oppress," this word for poverty emphasizes the pain felt by the powerless in society, whose poverty makes it impossible to resist the socially powerful. *'Ant* is often translated as "needy" or "afflicted" as well as "poor."

- *'ebyon*. This is an especially strong word that refers to a person who is in desperate material need, often lacking for basic necessities such as food or clothing. Utterly helpless, such poor are utterly dependent on others. The word occurs often

go to

laziness or irresponsibility
Proverbs 10:4;
20:13; 21:17; 23:21

social oppression
Psalm 74:21;
Proverbs
13:23;14:31

condemn exploitation
Ezekiel 22:29;
Zechariah 7:9–12

with the poor and oppressed
Psalms 69:33; 113:7;
Proverbs 19:22;
Jeremiah 22:16

glean in others' fields
Leviticus 19:10;
23:22;
Ruth 2

in the Psalms, and typically pictures a righteous person who has lost everything because of wicked enemies.

- *Rus*. This is another word that pictures the lower classes as deeply mired in poverty.

The way these words are used in the Old Testament gives us a vivid picture of poverty and its impact. The poor lack the material resources needed for even a reasonable quality of life. Even more devastating is the fact that they have no social standing, and are at the mercy of the wealthy and powerful. This vulnerability makes it almost certain they will be treated unfairly in the courts. Thus poverty strips the poor of basic human rights and their dignity.

It's true that some poor are responsible for their own condition, due to <u>laziness or irresponsibility</u>. But it is also true that most poverty in Old Testament society was rooted in <u>social oppression</u>. Again and again the Old Testament prophets <u>condemn such exploitation</u>. And it is clear that the Lord takes His stand <u>with the poor and oppressed</u>.

Recognizing the demeaning and devastating impact of poverty, the Lord built into the *torah* six specific social mechanisms, which, if consistently utilized, would rescue the poor and ultimately eradicate poverty.

Access to Necessities

Israel's economy was based on land and on what the land produced. To survive, an individual or a family had to have access to the grain and other crops the land produced. While originally every family was allotted its own land in Canaan, in time some families would be dispossessed and become landless. How then could the dispossessed have access to the food required to survive?

apply it

The first social mechanism designed to give the poor direct access to life's necessities was the right given the poor to <u>glean in others' fields</u>. At harvesttime a landowner was to go through his fields only one time, cutting and stacking stalks of grain, picking figs or olives or other fruit, etc. In the process some stalks of grain would be missed, and some of the heads containing kernels would break off. Some unripened fruit would be left on the tree; other fruit would fall to the ground. Everything that had been missed or had fallen to the ground was to be reserved for the poor. They were to be allowed to follow the harvesters and glean (collect) everything that remained for themselves and their families.

The second social mechanism that gave the poor direct access to necessities was the Sabbatical year (Exodus 23:10–11). Each seventh year landowners were to allow their lands to rest. During the seventh year no crops were to be planted. Whatever grew "of itself" during the seventh year was to belong to the poor, who were allowed to harvest all the crops from the fields, vineyards, and orchards. God promised the landowners bumper crops during the sixth year, so they would suffer no loss by resting their lands during the seventh or by leaving the land's bounty for the poor.

Neither of these social mechanisms involved charity. Each simply made necessities available to the poor, who were expected to go into the fields and harvest the food themselves.

Aid for the Fatherless

> **DEUTERONOMY 14:28–29** *At the end of every third year you shall bring out the **tithe** of your produce of that year and store it up within your gates. And the Levite, because he has no portion nor inheritance with you, and the stranger and the fatherless and the widow who are within your gates, may come and eat and be satisfied, that the LORD your God may bless you in all the work of your hand which you do. (NKJV)*

Widows and orphans fell into a special class. These often not only lacked land but also had no adult male to provide for them. The social mechanism designed to provide for the needs of the destitute is described above.

The Old Testament views God as owner of the territory given to Israel as a homeland. The tithe was a tax owed to God for the use of His land. That tax was 10 percent of all that the land produced, in crops and in animals born to an Israelite landholder. The tithe was normally brought to the central worship center, to be used to support the Levites and the priests who ministered at the Tabernacle, and later at the Jerusalem Temple. There's some debate as to whether the tax of the third year, described here, is an additional 10 percent to be collected every third year, or whether the regular tithe was to be stored locally each third year. There is no doubt, however,

tithe
10 percent of the produce harvested

that this was used to supply the landless and those who were destitute. Even the poorest in society were to be cared for as persons of worth and value.

> ### what others say
>
> **Christopher J. H. Wright**
>
> This triennial tithe was an element of Israel's welfare system for the relief of poverty . . . Care for the poor was structured into the regular economic life of the nation. It was not left to *private charity*. Rather, it was a *public duty* that the weakest and poorest should also be enabled to eat and be satisfied from the blessing of Yahweh on the whole nation.[4]

Interest-Free, Forgivable Loans

DEUTERONOMY 15:1–2 *At the end of every seven years you shall grant a release of debts. And this is the form of the release: Every creditor who has lent anything to his neighbor shall release it; he shall not require it of his neighbor or his brother, because it is called the LORD's release. (NKJV)*

To understand this mechanism we need to remember two important things. First, Israel's was **not a credit economy**. No one purchased things such as wagons or lands on time. People paid for what they purchased with money, or in barter. If a person worked another person's field, it was with the understanding that the landowner and the farmer would share what the land produced.

Second, Israelites did not borrow in order to purchase luxuries. No one borrowed to purchase the equivalent of today's new TV or a second car. When an Israelite sought aid from a wealthy neighbor, what he needed might be clothing for his family, an ox that would allow him to work his fields, or seed for planting. These were necessities that enabled a man to care for his own.

The Law called for the well-to-do to lend freely to fellow Jews, and to do so without exacting interest. It was permissible to charge interest to a foreigner, and loans to foreigners need not be forgiven. But if a fellow Jew was unable to repay what he had borrowed, the Law introduced a unique "release of debts" provision.

This particular social mechanism relied on each party to deal honestly with the other. On the one hand, a lender might hesitate to advance a loan if the seventh year was near. On the other hand, the borrower might delay repayment if the seventh year was near at hand. Scripture, however, speaks directly to this concern:

decide impartially
Exodus 23:3, 6;
Deuteronomy 16:19

> DEUTERONOMY 15:7–10 *If there is among you a poor man of your brethren, within any of the gates in your land which the LORD your God is giving you, you shall not harden your heart nor shut your hand from your poor brother, but you shall open your hand wide to him and willingly lend him sufficient for his need, whatever he needs. Beware lest there be a wicked thought in your heart, saying, "The seventh year, the year of release, is at hand," and your eye be evil against your poor brother and you give him nothing, and he cry out to the LORD against you, and it become sin among you. You shall surely give to him, and your heart should not be grieved when you give to him, because for this thing the LORD your God will bless you in all your works and in all to which you put your hand.* (NKJV)

Equal Justice for Rich and Poor

> LEVITICUS 19:15 *You shall do no injustice in judgment. You shall not be partial to the poor, nor honor the person of the mighty. In righteousness you shall judge your neighbor.* (NKJV)

We've noted that Scripture shows great sensitivity to the vulnerability of the poor to exploitation by the wealthy. In the Old Testament legal system, justice was distributive; that is, cases were brought to and decided by local elders rather than in a tribal or national system of courts. Everyone with personal knowledge of the matter in dispute was to testify, and disputes were to be settled on the basis of the facts and *torah* legal principles.

apply it

In this passage and in others, judges are commanded to <u>decide cases impartially</u>. This means they are not to be swayed by the needs of a poor person, or influenced by the social position and power of the wealthy. In Israel's courts the wealthy and the poor were to meet on what today we'd call a "level playing field."

Voluntary Servitude

> DEUTERONOMY 15:12–14 *If your brother, a Hebrew man, or a Hebrew woman, is sold to you and serves you six years, then in the seventh year you shall let him go free from you. And when you send him away free from you, you shall not let him go away*

empty-handed; you shall supply him liberally from your flock, from your threshing floor, and from your winepress. From what the LORD has blessed you with, you shall give to him. (NKJV)

This unique social mechanism is thoroughly described in Deuteronomy 15 and in Leviticus 25:39–54. This mechanism recognizes the fact that in some cases a person might become so indebted that there was no way for him to provide for himself or his family. In this case a person might sell himself or a family member to a well-to-do fellow Israelite. The money obtained from the sale would be used to settle family debts and enable family members to survive.

key point

But there is much more to this approach to servitude in Israel. A person sold to a fellow Israelite was more an apprentice than a slave. The person who had been unable to provide for himself or his family and had sold himself into servitude would have six years to work for a successful fellow Israelite. Hopefully during those years the "slave" would develop the work habits and skills needed to provide for himself. At the end of six years, the "owner" was to free his Israelite slave and supply him "liberally" with all he needed to get a fresh start.

While this social mechanism clearly benefited the slave, it's not clear that the "owner" benefited as well. The owner had to pay an initial price for his servant, support him for six years, and at the end of that time pay out an equal or greater amount to give his ex-slave a fresh start!

There was no such obligation to free a foreign slave or to provision him if he should be freed. It made more economic sense to buy a foreigner than to "purchase" a Hebrew slave. The individual who benefited from this provision in the *torah* was the Israelite slave, not the master!

Preservation of Capital

LEVITICUS 25:23–24 *The land shall not be sold permanently, for the land is Mine; for you are strangers and sojourners with Me. And in all the land of your possession you shall grant redemption of the land. (NKJV)*

This is one of the most unusual of the social mechanisms designed to deal with poverty. We've noted that the land of Canaan was divided by lot, so that the plots allotted to each family were viewed as a gift given to them personally by the Lord. The *torah* follows up on this theme by insisting that no one was to sell his land permanently.

We've also noted that Old Testament Israel was an agrarian society. In such a society land is the basis of wealth, or **capital**. By insisting that houses and lands not be sold permanently, what the Lord did was to preserve a family's capital from generation to generation. If some disaster struck one generation and land had to be sold, or if the head of a house proved to be a poor manager and was forced to sell family land, future generations would not be deprived of the capital they needed to build a good life. Every fiftieth year, called the Year of Jubilee, land that had been sold would be returned to the family of the original owners.

In essence, rather than sell the land, an Israelite sold his right to what his land might produce between the time of sale and the fiftieth year. No one could transfer title to the land itself. The price for such a sale would be based on an estimate of the value of what the land might produce during the number of years that lay between the sale and the Year of Jubilee.

This concept of the preservation of capital as a mechanism for controlling poverty was a unique social invention. It's as if every fifty years an American family was given $5 million. The persons who received the five million might use it wisely and increase the family wealth. Or those persons might spend it all foolishly and leave the family penniless. But no individual's foolish choices would forever doom his descendants to struggle in abject poverty. God could not guarantee that His gifts would be used wisely. But this provision of the Law did guarantee that even the poorest would have a start fresh.

capital
A resource that can produce wealth; in ancient Israel, the land was the resource that produced wealth.

God's Plan to Eradicate Poverty

1. Permit the poor to glean.
2. Permit the poor to harvest all seventh-year crops.
3. Feed the needy locally from the third-year tithe.
4. Give the poor interest-free, forgivable loans.
5. Treat rich and poor the same in the courts.
6. Provide the poor with the option of a six-year slavery/apprenticeship.
7. Preserve each family's land from generation to generation.

God Loves the Poor

If anyone doubts that the Law is deeply rooted in the love of God, an understanding of the provisions made in the *torah* for the poor should convince them. We can see the link between love and law in God's promise to bless those who keep His law. We can see the link between love and law in the fact that *torah* moral provisions point us toward a life of joy and fulfillment while warning us away from choices that lead to despair. Yet perhaps the provisions built into the *torah* for the eradication of poverty are the most powerful expression of the love of God for all human beings.

How *Torah* Deals with Crime

Looking back, worship leaders in the time of Nehemiah praised God because:

NEHEMIAH 9:13
You came down also on Mount Sinai,
And spoke with them from heaven,
And gave them just ordinances and true laws,
Good statutes and commandments. (NKJV)

The NIV translates, "You gave them regulations and laws that are just and right." If God's people would only keep His regulations, not only would poverty be eradicated, justice would prevail.

To encourage the maintenance of a just society, God also designed a unique **justice system** and imbedded it in the *torah*. That system is strikingly different from our own legal justice system.

A Quick Look at Our System

Jimmy breaks into Kenny's house and steals a TV. When Kenny comes home he calls the police. In this case, Jimmy was seen taking Kenny's TV into a pawnshop, and the police arrest him. The police keep the TV as evidence, leaving Kenny without a TV at home until after Jimmy's trial.

The police take Jimmy to jail, where a prosecutor determines that there is enough evidence to charge Jimmy with breaking and entering and with burglary. Because Jimmy can't make bond, he's kept in jail awaiting trial to determine whether he is guilty or innocent. Jimmy is now called "the defendant," and his grandfather hires a lawyer to defend him.

When Jimmy goes on trial his case is presented as "The State of Maryland vs. Jimmy," because Jimmy violated the laws of Maryland. A prosecutor represents the state of Maryland, and Jimmy's lawyer represents Jimmy. This is called an "adversarial system" because there are lawyers on each side, one fighting to convict Jimmy and one fighting to have him declared not guilty.

A judge oversees the trial, and a jury of twelve people who have never seen Jimmy or each other listen to the lawyers as they question witnesses. It's up to the jury to decide whether the evidence presented by the prosecutor or the argument from the defense attorney is more convincing.

In this case the prosecutor wins and Jimmy is found guilty. The judge sentences Jimmy to one year and one day in prison. Three weeks later Kenny gets his TV back.

A Quick Look at the *Torah* System

Kelah breaks into Eblah's sheepfold and steals a lamb. Eblah is pretty sure Kelah took the lamb and asks his neighbors if they saw anything. One neighbor remembers seeing Kelah hurrying away from Eblah's sheepfold carrying a bundle of some sort. Eblah and the witness go to the men who serve as elders in his community.

The elders meet and ask Kelah to join them. Most of the town gathers to listen to the proceedings. When everyone has assembled, Eblah tells about the stolen sheep and the witness recounts where he saw Kelah. Another person in the crowd speaks up, and says he saw Kelah near there too, and that Kelah was definitely carrying a lamb.

The elders and Eblah go to check out Kelah's flock. They don't find Eblah's lamb, but they do find the remains of a young sheep Kelah's family ate recently. The elders ask neighbors who know Kelah well to count his sheep. They report that all of the sheep Kelah owns are alive. It's clear that Kelah has eaten the lamb he took from Eblah. Since everyone now knows what he has done, Kelah confesses.

The elders check the *torah* and find the ruling: "If a man steals an ox or a sheep, and slaughters it or sells it, he shall restore five oxen for an ox and four sheep for a sheep" (Exodus 22:1 NKJV). They order Kelah to give Eblah four sheep as repayment for the one he stole. After delivering the sheep, Kelah takes a ram and heads for the Tabernacle where a priest will offer a trespass offering on his behalf (Leviticus 6:4–6).

Comparing the Two Systems

There are a number of significant differences between the two types of legal justice systems. They're summarized on the following chart, and then discussed point by point.

Two Criminal Justice Systems

Issue	Torah Justice System	U.S. Justice System
Standards	Revealed by God	Legislated by Government
Enforcement	By Whole Community	By Police and Courts
Responsibility	Of the Whole Community	Of Criminal Justice Professionals
Crime	Against Victim, God	Against the State
Process	Cooperative, Interpersonal	Adversarial, Impersonal
Resolution	Restitution	Punishment

- *Standards.* Each criminal justice system has rules governing behavior imbedded in the society's laws. The *torah* system laws are revealed by God; the contemporary U.S. legal system laws have been established by legislation.

- *Enforcement.* Responsibility for enforcing *torah* laws is distributed throughout the entire community. Not only a victim in the *torah* system but anyone with knowledge of a crime is responsible for seeing justice done. In the contemporary U.S. system victims report crimes to the police, who are responsible to gather evidence and apprehend the criminal. At this point the criminal is turned over to the courts to be tried.

- *Responsibility.* In the *torah* system each person in the community is responsible to see justice done by coming forward to give testimony to whatever he or she may know. In the contemporary U.S. system citizens are supposed to testify, but often must be compelled to do so. They are not legally bound to come forward to testify.

- *Crime.* In the *torah* system the crime is deemed to have been committed against the victim and against God. In the contemporary U.S. system the crime is considered to have been committed against whatever government passed the laws.

- *Process.* In the *torah* system the process of dealing with a crime is cooperative and interpersonal. The investigation is conducted within a community in which both the violator and the victim as well as all witnesses are well known. And the goal of the investigation is to discover the truth. In the contemporary U.S. system the investigation is conducted by professionals who typically do not know either the criminal or the victim. Guilt or innocence is determined by a jury made up of individuals who are strangers to the victim and the criminal as well as to each other. Because of the trial process's adversarial nature, the goal of discovering the truth is often obscured and the trial becomes a contest between the prosecution and the defense to see which side will win.

- *Resolution.* In the *torah* system the case is resolved by the violator's making restitution to the victim and taking responsibility for his actions by presenting a guilt offering to God. In this way the victim is made whole, and social harmony in the community is maintained. In the contemporary U.S. system the case is resolved by releasing the violator, or by sending the violator to jail. In this process the victim is forgotten, and no provision is made to restore whatever he may have lost or to restore social harmony.

When we compare the two, the *torah* system seems superior in a number of respects, especially in the concern that the *torah* system shows for both the victim and the violator. In the *torah* system any loss suffered by the victim is made up for by the very individual who violated his or her rights. And in the *torah* system, once restitution has been made and the guilt offering sacrificed, the violator remains a member of the community. In that closely knit community, threat of the shame of exposure serves as at least as effective a deterrent to future crimes as the threat of imprisonment. And no wives or children are forced to struggle for years to support themselves while their husbands and fathers are imprisoned.

key point

heinous
wrong, terrible,
unjustified

But It Won't Work Here

It's certainly true that the *torah* system, which is designed to function in an agrarian society of smaller communities in which everyone knows everyone else, can't be transferred to a society like ours. But that's not the point. The point is that the criminal justice system imbedded in the *torah* is a distinctive expression of God's love for human beings. The *torah* criminal justice system shows a concern for the truth and provides a process for arriving at it. The *torah* criminal justice system shows a concern for the victims of crime. It calls for full and complete restitution of that which has been lost. The *torah* criminal justice system also shows concern for the criminal. It defines a way for the criminal to make up for his actions and to remain an integral member of the community while continuing to meet the needs of spouse and children.

The sensitivity of the *torah* criminal justice system to issues like these clearly demonstrates God's concern for people, and is compelling evidence that law is an expression of God's love.

A Look at Capital Punishment

NUMBERS **35:31** *Moreover you shall take no ransom for the life of a murderer who is guilty of death, but he shall surely be put to death. (NKJV)*

For many today, the execution of a murderer seems as **heinous** as the murder the killer committed. Scripture, however, takes a different view. Its verdict is that those who commit murder "shall surely be put to death."

The rational for the execution of a murderer is neither revenge nor the notion that the death sentence is a deterrent. The reason is stated succinctly in Genesis 9:6, words that the Lord spoke to Noah: "Whoever sheds man's blood, by man his blood shall be shed; for in the image of God He made man" (NKJV). We see a reflection of this dictum in Numbers 35:31, "You shall take no ransom for the life of a murderer" (NKJV). Nothing that exists can compare to the value of a human life. The only thing of comparable value to a human life is another human life.

Scripture requires capital punishment not as vengeance or as a deterrent, but as an affirmation of the value of human life. The value of life is cheapened when any society is willing to accept a lesser punishment for murder.

go to

justified killings
1 Kings 19:1;
Exodus 13:15;
2 Samuel 4:11–12;
Deuteronomy
13:6–11

unjustified killings
Genesis 4:25;
1 Samuel 22:21;
1 Kings 18:13

Thou Shalt Not Kill

The message has been distorted by the unfortunate translation of the commandment against murder. Hebrew has a number of words for killing, most of which make no moral judgment. For instance, *harag* describes both <u>justified</u> and <u>unjustified</u> killings. The tragic fact is that in this sinful world killing is a fact of life. But, strikingly, the commandment does not say, "You shall not *harag*."

The Hebrew word used in the commandment is *rasah*, which should be translated "murder" or "manslaughter." This word has no parallel in the other languages of the ancient Middle East, but is unique to Hebrew. It is used of what we might call "personal killings." That is, it is never used of killing in battle or of the execution of a criminal. It is used when an individual, for whatever motive, causes the death of another person. When we read the passages in the *torah* that speak of *rasah*, it becomes clear that the death penalty is called for only in the case of intentional personal killings.

Murder Versus Accidental Killing

NUMBERS 35:20–25 *If he pushes him out of hatred or, while lying in wait, hurls something at him so that he dies, or in enmity he strikes him with his hand so that he dies, the one who struck him shall surely be put to death. He is a murderer . . .*

However, if he pushes him suddenly without enmity, or throws anything at him without lying in wait, or uses a stone, by which a man could die, throwing it at him without seeing him, so that he dies, while he was not his enemy or seeking his harm, . . . the congregation shall deliver the manslayer. (NKJV)

It's clear from this passage that a number of factors were to be taken into account when someone died at another person's hand. Where there is motive (*hostile intent, enmity*), and an action showing intent (*hurling something, striking*) that leads to death, the verdict is murder and the murderer is to be put to death. Where there is no motive, and the action reveals no intent to harm, the verdict is accidental homicide and the killer's life is to be preserved.

what others say

Raymond Brown

What of a person who kills his neighbor accidentally? He must be protected or the situation will get worse. If the offender's blood is also shed, however transparent his innocence, then within a matter of hours two innocent people have died and the feud would inevitably spark further trouble between two families which had earlier been at peace.[5]

Other safeguards are built into the law on murder. "The murderer shall be put to death on the testimony of witnesses; but one witness is not sufficient testimony against a person for the death penalty" (Numbers 35:30 NKJV). There must be no question at all about the intent and actions of a person who kills another before he can be executed.

The Avenger of Blood

NUMBERS 35:19 *The avenger of blood himself shall put the murderer to death. (NKJV)*

apply it

We saw that the *torah* made no provision for national or local police forces. How then were murderers to be executed? The answer is that, just as the victim of a crime was responsible to bring it to the local elders, so the nearest relative of a murdered person was responsible to carry out God's death sentence on the murderer. This nearest relative was called the "avenger of blood," and might begin to hunt a killer as soon as he heard of the death of his relative.

This, however, created another problem. What if the death was accidental rather than premeditated? How could a person who committed accidental homicide be protected from the avenger of blood until the facts could be determined?

Cities of Refuge

The *torah* solution was establishment of six "cities of refuge." These cities were located so that no Israelite lived more than a day's journey from **sanctuary**. What's more, Moses commanded the Israelites to prepare roads to the cities of refuge to ensure that "whoever kills his neighbor unintentionally" might reach them quickly (Deuteronomy 19:4 NKJV)!

When any person who had killed another appeared at a city of refuge, he was taken in and protected from the avenger of blood until witnesses could be called and the elders of the city of refuge determined whether the killing was intentional or accidental. If the witnesses established a history of hostility between the killer and his victim, or provided other testimony suggesting intentionality, the killer was to be turned over to the avenger of blood and executed. If, however, no such evidence existed, the killing was deemed accidental. The killer was allowed to live in the city of refuge until the death of the current high priest. At that time the killer was free to return home, in no danger from the avenger of blood.

God's concern that justice be done in the case of personal killings, and that the innocent be protected, is reflected in the fact that no less than three major Old Testament passages discuss murder and the cities of refuge (Numbers 35; Deuteronomy 19; Joshua 20).

appropriate compensation
Exodus 21:26–27

sanctuary
safety

But . . . That Eye-for-an-Eye Stuff?

EXODUS 21:23–24 *But if any harm follows, then you shall give life for life, eye for eye, tooth for tooth, hand for hand, foot for foot . . . (NKJV)*

I've argued that *torah* provisions for the poor and the torah legal justice system demonstrate a deep love of God for human beings. But to many, the "eye-for-an-eye" provisions of *torah* personal injury law seem to rob it of all compassion.

This, however, is a misunderstanding of how the eye-for-an-eye provision functioned, and its underlying purpose.

First, the eye-for-an-eye provision did not mean that the eye of someone who injured another's eye was blinded. It does mean that appropriate compensation was to be provided. In practice when one person injured another, the families of the two parties sat down, perhaps with one or more of the city elders, and agreed on compensation. The *torah* did not define this compensation, as its criminal provisions define restitution. There were too many factors involved

key point

in personal injury cases, such as the age of the injured person, how the injury affected his or her capacity to work, etc. What the eye-for-an-eye ruling does require is that compensation be appropriate to the injury.

Second, the eye-for-an-eye provision was established to *limit* compensation. Various cultures are all too familiar with feuds between families or tribal groups that grew out of a simple injury, which led to a greater injury, and which quickly spiraled out of control. When the *torah* requires an eye-for-an-eye, it limits the injured party from demanding an "eye and an arm" for an eye. There is to be no escalation of any hostility that may emerge from an injury one person does to another. Compensation is to be appropriate, not excessive. And then the matter is to remain closed.

key point

what others say

John L. Mackay

This is described as the *lex talionis*, "the law of retaliation," or of giving like for like, and is often thought of as primitive and barbaric. It is more appropriate to understand this as "the law of equivalencies." It represents a significant concept in jurisprudence, limiting the extent of retribution to the nature of the injury caused. It is not a charter for seeking unlimited revenge. "You" is plural, and describes the action of the whole community. The penalties imposed are to be no more than the crime merits.[6]

What Happened?

When we look at the *torah* that God gave His people through Moses and catch a glimpse of the truly great society envisioned there, it's appropriate to ask, "What happened?" Anyone with an even passing familiarity with Old Testament history realizes that the bright prospect of a just and moral society that's held out in the *torah* was never realized.

The answer is found in the contrast that we've already drawn between the promise covenants that God made with Israel and the Law Covenant. The promise covenants state what God commits Himself to do. The Law Covenant states, "If you indeed obey His voice . . ." (Exodus 23:22 NKJV).

Law was a *conditional* covenant. The blessings it promised depended on the willingness of God's people to trust the Lord and obey Him fully. And, with the possible exception of the second Exodus generation, no generation of Israelites fully followed the Lord or kept His *torah*.

We see this clearly in the words of the prophets, who constantly call Israel back to the Lord and the *torah*. They picture the Israelites as a people who take pleasure in religion, but who ignore the issues of social justice that are essential expressions of a true faith in the Lord. Why was the promise of *torah* unfulfilled? Listen to Isaiah's words to a sinful generation:

ISAIAH 58:3b–4, 6–8
In fact, in the day of your fast you find pleasure,
And exploit all your laborers.
Indeed you fast for strife and debate,
And to strike with the fist of wickedness . . .
Is this not the fast that I have chosen:
To loose the bonds of wickedness,
To undo the heavy burdens,
To let the oppressed go free,
And that you break every yoke?
Is it not to share your bread with the hungry,
And that you bring to your house the poor who are cast out;
When you see the naked, that you cover him,
And not hide yourself from your own flesh?
Then your light shall break forth like the morning,
Your healing shall spring forth speedily,
And your righteousness shall go before you.
(NKJV)

Only when God's people show the same concern for others that is revealed in His *torah* can days of blessing arrive.

Chapter Wrap-Up

- We've looked at Moses's *torah* from several perspectives: as laws and regulations, as a suzerainty treaty establishing Yahweh as Israel's King, and as a total religious system designed to provide Israel with access to God.

- In this chapter we look at *torah* as the blueprint of a just and moral society that displays the depths of God's love for His people.

- In Deuteronomy, Moses presents God's love as the motive for His gift of the *torah*.

- That love is revealed in God's provisions for the welfare of the poor and ultimate eradication of poverty.

- That love is also revealed in God's provision of a unique criminal justice system that operates on very different principles from our own.

- That love is further revealed in rules governing murder and personal injury cases.

- Tragically, *torah*'s promise of a just and moral society was never realized because the Israelites failed to love and fully obey the Lord.

Study Questions

1. What are distinctive elements of *torah*'s rules and regulations?

2. What is the significance of the Hittite suzerainty treaty, and where does its structure appear in Moses's *torah*?

3. What are the critical elements in *torah* as a religious system designed to provide God's people with access to Him?

4. What are three benefits of the Law that establish it as God's loving gift?

5. What are five of the seven mechanisms built into the Law to relieve the poor and move toward a poverty-free society?

6. What are four significant contrasts between the *torah* legal justice system and the contemporary U.S. legal justice system?

7. Why does Scripture require capital punishment for murder?

8. How can the "eye-for-an-eye" principle that guides resolution in personal injury law be seen as an expression of God's love?

Chapter Highlights:
• Remember!
• Choose Life!
• What Lies Ahead
• Through It All
• Gone, but Not Forgotten

Chapter 15
The Long Good-Bye

Let's Get Started

Deuteronomy constitutes Moses's last words to the Israelites. His truly was a long good-bye! And we're not even through with what he had to say.

The long good-bye began with <u>a review</u> of what Yahweh had done for Israel, despite that people's rebelliousness. Moses continued with a passionate restatement of *torah* rules and regulations, cast in such a way that the deep <u>love of the Lord for His people shines</u> through. God yearns to bless the Israelites, and in the *torah* lays the <u>foundation of a just and moral society</u> in which each individual can prosper.

But there's more that Moses must say. As the Israelites promise to obey God's law, their leader urges them to remember their commitment, and he describes what awaits the nation should they obey . . . and should they disobey. Despite the dark vision of the future that Moses shares, he remains convinced that, through it all, God firmly intends to redeem and to bless.

go to

a review
Deuteronomy 1–4

love shines through
Deuteronomy 5–11

foundation of a just and moral society
Deuteronomy
12:1–26:15

Remember!

DEUTERONOMY 26:16–17 *This day the LORD your God commands you to observe these statutes and judgments; therefore you shall be careful to observe them with all your heart and with all your soul. Today you have proclaimed the LORD to be your God, and that you will walk in His ways and keep His statutes, His commandments, and His judgments, and that you will obey His voice. (NKJV)*

what others say

Eugene H. Merrill

The net result of covenant obedience was to be Israel's exaltation above all nations, an exaltation that would render them "praise, fame and honor" (v.19) . . . It is true that Israel's selection as a "kingdom of priests" and a "holy nation" carried with it a heavy responsibility. Their faithful discharge of that responsibility would, however, result in the greatest privilege and honor.[1]

covenant renewals
Joshua 24:14–19;
2 Kings 23:3;
2 Chronicles 15:12;
29:10; 34:31

Mount Horeb
Mount Sinai

Moses's restatement of the Law's stipulations in Deuteronomy 5–26 culminated in this renewal of the <u>covenant</u> relationship. Such <u>renewals</u> appear a number of times in the Old Testament. These ceremonies had no effect on God's commitment to bless or punish His people based on their obedience to Mosaic Law. It did, however, impact the generation that formally submitted to the Lord as King and committed to obey Him.

As Moses put it, "I make this covenant and this oath, not with you alone, but with him who stands here with us today before the LORD our God, as well as with him who is not here with us today . . . So it may not happen, when he [a man or a woman whose heart turns from God to idols] hears the words of this curse, that he blesses himself in his heart, saying, 'I shall have peace, even though I follow the dictates of my heart . . .' The LORD would not spare him" (Deuteronomy 29:14–15, 19–20 NKJV).

In renewing the law covenant, a generation of Israelites not only reviewed its obligations to the Lord, but also the significance of obedience and disobedience. Such a generation was reminded that it is impossible for a human being to "bless himself" or to actually "have peace, even though I follow the dictates of my heart . . ." Only Yahweh is able to bless. And blessing for Israel depended on following the dictates of God's law.

what others say

Eugene H. Merrill

it is important to remember that this was not so much a ceremony of covenant making as it was one of covenant affirmation or covenant renewal. The original covenant had been made at **Horeb**. What was in view here was the Lord's offer of the same covenant (albeit, with necessary amendments) to the next generation of Israelites. Arrangements agreed to by their parents were not sufficient for them. They also had to go on record as committing themselves to the Lord and his theocratic program.[2]

How About "Lordship"?

Christians today sometimes debate something called "lordship salvation." It's the idea that a person isn't really a Christian unless he or she acknowledges Christ as Lord and seeks to do His will daily.

There's a parallel here between New Testament believers and ancient Israel. The Israelites were God's people. As descendants of Abraham, they were inheritors of the covenant promises and beneficiaries of redemption from Egypt. The issue each generation of Israelites faced was not to choose whether or not they would be God's chosen people—they *were* God's chosen people. The choice the Israelites faced was whether they would follow the dictates of their own hearts, and lose God's blessing, or follow the dictates of God's law, and experience His best.

go to

new covenant
promises
Jeremiah 31:31–34;
Hebrews 8:8–12

Similarly, Christian salvation is rooted in God's <u>new covenant promises</u> and depends on Christ's redeeming death on the cross. Whether or not to acknowledge Christ's lordship isn't a decision non-Christians can make. Their only choice is to trust Christ as Savior, or to reject Him. But once we become Christians, we face a choice much like that faced by the Israelites. Will we continue to follow the dictates of our own hearts, or will we acknowledge Christ as Lord and choose the dictates of *His* heart?

key point

The choice between obeying and disobeying the precepts of the Law Covenant was for Israel only, not for pagan peoples around them. In the same way, the choice between living under the lordship of Christ is available only to those who already have a by-faith relationship with God.

For both peoples, the choice is between walking a path that leads to blessing, or walking a path that leads to an empty, disappointing life.

Choose Life!

DEUTERONOMY 30:15–19 *See, I have set before you today life and good, death and evil, in that I command you today to love the LORD your God, to walk in His ways, and to keep His commandments, His statutes, and His judgments, that you may live and multiply; and the LORD your God will bless you in the land which you go to possess. But if your heart turns away so that you do not hear, and are drawn away, and worship other gods and serve them, I announce to you today that you shall surely perish; you shall not prolong your days in the land which you cross over the Jordan to go in and possess. I call heaven and earth as witnesses today against you, that I have set before you life and death, blessing and cursing; therefore choose life, that both you and your descendants may live. (NKJV)*

Doug McIntosh

Moses places before Israel the two broad possibilities. Either
they would choose life and prosperity, or they would decide
on death and destruction. Death in this context did not suggest that unfaithful Israelites would die physically because of
their failure to comply with the terms of the covenant, though
physical death at some point was a certainty. Instead, the
death in question is a form of existence that is hateful, miser-
able, and unproductive, such as that described by the apostle
Paul: "The widow who lives for pleasure is dead even while
she lives" (1 Timothy 5:6).[3]

Reading this impassioned plea, we can sense how ardently Moses
desires the best for the people he's led the past forty years. Oh, that
they might heed God's Word always!

We can see this concern in several initiatives Moses takes to ensure
that God's people remember the words of the *torah*:

key point

- *Copies for all?* Deuteronomy 31:9 tells us that "Moses wrote
this law and delivered it to the priests, the sons of Levi, who
bore the ark of the covenant of the LORD, and to all the elders of Israel" (NKJV). While there was only one **autographa**,
this verse suggests that Moses expected copies to be made for
the priests and "all the elders of Israel." Today there are millions of copies of Scripture available in hundreds of different
languages. How important that we take advantage of
Scripture's availability to read and study God's Word.

- *Post it.* Deuteronomy 27:2–3 records Moses's command that
"when you cross over the Jordan . . . you shall set up for
yourselves large stones, and whitewash them with lime. You
shall write on them all the words of this law . . ." (NKJV). Not
just the leaders, but every person who could read was to have
access to the divine law.

- *Shout it out!* Deuteronomy 27 records another way that
Moses sought to imbed key provisions of the Law in his people's hearts and minds. Moses commanded that after crossing the Jordan half the tribes stand on Mount Gerizim and
half on Mount Ebal. The tribes on Gerizim were to chant the
blessings of the Law to the tribes across the valley between,

and those on Ebal to chant its curses (Deuteronomy 27:11–26).

- *Sing it!* Moses also wrote <u>a song</u> which the people were to memorize. The purpose of the song is described in Deuteronomy 31:21: "Then it shall be, when many evils and troubles have come upon them, that this song will testify against them as a witness; for it will not be forgotten in the mouths of their descendants" (NKJV).

a song
Deuteronomy 32

Shoutin' Against Thunder

DEUTERONOMY 30:1–3 *Now it shall come to pass, when all these things come upon you, the blessing and the curse which I have set before you, and you call them to mind among all the nations where the LORD your God drives you, and you return to the LORD your God and obey His voice, according to all that I command you today, you and your children, with all your heart and with all your soul, that the LORD your God will bring you back from captivity. (NKJV)*

My wife's father had an expression for futile efforts. He'd say, "That's like shoutin' against thunder." Shout as loudly as you can, the thunder is louder.

Moses has used device after device to anchor God's law in the hearts and minds of the Israelites. He's reviewed Israel's history. He's preached the Law to them. He's written it down and delivered it to the priests and tribal leaders. He's had the Law's provisions posted on whitewashed rocks for everyone to read. He's had the people chant the laws, and he's had them memorize an educational song. But despite all that Moses has done, he is all too aware that in the future this generation's offspring will ignore God's *torah* and leave the path to blessing.

All Moses's efforts have been no more effective than shoutin' against thunder.

But while God's people will forget Him and His law, the Lord will never forget them. Thus Moses looks beyond the centuries of apostasy and the exile of Israel from the Promised Land to a day when "you return to the LORD your God and obey His voice" (Deuteronomy 30:2 NKJV).

go to

possess the Promised Land
Genesis 12:7;
15:18–21

David's descendant will reign
2 Samuel 7:16;
Psalm 89:2–4

inner spiritual transformation
Jeremiah 31:31–34

promise covenants
the Abrahamic, Davidic, and New Covenants

second coming
the return of the resurrected Christ to rule

what others say

Duane L. Christensen

Unlike most judges today, God never closes the case in his dealings with his people. The terrifying list of curses that reaches its climax in the horrors of siege warfare and exile to a foreign land are followed by an affirmation that the door remains open for the return of the prodigal son.[4]

Whatever heartaches coming generations must endure because of their unfaithfulness, God will remain faithful to His covenant promises. In the end, God will bring His people home.

Now Versus History's End

In an earlier chapter we looked at the difference between the unconditional **promise covenants**, which state what God is committed to do and the Law Covenant given by Moses. We noted the key difference: Law is an "if . . . then," or conditional, covenant. Whether a given generation is blessed or punished depends on whether that generation keeps God's law.

There's another difference that we need to understand. The promise covenants are eschatological. That is, they are promises to be kept at history's end. Thus, the Abrahamic Covenant's provision that Israel will possess the Promised Land has always been about the still-distant future. The Davidic Covenant's promise that King David's descendant will reign over the whole earth has always been a promise about Jesus's **second coming**. And the New Covenant's promise of an inner spiritual transformation has always been about what will happen at our resurrection (1 John 3:2).

At the same time, these eschatological promises have an impact on the present. While fulfillment of the Abrahamic Promise concerning Palestine lies in the still-distant future, God also promised that *obedient generations of Israelites would enjoy life in the land*.

In a sense, the Law was the key that unlocked future blessings so they could be enjoyed by any present generation. If any generation of Israelites would love the Lord and keep His *torah*, the Lord would bless them with a good life in the Promised Land.

Now, whether a particular generation of Israelites kept the Law or rejected the Law had no effect on the covenant promises. The promises, which have always been about history's end, could not be annulled by the failures of any number of generations of Israelites. But whether a particular generation of Israelites was granted some of the blessings guaranteed for history's end *was* determined by their response to God and His *torah*.

How About Us?

When Jesus died on the cross, He <u>inaugurated the New Covenant</u> promised in Jeremiah. Among the New Covenant promises is the promise of an inner transformation. God intends not only to forgive our sins but to write His law on our hearts, performing an extreme makeover that will refashion us into the very likeness of Christ. This promise too is eschatological; it is to be kept at history's end.

But like obedient generations of Israelites that were permitted to experience then and there some of the blessings associated with possession of the land, so too God makes it possible for Christians to experience some of the <u>blessings associated with transformation</u>.

We will never be perfected in this life. But if we love the Lord and seek to please Him, God will begin His transforming work within us now, and we will grow more Christlike year by year.

All God's Best, Now!

This is what Moses so desperately wants for the Israelites. Moses has <u>reviewed the history</u> of God's dealings with the Exodus generation to drive home the importance of obedience to the *torah*. He's gone over the provisions of the Law with the people. He's had the Law written down. He's had the Law posted. He's had the Israelites shout out the Law, and he's had them memorize a song that emphasizes the importance of keeping it. There's not much more Moses can do. And although Moses realizes that all his efforts will have little more effect than shoutin' against thunder, he takes comfort in the conviction that God will live up to His commitments. At history's end, God's people will return to Him, and He will bless them just as He promised Abraham He would. Yet Moses wants each gen-

go to

inaugurated the New Covenant
Matthew 26:28;
Hebrew 9:15–20

blessings associated with transformation
Romans 8:3–5;
2 Corinthians 3:18

reviewed history
Deuteronomy 1–4

eration to experience God's best—the blessings assured in the Abrahamic Covenant—now!

What Lies Ahead

DEUTERONOMY 28:1 *Now it shall come to pass, if . . . (NKJV)*

Within the suzerainty treaty structure of Deuteronomy, chapter 28 serves as the clause that specifies the benefits to be provided good subjects by the ruler, and the punishments to be inflicted should subjects rebel. These are called the blessings and the curses.

As noted above, the blessings of obedience, listed in Deuteronomy 28:1–13, are essentially the present experience by an obedient generation of the blessings guaranteed Israel at history's end.

The curses listed in Deuteronomy 28:15–68 are different. They spell out punishments that God has a right to inflict on any rebellious generations that lie between Sinai and the end times. But they have even more significant functions in Scripture. First, this passage containing the curses provides the basis for the prophets' later interpretation of current events. And second, the passage is also predictive, sketching the course that Israel's history will follow.

> **what others say**
>
> ### W. Gunther Plaut
>
> Jewish tradition has held that at one time or another all the curses of chapter 28 were fulfilled: still, Israel survived. It became the custom when the annual cycle of Torah readings would reach this chapter, to call up a volunteer for the curses (sometimes the synagogue's contract with the sexton included his obligation to "volunteer"). Such a person would often be called up, not in customary fashion, by his name, but rather as "He who wishes." The chapter itself would be read without interruption and in a low voice, a rule that applies also to the reading of Lev. 26:14–43. This practice reflects an old fear that if one spoke too loudly of possible adversity, it might, in some mysterious fashion, be invited to happen.[5]

Flash Forward

It's some 650 years after Moses has recorded the curses found in Deuteronomy 28. The prophet Amos is God's spokesman to a rebellious generation of Israelites. Amos reminds the people of a series of disasters that have struck Israel in recent decades, and calls for a return to the Lord:

Look in the Mirror

What's striking about the prophet's words is that the events he describes mirror perfectly the curses the Lord announced in Deuteronomy 28. By looking back into Deuteronomy, Amos and the other prophets God sent to His people discovered the key to interpreting the events of their own time.

The disasters that overtook Israel were predicted in Deuteronomy 28. Surely such events were caused by Israel's departure from the Lord. And just as surely such events were a call by the Lord to return to Him.

Current Events and Deuteronomy 28 Curses

The Events	Disasters in Amos's Day	Curses for Disobedience
Starvation, lack of bread	Amos 4:6	Deuteronomy 28:17
Drought	Amos 4:7	Deuteronomy 28:24
Dispossession	Amos 4:8	Deuteronomy 28:36–37
Blight and mildew	Amos 4:9	Deuteronomy 28:22
Locust invasions	Amos 4:9	Deuteronomy 28:38, 42
Plagues of Egypt	Amos 4:10	Deuteronomy 28:21, 27
Death of children	Amos 4:10	Deuteronomy 28:32
Destruction	Amos 4:11	Deuteronomy 28:20

The Long Look Ahead

DEUTERONOMY 28:36 *The LORD will bring you and the king whom you set over you to a nation which neither you nor your fathers have known. (NKJV)*

As Moses continues to pen the words of Deuteronomy 28, he seems to look farther and farther into Israel's future. Despite the disasters that will devastate God's people, they will remain stubbornly intent on having their own way. And the Lord will increase the intensity of the curses. Looking far beyond his own time, Moses foresees foreign peoples invading the Jewish homeland. He describes the intense suffering of a people under siege. And he predicts that a day will come when God will fling His people out of the Promised Land, to live among the nations. They will be "[scattered] among all peoples, from one end of the earth to the other" (Deuteronomy 28:64 NKJV).

Someone has called predictive prophecy "history that hasn't happened yet." Reading Deuteronomy 28, a person familiar with the Old Testament senses the validity of this saying. Image after image in Deuteronomy 28 seems to fit the experience of the generations that lay between the conquest and the appearance of Christ, the Messiah.

While we shouldn't attempt a too-detailed analysis of Deuteronomy 28 as a prophetic look at Israel's future, there are striking parallels that simply cannot be ignored.

go to

450 years
Acts 13:20

> **what others say**
>
> **Mark. E. Biddle**
>
> The covenant blessings and curses contained in Deuteronomy 28 insist on one key assertion: namely, that faithful adherence to the requirements of YHWH's covenant will result in success, security, and status for Israel, while the opposite, rebelliousness, will bring a reversal of Israel's fortunes. For Deuteronomy 28, this linkage between obedience and blessing, defiance and curse is direct, immediate, and invariable. Explicitly and implicitly, this understanding of Israel's fate relies on absolute confidence in YHWH's sovereignty over the natural world and over human history.[6]

key point

The Days of the Judges

Under Joshua, the generation to which Moses has been speaking will force its way into Canaan. In a series of battles with the people who live there, the Israelites will establish their control over the Promised Land. But not all the Canaanites will be destroyed or driven out. After the death of Joshua, succeeding generations will prove susceptible to the practices of the surrounding peoples and abandon the Lord and His law.

For about <u>450 years</u> the Israelites will barely survive in their hard-won homeland. Those centuries will be marked by times of apostasy followed by the emergence of a judge—a charismatic religious, political, and military leader—who will break the power of foreign oppressors. During the lifetimes of most of the judges the Israelites will remain true to the Lord. But after the judges die the people will quickly return to idolatry. Then they will experience the curses until desperation drives them to pray to God for help, and a new judge arises.

go to

golden age
from about 1010 BC
to 930 BC

crushed by Assyria
2 Kings 17:7–41

How powerfully Deuteronomy 28:1–35 depicts Israel's condition during those centuries:

- "The LORD will send on you cursing, confusion, and rebuke in all that you set your hand to do, until you are destroyed and until you perish quickly, because of the wickedness of your doings in which you have forsaken Me" (28:20 NKJV).

- "The LORD will cause you to be defeated before your enemies; you shall go out one way against them and flee seven ways before them" (28:25 NKJV).

- "You shall betroth a wife, but another man shall lie with her; you shall build a house, but you shall not dwell in it; you shall plant a vineyard, but shall not gather its grapes. Your ox shall be slaughtered before your eyes, but you shall not eat of it; your donkey shall be violently taken away from before you, and shall not be restored to you; your sheep shall be given to your enemies, and you shall have no one to rescue them" (28:30–31 NKJV).

The Age of Kings

In time the people of Israel will insist on having a king to lead them and fight their battles for them. After a brief golden age during the reigns of David and Solomon, the United Hebrew Kingdom will be divided into two hostile entities: Israel in the North, and Judah in the South.

key point

Not a single king of Israel will be true to the Lord or observe His law. Although Israel will flourish briefly during the reign of Jeroboam II, the nation will experience disaster after disaster until the Northern Kingdom is crushed by the Assyrians and its people are deported and resettled throughout the Assyrian Empire.

Verses in Deuteronomy 28:36–48 seem particularly applicable to the history of the Northern Kingdom:

- "The LORD will bring you and the king whom you set over you to a nation which neither you nor your fathers have known, and there you shall serve other gods—wood and stone" (28:36 NKJV).

- "You shall carry much seed out to the field but gather little in, for the locust shall consume it. You shall plant vineyards and tend them, but you shall neither drink of the wine nor gather the grapes; for the worms shall eat them" (28:38–39 NKJV).

- "You shall beget sons and daughters, but they shall not be yours; for they shall go into captivity" (28:41 NKJV).

- "They shall be upon you for a sign and a wonder . . . Because you did not serve the LORD your God with joy and gladness of heart, for the abundance of everything, therefore you shall serve your enemies, whom the LORD will send against you, in hunger, in thirst, in nakedness, and in need of everything; and He will put a yoke of iron on your neck until He has destroyed you" (28:46–48 NKJV).

overrun by Babylonians
2 Kings 25;
2 Chronicles
36:15–21

The Surviving Kingdom

The Southern Hebrew Kingdom, Judah, will survive the fall of Israel for some 130 years. Unlike the Northern Kingdom, the South will be blessed with several godly rulers who lead revivals that for a time preserve the nation. But Judah too will be caught in apostasy's downward spiral. In the end Judah will be overrun by the Babylonians, the city of Jerusalem will be destroyed after a terrible siege, and Judah's people will also be exiled from the Promised Land.

Deuteronomy 28:49–68 seems to describe the desperate situation of the Israelites before the last of them are exiled from the Promised Land:

- "The LORD will bring a nation against you from afar, from the end of the earth, as swift as the eagle flies, a nation whose language you will not understand, a nation of fierce countenance, which does not respect the elderly nor show favor to the young" (28:49–50 NKJV).

- "They shall besiege you at all your gates until your high and fortified walls, in which you trust, come down throughout all your land; and they shall besiege you at all your gates throughout all your land which the LORD your God has given you. You shall eat the fruit of your own body, the flesh of your sons and your daughters whom the LORD your God has given you, in the siege and desperate straits in which your enemy shall distress you" (28:52–53 NKJV).

- "If you do not carefully observe all the words of this law that are written in this book, that you may fear this glorious and awesome name, THE LORD YOUR GOD, then the LORD will bring upon you and your descendants extraordinary plagues—great and prolonged plagues—and serious and prolonged sicknesses" (28:58–59 NKJV).

- "Then the LORD will scatter you among all peoples, from one end of the earth to the other, and there you shall serve other gods, which neither you nor your fathers have known—wood and stone. And among those nations you shall find no rest, nor shall the sole of your foot have a resting place; but there the LORD will give you a trembling heart, failing eyes, and anguish of soul. Your life shall hang in doubt before you; you shall fear day and night, and have no assurance of life. In the morning you shall say, 'Oh, that it were evening!' And at evening you shall say, 'Oh, that it were morning!' because of the fear which terrifies your heart, and because of the sight which your eyes see" (28:64–67 NKJV).

key point

what others say

Clifton J. Allen

This section presumes a breach of the covenant, a judgment already decreed in a terrible siege and military defeat with all their consequences. The situation pictured fits the situation preceding the Exile (cf. 2 Kings 24–25). The section gives no evidence of knowing the Exile itself and may well be a kind of sermonic and prophetic expansion of the chapter.[7]

The Choice

DEUTERONOMY 30:15–16 *See, I have set before you today life and good, death and evil, in that I command you today to love the LORD your God, to walk in His ways, and to keep His commandments, His statutes, and His judgments, that you may live and multiply; and the LORD your God will bless you in the land which you go to possess. (NKJV)*

what others say

Clifton J. Allen

It is clear in these speeches that the covenant preacher pleads to win acceptance of the covenant. But then his exhortations

> continue to the very last to lead for reality of faith and obedience to the opportunities which the covenant offers. This battle, it seems is never won. Each new generation must be exhorted anew. God's invitation is always new and is repeated with full meaning to each generation.[8]

go to

peace
John 14:27;
Romans 5:1

fulfillment
John 10:10

guilt
Psalm 51:14;
Joel 3:21

never alone
Hebrews 13:5–6

accept God's offer
John 3:16

reject and be punished
John 3:18

the eternal destiny
Matthew 25:41;
Revelation 19:20;
20:10, 13–15;
John 3:18

unconverted
not Christians

It's no wonder that Moses has been so impassioned in his presentation of God's law and has tried so hard to help it take root in the Israelites' hearts. For God's Old Testament people, response to the *torah* truly involved a choice between "life and good, death and evil."

It's important when we read the awful punishments laid out in Deuteronomy 28 to understand that their statement is as much an expression of God's love as is the same chapter's statement of blessings. If any person is to make an intelligent choice, he or she needs to fully understand its consequences. Through Moses the Lord made sure that His people were fully informed of the significance of the choice that lay before them.

The Gospel Choice Today

There's a tendency today to present the Christian gospel only in its most positive form. Those seeking to appeal to the **unconverted** have a tendency to emphasize the blessings provided by a present relationship with Jesus. Accept Christ, and He'll give you peace. Accept Christ, and God will lead you into a life of fulfillment. Accept Christ, and be released from guilt. Accept Christ, and you'll never need to feel alone again.

These and other benefits of our faith do appeal to moderns, for we live in a culture that values the present and that tends to ignore the future. In an age when people focus on instant gratification, talk of heaven or hell seems to have little appeal.

Yet the Christian gospel also calls for a choice between *life and good, death and evil.* The choice that a modern makes, to trust Christ and accept God's offer of forgiveness and eternal life, or to reject Him and be punished for one's sins forever, is of ultimate concern. Surely the consequences to Israel of disobeying God's law, as terrible as they were, can hardly compare with the eternal destiny that hinges on our decision today to trust or reject the Savior.

Something to ponder

Mentored by Moses

DEUTERONOMY 30:15 *See, I have set before you today life and good, death and evil.* (NKJV)

As Moses's death approaches, his greatest concern is for those he must soon leave. Like the Lord Himself, Moses's primary concern now is the choice that this and future generations of Israelites will make concerning their relationship with God.

As Moses's concern reminds us, a healthy relationship with God generates a concern for others and the life-or-death choice each must make about a personal relationship with the Lord. This brings up guideline #12, at which point we have now assembled them all together, as follows:

1. A healthy relationship with God is marked by a humble reliance on Him rather than on our natural strengths, gifts, or abilities.

2. A healthy relationship with God is rooted in complete confidence in God's presence, goodness, and power.

3. A healthy relationship with God is displayed when things go wrong by the assurance that God has a purpose, and that He intends to do us good.

4. A healthy relationship with God is reflected in the expectation that He will act to deliver us in difficult and stressful situations.

5. A healthy relationship with God calls for us to go to the Lord with our complaints, frustrations, and fears.

6. A healthy relationship with God is expressed in prayers whose primary concern is the glory and reputation of our God.

7. A healthy relationship with God is nurtured by keeping His goodness in view when we face difficult times.

8. A healthy relationship with God is promoted by a free and honest expression of our feelings and our needs to the Lord.

9. A healthy relationship with God is marked by a humble and self-less submission of our will to His.

10. A healthy relationship with God is maintained by consistently setting aside every selfish ambition and making it our sole concern to glorify our Lord.

11. A healthy relationship with God is best communicated when we are honest about our weaknesses and our total dependence on the forgiving grace of God.

12. A healthy relationship with God generates a concern for others and the life or death choice they must make about a personal relationship with the Lord.

high places
places where pagans worshipped

Through It All

DEUTERONOMY 33:1 *Now this is the blessing with which Moses the man of God blessed the children of Israel before his death. (NKJV)*

Moses is under no illusions. He's never been a man for wishful thinking. Moses knows that the people he has loved and prayed for will stray, and that the "curse which I have set before you" will "come upon you" (Deuteronomy 30:1 NKJV). But Moses also knows that the Lord will remain faithful to His promises. Despite tragedy and suffering as God's people travel along history's long highway, blessings lie ahead.

In one of Scripture's most powerful passages Moses blesses the tribes of Israel before his death. The passage concludes with Moses's affirmation of a wonderful future for the people of God:

DEUTERONOMY 33:27–29
The eternal God is your refuge,
And underneath are the everlasting arms;
He will thrust out the enemy from before you,
And will say, "Destroy!"
Then Israel shall dwell in safety,
The fountain of Jacob alone,
In a land of grain and new wine;
His heavens shall also drop dew.
Happy are you, O Israel!
Who is like you, a people saved by the LORD,
The shield of your help
And the sword of your majesty!
Your enemies shall submit to you,
*And you shall tread down their **high places**. (NKJV)*

prophecy

Gone, but Not Forgotten

DEUTERONOMY 34:1–6 *Then Moses went up from the plains of Moab to Mount Nebo, to the top of Pisgah, which is across from Jericho. And the LORD showed him all the land . . . So Moses the servant of the LORD died there in the land of Moab, according to the word of the LORD. And He buried him in a valley in the land of Moab, opposite Beth Peor; but no one knows his grave to this day. (NKJV)*

Moses was 120 years old when he died. For thirty days the Israelites mourned the loss of the only leader they had known since their release from slavery in Egypt. Moses was gone, but he would never be forgotten.

Moses is one of history's most amazing characters. He was brought up as a son in Egypt's royal family, "learned in all the wisdom of the Egyptians, and was mighty in words and deeds" (Acts 7:22 NKJV). Yet he retained his identity with the covenant people. His choice must have been a traumatic one. Moses could be one with the wealthy and powerful, or one with the oppressed. Confident in God, Moss took his stand with the people of Israel.

key point

We cannot tell what dreams the young Moses had of freedom for his people. We do know something of the high ideals he had for brotherhood among the enslaved, rooted in their family relationship with God (Exodus 2:14). When his commitment to his oppressed brothers exploded in violence, Moses was forced to flee Egypt. He was forty years old.

Moses traveled to Midian. That land was broad, with undefined borders. It included within its vast desert landscapes Mount Sinai and much of the wilderness through which Israel would later wander. For forty more years of his life Moses lived as a humble shepherd with the nomadic Midianites. Finally, at eighty, his dream of freeing Israel was long dead (cf. Exodus 3:11). Then God spoke to Moses and announced the emancipation of his people!

The final four decades of Moses's life were dedicated to the work that has assured his place in history. Constantly under pressure, confronting enemies without and rebelliousness within Israel, Moses's flaming faith never failed. Though often discouraged, he was a model of faithfulness for every succeeding generation (Hebrews 3:2). The Law given through him has shaped the lives of the covenant people for millennia. And the five books of the OT ascribed to him have been revered above all others by the Jewish people.

Chapter Wrap-Up

- Moses leads Israel in a recommitment to God and His law, a covenant renewal ceremony.

- Moses uses several approaches to anchor God's law in the hearts and minds of the Israelites.

- If any generation of Israelites will keep God's law, the Lord will provide that generation with blessings that will be Israel's at history's end.

- In Deuteronomy 28, Moses defines blessings and curses, the consequences of either obeying or disobeying the Lord.

- The curses of Deuteronomy 28 serve as the key used by later prophets to interpret the significance of current events.

- The curses of Deuteronomy 28 also provide an overview of the future history of God's Old Testament people.

- While Moses knows what lies ahead for Israel, he also knows the blessings that await at history's end, and so blesses each Israelite tribe as well as the whole people.

- Moses dies at age 120, but he has never been forgotten by God's people.

Study Questions

1. What strategies did Moses use to implant God's law in the hearts and minds of the Israelites?

2. What is the content of Deuteronomy 28?

3. What does it mean to say that the biblical promise covenants are eschatological? What is the relationship between the Law Covenant and the promise in the Abrahamic Covenant that Israel will inherit the land?

4. Beyond spelling out punishments should Israel disobey, what is the significance of Deuteronomy 28?

5. In what way can the listing of punishments in Deuteronomy 28 be considered a gift expressing God's love for His people?

6. What deep concern of Moses is seen in the final chapters of Deuteronomy? What can Christians learn from the ways Moses expressed that concern?

7. How did Moses die?

Chapter 16
Moses: A Backward Look

Chapter Highlights:
• The God of Moses
• The Books of Moses
• The Foundational Five
• The Law of Moses
• Moses as Mentor

Let's Get Started

Moses is long dead, buried in an unknown grave. Yet few in history have had such a lasting impact. Moses seems even more significant when we look back and summarize his impact on the Western world. The revelation given through Moses laid the foundation of our concept of God. The Old Testament books that Moses penned anchor our faith securely in history. The Law of Moses so powerfully shaped a people that despite being without a homeland, that people has retained its unique identity through millennia. And, should we look to him, Moses can mentor us in deepening our personal relationship with the Lord.

The God of Moses

The story of Moses begins in the Old Testament book of Exodus. At that time the descendants of Abraham, Isaac, and Jacob were slaves in Israel. The Israelites' identity had been shaped by their verbal history, stories passed on from generation to generation of an ancestor who was given wonderful promises by a God who was above all gods. Later, when Moses was an adult, those stories were woven together and expanded through a direct revelation the Lord gave Moses at Sinai. In that revelation, recorded in the Old Testament book of Genesis, two vital truths about God are emphasized. Then, at age eighty, Moses began a ministry during which more and more of the nature and character of God became known.

God in Genesis

Genesis reveals two vital truths about God. First, God is the Creator, the source of all that exists. And second, God has a purpose that is being worked out through human history.

- ***The Revelation of God as Creator.*** All the religions of the ancient world assumed that there were many deities. These deities were very much like humans, driven by passion and jealousy, essentially unconcerned with humans. Human beings worshipped the deities to avoid the gods' displeasure and in an attempt to win their favor. While in some ancient religions the body of a dead deity might become the material universe, or drops of a slain god's blood might be deemed the source of humanity, no ancient faith pictured its gods standing outside the material universe or as the universe's source.

key point

Genesis thus introduces a God who is wholly different from the gods of the ancient world. This God is One. He has existed forever. He is the source of all that exists. He is all-powerful, for He is the Creator of all things. Even more stunning, this God has a vital interest in human beings, whom He created in His own image and likeness.

Living as we do in a world where our concept of God has been shaped by the Bible, we can't begin to imagine what a stunning and unexpected deity Scripture introduced into the ancient world. The God of the Bible is completely different from the gods invented by humans and enshrined in their religions.

- ***The revelation of God as God of history.*** This is the other stunning revelation in Genesis. It comes to us through promises made to Abraham. Ancient religions tended to view the universe as static. That is, ancient faiths did not sense either direction or purpose in history. What is simply is. The universe isn't moving toward a particular end. Some Greek philosophers speculated that the universe expanded for ten thousand years and then fell in upon itself, only to repeat the process endlessly. But most ancients simply assumed that what existed then would exist forever.

something to ponder

When God spoke to Abraham of a future in which all humankind would be blessed through one of his descendants, a stunning new concept was introduced. History was flowing toward God's intended end. The God who existed "in the beginning" and had brought the universe into existence had purpose for the creation, and He was shaping history so that events flowed toward His intended end.

This too was a stunning innovation. In ancient religions, deities—like humans—were trapped within the present. They might struggle for dominance—i.e., one deity might fade in significance while another assumed his powers; but there was no sense of a grand plan or of movement toward an end shaped by the gods.

Ancient Concepts of Origins[1]

	Mesopotamian	Egyptian	Greek	Genesis
VIEW OF GOD(S)	Many competing gods/goddesses	Many related gods/goddesses	Many warring gods/goddesses	One God
NATURE GOD(S)	Good/evil, petty, warring	Represent natural phenomenon, & abstract ideas	Adulterous, petty, limited	Good, All-Powerful
RELATION MAN/GODS	Man vastly inferior, from blood of the demon/god Kingu	Little moral or personal relationship	Both subject to fate; gods intervene capriciously	Mankind is created by, loved by God
SOURCE OF MATERIAL UNIVERSE	Corpse of slain deity, Tiamat	Five myths give different explanations	Universe pre-existed the gods	The One God is Creator and Designer

Designer God in Exodus–Deuteronomy

Exodus continues God's revelation of His nature and character of God. Here the revelations come more quickly, squeezed into the last forty years of Moses's life.

- *The revelation of the name Yahweh.* God appears to the eighty-year-old Moses and reveals the name Yahweh. The name, meaning "The One Who Is Always Present," emphasizes God's presence and His involvement in the life of His people. This is no deity whose attention needs to be attracted by religious rites that draw blood or provoke sexual passion, as was common in pagan rites. The God of the Bible was with His people always, ever aware of their situation and their needs.

- *The revelation of God's faithfulness.* The Lord announces to Moses that He has heard Israel's cries, and has come to rescue them. The Lord will keep the covenant promises He made to Abraham, and will bring Abraham's descendants back to Canaan and give them that land. Throughout the books that span Moses's life, the fact that God keeps His promises—even when provoked by the rebelliousness of the

Israelites—is a repeated theme. God is trustworthy. He will do what He says He will do.

- *The revelation of God's power to save.* When Moses arrives in Egypt he finds a pharaoh who has nothing but contempt for the demands of the God of his slaves. It takes a series of punishing miracles that devastate Egypt to force the arrogant ruler to submit and to free God's people. This series of mighty deeds makes it clear that there is no limit to the power of God, or of His ability to act in the material universe. The series of miracles also makes it clear that God will use His power to save His people. With Creation, the Exodus stands as the most powerful defining act of God. Forever He will be known as the Creator and the Savior of His people.

- *The revelation of God's moral character.* At Mount Sinai the Lord gives Israel a Law whose principles and precepts reflect His own moral character. Earlier law codes from the ancient Middle East show that human beings have an innate sense of right and wrong. The Law of Moses makes it clear that God is the source of humankind's moral awareness. Moreover, Mosaic Law more accurately defines right and wrong acts, and links those acts to relationship with God. God's concern with morality provides vital insight into His nature.

Strikingly, the deities of other ancient religions show little or no concern with human moral behavior. While the gods are quick to avenge the slightest affront to themselves, the gods and goddesses show no concern for how humans treat each other. Nor do they display any moral compunction in how they, the gods, treat humans.

What a contrast with the God of Scripture! He is so deeply concerned with how humans treat one another that He designs mechanisms in His law to protect the poor. He commits Himself to judge those who violate His laws and oppress others. Yet God Himself waits to punish the Canaanites until their iniquity is "full." Only Scripture presents a God who is the source and standard of morality, and who anchors human moral behavior in a personal relationship with Himself.

key point

- *The revelation of God's desire to have a relationship with sinful human beings.* God's intent to have a relationship with human beings is expressed in the covenant He made with Abraham (Genesis 12:1–3). It is seen even more clearly in the provision made in Mosaic Law for sinful human beings to approach Him through sacrifices offered by Israel's priests. Old Testament rules and regulations as well as those institutions that allow sinners to approach God, are rightly described in Deuteronomy as rooted in God's love for His people.

God's love is also seen in the Lord's description of Himself as a "jealous" God. The opposite of jealousy is indifference, and God cares so intensely about His people that He can never be indifferent toward them or their actions. Even God's punishments and discipline are designed to lead human beings to a saving relationship with Him, so they can be blessed.

The picture of God that emerges from the first five books of the Old Testament lays the foundation for our knowledge of God. In these books penned by Moses, the Lord reveals Himself to be the opposite, in nearly every respect, of the deities worshiped by pagans.

The true God is the Creator of all that exists. He created human beings in His own image, and He continues to love humankind. God is also the God of history; He has a plan and is shaping history so that it moves toward His intended end. God has expressed His plan in covenant promises, first those made to Abraham, and in subsequent promises made to David and, through Jeremiah, to Israel the promise of a New Covenant. God is totally reliable and faithful in keeping those promises. As history flows, God is always present with His people. His power to save is unlimited; He can and does intervene in history on behalf of His own.

God is a moral being who truly cares about human beings. He expects His people to do what is right, both in their relationship with Him and in relationships with other human beings. Because the Lord loves us so, He is passionately concerned that we do what is right, and so experience His richest blessings. Because He loves us so, God will not hesitate to punish or disciple when we do wrong. God's desire to have a personal relationship with human beings is powerfully expressed in the fact that God imbedded in His law a way for sinful people to approach Him through blood sacrifice.

The vision of God introduced through Moses is expanded upon and developed in the rest of Scripture. As history flows, and more and more elements of His grand plan are unveiled, we see Him ever more clearly. Then, in history's greatest revelation we are overcome as the depths of divine love are displayed in Jesus.

It's vital that we come to see God as He truly is. Our thoughts about God must be consistent with who He has revealed Himself to be. And the earliest pages of Scripture, penned by Moses, are intended to shape an accurate understanding of the Lord.

The Books of Moses

key point

One of the benefits in studying the life and mission of Moses is that, as we journey with him, we learn so much about God. In personal revelations such as the experience of Moses at the burning bush; in historic events such as the plagues that struck Egypt; in the moral vision and the institutions of Mosaic Law; and in God's relationship with rebellious Israel, a clearer and clearer picture of God emerges. The foundation of an accurate God concept is laid in the story of Moses and his mission.

This story is recorded in the first five books of the Old Testament, which were penned by Moses himself. Perhaps without even noticing it, as we've journeyed with Moses we've begun to develop a grasp of what these books contain. At any rate, the story of Moses and his mission gives us tools to see what is significant in each early Old Testament book.

Genesis

Genesis is the book of origins. It opens with the story of God's creation of the universe and His creation of human beings in His own image and likeness. While we haven't touched on this, the early chapters of Genesis also reveal the origin of sin and the impact that evil has on the human race.

Chapter 12 of Genesis introduces Abraham and the covenant promises given to him. As we've seen, these covenant promises reveal that history is moving toward an end designed by God. The rest of Genesis, from chapter 12 through chapter 50, traces the transmission of the covenant promises from Abraham to his son

Isaac and his grandson Israel, and to Israel's (Jacob's) twelve sons. Genesis ends with the descendants of Abraham, Isaac, and Jacob welcomed as guests in Egypt.

If we keep in mind that early Genesis reveals origins, and that from Genesis 12 on the theme is the transmission from generation to generation of the covenant promises God made to Abraham, we'll have a basic grasp of Genesis.

Exodus

Exodus opens with the birth of Moses to Israelite slaves. It tells of his adoption into Egypt's royal family, and of Moses's loyalty to his own people. At eighty Moses is commissioned by God to free the Israelites. Encouraged by the revelation of the divine name Yahweh, Moses returns to Egypt. There God performs miracles which devastate that land and force Pharaoh to release his slaves. After various adventures Moses leads the Israelites to Mount Sinai. God appears to Israel there, and enters into a covenant relationship patterned on the Hittite suzerainty treaty. The people accept the covenant and acknowledge the Lord as Israel's King.

At Sinai the Lord lays out a unique religious system intended to provide a sinning Israel with access to God. That system involves a lifestyle based on moral and nonmoral rules of behavior, a priesthood to represent the people to God, blood sacrifices to cover sins, a tabernacle worship center to which the Israelites may come to appeal to the Lord, a worship calendar, and other features.

Leviticus

Leviticus opens with the Israelites still at Sinai. Its first ten chapters define the sacrifices to be offered by Israel's priests. The book then continues to describe the way of life God's people are expected to live, laying down ceremonial laws—practices not related to morality which affect the "cleanness" or "uncleanness" of God's people—and going into details on sexual practices and other moral issue.

Leviticus 16 is the pivotal passage in this book, for it contains instructions for the Day of Atonement and the one annual sacrifice that covered all of Israel's sins.

The book continues with additional detailed instructions and the laying out of a religious calendar the Israelites are to follow.

Key Passages in the Books of Moses

Book	Biblical Event
Genesis 1	Creation of the universe.
Genesis 2	Creation of humankind.
Genesis 3	The first humans sin.
Genesis 12, 15	God makes covenant promises.
Exodus 1	Israel is enslaved. Moses is born.
Exodus 3, 4	God reveals that his name is Yahweh.
Exodus 5–11	God's mighty acts free the Israelites.
Exodus 12	Passover is introduced.
Exodus 20	The Ten Commandments.
Exodus 19–23	Law takes covenant form.
Exodus 25–31	The Tabernacle and priesthood.
Leviticus 1–10	Sacrifices and offering.
Leviticus 16	The Day of Atonement.
Numbers 14	The Israelites rebel.
Deuteronomy 5–11	Law is rooted in love.
Deuteronomy 27	The Covenant is renewed.
Deuteronomy 28	Blessings and curses.
Deuteronomy 34	Moses dies.

Numbers

After taking a census of men of military age, the Israelites leave Mount Sinai and travel toward Canaan. Events along the way make it clear that the generation that escaped from Egypt remais critical and rebellious. When the people reach the borders of Canaan they are gripped by fear. They refuse to trust God and rebel when told to enter the land and possess it. God dooms that generation to forty years of wandering in the wilderness until all the rebels have died.

The rest of Numbers features highlights of those forty years and continuing rebellions that lead to the death of the first Exodus generation. When all in the first generation have died Moses takes a census of men of military age in the new generation. The numbers are nearly the same. The forty-year delay has caused no decline in strength, and the new generation that emerges is ready to trust God and take the land. Wars with peoples on the east side of the Jordan River have also produced a battle-tested force, and some of the tribes ask to occupy the conquered eastern lands.

Deuteronomy

The whole book follows the pattern established in Hittite suzerainty treaties. It contains three speeches of Moses: one tracing travels from Egypt to Canaan; one restating Covenant rules and laws; and one urging the Israelites to remain ever faithful to the Lord.

As Moses prepares to turn over leadership of Israel to his successor, Joshua, he does all that he can to imbed God's law in the hearts and minds of the people. He also lays out clearly what will follow should Israel continue to obey the Lord, and what will happen if they abandon Yahweh and his *torah*.

The book ends with an account of Moses's death. Moses is given a glimpse of the Promised Land before he dies. Then the Lord Himself buries Moses's body in an unknown grave.

The Foundational Five

These five books of Moses are the foundation on which the rest of Scripture is constructed. In one sense they are the story of one man, Moses, and of his mission. In another sense they are the story of a people chosen and fashioned by God. In yet another sense they are the stunning revelation of a God totally unlike the deities worshipped in the ancient world, a God whose character and purposes will continue to be revealed through all the subsequent books that make up our Bible.

One of the benefits of studying Moses and his mission is that such a study incorporates a survey of each of these five foundational Bible books.

The Law of Moses

There are few aspects of Scripture so little understood as the Law of Moses. This misunderstanding is serious, for all too many non-Christians assume that they can make themselves acceptable to God by trying to keep the Ten Commandments. Too many Christians assume that a similar effort to keep God's commandments is all that God expects of them. Only when we see Mosaic Law for what it truly was will we begin to understand the authentic Christian life. So let's review what we've learned in this study about the Law of Moses.

key point

- *"Law" is a broad term with many meanings.* The Hebrew word translated "Law," *torah*, may refer to any of a number of things. The whole revelation given through Moses—the first five books—are *torah*. Any specific biblical ruling is *torah*. The Ten Commandments are *torah*. Moral rules and ceremonial rules are *torah*. The religious system of the Old Testament, with its laws, its priesthood, its sacrifices, etc., is *torah*. And any of these elements, such as the priesthood, is *torah*. Thus when we come across the word *law* in the Old Testament, or references to Old Testament "law" in the New Testament, we need to discern what feature of Old Testament religion the writer is referring to. Too often we assume that such references to "the law" are references to the Ten Commandments, when in fact such references often are not!

- *"Law" may refer to rulings concerning practices which are morally right or wrong.* Like other law codes of the ancient Middle East, the Bible contains laws governing specific practices. Both biblical and other law codes reflect a common moral vision, in that each deals with the same kinds of issues, and each reflects a common conviction that certain acts are morally wrong and that others are morally right.

The similarity between the biblical code and the other law codes doesn't mean that any one is necessarily dependent on any other. The similarities do suggest that in creating humans in His own image, God implanted an awareness of the kinds of issues which are moral in character. Thus all ancient codes regulate sexual behavior, property rights, etc. Where the details differ, the biblical code is morally superior.

- *"Law" may refer to moral principles, such as those expressed in the Ten Commandments.* Here biblical law departs from other ancient law codes, which deal with specifics rather than principles. The Old Testament frequently refers to principles, such as we see in the Ten Commandments or in the saying, "You shall love your neighbor as yourself."

The moral principles stated in Moses's *torah* serve as a revelation of the moral character of God. They also serve as an expression of the moral character He desires in human beings. As we noted in this study, the commandments establish both external (behavioral) and internal (character) boundaries. Thus, "You shall not murder" is not simply about committing murder, but is also about the hostility and hatred that lead to murder.

Moral principles stated as commandments remind us that to truly meet God's expectations we must experience an extreme inner makeover; an inner transformation that only God can work. Thus in a sense such commandments are prophecy, revealing what God intends to do in the hearts and lives of those who trust Him.

- *"Law" may refer to the nonmoral, or ceremonial, requirements laid down by Moses.* Rules governing what a person may eat, the kind of clothing he or she may wear, etc., have no moral implications. Generally the violation of ceremonial rulings makes a person "unclean"—unfit to participate in Israel's worship or in the life of the community. Generally also, a person may be restored to a state of "cleanness" by the passage of time and washing with water, although for some violations of ceremonial rules a blood sacrifice may also be required. There are no parallels to the ceremonial rules of Scripture in the other law codes of the ancient Middle East.

- *"Law" is presented in the form of a Hittite suzerainty treaty.* Such a treaty governed the relationship between a ruler and his subjects. Thus biblical law is to be understood as a constitution, formalizing the relationship between Yahweh as King and Israel as His subjects. It is significant that the Law Covenant was between Yahweh and "the children of Israel" (Exodus 19:3 NKJV). The Old Testament Law Code, which is an integral part of the treaty, was *never binding on any pagan people or on Christians.* Mosaic Law defined the relationship between God and Israel. The Christian's relationship with God is governed by the provisions of the New Covenant, not the Law Covenant.

- *Mosaic Law is a religious system designed to provide a sinful people with limited access to God.* The *torah* spelled out rules and regulations which the Israelites were unable to keep. Yet God desires a relationship with sinful human

go to

temporary
Galatians 3:16–19

faithful
Numbers 12:7;
Hebrews 3:2

beings. God's solution was a religious system which provided the Israelites with limited access to God. The system required a priesthood to offer sacrifices, blood sacrifices to cover Israel's sins, a worship center where God might be approached, and a religious calendar with special holy days and holidays to keep the Israelites mindful of the Lord.

This religious system was imperfect, for the blood of bulls and goats could never compensate for sin. And it was <u>temporary</u>, intended to function only until God's Son could take on human flesh and die on a cross, instituting the New Covenant, which provides those who believe in Jesus with an eternal salvation. Thus, Mosaic Law was in force only from the events on Mount Sinai to the events on Calvary.

When the apostle Paul writes, "You are not under law but under grace" (Romans 6:14 NKJV), he is not suggesting that God is no longer concerned with morality. What he is teaching is that the *torah* approach to God has been replaced by a grace system that is far more effective. In fact, in the same letter Paul promises that through the power of the Holy Spirit, who is available to us under the New Covenant, "what the law could not do" God will do in us, "that the righteous requirement of the law might be fulfilled in us" (Romans 8:3–4 NKJV).

key point

The Law of Moses is far more than the Ten Commandments and other moral principles. In our study of Moses and his mission we've seen how complex Mosaic Law truly is. Hopefully, this will keep us from jumping to conclusions when we come across references to the Law in our own Bible reading. And hopefully the discussion of Mosaic Law will motivate us to learn more about the far better way to approach and to please God that is God's gift to us under His New Covenant.

Moses as Mentor

One of the greatest benefits in studying Moses and his mission is the insight we gain into developing and maintaining a healthy relationship with God. Moses is not only commended by God as a <u>faithful</u> individual; he is also enshrined with other heroes of the faith in Hebrews 11.

As we've studied Moses, we've paused now and then to discover how Moses can mentor us in our own relationship with the Lord. The principles we've discovered are worth reviewing.

- *A healthy relationship with God is marked by a humble reliance on Him rather than on our natural strengths, gifts, or abilities.* Moses had many natural talents and the best education available in his era. He had position, power, and wealth. It took Moses forty years in the desert as a lowly shepherd to become humble enough to rely wholly on the Lord. Such reliance is freeing for the talented, and encouraging for the person who feels he or she has no great strengths. For the multitalented individual, relying on the Lord frees us from the fear of failure and the pressure to try harder. For the person who feels he or she has no great strengths, it's encouraging to realize that ministry is what God does through us, not what we can do for Him. For both, the divine prescription is to trust God, as Moses did, and to step out in faith to follow where the Lord leads.

- *A healthy relationship with God is rooted in complete confidence in God's presence, goodness, and power.* This was hard for Moses to grasp. He rightly felt weak and inadequate, and hesitated to accept God's commission. But Moses finally grasped the fact that he was to let go, and let God. There are times when anyone will feel inadequate, or even feel abandoned by God. There may be times when we seem paralyzed by fear. Yet God has revealed Himself as The One Who Is Always Present. We don't need to feel His presence to know that the Lord is with us. All we need to do is trust Him to be who He has revealed Himself to be. When God is present, we have no need to fear.

- *A healthy relationship with God is displayed when things go wrong by the assurance that God has a purpose, and that He intends to do us good.* Moses couldn't understand Pharaoh's harsh response to his request to let his slaves go out in the desert to worship. Moses had obeyed God, but the result was even greater sufferings for God's people. The saying "God works in mysterious ways" is surely true. If we were in charge there would be no such setbacks or disappointments. Those things we yearn to do for God would proceed from victory to victory. But God is One who works through failure. Each setback, each disappointment, is part of His plan. God explained to Moses that it would take a series of miracles that forever established His power to force Pharaoh to release his slaves. Somehow it all fit together, and the result was the accomplishment of God's purpose and His people's good. Somehow those things that go wrong in our lives will fit together as well, for God's glory and for what is best for us.

- *A healthy relationship with God is reflected in the expectation that He will act to deliver us in difficult and stressful situations.* All too often we expect the worst when we should expect the best. When the Israelites saw Pharaoh's army pursuing them, they were sure they were about to die. Moses told them to simply stand still and see God's deliverance. Our God is still One who overcomes difficulties and stands with us when we are in danger. Being confident God will act isn't foolish optimism; it's a realistic approach to the challenges we all face. God is present with us, and we can be confident He will save.

- *A healthy relationship with God calls for us to go to the Lord with our complaints, frustrations, and fears.* As soon as the water ran out the Israelites began to complain about Moses. In contrast, Moses went directly to the Lord with his complaints. Complaining about situations we find ourselves in is a denial of God's sovereignty. Bringing our frustrations to God honors Him, for it acknowledges His control over our situation. Bringing our feelings to God—even the most negative—also honors Him as loving. Complaining to God is an expression of confidence that He cares for us even when circumstances suggest otherwise.

- *A healthy relationship with God is expressed in prayers whose primary concern is the glory and reputation of our God.* Moses cared about the people he led. He pleaded with God to be gracious to them after the incident with the golden calf stirred God's wrath. But Moses was most concerned about the reputation of God as a faithful, covenant-keeping God whose purposes could not be thwarted even by a rebellious Israel. It's all right to pray for people we care about, whatever their needs. But our prayers should all be motivated by a desire that God will glorify Himself in whatever answer He gives.

key point

- *A healthy relationship with God is nurtured by keeping His goodness in view when we face difficult times.* Under tremendous pressure because of the rebelliousness and stubbornness of the people he led, Moses cried out, begging to know God better. God was unable to reveal everything about Himself to Moses. But God did make His goodness pass before His servant. When we find ourselves under intense pressure and feel a need to know God better, we need to keep one things in the forefront of our thoughts: God is good. We may not see the good in the circumstance that troubles us, yet His goodness is all around us. God taught Moses to focus on the good that he could see, and ascribe that good to God. In time we may even see His good in the things that have distressed us the most.

- *A healthy relationship with God is promoted by a free and honest expression of our feelings and our needs to the Lord.* Moses let all his frustrations out when he spoke with the Lord. He even shared negative thoughts he had about the Lord Himself. Honest expression of our thoughts, our feelings, and our needs to the Lord is an affirmation of confidence in Him. Such expression shows that we've come to the place where we know He loves us as we are, not as we sometimes pretend to be to impress others. Honesty in our relationship with God is one of the keys to significant spiritual growth.

- *A healthy relationship with God is marked by a humble and selfless submission of our will to His.* Moses was crushed when he learned that God would not permit him to enter Canaan with the Israelites. Yet he shows us the only way to deal with our own crushing disappointments. We are to say— and to mean it!—"not what I will, but what You will, be done."

- *A healthy relationship with God is maintained by consistently setting aside every selfish ambition and making it our sole concern to glorify our Lord.* Aaron and Miriam were driven by a selfish ambition to supplant Moses as the leader of God's people. Moses had no concern for self-promotion or for the limelight. Moses realized that to lead means to serve; not to be the star, but to be the servant of all. It is by serving others that we glorify God. It is by serving others that we find our place in God's family. As long as your sole concern is to glorify our Lord you will be protected from the dangers of selfish ambition.

key point

- *A healthy relationship with God is best communicated when we are honest about our weaknesses and our total dependence on the forgiving grace of God.* One of the few incidents where we noted a flaw in Moses's character was when he was unable to bring himself to admit that the reason God wouldn't let him enter Canaan was that he had been disobedient. Instead Moses tried to shift the blame to the rebelliousness of the people he led. In doing this, Moses missed an opportunity to remind the people he led that God requires obedience in all His people. He missed an opportunity to show them that disobedience has consequences. And he missed an opportunity to model honest confession as the best way to deal with the sins that plague us all. It's unusual, but in this one case we learn *not* to follow Moses's example.

- *A healthy relationship with God generates a concern for others and the life-or-death choice they must make about a personal relationship with the Lord.* Moses's deep concern for the welfare of the people he leads is apparent in the last chapters of Deuteronomy. Before he dies, Moses's thoughts turn to the future of those he has led. He yearns for them to choose life and good, not death and evil. In our day friends and neighbors must choose Christ and find eternal life, or fail to choose Him and find that death and evil await them. Like Moses we are to take to heart the reality of what lies ahead for everyone, and to make the life-and-death issue of faith in Christ as clear to others as possible.

Chapter Wrap-Up

- In studying Moses and his mission, we learn key truths that help us develop an accurate concept of who God is.

- In studying Moses and his mission, we develop a general understanding of the content of the first five books of the Old Testament.

- In studying Moses and his mission, we begin to realize how multifaceted the "Law of Moses" truly is.

- In studying Moses, we discover how to relate to the Lord in ways that help us deepen our personal relationship with Him.

Study Questions

1. List three things that we learn about God through a study of Moses and his mission. Which of the three you listed seems most important for you to remember when you think about the Lord?

2. What does Romans 6:14 mean by "You are not under law but under grace" (NKJV)?

3. Explain why Romans 6:14 does not mean that Christians are not expected to live moral lives.

4. List three things that you have learned about relationship with God from Moses's mentoring. Which of these is the most important to you, and why?

Appendix A—The Answers

Chapter 1

1. Their ancestors had entered Egypt during a time of famine and settled there.

2. Foreign peoples that had ruled Egypt were driven out by the Egyptians.

3. Pharaoh had ordered the death of all male infants born to the Hebrews, potentially exterminating the race.

4. His mother, who told him stories of his Hebrew heritage, and his education as an adopted prince of Egypt.

5. He killed an Egyptian who was beating a Hebrew.

6. He went into the Sinai, and he lived there for forty years.

7. God promised to bless Abraham and his offspring, and give them the land of of Canaan as a homeland. He promised that all peoples would be blessed through the Jews.

8. The enslaved Israelites were suffering intensely, and cried out to the Lord.

Chapter 2

1. God Himself, appearing in cloaked form.

2. "Holy" means set apart from the ordinary, for God's use.

3. Yahweh means "The One Who Is Always Present." Israel hadn't yet experienced God as present for them during their enslavement.

4. God specifically said that His was the name by which He was to be known by His people for all time. It is a personal, revelatory name rather than simply a descriptive name.

5. The "new Moses" is humble, self-effacing, and unwilling to rely on himself, unlike the "old" confident man of action. This is revealed in his hesitation to accept Yahweh's commission to deliver the Israelites from Egypt.

6. God promised to be with him, explained what He

intended to do, equipped Moses with "signs," and gave him Aaron as a spokesperson.

7. Don't rely on your own gifts and talents; do rely completely on God and have confidence in Him.

Chapter 3

1. He was arrogant and boastful. To free the slaves would have been humiliating.

2. The Israelites blamed Moses and complained. Moses asked God why this had happened.

3. By revealing more of Himself and His power. The method is significant because it meant Pharaoh remained responsible for his actions and their consequences.

4. Because natural laws describe how the universe functions without the intervention of a person.

5. That the Israelites and the Egyptians might know the Lord, and that all the gods of Egypt should be judged and exposed as frauds.

6. See pages 52–53 for all ten.

7. The miracle judgments did not touch the Israelites in Goshen but devastated the rest of Egypt.

Chapter 4

1. The decades of oppression in which all Egyptians took part.

2. It is a *zikkaron*, a means by which future generations can participate in what God did for His people.

3. It too is a *zikkaron*, inviting us to see ourselves at the foot of Jesus's cross and to realize Christ died for us.

4. Many suggest this hardening was a divine judgment. Pharaoh had gone too far in resisting the Lord to be permitted to repent.

5. They failed to remember God's miracles or trust Him.

6. He opened a path in the sea for the Israelites;

when the Egyptian army pursued, He caused the waters to flow back and drown them.

7. Because they seemed unable to trust God despite all He had done for them so recently.

8. The Israelites murmur, complain, and seem totally unable to trust God. Moses looks to the Lord whenever any need arises.

Chapter 5

1. God intended Israel to be His special people, a kingdom of priests and a holy nation.

2. Because of the awe-inspiring effects of God's presence on the mountain.

3. A covenant is an agreement between two or more parties that defines the relationship between them.

4. The Abrahamic, the Davidic, and the New. The last two are revelations of how God intends to keep the promises made in the first.

5. Because it's an "if . . . then" (i.e., conditional) structure.

6. It tells us that God intends to rule His people personally, as Israel's King.

7. General principles, as in the Ten Commandments. And both moral rulings and nonmoral rulings in case-by-case law.

8. Moral case-by-case rulings are found in other ancient law codes. The other two are not.

9. The parallels show that God created human beings with an awareness of the kinds of issues which are essentially moral.

Chapter 6

1. No other nation had a God so near to answer prayer, and no other nation had such righteous laws.

2. By tracing the inner attitudes and that led to the behavior.

3. Check the list on page 115.

4. Four.

5. Six.

6. Check the chart on pages 135–136.

Chapter 7

1. The first two: no other gods before Me, and no graven images.

2. Intense anger.

3. It is caused by sin. It is expression balanced by His traits of love and compassion. Actions it may lead to are always intended for good.

4. For God to forgive the Israelites' sin. For the Lord to be present with His people. For Moses to see God's glory.

5. By showing Moses as much as he could take, i.e., His "back." His goodness.

6. Our prayers should be motivated by concern for the glory of God. We should always keep God's goodness in view whatever happens.

7. Paul says the veil was to keep the Israelites from seeing that the splendor on his face faded. Paul says we need to take our veils off, because others see Christ as He transforms us with an increasing splendor.

Chapter 8

1. Genesis.

2. Leviticus.

3. General principles, moral case-by-case, and non-moral case-by-case.

4. Plans for the Tabernacle, the priesthood, the sacrificial system, the priesthood, a religious calendar, etc.

5. We mistakenly assume that every reference to Mosaic Law is "do and don't."

6. He means that the Old Testament system for relating to God has been replaced by a grace system.

7. By explaining what "law" means, or by showing in the New Testament that standards of right behavior have not been abandoned.

8. Both are concerned with righteousness, priesthood, sacrifice, and access to God. For comparison/ contrast, see the discussion on pages 174–78.

Chapter 9

1. The biblical numbers are correct. Or a word intended to mean "units" was mistakenly translated as "thousands," giving an unrealistically high count.

2. By tribes. The Levites were organized by families.

3. Because they had been set aside to serve God and were not to see military service.

4. The camp was cleansed of everything unclean, the people were taught about jealousy and the Nazirite vow, the whole community worshipped, and Moses reviewed what God had done for them.

5. They faced similar situations and responded in the same way, with complaint and rebelliousness.

6. From the Red Sea to Sinai the Lord met every need. From Sinai on, the Lord met their needs, but disciplined them for their attitude.

7. All three had significant leadership roles. Moses was humble, and saw his role as that of a servant. Aaron and Miriam were jealous, and wanted higher positions for selfish reasons.

Chapter 10

1. The fertility of the land, and the size and strength of the Canaanites.

2. They were terrified and refused to trust God and enter the land.

3. God was angry and threatened to wipe the Israelites out.

4. Each prayer was for the preservation of the Israelites. Each appeal was based on preserving God's reputation. Each prayer emphasized God's faithfulness to His covenant promises. The prayer at this time also appealed to God's character as merciful and just, forgiving, but not overlooking sin.

5. God forgave the people in each case. But in this second case the Lord also imposed a just penalty.

6. They were to spend one year in the desert for each day that the spies had spent in Canaan.

7. Fact-level faith is an agreement that something is true. True faith is trust, a commitment to the One who makes promises to us. Fact-level faith is abstract. Those who have true faith trust God and respond by obeying Him.

Chapter 11

1. They were jealous. They charged Moses and Aaron with "exalting themselves."

2. Korah and his followers were swallowed by the earth, and a plague struck the camp.

3. As high priest, Aaron was the only one who could offer sacrifice for willful sins, such that the Israelites had committed, just as Christ our High Priest is the only One who could offer the sacrifice that saves us.

4. The rock represented Christ. Jesus had to be struck by death only once to provide us with salvation and all we need.

5. First Corinthians 10.

6. The event is referred to in John 3 by Jesus. Faith, expressed in coming to look at the serpent, saved the snakebitten Israelites. Faith, expressed in looking to Jesus on the cross for salvation, saves the sinner.

Chapter 12

1. Usually, "curse" means a solemn warning or an explanation of consequences. In the story of Balaam, to "curse" is to call on occult powers to cripple an enemy.

2. His eagerness to earn his fee despite being told by God not to go. Also, his willingness to try to turn God against the Israelites even though he knows God intends to bless them.

3. General guidance is provided through principles and precepts in Scripture. Specific guidance has to do with choices in a specific situation which are not covered in Scripture. Israel was not to look to the occult for specific guidance, but to Urim and Thummim or to prophets God would send. Today the Holy Spirit is present in Christians to provide specific guidance.

4. He advised Balak to get women to use sex to turn the Israelites to idolatry.

5. Balaam assumed that the Israelites would sin and that God would have to turn against them. The Israelites did sin, and the Lord punished them. But He did not reject them totally.

6. The New Testament warns against the way of Balaam (using religion to seek wealth), the doctrine of Balaam (sanctioning immorality), and the error of Balaam (choosing wealth over obedience).

7. One was faithful to God, the other driven by greed. One sought to serve God, the other to manipulate him. One protected God's people, the other sought to harm them.

Chapter 13

1. The total number of men available for military duty was about the same as during the first census.

2. Moses appointed his successor, emphasized Israel's duty to worship God, clarified the issue of vows, and punished the Midianites for their role in Balaam's plot to turn God against Israel.

3. First, because the people were evil and required divine punishment. Second, to protect the Israelites from moral and spiritual corruption.

4. The Canaanites were to be driven out or exterminated. Those outside Canaan were to be given the option of surrender and payment of tribute. Even those who fought were not to be exterminated.

5. Moses emphasizes the faithfulness of God despite the Israelites' persistent rebelliousness.

Chapter 14

1. They present moral principles as well as specific moral rulings, and unlike other ancient law codes they also include nonmoral (ceremonial) rules.

2. The use of the treaty format in Exodus 19–23 and in Deuteronomy makes it clear that Mosaic Law is viewed as a national constitution acknowledging God as King.

3. The critical elements are the priesthood, the sacrifices, and the place (the Tabernacle) where God can be approached.

4. It reveals the moral character of God. It shows us how to receive God's blessings. It warns us away from behavior that would bring us unhappiness and misery.

5. The seven mechanisms are: gleaning; the sabbatical year; the third-year tithe; interest-free, forgivable

loans; servitude/apprenticeship; the Year of Jubilee; and return of lands.

6. The goal of restoration versus punishment, cooperative versus adversarial, personal, community-based versus impersonal, and the idea that crime is against the state rather than against the victim.

7. Because people are made in the image of God. Capital punishment teaches the lesson that there is nothing of comparable value.

8. The principle is intended to prevent escalation of accidents into feuds.

Chapter 15

1. He reviewed the law, had it written down, posted it on whitewashed rocks, had Israel chant it, and had them memorize a song.

2. The first fourteen verses list the blessings that will follow obedience; the rest of the chapter lists punishments that disobedience will bring on God's people.

3. Biblical covenant promises will be kept at history's end. The Law Covenant showed Israel how any generation could experience some of the blessing promises for history's end during their own lifetimes.

4. Deuteronomy 28 provided the key later prophets used to interpret events during their lifetimes. In addition, the passage is prophetic, revealing future experiences of God's people.

5. By spelling out the consequences of obedience and disobedience God motivated the people to remain faithful.

6. Moses was deeply concerned for the life-or-death choices the Israelites would make. We need to be equally concerned about the life-or-death choice of Christ that people make today, and be as bold as Moses in spelling out the consequences of that choice.

7. He died in God's presence, and the Lord buried his body.

Chapter 16

1. That God is the Creator, that He has a purpose being worked out through history, that He is always present with us, that His power is unlimited and that He can act in our world, that He is faithful, that He uses His power to save His people, that He is a moral being, that He loves human beings and desires to have a personal relationship with us despite our sinfulness.

2. It means that the law's approach to relationship with God has been replaced by a grace approach explained in the New Covenant.

3. Romans 6:14 is not referring to the moral con-

cepts expressed in the law. Because these concepts are rooted in the very nature of God as a moral being, believers of every age are expected to live moral lives.

4. There are no right or wrong answers to this very personal question.

Appendix B–The Experts

Aldred, Cyril was Keeper of the Department of Art and Archaeology at the Royal Museum of Scotland.

Arnold, Bill T. is director of Hebrew Studies as Asbury Theological Seminary.

Ashley, Timothy R. was professor of Biblical Studies at Acadia University for over twenty years, and now pastors the First Baptist Church of La Crosse, Wisconsin.

Barclay, R. A. was the author of an exhaustive study of Israel's lawgivers, focusing on the books of Leviticus and Deuteronomy.

Barclay, William was a popular Scottish theologian who taught for twenty-eight years at the University of Glasgow and who died in 1978.

Benjamin, Don C. teaches biblical and ancient Near Eastern Studies at Arizona State University.

Beyer, Bryan E. teaches Old Testament Hebrew and Semetic Languages at Columbia Biblical Seminary and School of Missions in Columbia, South Carolina.

Biddle, Mark E. is professor of Old Testament at Baptist Theological Seminary of Richmond.

Brown, Raymond is retired as principal of Spurgeon's College in London, and now pastors Victoria Baptist Church in Eastbourne, England.

Cairns, Ian taught theology in Indonesia for twenty years, and is now a parish minister in New Zealand.

Carson, D. A. is professor of New Testament at the Trinity Evangelical Divinity school and author of several influential books.

Chrysostom, John was archbishop of Constantinople around AD 400. He is recognized as one of the fathers of the early church.

Coats, George was the author of several books dealing with events in the Old Testament, with particular emphasis on the books of Moses.

Cole, R. Dennis is professor of Old Testament and Archaeology at New Orleans Baptist Theological Seminary.

Cole, Robert L. is associate professor of Old Testament and Semetic Languages at Southeastern Baptist Theological Seminary in Wake Forest, North Carolina.

Cottrell, Leonard is a writer-producer at the BBC and editor of *The Encyclopedia of Archaeology.*

Currid, John D. is professor of Old Testament at Reformed Theological Seminary.

Dunnam, Maxie D. is senior minister of Christ United Methodist Church in Memphis, Tennessee.

Durham, John I. is a specialist in the Hebrew Bible who has taught extensively in the United States, Great Britain, and Switzerland.

Enns, Peter is associate professor of Old Testament at Westminster Theological Seminary.

Forty, Jonathan has written a number of books about ancient Egypt.

Getz, Gene taught at Dallas Theological Seminary and founded Fellowship Bible Church in Plano, Texas, where he is senior pastor.

Green, Wilda, now retired, was a well-known curriculum writer for the Southern Baptist Convention Press.

Grudem, Wayne A. is associate professor of Biblical and Systematic Theology at Trinity Evangelical Divinity School in Deerfield, Illinois.

Harris, R. Laird was a founding faculty member of Covenant Theological Seminary, and chair of the Old Testament department from 1956 until he retired in 1981.

Harrison, R. K. is professor emeritus of Old Testament at Wycliffe College, University of Toronto.

Hill, Steve is pastor of Heartland World Ministries Church in Dallas.

Hillyer, Norman was formerly librarian of Tyndale House, Cambridge, England.

Hoerth, Alfred J. recently retired as director of

archaeology at Wheaton College, where he taught for almost thirty years.

Janzen, J. Gerald is MacAllister-Petticrew Professor of Old Testament at Christian Theological Seminary in Indianapolis.

Josephus was a Jewish general in the war against Rome in the late AD 60s. Later he wrote extensively about the war and Jewish history.

Kaster, Joseph was a noted Egyptologist whose works on ancient Egypt became the standard quoted by all.

Lewis, C. S. was a British scholar who authored many apologetics books and the popular Narnia series recently being made into movies.

MacIntosh, Doug is senior pastor at Cornerstone Bible Church near Atlanta.

Matthews, Victor H. is professor of Religious Studies at Southwest Missouri State University and a specialist in Ancient Near Eastern law and culture.

McGee, J. Vernon retired as pastor of the Church of the Open Door in Los Angeles. After retiring, McGee taught the popular *Through the Bible* radio Bible class.

McKnight, Scott is associate professor of New Testament at Trinity Evangelical Divinity School in Deerfield, Illinois.

Merrill, Eugene H. is professor of Biblical Studies at Dallas Theological Seminary, Dallas, Texas.

Nystrom, David P. is associate professor of theology and history and director of the Institute of Christian Studies at North Park Theological Seminary.

Olson, Dennis T. is assistant professor of Old Testament at Princeton Theological Seminary.

Payne, David is senior lecturer in Semitic Studies, Queens University of Belfast, Ireland.

Philip, James is minister of Holyrood Abbey Church of Scotland in Edinburgh.

Plaut, W. Gunther is a Jewish rabbi.

Prichard, James B. was cannon to the ordinary of the Diocese of Rochester of the Episcopal Church.

Ross, Allen P. is Professor of Old Testament at Beason Divinity School and taught Old Testament at Dallas Theological Seminary and Trinity Episcopal School of Ministry.

Ryle, J. C. was an Anglican bishop who died in 1900. He was a leader of the evangelical branch of the Church of England, and author of many works.

Stifler, James M. was the author of books dealing with Paul's epistle to the Romans and the Apostles of the book of Acts.

Wiersbe, Warren W. is a retired pastor of Moody Church in Chicago. He is a popular speaker and the author of many books on the Bible.

Wright, Christopher J. H. is the principal of All Nations Christian College, in Ware, United Kingdom.

Youngblood, Ronald has served as professor of Old Testament at several schools and currently teaches in that capacity at International College and Bible Graduate School in Honolulu.

Endnotes

Introduction

1. Gene Getz, *Moses* (Nashville: Broadman, 1997), 139.
2. Bill T. Arnold and Bryan E. Beyer, *Encountering the Old Testament* (Grand Rapids: Baker, 1993), 108.

Chapter 1

1. Josephus, *Against Apion*, book 1, section 73, http//www.touregypt.net/manethohyksos.htm.
2. Robert L. Cole, *Layman's Bible Commentary*, vol. 2, *Exodus* (Nashville: Broadman, 1979), 22.
3. Chrysostom, as quoted in William Barklay, *Educational Ideals in the Ancient World* (Grand Rapids: Baker, 1974), 258.
4. Koot van Wyk, *Archaeology in the Bible and the Text in the Tel* (Berrian Springs, MI: Louis Hester, 1996), 120.
5 Cyril Aldred, *The Egyptians* (London: T&H, 1984), 182.
6. See http://www.touregypt.net/18dyn05.htm.
7. Quoted in Leonard Cattrel, *Queens of the Pharaohs* (London: Evans Brothers, 1966), 26.
8. Adolph Erman, *Life in Ancient Egypt* (London: Macquillen, 1903), 348.
9. Aldred, 184.
10. *The Revell Bible Dictionary* (Grand Rapids, Revell, 1990), 926.

Chapter 2

1. J. Vernon McGee, *Exodus* (Nashville: Nelson, 1991), 30.
2. D. A. Carson, *How Long, O Lord?* (Grand Rapids: Baker, 1990), 73.
3. Robert L. Cole, *The Layman's Bible Commentary*, vol. 2, *Exodus* (Waco, TX: Word, 1979), 31.

4. R. Laird Harris et al. *Theological Wordbook of the Old Testament*, vol. 1 (Chicago: Moody Press, 1980), 44.
5. Lawrence O. Richards, *Every Name of God* (Nashville: Nelson, 2000).
6. *Broadman Bible Commentary* (Nashville: Broadman, 1969), 333.
7. John I. Durham, *Word Biblical Commentary*, vol. 3, *Exodus* (Waco, TX: Word, 1987), 193.
8. John L. Mackay, *Exodus* (Ross-Shire, Scotland: Christian Focus, 2001), 77.

Chapter 3

1. A. Lucas and J. R. Harris, *Ancient Egyptian Materials and Industries* (Mineola, NY: Dover, 1999), 49.
2. Alfred J. Hoerth, *Archaeology and the Old Testament* (Grand Rapids: Baker, 1998), 163.
3. Adolf Erman, *Life in Ancient Egypt* (London: Macquillen, 1903), 58.
4. Joseph Kaster, *The Wisdom of Ancient Egypt* (New York: Barnes and Noble, 1968), 46.5.
5. John D. Currid, *A Study Commentary on Exodus* (Philadephia: Evangelical Press, 2000), 155.
6. James M. Stifler, *The Epistle to the Romans* (Chicago: Moody Press, 1968), 30.
7. Norman Hillyer, *1 and 2 Peter, Jude* (Peabody, MA: Hendrickson, 1992), 108.
8. J. Gerald Janzen, *Exodus* (Louisville, KY: Westiminster, 1997), 70–71.
9. C. S. Lewis, *Miracles* (London: Geoffrey Bles, 1952), 161.
10. Joseph Kaster, *The Wisdom of Ancient Egypt*, 154.

Chapter 4

1. John D. Currid, *A Study Commentary on Exodus* (Darlington, UK: Evangelical Press, 2000), 234.

2. Joseph Kaster, *The Wisdom of Ancient Egypt* (New York: Barnes and Noble, 1968), 111.

3. Jo Forty, *Ancient Egyptian Pharaohs* (London: PRC, 1998), 98.

4. Maxie D. Dunnam, *The Communicator's Commentary: Exodus* (Waco, TX: Word, 1987), 141.

5. See http://judaism.about.com/passover/ss/ pesach_seder_4.htm.

6. Dunnam, *The Communicators Commentary*, 156.

7. James M. Stifler, *The Epistle to the Romans* (Chicago: Moody Press, 1968), 33–34.

8. J. Gerald Janzen, *Exodus* (Louisville, KY: Westiminster, 1997), 70–71.

Chapter 5

1. John L. Mackay, *Exodus* (Ross-Shire, Scotland: Christian Focus, 2001), 246.

2. Wayne A. Grudem, *The First Epistle of Peter* (Leicester, England: InterVarsity, 1997), 113.

3. Peter Enns, *Exodus, The NIV Application Commentary* (Grand Rapids, MI: Zondervan, 2000), 408.

4. James B. Prichard, ed., *The Ancient Near East*, vol. 2 (Princeton, NJ: Princeton University Press, 1975), 72.

5. Warren W. Wiersbe, *Be Confident* (Wheaton, IL: Victor, 1962), 68.

6. Ronald Youngblood, *The Book of Genesis* (Grand Rapids: Baker, 1991), 165.

7. Mackay, *Exodus*, 358.

8. *The Code of Hammurabi*, from James B. Pritchard, *The Ancient Near East*, vol. 1 (Princeton, NJ: Princeton University Press, 1973), 138–67.

9. Victor H. Matthews and Don C. Benjamin, *Old Testament Parallels* (New York: Paulist, 1991), 62-74.

10. C. S. Lewis, *Mere Christianity*, 19.

Chapter 6

1. J. C. Ryle, *Matthew* (Wheaton, IL: Crossway, 1993), 30.

2. *Encyclopedia of Bible Words* (Grand Rapids, MI: Zondervan, 1985), 392.

3. Peter Enns, *Exodus, The NIV Application Commentary* (Grand Rapids, MI: Zondervan, 2000), 427.

Chapter 7

1. Maxie D. Dunnam, *The Communicator's Commentary: Exodus* (Waco, TX: Word, 1987), 350.

2. Peter Enns, *Exodus, The NIV Application Commentary* (Grand Rapids, MI: Zondervan, 2000), 589.

Chapter 8

1. R. A. Barclay, *The Law Givers* (New York: Abingdon Press, 1964), 35.

2. Ibid., 13.

3. Allen P. Ross, *Holiness to the LORD* (Grand Rapids: Baker, 2002), 30.

4. Ibid., 246.

5. Scott McKnight, *Galatians: The NIV Application Commentary* (Grand Rapids, MI: Zondervan, 1995), 155.

Chapter 9

1. Timothy R. Ashley, *The Book of Numbers* (Grand Rapids, MI: Eerdmans, 1993), 66.

2. Preston A. Taylor, *Numbers: In the Wilderness* (Preston A. Taylor, 1995), 15.

3. Christopher J. H. Wright, *Deuteronomy* (Peabody, MA: Hendrickson, 1996), 53.

4. Dennis T. Olson, *Numbers* (Louisville, KY: John Knox Press, 1996), 40–41.

5. James Philip, *The Communicator's Commentary: Numbers* (Waco, TX: Word, 1987), 83.

6. Olson, *Numbers*, 53.

7. R. K. Harrison, *Numbers, an Exegetical Commentary* (Grand Rapids: Baker, 1992), 188.

Chapter 10

1. Preston A. Taylor, *Numbers: In the Wilderness* (Preston A. Taylor, 1995), 52.

2. R. K. Harrison, *Numbers, an Exegetical Commentary* (Grand Rapids: Baker, 1992), 210.

3. George Coats, *Rebellion in the Wilderness* (Nashville: Abingdon, 1965), 146.

4. David P. Nystrom, *The NIV Application Commentary* (Grand Rapids: Zondervan, 1997), 149.

5. Dennis T. Olson, *Numbers* (Louisville, KY: John Knox Press, 1996), 88.

6. R. Dennis Cole, *The New American Commentary, Numbers* (Nashville: Broadman, 2000), 229.

7. James Philip, *The Communicator's Commentary: Numbers* (Waco, TX: Word, 1987), 162.

8. Wilda Green, *Finding Rest* (Nashville, Broadman, 1973), 231

9. Cole, *Numbers* 240

Chapter 11

1. R. K. Harrison, *Numbers, an Exegetical Commentary* (Grand Rapids: Baker, 1992), 234.

2. Ibid., 238.

3. Steve Hill, "Keep Your Mind Closed," *Charisma* magazine, July 2006, 51.

4. Dennis T. Olson, *Numbers* (Louisville, KY: John Knox Press, 1996), 128.

5. R. Dennis Cole, *The New American Commentary, Numbers* (Nashville: Broadman, 2000), 328.

6. Preston A. Taylor, *Numbers: In the Wilderness* (Preston A. Taylor, 1995), 82.

7. James Philip, *The Communicator's Commentary: Numbers* (Waco, TX: Word, 1987), 234.

Chapter 12

1. Dennis T. Olson, *Numbers* (Louisville, KY: John Knox Press, 1996), 140.

2. R. Laird Harris, *Theological Wordbook of the Old Testament* (Chicago: Moody Press, 1980), 1:132.

3. R. Dennis Cole, *The New American Commentary, Numbers* (Nashville: Broadman, 2000), 381.

4. R. K. Harrison, *Numbers, an Exegetical Commentary* (Grand Rapids: Baker, 1992), 293.

5. Christopher J. H. Wright, *Deuteronomy* (Peabody, MA: Hendrickson, 1996), 216.

6. David Payne, *Deuteronomy* (Philadelphia, PA: Westminster, 1985), 111.

7. James Philip, *The Communicator's Commentary: Numbers* (Waco, TX: Word, 1987), 262.

8. William Barclay, *The Letters of John and Jude* (Philadelphia, PA: Westminster, 1960), 325.

Chapter 13

1. James Philip, *The Communicator's Commentary: Numbers* (Waco, TX: Word, 1987), 281.

2. R. Dennis Cole, *The New American Commentary, Numbers* (Nashville: Broadman, 2000), 530.

3. Dennis T. Olson, *Numbers* (Louisville, KY: John Knox Press, 1996), 169.

4. Cole, *Numbers*, 498.

5. J. Vernon McGee, *Deuteronomy* (Nashville: Nelson, 1991), 62.

6. Christopher J. H. Wright, *Deuteronomy* (Peabody, MA: Hendrickson, 1996), 111.

7. J. A. Thompson, *The Bible and Archaeology* (Grand Rapids, MI: Eerdmans, 1962), 84.

Chapter 14

1. Raymond Brown, *The Message of Deuteronomy* (Downers Grove, IL: InterVarsity, 1993), 72.

2. Christopher J. H. Wright, *Deuteronomy* (Peabody, MA: Hendrickson, 1996), 47.

3. Ian Cairns, *Word and Presence* (Grand Rapids: Eerdmans, 1992), 148.

4. Wright, *Deuteronomy*, 184.

5. Brown, *The Message of Deuteronomy*, 191.

6. John L. Mackay, *Exodus* (Ross-shire, Scotland: Christian Focus, 2001), 376.

Chapter 15

1. Eugene H. Merrill *The New American Commentary: vol. 4, Deuteronomy* (Nashville: Broadman, 2002), 338

2. Ibid., 379.

3. Doug McIntosh, *The Holman Old Testament Commentary: Deuteronomy* (Nashville: Broadman, 2001), 341

4. Duane L. Christensen, *Word Biblical Commentary, vol. 6B, Deuteronomy 21:10–34:12* (2002: Nashville, Nelson), 739

5. W. Gunther Plaut, *The Torah: a Modern Commentary*, vol. 5 (New York: Union of American Hebrew Congregations, 1983), 311

6. Mark E. Biddle *Symth & Helwys Bible Commentary: Deuteronomy* (London: Smyth & Helwys, 2003), 427.

7. Clifton J. Allen, general editor, *The Broadman Bible Commentary* (Nashville: Broadman, 1977), 276.

8. Ibid., 282.

Chapter 16

1. *Nelson's Illustrated Bible Handbook* (Nashville: Nelson, 1997), 17.

Index

beneath the desert sun, 21
Benjamin, 9, 182, 262
Beor, 239, 241, 257
best and most perfect of its kind, 72
biblical Aramaic, 28
biblical literature, 251
biblical teachings, 7
Biddle, Mark E., 319
bitter with hard bondage, 2, 3, 67
black magic, 242
blasphemy, 34, 265
  definition, 34
blessed, 18, 50–51, 69–70, 72, 90, 93, 96, 99, 187, 239–40, 243, 254–55
  definition, 50
blessings, 24, 67, 70, 100, 101, 118, 177, 218, 312, 315, 316, 327
blessings and curses, 316, 327, 336
blood of the lamb, 72
blood-sprinkled doors, 72
Bochim, 274
boils and sores, 58, 60
bondage, 2, 3, 17, 36, 50, 51, 74
  definition, 50
book of Acts, 11, 15
book of Deuteronomy, 101, 276, 283, 284
book of Exodus, 1, 5, 8, 72, 161, 329
book of Genesis, 8, 181, 329
book of Habakkuk, 4
book of Hebrews, 11, 93, 98, 154, 173, 227, 233
book of Jude, 258
book of Leviticus, 163, 169
book of Numbers, 221
book of origins, 334
book of Proverbs, 128
book of Romans, 47
Book of the Dead, 67, 107
  definition, 67
books containing God's Law
  definition, 102
born a slave, 1
bread and wine are passed, 74
brethren, 14–15, 229–30, 232, 251–52, 293

Brown, Raymond
  on God's love for us, 285
  on the shedding of innocent blood, 302
brutal Babylonians, 4
burnt sacrifice, 170, 172

C

Cairns, Ian, 289
Caleb, 205, 214, 257, 261
Caleb and Joshua, 205, 261
Calvary, 74, 97
Calvin, 153
Canaan, 8, 13, 204–5, 211, 215, 237, 262, 265, 270–71, 276
  definition, 8
Canaanites, 34, 117, 203–4, 219, 261, 272, 274–76, 281, 319, 332
  definition, 261
capital, 29, 126, 251, 295, 300–301, 307
  definition, 295
Carson, D. A., 25
casual sex, 287
casualties of war, 256
cattle, 60, 61, 120, 286
censers, 224, 225, 226
  definition, 224
census, 181, 183, 184, 195, 201, 261, 262, 263, 276, 281
ceremonial laws, 164, 165, 335
ceremonially cleansed, 188
chastening
  definition, 24
child molester, 68
children of Israel, 2, 9, 15, 17, 23, 25, 29, 39, 50–52, 58, 67, 72, 76, 79, 82, 89, 113, 155–56, 163, 181, 184–85, 187, 189–90, 205, 227–28, 231, 256, 261, 268, 270, 279–80
Christensen, Duane L., 314
Christlike, 315
Christlikeness, 246
Chrysostom, 10, 11
church, 10, 54, 56, 92, 124, 149, 196, 210, 222, 224, 257

church fathers, 10
church prayer meeting, 149
cisterns
  definition, 140
cities of refuge, 163, 265, 302, 303
clean and unclean, 169
Coats, George, 207
Code of Hammurabi, 105
Cole, R. Dennis
  on consequences of sin, 218
  on expressions of faith, 211
  on power of priests and prophets, 241
  on the holy war, 269
  on the Promised Land, 264
  on trusting in Yahweh, 231
Cole, Robert C.
  on baby Moses, 11
  on Moses and the Divine presence, 26
colorless afterlife, 70
command the whole Hebrew population to throw their newborn sons into the Nile, 3
commemorate God's victory over Pharaoh, 81
commemorative meal, 71
commentaries, 1
common names, 6
communion, 74, 87
compassion, 9, 29, 44, 68, 125, 150, 152, 153
concubine, 95
conjugate a verb
  definition, 30
consecrate, 75, 172, 185, 187, 188
  definition, 75
constitution, 18, 95, 100, 121, 175, 187
contemporaries, 208, 253
contemporary false prophets, 257
contemporary U.S., 298, 299
contended, 82, 230
  definition, 82
contract, 18, 95, 98
corpse, 185, 209
corrects, 145, 193
corrupted, 58, 59
corruptible man, 79

counterfeit, 59, 89
covenant, 17–20, 22, 30–31, 74, 93–100, 110–11, 172, 175, 304
  definition, 18
covenant ceremony, 19
covenant is renewed, 336
covenant with Abraham, 17, 18, 20, 96, 97
coveting, 134, 135
creation of humankind, 336
creation of the universe, 334, 336
Creator, 28, 66, 94, 197, 329–33
criminal, 68, 130, 288, 298–301
Crucified One, 235
cruel bondage, 51
cry of the Israelites, 18
cry out to the Lord, 24, 293
cup of iniquity, 272
cup of wine, 74
Currid, John D.
  on Pharaoh, 47
  on Yahweh's protection at night, 65–66
curse on the Nile, 59
cut them off, 270, 271
  definition, 270

D

daily worship, 173
Dal, 289
Dallah, 289
damage caused by ill treatment, 68
Dan, 262
dark, 58, 60
Dathan, 224, 225
dating monuments or documents, 6
daughters of Zelophehad, 262, 263
Davidic Covenant, 98, 99, 314
David's descendant will rule, 98, 314
Dayenu, 73
Day of Atonement, 167, 169, 171, 172, 200, 226, 227
Day of Forgiveness of all sins, 267
Decision Makers, 206

define who God is, 33
defining act, 24, 332
  definition, 24
definitively
  definition, 133
Deir 'Alla, 241
Deir el Bahan, 12
deliverance, 24, 40, 57, 73, 75, 166, 206, 267, 278
deliver from sin's power and penalty
  definition, 166
deliver His people, 14, 36
demands of justice, 68
demon
  definition, 33
demonic forces, 70
demon possessed
  definition, 34
demons, 59, 71, 209, 242
  definition, 59
descendant of Levi, 38
descendant of pagans, 34
descendants of Abraham, 1, 8, 51, 96, 168, 271, 311
descendants of Jacob, 8, 9
deserved punishment, 4
deserving of punishment, 68
desolate places, 16, 89
desolate ruin, 65
deteriorated
  definition, 86
detestable to the Lord, 242
Deuteronomy, 101, 122, 126, 132, 241, 250–51, 271, 273, 275–76, 278–79, 283, 287
  definition, 276
disciplines, 145, 193
  definition, 193
disease, 53, 58, 60, 73, 84, 165, 185, 287
disfiguring illness, 26
disobedience, 22, 208, 240, 277, 310, 318
divine presence, 26
divorce, 95, 268
doctrine of Balaam, 258
doll-like child, 12
do not make carved images, 115, 135
do not take God's name in vain, 115, 119, 135

drowning Egyptians, 80, 87
Dunnam, Maxie D.
  on firstborn, 75
  on Passover, 72
  on stiff-necked people, 141
Durham, John I., 31

E

eastern Mediterranean people, 1
eat every herb of the land, 61
'ebyon, 289
Egypt, 5–6, 8, 13, 17, 34, 45, 58, 65–66, 69–71, 81, 212, 277–78, 281
Egyptian love of bureaucracy, 6
Egyptian overseer, 25, 278
Egyptian propaganda, 44
Egypt's deities, 45, 52, 70
18th Dynasty, 12
elders of the people, 195, 200
  definition, 195
eldest son, 75, 263
Eleazar, 233, 261
Elijah, 22, 56
Elisha, 56
Elkanah, 268
Elohim, 27, 28, 32
Elohist, 32
Emenhotep II Pharaoh, 13
Empathize, 66, 194
  definition, 66
empty-handed, 34, 69, 294
enchantments, 59
enemy, 2, 44, 78, 80, 207–8, 210, 240, 270, 275, 301, 321, 325
Enishru, 95
Enns, Peter
  on intercessory work, 93–94
  on the rejection of God, 141
  on the ten commandments, 123
enslave the Israelites, 3, 11, 20
ephod, 249, 250
Ephraim, 191, 262
eradicating poverty, 288, 289, 290, 295, 296, 306
Erman, Adolph, 13
eternal death, 70, 234, 323
Eternal God, 28, 325
ethical dilemmas, 7
ethics

definition, 7
Ethiopian woman, 197
evening, 54, 69, 84, 104, 164, 189, 322
definition, 164
Everlasting God, 28
everlasting life, 70, 229, 236
everlasting ordinance, 71, 73
every other deity is a human invention, 117
evil, 4–5, 47–48, 127, 140, 214–15, 242, 258, 287, 311, 322–23
definition, 48
execute judgment
definition, 52
execution of judgment, 70
expiation
definition, 172
exposed Egypt's deities as frauds, 70
extermination of the Hebrew people, 5

F

fail to apply standards fairly, 68
faith, 16, 118, 176, 208, 209, 210, 211, 216, 220, 323
fall short of, 155, 227
false witness, 104, 115, 131, 132, 133, 136
family, 13, 66, 69, 71, 72, 73, 75, 181, 184, 262, 264
definition, 181
family's fortune, 66
farmer, 292
father Abraham, 33
Father's flock, 17
fear but also trust, 77
feared, 6, 81, 210
definition, 6, 81
fear is appropriate, 76
fears paralyze us, 77
feast and drink beer, 70
Feast of Unleavened Bread, 71
feed the needy locally from the third-year tithe, 295
female deities
definition, 274
female servant, 65, 66, 120, 134
festival to celebrate a restoration of temple worship, 267

festival to recall deliverance under Queen Esther, 267
1527 BC, 7
1567 BC, 2
final judgment, 68
firstborn, 5, 53, 65, 66, 75, 87, 184
first humans sin, 336
first Passover meal, 71
first plague, 52
first temple period
definition, 188
flax and barley, 60
flies, 59, 60, 321
floating cradle, 1
follows Satan, 33
foolish arrogance, 61
forsaken the right way, 257
forthcoming miracles, 51
1447 BC, 44
fourth judgment, 60
free labor, 3
fresh infusion of faith, 76
frogs, 53, 58, 73

G

Gad, 9, 22, 262, 269, 270
Gadites, 265, 276
gain blessings, 67
G-d, 72
general guidance, 248, 249, 251, 253, 254, 259
generic name
definition, 27
Gentile Christians, 74
Germany, 5, 68
Gershom
definition, 17
Gethsemane, 245
Gideon, 22
give the poor interest-free, forgivable loans, 295
glory, 22, 28, 83, 149, 159, 212
definition, 83
God acts, 80, 145
God Almighty, 28
god Baal, 117
God "heard their groaning," 17, 18, 96
God in Heaven, 28
godliness, 118
godly men and women

definition, 24
God makes covenant promises, 336
God Most High, 28
God of Glory, 28
God of His slaves, 45, 332
God of history, 330
God of Hosts, 28
God of Justice, 28
God of Knowledge, 28
God of My Salvation, 28
God our Healer, 28
God "remembered His covenant with Abraham," 17, 18, 19
God remembers, 19, 96
God reveals that His name is Yahweh, 336
God's appearance to Moses, 89
God's disapproval, 118
God's faithfulness, 89, 213, 254, 331
God's grace, 43, 154, 155, 172, 193, 229
definition, 154
God's mighty acts free the Israelites, 336
God's miracle-working power, 43, 79
God's new covenant people, 74
gods of Egypt, 13, 52, 69, 70, 71
God's plan to eradicate poverty, 288, 290, 295, 306
God's presence, 23, 37, 148, 156, 157, 166, 175, 190, 207, 324
God's redeeming power, 73
God's Sovereignty, 28, 153
God's Word, 6, 61, 117, 127, 198, 210, 213, 227, 231, 252, 254, 280, 312
God Who Sees, 28
golden age
definition, 320
Goliath, 78
gone astray, 257
Goshen, 60
grace, 37, 43, 125, 146, 149–50, 154–55, 167, 174–77, 179, 280, 315
gracious acts, 57, 141
definition, 57
grain offerings, 170, 172

great God, 28, 45
Green, Wilda, 216
green and prosperous, 65
grow more Christlike, 315
Grudem, Wayne A., 92
grumble against, 82
guild of midwives, 6
guilt offerings, 163, 171, 172
guilty, 68, 116, 132, 146,
    153–54, 170, 186, 212,
    214, 258–59, 297, 300
    definition, 68

H

Habakkuk, 4
Haggadah
    definition, 73
hail, 25, 58, 61
hailstones, 53, 60, 61, 65, 73
hamad, 134
Haman, 5
Hananiah, 119, 120, 267
handmill, 65, 66
Hanukkah, 267
Hapuseneb, 12
harlotry
    definition, 256
Harris, R. Laird, 28
Harrison, R. K.
    on an Aramaic prophet text on
        Balaam, 241
    on Korah's destruction, 225
    on Korah's rebellion, 224
    on the reconnaissance report,
        206
    on the spirit of the seventy,
        196
harvest feast of thanksgiving,
    267
Hatala, 95
hatred and resentment, 4
Hatshepsut, 12, 14, 15
headship of the family, 75
healthy relationship with God,
    26, 37, 41, 49, 78, 83, 147,
    155, 159, 199, 214
Hebrew and Egyptian
    mothers-to-be, 6
Hebrew children, 67
Hebrews, 1, 3, 11, 13, 16, 24,
    93, 98, 168, 173–174, 177,
    208, 215, 219, 227, 233

definition, 1
hegakhases, 2
heinous
    definition, 300
He's God, 66
hierodule
    definition, 95
highly moral people, 67
high places
    definition, 325
Hill, Steve, 229
Hillyer, Norman, 49
His commandments, 24, 218,
    309, 311, 322
His disciples, 74, 77, 120, 228
His identity, 27, 51, 56, 326
His righteousness
    definition, 89
His right to rule, 28
His rule over every earthly
    power, 28
historian, 2
His universal rule, 28
Hitler, 5, 68
Hittite codes, 106
Hittites, 100, 101, 106, 110,
    111, 270, 271, 276, 284,
    307
    definition, 100
holy, 21, 23, 29, 72, 91, 92,
    135, 157, 169, 222, 235,
    254, 340
Holy One of Israel, 28, 208
Holy Spirit, 125, 127, 135, 157,
    169, 242, 246, 254
homosexuals practice the
    doctrine of Balaam, 258
"honey pot," 256, 269, 272
honor father and mother, 115,
    123
Hope of Israel, 28
Horeb
    definition, 310
horoscope, 242
Horus, 45
Hosea, 191
hostile leaders, 34
hostility, 60, 82, 87, 114, 126,
    127, 303, 304
house full of silver and gold,
    244, 256
household came with Jacob, 9
House of Israel, 98

hubris
    definition, 61
human being, 22, 47, 80, 90,
    108, 109, 157, 168, 176,
    234, 287
humankind, 56, 89, 90, 137,
    139, 166, 242, 289, 330
humble home, 66
Hyksos, 2, 3, 8, 13
Hyksos invasion, 2
hymn to Aton, 66
hypocritical, 83, 223, 247

I

I AM WHO I AM, 29, 30
identify with
    definition, 14
idol, 117, 118, 134, 136, 139,
    140, 143, 159
idols, 35, 118, 135, 140, 141,
    242, 273
    definition, 35
imperatives, 7, 286
    definition, 286
import pagan priests and
    prophets, 56
imprecator
    definition, 241
incantation
    definition, 59
increasing brutality, 4
Ineni, 12
infectious skin disease, 185
influential religious leaders, 94
information or facts, 33
instructs, 184, 187, 193
intercession, 213
intercessory work
    definition, 93
interpreter of dreams, 8
interpreting
    definition, 251
interprets omens, 241
introduce monotheism in Egypt,
    70
in vain, 104, 115, 119, 120,
    135
Israel is enslaved, 336
Israelites, 1–8, 11, 15, 17–20,
    24, 31, 43–44, 48–49, 51,
    57, 60, 63, 68, 71, 76,
    78–87, 90–91, 101, 103,

M

Mackay, John L.
on codes of behavior, 103
on God's presentation of
Himself, 31
on the holy nation, 91
on the law of retaliation, 304
made perfect
definition, 26
magic and spells, 59
magnificent stone temples, 65
major religious revivals, 74
make their lives bitter with hard
bondage, 3
Malachi, 31
male deities
definition, 274
male infant, 3, 7, 67
Manetho, 2
manna
definition, 84, 192
Marah, 81, 82, 84
mastery of skills, 33
matza, 72
McGee, J. Vernon
on the angel of the Lord, 22
on the God of mercy, 272
McIntosh, Doug, 312
McKnight, Scott, 176
mediator
definition, 141, 278
Mediterranean Sea, 53
Mediterranean shore, 75
members of a slave race, 1
memorial
definition, 71
memorial to all generations
definition, 29
Mendenhall, George, 100
merciful God, 29, 277
Merrill, Eugene H.
on covenant obedience, 309
on covenant of Horeb, 310
Mesopotamia, 18, 102
Mesopotamian law codes, 107
messenger, 21, 34, 236
Messiah, 228, 233, 251, 319
Middle Eastern deities, 27
Midian, 17, 239, 256, 268, 269,
272, 326
Midianites, 17, 239, 256, 268,
270, 326

mighty hand, 34, 72, 122, 147,
212, 278, 285
definition, 34
military units, 195
mina
definition, 95
mined turquoise, 17
miracle chapters, 46
miracles, 23, 33, 36, 43, 51–57,
61, 63, 87, 141
miraculous judgment, 53, 58,
59, 238
miraculous signs, 211
Miriam, 1, 10, 39, 197, 199,
200, 201, 221, 230
mission, 22, 25, 91, 157, 176,
198, 258
Moab, 236, 237, 239, 243,
254, 259, 285, 326
Moabites, 239, 240, 256, 261
modern Israel and Palestine, 8
modern Turkey, 100
monarchy
definition, 268
monotheism, 70
moral code, 286
moral correctness, 66
moral imperatives, 7, 286
definition, 7
moral sensibilities, 66
morals in Egypt, 67
moral universe, 5, 154
mosaic codes, 106, 263
Mosaic Covenant, 99, 100, 110,
111
Moses dies, 336
Moses is born, 9, 336
Moses's dream, 15, 17
Moses's face, 65, 155, 156
Moses's infancy, 1
Motive, 156, 224, 273, 301
Mount Ebal, 312
Mount Gerizim, 312
Mount of Nebo, 326
Mount Sinai, 39, 82, 86, 94,
111, 113, 137, 139, 155,
156, 190
multi-breasted clay model of
Ashtoreth, 117
multiply my signs and my
wonders, 52, 58
multiply your descendants, 147,
212

murmur, 81, 82, 207

N

Naboth, 264, 265
names have great significance, 27
Naphtali, 9, 262
national constitution, 95
national sacrifices, 172
nation led by a hereditary king,
268
natural consequences of evil
behavior, 4
natural events
definition, 53
natural law, 53, 54, 55, 63
definition, 53
natural leaders, 26
Nazirite, 187, 268
Nazirite vow, 187
Nazis, 5
negative confessions, 67, 107
New Covenant, 74, 98, 99, 110,
314, 315, 333
New King James Version, 123
new kingdom dynasties, 2
new revelation, 56, 89, 91, 251
definition, 251
Nicodemus, 234, 236
nighttime, 65
Nile River, 53
Nile to blood, 53, 58, 73
1917, 204
Noah, 300
nonbelievers, 49
non-Christians, 120, 311, 337
non-miraculous Christianity, 54
no other gods before Me, 102,
115, 116, 135, 140, 210
northwestern Arabia, 17
not a credit economy
definition, 292
Nystrom, David P., 209

O

oath, 97, 98, 100, 101, 106,
233, 267, 285, 310
oath of acceptance, 100, 101
obedience, 215, 217, 258, 277,
289, 315
occult, 240, 241, 242, 248,
250, 259, 272

definition, 241
offered sacrifices for sins, 227
offered the blood of animals, 227
offerings at religious festivals, 173
older law codes, 107
Olson, Dennis T.
  on Balaam, 239
  on central theme of Numbers, 190
  on faith as fear and trust in God's power, 210
  on first temple period, 188
  on Joshua, 266
  on Moses' and Aaron's disobedience, 231
One Who Is Always Present, 31, 34, 51, 61, 78, 113, 120, 135, 152, 331
one who suffers at the hands of others, 68
oppressed Hebrew slaves, 68
oppression of the Israelites, 3, 4, 5, 62
optimistic view of the afterlife, 70
order midwives to kill male infants, 3
ordinance
  definition, 71
orgy
  definition, 148
orphans, 291
Osiris, 67
other codes of law, 106, 338
other gods, 102, 104, 113, 115–17, 135, 140, 210, 252, 274, 311
Ouija board, 242
overreaching pride, 61

P

pagan, 4, 34, 35, 116, 170, 242, 243, 256, 325, 331, 339
  definition, 35
pagan Babylonians, 4
papyrus plants, 10
Paran, 203
paranoia
  definition, 2

passive resistance, 6
Passover, 65, 71, 72, 73, 74, 87, 173, 188, 189, 228, 267, 336
Passover is introduced, 336
Passover sacrifice, 92
pass through fire
  definition, 241
patriarch of Constantinople, 10
Payne, David F., 242
peace offerings, 171, 172
penalties, 57, 95, 304
penalty was death, 68, 301
Pentecost, 267
perfect, 26, 72, 168, 176
  definition, 176
Perizzites, 270, 271
permit the poor to glean, 295
permit the poor to harvest all seventh-year crops, 295
Persian Empire, 5
persistent, 84, 219
  definition, 219
personal killings, 301, 303
person of Jesus, 78
Peter, 50, 257
Pethor, 239
Pharaoh, 2–3, 5–15, 25, 38, 43–48, 52, 58–59, 63, 65–67, 70–72, 79–80, 87, 332
  definition, 2
Pharaoh's chariot army, 80
Pharaoh's daughter, 9, 10, 11, 13, 14, 16
Pharaoh's heart, 46, 52, 63, 87
Pharaoh's oppression of the Israelites, 3
Pharaoh's stubbornness, 58, 75
Pharisees
  definition, 94
Philip, James
  on Balaam, 247
  on keeping the Passover, 189
  on model for prayer and intercession, 213
  on mosaic code, 263
  on a symbol of the substitutionary atonement, 235
Philistines, 78, 124, 249
philosophical
  definition, 54
physical adultery, 256

pillar of fire, 76, 212
Pisgah, 326
Pithom, 2, 3
Plaut, W. Gunther, 316
pleasures of sin, 16
"plural of majesty," 27
polytheism of many altars and idols, 273
polytheistic, 274
pornography, 129
powerlessness, 52, 70
power of the wealthy, 293
pre-Christian and Christian eras, 32
predicted, 8, 35, 318
  definition, 35
preserve each family's land from generation to generation, 295
presumptuously
  definition, 218
priest of Midian, 17
primary heir, 66
princess, 1, 10, 11, 12, 20
principles of judgment
  definition, 4
private charity, 292
private property, 131, 136
promiscuous sex, 287
promise, 18, 40, 58, 98, 111, 234, 235, 304, 314, 315, 327
promise covenants, 98, 99, 100, 102, 110, 111, 304, 314
  definition, 314
Promised Land, 148, 200, 203, 217, 231, 233, 277
prophet, 33, 140, 197, 241, 251
  definition, 251
prostitute, 128, 134, 274
provide the poor with the option of a six-year slavery/apprenticeship, 295
provoke others to envy, 4
psalmist, 61, 146, 152
Puah, 5, 6, 7
public duty, 292
punishes, 154, 193, 256
punishment decree, 68
punishments, 57, 101, 154, 178, 316, 323
purifications, 172, 175
Purim, 267

U

unbelief, 49, 203, 205, 208, 210, 215, 219, 220, 231
  definition, 49
unbeliever, 120, 152
unconverted
  definition, 323
unique "release of debts," 292
unique religious system, 335
United Hebrew Kingdom, 320
University of Michigan, 100
unjustified, 142, 143, 300, 301
unjustified killings, 301
unmistakable miracles, 61
unmovable, 57
unreasonable fear, 2
Urim, 169, 249, 250, 254, 259
Ur-Nammu, 106, 108
Ur-Nammu Code, 106, 108

V

vengeance, 162, 268, 301
  definition, 268
very humble, 198
victim, 68, 103, 129, 130, 298, 299, 300, 302, 303
  definition, 68
victory, 241
volunteer, 316
vows, 92, 265, 267, 268
  definition, 265

W

wafer-like food, 84
wafers made with honey, 192
weapons, 44, 239
well-being of the family, 75
we see Christ's agony, 74
Wesleyans, 153
western Semitic languages, 27
white coriander seed, 192
widows, 291
Wiersbe, Warren W., 97
wife beater, 68
wilderness of Paran, 203
wilderness of Shur, 81
wilderness of Sinai, 89, 183, 261
willful blindness, 178
win their release from Egypt, 68, 183

witchcraft, 241
worked to exhaustion, 1
worshipping pagan deities, 19, 117
worthless bread
  definition, 233
would eat no bread made with yeast, 71
wretchedness, 194
Wright, Christopher J. H.
  on God of the Shema, 273
  on our jealous God, 186
  on the phenomenon of Israel, 288
  on the triennial tithe, 292
  on what's detestable to the Lord, 242

X

x-rays, 57

Y

yada', 33
Yahweh, 28, 30, 32–33, 36, 56, 61, 70, 83, 89, 101, 116, 141, 146–47, 156, 177, 231
Yahweh Elohim, 32
Yahweh struck Egypt, 70
Yahwist, 32
Year of Jubilee, 173, 295
YHWH, 29, 30, 319
yoke of iron, 321
you fool, 127
Youngblood, Ronald, 97
younger brother, 39
your fathers, 22, 270, 277, 285–86, 320, 322
  definition, 277
you shall not bear false witness, 115, 131, 136
you shall not commit adultery, 115, 128, 136
you shall not covet, 102, 115, 134, 136
you shall not murder, 115, 126, 136, 339
you shall not steal, 115, 129, 131, 136

Z

Zebulon, 182
Zebulun, 9, 262
Zelophehad, 262, 263
Zikkaron, 73, 74, 189, 225
Zippor, 239, 243
Zipporah, 17
Zoan, 208